to

Naomi
Shira, Matityahu, Kedem and Adi
Hillel
Yishai
Shoval, Yosef, HiLi and Rom
Elisheva

Explorations
EXPANDED

Bereishit

Rabbi Ari Kahn

KODESH PRESS

Exporations Expanded: Bereishit

© Ari Kahn, 2019

ISBN: 978-1-947857-29-2
Paperback edition

All rights reserved. Except for brief quotations in printed reviews, no part of this publication may be reproduced, stored in a retrieval system, or transmitted in any form or by any means (printed, written, photocopied, visual electronic, audio, or otherwise) without the prior permission of the publisher.

Cover Design by S. Kim Glassman

Contents

Introduction 9

Parashat Bereishit
The First Argument 15
The Missing 974 Generations 33

Parashat Noach
Was Noach a *Tzaddik*? 59

Parashat Lech Lecha
Avraham's Discovery 83

Parashat Vayeira
The Trial 101

Parashat Chayei Sarah
The First Matriarch 123

Parashat Toldot
Yaakov and Esav 143

Parashat Vayeitzei
Antecedents of a Nation 169

Parashat Vayishlach
The Struggle 189

Parashat Vayeshev
The Light of *Mashiach* 213
Worse Than You Thought 233

Parashat Miketz
Yosef HaTzaddik 241
A Cherished Chalice 255

Parashat Vayigash
The Beauty of Yosef 267
Emotional Truth: Becoming Brothers Once Again . . 291

Parashat Vayechi
Who Is First? 309
The Death of Yaakov 329

Introduction

Over twenty years have elapsed since I wrote and subsequently published my first book, *Explorations*; over twenty years have passed since I was warned that the shelves of Jewish book stores are packed with volumes on the *parashah*, and every year, as new ones are published, the older ones are quickly forgotten. Twenty years—and I am extremely thankful that *Explorations* is still in demand, has been reprinted a number of times, and has since been translated into a five-volume edition in French.

Even more gratifying than its longevity is its impact: So many thoughtful readers have reached out to me to express their excitement with the ideas and the Torah insights in *Explorations*. Over the years, these ideas have been quoted and cited, used as the basis for study of the weekly Torah portion, and served as a guide for teachers and pulpit rabbis.

In the interim, I have had the privilege to write and publish other volumes, including a five-volume series titled *Echoes of Eden*, which unlike *Explorations*, included Hebrew source materials and detailed footnotes. My goal for *Echoes of Eden* was to produce not merely a set of books to be read, but *sefarim* to be studied. Although I labored to make the ideas accessible to "entry-level" readers, more advanced students found full-text sources on each page, and scholars were able to use the referenced materials for *chavruta* study or in the classroom. Countless readers, scholars, and laypeople alike, have expressed their appreciation for the access *Echoes of Eden* provides to the insights and conclusions in those books, as well as to primary sources, especially those that are relatively obscure.

The present volume, *Explorations Expanded: Bereishit*, is both old and new. It contains new essays as well as the essays that comprised the original volume, which have now been freshly edited. The original ideas have been expanded, sources have been included and annotated, and major concepts have been cross-referenced with *Echoes of Eden*, other books I have published, and some not-yet published manuscripts. As in the *Echoes of Eden* series, Hebrew sources and detailed footnotes have been added. I hope that readers who enjoyed the original *Explorations* will find the present volume more useful and more enlightening.

I am eternally grateful to my first teachers, my parents, who brought me into the world—and into the world of Torah. I would also like to thank the mentors, colleagues, congregants, and students who have given me so much encouragement over the years.

There are a number of people who have facilitated the publication of my work, but they are more than mere facilitators. They are dear friends who believed that my writings were worthy of publication, and their support has helped to create a growing library of Torah thought:

Chaya and Rabbi Howard Balter, Deena and Ben Zion Fuchs, Elizabeth and Raymond Gindi, Natalie and Davidi Jonas, Joleen and Mitch Julis, Ora and Rich Rabinovitch, and June and Joe Silny have all been instrumental in helping me publish a dozen books over the past twenty years.

I thank Rabbi Alec Goldstein of Kodesh Press for publishing two of my earlier volumes, *A River Flowed from Eden: Torah for the Shabbat Table*, and *A Taste of Eden: (More) Torah for the Shabbat Table*. I thank him for believing in our current project, and for adding his professional touch to this volume. With God's help, we hope to publish *Explorations Expanded* on all five books of the Torah.

It is my pleasure, once again, to thank my wife Naomi for her sensitive reading, capable editing, critical thinking, and constant inspiration. The dedication included in the original version of Explorations still rings true:

Many years ago, a young woman told me that her idea of the study of Torah is a pursuit of revelation. Her comment was so simple yet so profound, for at times those of us who spend many years in yeshivah run the risk of focusing on the ideas and losing sight of the revelation. In all Torah learning one should experience what Rav Soloveitchik described as "feeling the breath of eternity on your face." I wish to thank that young woman for helping me focus my learning and teaching, for making sure that I never lose sight of the rendezvous with the Divine. I would like to thank her for editing and proofreading my writings, for being my best critic and greatest fan. I would like to thank her for marrying me, for raising our children, for creating a home of Torah and *chesed*. I would like to thank her for encouraging me to write (even on *erev Shabbat* when the house could have used an extra hand!) and teach (all over the world—even if it meant long travel and weeks apart), and for sharing with me the excitement of a new idea—at any hour of the day or night.

Naomi, thank you for inspiring me and helping me inspire others.

May the merit of this Torah protect us and our children. May our children and descendants be among those who study Torah, fear God, follow His commandments, and bring *nachat* to their grandparents, parents, and the entire community of Israel.

Over the past twenty years we have grown older together and watched (some of) those young children become parents. May God bless us with health and strength to begin and to complete many more works of Torah together. May we continue to share *nachat* from our children, our grandchildren, and our growing extended family.

No writer can be certain how the fruit of his or her labor will be received, but when Torah is transmitted through the written word, something magical can happen. If the community of Israel is receptive to the work, it enters a corpus which has a life-force of its own. It attains a level of holiness.

A short time after *Explorations* was first published, I happened to be learning in an unfamiliar *Beit Midrash*, and I noticed a young man sitting nearby, raptly reading from an open volume; nothing unusual, given the setting—other than the fact that this student was reading *Explorations*. Although I tried to continue my own learning without being distracted, I couldn't help but glance his way every now and again, hoping that his facial expressions might tell me if he was enjoying what he was learning, or perhaps not. What happened next was also not unusual: He finished the chapter he was reading and closed the book. But as he did so, he gave the *sefer* a gentle kiss. More than any positive assessment by a reviewer or any admiring citation by another author, more than any of the words of praise that have been written or spoken about my work in the years since, it was that gesture, in that fleeting moment, that gave me an overwhelming sense of gratitude. In my own small way, I had written a book that had been included in the *Masorah* of the Jewish people, and I had been allowed to enter the most holy fraternity.

I have never hoped for any greater accomplishment.

Rabbi Ari Kahn
9 Elul 5779
Givat Ze'ev

Parashat Bereishit

The First Argument

ספר בראשית פרק א:א
בְּרֵאשִׁית בָּרָא אֱלֹהִים אֵת הַשָּׁמַיִם וְאֵת הָאָרֶץ:

In the beginning God created the heavens and the earth.
(*Bereishit* 1:1)

The Torah begins with a description of the events that unfolded at the dawn of history, yet it has long been the understanding of the Rabbis of the Talmud, Midrash, and *Zohar* that, as important as the literal text may be, the primary message of the Torah lies in its theological teachings. The Torah is, first and foremost, a book of theological truth. It is the word of God, and, therefore, it is historically accurate as well. Consequently, verses which may seem mundane or simplistic to the uninitiated reader often contain the most profound teachings and secrets of the Torah.[1]

The Midrashic treatment of the first *parashah* of the Torah is based on inference, not from the famous words of the verses but from what is missing:

בראשית רבה (וילנא) פרשת בראשית פרשה ד סימן ו
לָמָה אֵין כְּתִיב בַּשֵּׁנִי כִּי טוֹב, רַבִּי יוֹחָנָן תָּנֵי לָהּ בְּשֵׁם רַבִּי יוֹסֵי בֶּן רַבִּי חֲלַפְתָּא, שֶׁבּוֹ נִבְרֵאת גֵּיהִנֹּם, שֶׁנֶּאֱמַר (ישעיה ל, לג): כִּי עָרוּךְ מֵאֶתְמוּל תָּפְתֶּה, יוֹם שֶׁיֵּשׁ בּוֹ אֶתְמוֹל וְאֵין בּוֹ שִׁלְשׁוֹם. רַבִּי חֲנִינָא אוֹמֵר שֶׁבּוֹ נִבְרֵאת מַחֲלֹקֶת, שֶׁנֶּאֱמַר: וִיהִי מַבְדִּיל בֵּין מַיִם לָמָיִם. אָמַר רַבִּי טַבְיוֹמֵי אִם מַחֲלֹקֶת שֶׁהִיא לְתִקּוּנוֹ שֶׁל עוֹלָם וּלְיִשּׁוּבוֹ, אֵין בָּהּ כִּי טוֹב, מַחֲלֹקֶת שֶׁהִיא לְעִרְבּוּבוֹ עַל אַחַת כַּמָּה וְכַמָּה.

---

1. This is particularly true in the teachings of the Zohar. The list of kings of Edom (*Bereishit* 36) is one example of this phenomenon.

> Why is [the phrase] "that it was good" not written in connection to the second day? Rabbi Yochanan explained in the name of Rabbi Yosi bar Chalafta: Because on it the Gehenna [Hell] was created…. Rabbi Chanina said: Because on it schism came into the world, [as it is written,] (*Bereishit* 1:6). "[God said, 'Let there be a firmament in the midst of the waters, and] let it divide the waters from the waters.'" (*Bereishit Rabbah* 4:6)

The Midrash teaches that the Divine act of separating the upper and lower waters is the power that allowed dissension to come into being. However, the term used to describe this act of separation, *va-yavdeil*, "He divided," was used on the first day as well, when God differentiated between light and darkness. Why, then, is the power of dissension expressed only on the second day? Apparently, argument occurs when two entities or two people do not have clearly defined boundaries. The separation between light and darkness is absolute, qualitative, objective; they are opposites, and therefore no dissension follows their separation. However, the separation between water and water, two things that are ostensibly the same, is where the power of dissent originates. God separated the higher waters from the lower waters—seemingly, two halves of a uniform whole. With this act of seemingly-arbitrary division, dissension was created.

This Midrash serves as an introduction to one of the most tragic events recorded in *Sefer Bereishit*. Chapter 4 records the birth of Kayin and Hevel, their difference of opinion, and finally, the horrifying murder of Hevel.

ספר בראשית פרק ד:א-ב

(א) וְהָאָדָם יָדַע אֶת חַוָּה אִשְׁתּוֹ וַתַּהַר וַתֵּלֶד אֶת קַיִן וַתֹּאמֶר קָנִיתִי אִישׁ אֶת ה': (ב) וַתֹּסֶף לָלֶדֶת אֶת אָחִיו אֶת הָבֶל וַיְהִי הֶבֶל רֹעֵה צֹאן וְקַיִן הָיָה עֹבֵד אֲדָמָה:

Adam knew Chavah [Eve], his wife. She conceived and gave birth to Kayin, and she said, "I have acquired a man from God."

She gave birth again, to his brother Hevel. Hevel was a shepherd, and Kayin worked the land. (*Bereishit* 4:1–2)

These verses lack symmetry. When Kayin is born, his name is immediately explained; when Hevel is born, no reason is given for his name. From the outset, Hevel is described in relation to his brother. His identity is somehow less than independent; he is Kayin's brother—"and she gave birth again, to his brother"—no more, no less.

The background of this episode is crucial: Let us consider the name given to Kayin. The section began with the words, "Adam knew Chavah, his wife." In the previous chapter, Adam and Chavah were banished from the Garden of Eden because they had partaken of the fruit of the Tree of Knowledge. And then, immediately afterward, we are told that "Adam knew Chavah." Evidently, they took the knowledge they had acquired by eating the fruit of the Tree of Knowledge—and applied it. When Chavah names her firstborn son Kayin, she seems to be seeking a way to rekindle her relationship with God in the aftermath of the sin and ensuing estrangement from God: The root of this child's name denotes acquisition, as if to say that Chavah hopes, through his birth, to reclaim the lost intimacy with God.

In the Garden of Eden, God's presence was not an abstract concept; it was a reality, immediate and concrete. God, the Creator, was a part of their experience; He gave them names and He gave them purpose. In his own way, Adam, too, was a creator. By giving names to the animals, by categorizing and describing them, Adam created order and purpose in the natural world that surrounded him. The fact that Adam used speech to "create" is no coincidence: God, too, created with the use of speech.

בראשית פרק א, ג
וַיֹּאמֶר אֱלֹהִים יְהִי אוֹר וַיְהִי־אוֹר:

"God said, 'Let there be light,' and there was light" (*Bereishit* 1:3)

Surely, God could have created by simply willing the universe into being. Instead, He chose to create with speech. When the Torah tells us that man was created in the image of God, the Targum explains that this refers specifically to the unique endowment of the power of speech.[2] As God created with speech, man created with speech. God's creation is *ex nihilo*, creating something from nothing, while man's creative act is in categorizing and understanding God's creation. When man is expelled, he is told that he must work the land, engaging in a different type of creative activity. Chavah, for her part, seeks to repair her damaged relationship with God and sees in the birth of Kayin a reacquisition of her own partnership in Creation.[3]

---

2. *Bereishit* 2:7:

בראשית פרק ב:ז

וַיִּיצֶר ה׳ אֱלֹהִים אֶת־הָאָדָם עָפָר מִן־הָאֲדָמָה וַיִּפַּח בְּאַפָּיו נִשְׁמַת חַיִּים וַיְהִי הָאָדָם לְנֶפֶשׁ חַיָּה:

The Eternal, Almighty God formed man from the dust of the earth. He blew into his nostrils the breath of life, and man became a living being."

תרגום אונקלוס בראשית פרק ב:ז

וּבְרָא יְיָ אֱלֹהִים יָת אָדָם מִן עַפְרָא מִן אַדְמְתָא וּנְפַח בְּאַפּוֹהִי נִשְׁמְתָא דְחַיֵּי וַהֲוַת בְּאָדָם לְרוּחַ מְמַלְלָא:

And the Eternal, Almighty God created man, dirt from the ground, and He blew into his nostrils a living soul, and it became, in man, a speaking spirit.

3. There are two approaches recorded in the Midrash (*Bereishit Rabbah* 22:2). One midrash sees the name as an expression of a feeling, that she had now mended the relationship with her husband which may have been damaged by the sin and subsequent expulsion. The other sees her act of childbirth as a type of partnership with God (and her husband):

בראשית רבה כב:ב

וַתֹּאמֶר קָנִיתִי אִישׁ אֶת ה׳, חָמַת לָהּ הָא אִיתְּתָא בְּנִין, אָמְרָה הָא קִנְיָנוֹ בַּעֲלִי בְּיָדִי. רַבִּי יִשְׁמָעֵאל שָׁאַל אֶת רַבִּי עֲקִיבָא אָמַר לוֹ בִּשְׁבִיל שֶׁשִּׁמַּשְׁתָּ נַחוּם אִישׁ גַּם זוֹ עֶשְׂרִים וּשְׁתַּיִם שָׁנָה, אָכִין וְרַקִּין מִעוּטִים, אֶתִין וְגַמִּין רִבּוּיִים, הַאי אֶת דִּכְתִיב הָכָא מַהוּ, אָמַר אִלּוּ נֶאֱמַר קָנִיתִי אִישׁ ה׳, הָיָה הַדָּבָר קָשֶׁה, אֶלָּא אֶת ה׳. אָמַר לֵיהּ (דברים לב, מז): כִּי לֹא דָבָר רֵק הוּא מִכֶּם, וְאִם רֵק הוּא מִכֶּם, שֶׁאֵין אַתֶּם יוֹדְעִים לִדְרשׁ, אֶלָּא אֶת ה׳, לְשֶׁעָבַר אָדָם נִבְרָא מֵאֲדָמָה, וְחַוָּה נִבְרֵאת מֵאָדָם, מִכָּאן וָאֵילָךְ (בראשית א, כו): בְּצַלְמֵנוּ כִּדְמוּתֵנוּ, לֹא אִישׁ בְּלֹא אִשָּׁה וְלֹא אִשָּׁה בְּלֹא אִישׁ, וְלֹא שְׁנֵיהֶם בְּלֹא שְׁכִינָה.

Conversely, the text offers no explanation of Hevel's name. In fact, his birth seems to be an afterthought; his very name, *Hevel*, means "nothingness." It is difficult to interpret what significance Adam and Chavah saw in the birth of Hevel, but it does not seem to inspire the same fanfare as the arrival of Kayin.

Kayin becomes a farmer. He relates to God as per the rules of exile; he works the land, by the sweat of his brow, for his sustenance. Hevel, however, becomes a shepherd; he seems to ignore the rules of exile and tries to relate to God in the way his father did before the sin.

בראשית פרק ד:ב
וַיְהִי־הֶבֶל רֹעֵה צֹאן וְקַיִן הָיָה עֹבֵד אֲדָמָה:

Hevel was a shepherd, and Kayin worked the land. (*Bereishit* 4:2)

The Midrash tells us something interesting about the births of Kayin and Hevel. Kayin, we are told, was born with a twin sister; Hevel, however, was born with two sisters.[4]

"And she said: I have gotten a man…" —R. Yitzchak said: When a woman sees that she has children she exclaims, Behold, my husband is now in my possession.

"With the help of [*et*] the Lord…" —R. Ishmael asked R. Akiva: Since you have served Nahum of Gimzo for twenty-two years, [and he taught], Every *akh* and *rak* is a limitation, while every *et* and *gam* is an addition, tell me what is the purpose of the *et* written here? ' If it said, "I have gotten a man the Lord," ' he, replied, it would have been difficult [to interpret]; hence "with the help of [*et*] the Lord" is required. At that point he quoted to him: For it is no empty thing from you (*Devarim* 32:47), and if it is empty, it is so on your account, because you do not know how to interpret it. Rather, "[*et*] the Lord" [teaches this]: In the past, Adam was created from the ground, and Chavah from Adam; but henceforth it shall be, "in our image, after our likeness" (*Bereishit* 1:26): neither man without woman nor woman without man, nor both of them without the *Shechinah*.
4. *Bereishit Rabbah* 22:2:

בראשית רבה כב:ב
וַתַּהַר וַתֵּלֶד אֶת קַיִן, אָמַר רַבִּי אֶלְעָזָר בֶּן עֲזַרְיָה שְׁלשָׁה נַעֲשׂוּ בְּאוֹתוֹ הַיּוֹם, בּוֹ בַּיּוֹם נִבְ־רְאוּ, בּוֹ בַּיּוֹם שִׁמְּשׁוּ, בּוֹ בַּיּוֹם הוֹצִיאוּ תוֹלָדוֹת. אָמַר לֵיהּ רַבִּי יְהוֹשֻׁעַ בֶּן קָרְחָה עָלוּ לַמִּטָּה שְׁנַיִם וְיָרְדוּ שִׁבְעָה, קַיִן וּתְאוֹמָתוֹ, וְהֶבֶל וּשְׁתֵּי תְאוֹמוֹתָיו,
"And she conceived and gave birth to Kayin" — R. Eleazar b. Azariah said: Three

Perhaps this is the origin of the friction between Kayin and Hevel.[5] Kayin is the older brother, the "golden child." Chavah's hopes and aspirations rest upon him. Kayin may question the propriety of God's giving the younger brother two sisters, when he himself had only one. After all, if anyone should have received a double share, it should have been Kayin, the firstborn.[6] This sets the stage for the rest of *Sefer Bereishit*, in which the younger brother consistently achieves superiority over the older brother, who inevitably fails.

Kayin, nonetheless, sets about his task, working the land and bringing an offering to God. Hevel, too, brings an offering from his flock.

בראשית פרק ד:ד-ז

(ד) וְהֶבֶל הֵבִיא גַם־הוּא מִבְּכֹרוֹת צֹאנוֹ וּמֵחֶלְבֵהֶן וַיִּשַׁע ה' אֶל־הֶבֶל וְאֶל־מִנְחָתוֹ: (ה) וְאֶל־קַיִן וְאֶל־מִנְחָתוֹ לֹא שָׁעָה וַיִּחַר לְקַיִן מְאֹד וַיִּפְּלוּ פָּנָיו: (ו) וַיֹּאמֶר ה' אֶל־קָיִן לָמָּה חָרָה לָךְ וְלָמָּה נָפְלוּ פָנֶיךָ: (ז) הֲלוֹא אִם־תֵּיטִיב שְׂאֵת וְאִם לֹא תֵיטִיב לַפֶּתַח חַטָּאת רֹבֵץ וְאֵלֶיךָ תְּשׁוּקָתוֹ וְאַתָּה תִּמְשָׁל־בּוֹ:

---

wonders were performed on that day: on that very day they were created, on that very day they cohabited, and on that very day they produced off- spring. R. Joshua b. Karhah said to him: Only two entered the bed, and seven left it: Cain and his twin sister, Abel and his two twin sisters.

5. This suggestion is found in *Pirkei de-Rabbi Eliezer*, chapter 21.

פרקי דרבי אליעזר פרק כא

רַבִּי צָדוֹק אוֹמֵר נִכְנְסָה קִנְאָה וְשִׂנְאָה גְדוֹלָה בְּלִבּוֹ שֶׁל קַיִן, עַל שֶׁנִּתְרַצֵּית מִנְחָתוֹ שֶׁל הֶבֶל. וְלֹא עוֹד אֶלָּא שֶׁהָיְתָה אִשְׁתּוֹ תְּאוֹמָתוֹ יָפָה בַּנָּשִׁים, אָמַר אֲנִי אֶהֱרֹג אֶת הֶבֶל אָחִי וְאֶקַּח אֶת אִשְׁתּוֹ, שֶׁנֶּאֱמַר [בראשית ד, ח] וַיֹּאמֶר קַיִן אֶל הֶבֶל אָחִיו וַיְהִי בִּהְיוֹתָם בַּשָּׂדֶה. וְאֵין בַּשָּׂדֶה אֶלָּא הָאִשָּׁה שֶׁנִּמְשְׁלָה כַּשָּׂדֶה, שֶׁנֶּאֱמַר [דברים כ, יט] כִּי הָאָדָם עֵץ הַשָּׂדֶה.

6. See *Midrash Tanchuma Bereishit* 9:4

מדרש תנחומא (ורשא) פרשת בראשית (ט) [ד, ג]

וַיְהִי מִקֵּץ יָמִים וַיָּבֵא קַיִן וְגוֹ'. יֵשׁ מִקֵּץ שָׁנָה וְיֵשׁ מִקֵּץ שְׁנָתַיִם, וְיֵשׁ יָמִים, וְיֵשׁ אַרְבָּעִים שָׁנָה. אָמְרוּ חֲכָמֵינוּ זִכְרוֹנָם לִבְרָכָה, בְּנֵי אַרְבָּעִים שָׁנָה הָיוּ קַיִן וְהֶבֶל. וַיָּבֵא קַיִן מִפְּרִי הָאֲדָמָה, מַהוּ? מִן מוֹתַר מַאֲכָלוֹ. וְרַבָּנָן אָמְרֵי, זֶרַע פִּשְׁתָּן הָיָה, וְהֶבֶל הֵבִיא גַם הוּא מִבְּכֹרוֹת צֹאנוֹ וּמֵחֶלְבֵהֶן לְפִיכָךְ נֶאֱסַר צֶמֶר וּפִשְׁתִּים, שֶׁנֶּאֱמַר: לֹא תִלְבַּשׁ שַׁעַטְנֵז וְגוֹ' (דברים כב, יא). וְאָמַר הַקָּדוֹשׁ בָּרוּךְ הוּא, אֵינוֹ דִין שֶׁיִּתְעָרֵב מִנְחַת הַחוֹטֵא עִם מִנְחַת הַזַּכַּאי לְפִיכָךְ נֶאֱסַר. וַיֹּאמֶר קַיִן אֶל הֶבֶל אָחִיו, מָה אָמַר לוֹ? נַחֲלֹק הָעוֹלָם וַאֲנִי בְּכוֹר וְאֶטֹּל פִּי שְׁנַיִם. אָמַר לוֹ הֶבֶל, אֶפְשָׁר. אָמַר לוֹ קַיִן, אִם כֵּן אֲנִי נוֹטֵל יֶתֶר חֵלֶק עַל חֶלְקִי מָקוֹם שֶׁנִּתְקַבֵּל בּוֹ קָרְבָּנֶךָ. אָמַר לוֹ הֶבֶל, לֹא תִטֹּל. וְעַל דָּבָר זֶה נָפְלָה קְטָטָה בֵּינֵיהֶם, שֶׁנֶּאֱמַר: וַיְהִי בִּהְיוֹתָם בַּשָּׂדֶה.

Hevel, for his part, brought the choicest of the firstlings of his flock. God paid heed to Hevel and his offering, but to Kayin and his offering He paid no heed. Kayin was very distressed and his face fell. God said to Kayin, "Why are you distressed and why has your face fallen? Surely, if you do well, you shall be uplifted, but if you do not well, sin crouches at the door. It longs to overcome you, and yet you may overpower it." (*Bereishit* 4:4–7)

Kayin repeatedly compares himself to his brother Hevel, and finds himself holding the short end of the stick. First, he felt slighted that his brother had two sisters, and now Hevel's offering is accepted by God while his own offering is not. Kayin defines himself in terms of his relationship with his brother; he judges his accomplishments by comparing them with his brother's. When Kayin sees that he has not been as successful as Hevel, he becomes bitter, angry, and depressed.

Kayin's mistake was that he assumed that he and his brother were the same and were therefore deserving of equal opportunities and equal success. This reminds us of the second day of Creation, when God separated between the waters: When two things are assumed to be equal, dissension follows.

בראשית פרק ד:ח

(ח) וַיֹּאמֶר קַיִן אֶל־הֶבֶל אָחִיו וַיְהִי בִּהְיוֹתָם בַּשָּׂדֶה וַיָּקָם קַיִן אֶל־הֶבֶל אָחִיו וַיַּהַרְגֵהוּ:

Kayin said to his brother Hevel; and it came to pass, when they were in the field, that Kayin rose up against his brother Hevel and killed him. (*Bereishit* 4:8)

Although the Torah reports that Kayin spoke to Hevel, it does not record what he said, nor are we told what Hevel answered. Hevel seems uninvolved in this argument; it is one-sided. Although Kayin is haunted by the competition, Hevel concerns himself with his flock, with the offering of gifts to God, and with his relationship to God. Once again, there is a lack of symmetry in the verses:

בראשית פרק ד:ט-יב

(ט) וַיֹּאמֶר ה' אֶל־קַיִן אֵי הֶבֶל אָחִיךָ וַיֹּאמֶר לֹא יָדַעְתִּי הֲשֹׁמֵר אָחִי אָנֹכִי: (י) וַיֹּאמֶר מֶה עָשִׂיתָ קוֹל דְּמֵי אָחִיךָ צֹעֲקִים אֵלַי מִן־הָאֲדָמָה: (יא) וְעַתָּה אָרוּר אָתָּה מִן־הָאֲדָמָה אֲשֶׁר פָּצְתָה אֶת־פִּיהָ לָקַחַת אֶת־דְּמֵי אָחִיךָ מִיָּדֶךָ: (יב) כִּי תַעֲבֹד אֶת־הָאֲדָמָה לֹא־תֹסֵף תֵּת־כֹּחָהּ לָךְ נָע וָנָד תִּהְיֶה בָאָרֶץ:

God said to Kayin, "Where is Hevel, your brother?" He said, "I do not know. Am I my brother's keeper?" [God] said, "What have you done? The voice of your brother's blood cries to me from the ground. Now you are cursed from the earth, which has opened her mouth to receive your brother's blood from your hand. When you till the ground, it shall not henceforth yield to you its strength; a fugitive and a wanderer shall you be on the earth." (*Bereishit* 4:9-12)

The earth, which had already been cursed because of Adam's sin and now yielded its fruit only when worked by man, is now cursed a second time, because it opened its mouth and swallowed the blood of Hevel. Kayin is banished—even more banished, as it were, than Adam was after the first sin; he is doomed to wander the earth, finding no respite.

The tragic relationship between Kayin and Hevel unleashed the spiritual power that lies behind other arguments throughout history. One such argument is found in *Sefer Bamidbar*:

במדבר פרק טז:ג

וַיִּקָּהֲלוּ עַל־מֹשֶׁה וְעַל־אַהֲרֹן וַיֹּאמְרוּ אֲלֵהֶם רַב־לָכֶם כִּי כָל־הָעֵדָה כֻּלָּם קְדֹשִׁים וּבְתוֹכָם ה' וּמַדּוּעַ תִּתְנַשְּׂאוּ עַל־קְהַל ה':

[Korach and his followers] gathered themselves together against Moshe and Aharon and said to them, "You take too much upon yourselves, since all the congregation is holy, every one of them, and God is among them. Why then do you lift yourselves up above the congregation of God?" (*Bamidbar* 16:3)

Korach's populist message attracted the masses. He claimed that all people are holy, all people are equal, and therefore should have the same rights and opportunities to fulfuill any and all positions and perform any and all tasks. This notion can be traced back to the second day of Creation, before God separated the upper and lower waters; Korach's argument is the same as Kayin's. In fact, according to Kabbalistic tradition, Korah was a reincarnation of Kayin,[7] and Moshe of Hevel.[8]

---

7. See *Torat Chaim* to *Sanhedrin* 110a, who cites the *Zohar*'s statement that Moshe was a reincarnation of Hevel (the name "Hevel" means "nothing", and Moshe being the most modest of men, thought "nothing" of himself). He also cites a passage in the Talmud that the conspirators accused Moshe of being a philanderer. He links this with the midrashic tradition that the core of the fight between Kayin and Hevel was Kayin's desire to steal Hevel's wife.

ספר תורת חיים על סנהדרין דף קי/א

ובספר הזוהר כתוב דנשמתו של משה מגולגלת היתה מנשמתו של הבל והסימן מש״ה ש״ת ה״בל ובספר הציוני פ׳ קרח משמע מגולגלת דנשמתו של קרח היתה מנשמתו של קין זה לשונו שם אבאר ברמיזה כאשר קבלתי דע איש המעיין שהוא סוד שופך דם האדם באדם באותו אדם עצמו וההרגו הורג את הורגו ע״ד דאטפת אטפוך וכו׳ וכן הבל הרג קין בימי משה ומיתת קרח נמי בבליעה מדה כנגד מדה ידוע ובקרח חקר ודרש בשתי שים ערב ותמצא סוד מופלא עכ״ל. ולפי זה יש לומר דלכך חשד קרח למשה באשת איש משום דבמדרש רבה פרשת בראשית איתא על מה היו מדיינין קין והבל אמר רב הונא תאומה יתירה נולדה עם הבל זה אומר אני נוטלה שאני בכור וזה אומר אני נוטלה שנולדה עמי מתוך כך ויקם קין נמצא שכבר חשדו באשת איש משמת ימי בראשית כלומר שרוצה ליטול ממנו אשתו המיוחדת לו בטענה שהיא שלו כיון שהוא בכור לכך גם עתה בגלגולו לא שב מטבעו ומזגו הרע וחשד למשה באשת איש וקנא אשתו ממשה כמו שעשה לשעבר:

8. For example, see *Zohar Bereishit* 28b, *Tikkunei Zohar* 99b, *Shaar Ha-Gilgulim*, hakdamah 32, 33:

זוהר חלק א דף כח/ב

וְעֲלַיְיהוּ אִתְּמַר. וְהַנָּחָשׁ הָיָה עָרוּם מִכֹּל חַיַּת הַשָּׂדֶה וְגוֹ׳ עָרוּם לְרַע מִכָּל חֵיוָן דְּאָמִין לְעָלְמָא עוֹבְדֵי כּוֹכָבִים וּמַזָּלוֹת. וְאִנּוּן בְּנוֹי דְּנָחָשׁ הַקַּדְמוֹנִי דְּפַתֵּי לְחַוָּה. וְעֶרֶב רַב וַדַּאי אִנּוּן הֲווֹ זוּהֲמָא דְּאָטִיל נָחָשׁ בְּחַוָּה. וּמֵהַהִיא זוּהֲמָא נְפַק קַיִן וְקַטִּיל לְהֶבֶל רוֹעֵה צֹאן דְּאִתְּמַר בֵּיהּ בְּשָׁגַּם הוּא בָשָׂר בְּשָׁגַּם זֶה הֶבֶל. בְּשָׁגַּ״ם וַדַּאי אִיהוּ מֹשֶׁ״ה וְקַטִּיל לֵיהּ וְאִיהוּ הֲוָה בְּרָא בּוּכְרָא דְּאָדָם:

וְעִם כָּל דָּא מֹשֶׁה בְּגִין לְכַסָּאָה עַל עֲרְיָיתָא דְאֲבוּהִי נָטַל בַּת יִתְרוֹ דְּאִתְּמַר בֵּיהּ (שופטים א) וּבְנֵי קֵינִי חוֹתֵן מֹשֶׁה, וְהָא אוּקְמוּהָ אֲמַאי אִתְקְרֵי קֵינִי שֶׁנִּפְרַד מִקַּיִן. כְּמָה דְאַתְּ אָמֵר, (שופטים ד) וְחֶבֶר הַקֵּינִי נִפְרָד מִקַּיִן. וּלְבָתַר בָּעָא לְאַהֲדְרָא עֶרֶב רַב בִּתְיוּבְתָּא לְכַסָּאָה עֲרְיָיתָא דְּאֲבוּהִי. דְּקוּדְשָׁא בְּרִיךְ הוּא מַחֲשָׁבָה טוֹבָה מְצָרְפָהּ לְמַעֲשֶׂה, וְאָמַר לֵיהּ קוּדְשָׁא בְּרִיךְ הוּא מִגִּזְעָא בִישָׁא אִנּוּן, תִּסְתַּמַּר מִנַּיְיהוּ. אִלֵּין אִנּוּן חוֹבָה דְּאָדָם דְּאָמַר לֵיהּ וּמֵעֵץ הַדַּעַת טוֹב וָרָע לֹא תֹאכַל מִמֶּנּוּ. אִלֵּין אִנּוּן חוֹבָה דְּמֹשֶׁה וְיִשְׂרָאֵל:

It is surely no coincidence, then, that Moshe asks for a very specific punishment for Korach's rebellion: He asks that the earth "open up its mouth" and swallow Korach and his co-conspirators:

במדבר פרק טז:כח-לב

(כח) וַיֹּאמֶר מֹשֶׁה בְּזֹאת תֵּדְעוּן כִּי־ה' שְׁלָחַנִי לַעֲשׂוֹת אֵת כָּל־הַמַּעֲשִׂים הָאֵלֶּה כִּי־לֹא מִלִּבִּי: (כט) אִם־כְּמוֹת כָּל־הָאָדָם יְמֻתוּן אֵלֶּה וּפְקֻדַּת כָּל־הָאָדָם יִפָּקֵד עֲלֵיהֶם לֹא ה' שְׁלָחָנִי: (ל) וְאִם־בְּרִיאָה יִבְרָא ה' וּפָצְתָה הָאֲדָמָה אֶת־פִּיהָ וּבָלְעָה אֹתָם וְאֶת־כָּל־אֲשֶׁר לָהֶם וְיָרְדוּ חַיִּים שְׁאֹלָה וִידַעְתֶּם כִּי נִאֲצוּ הָאֲנָשִׁים הָאֵלֶּה אֶת־ה': (לא) וַיְהִי כְּכַלֹּתוֹ לְדַבֵּר אֵת כָּל־הַדְּבָרִים הָאֵלֶּה וַתִּבָּקַע הָאֲדָמָה אֲשֶׁר תַּחְתֵּיהֶם: (לב) וַתִּפְתַּח הָאָרֶץ אֶת־פִּיהָ וַתִּבְלַע אֹתָם וְאֶת־בָּתֵּיהֶם וְאֵת כָּל־הָאָדָם אֲשֶׁר לְקֹרַח וְאֵת כָּל־הָרְכוּשׁ:

ספר תיקוני זהר מנוקד דף צט/ב

וַתּוֹסֶף לָלֶדֶת אֶת אָחִיו אֶת הָבֶל, פָּתַח וְאָמַר (תהלים קד כט) תּוֹסֵף רוּחָם יִגְוָעוּן וְאֶל עֲפָרָם יְשׁוּבוּן, הָכָא רָמִיז גִּלְגּוּלָא דְּצַדִּיקַיָּא, וְאַחֲזֵי לֵיהּ קוּדְשָׁא בְּרִיךְ הוּא גִּלְגּוּלָא דִּילֵיהּ בְּכָל דָּרָא וְדָרָא, אֵיךְ הֲוָה אָזִיל מְצַדִּיק לְצַדִּיק, עַד שִׁתִּין רִבּוֹא, עַד דְּמָטֵי לְהַהוּא דְּאִתְּמַר בֵּיהּ (בראשית ו ג) בְּשַׁגַּם הוּא בָשָׂר, בְּשַׁגַּם זֶה הֶבֶל, וְאוּקְמוּהָ קַדְמָאֵי בְּשַׁגַּם דָּא מֹשֶׁה, וּמִיָּד דְּחָמָא דַּעֲתִידָא אוֹרַיְתָא לְאִתְיַהֲבָא עַל יְדֵיהּ, אוֹסִיפַת בְּגִינֵיהּ כַּמָּה קָרְבָּנִין לְקוּדְשָׁא בְּרִיךְ הוּא, וְכַמָּה צְלוֹתִין וּבָעוּתִין, וְדָא אִיהוּ וַתּוֹסֶף לָלֶדֶת:

שער הגלגולים - הקדמה לב

וז"ס מה שצחקו בו הילדים, וא"ל של קרח עלה קרח, והענין הוא, במה שיתבאר לקמן, כי קרח בן יצהר, הוא רוחו של קין מצד הרע, ולכן ירד חיים שאולה, וא"ל הילדים לביישו ולגדפו, כי הנה קרח ירד שאולה, וצריך לעלות, ואתה נמשך משרש קרח, ואיך אתה רוצה לעלות. גם רמזו, כי הנה קרח בן יצהר גלחו משה, והיה קרח בשערותיו כנודע, ולכן גם אלישע היה קרח בשער רותיו כמוהו, כי שרש נשמתו יש בה חלק ואחיזה מן קרח. וזה גרם שנתעברו בו אחר כך נפש נדב ואביהוא, שגם הם משרש נשמת קרח. גם כמו שמרע"ה הזכיר שם בן מ"ב, והרג את המצרי שהוא נפש קין מצד הרע, כן אלישע הזכיר שם בן מ"ב, והרג מ"ב ילדים אלו כנזכר בזוהר:

שער הגלגולים - הקדמה לג

ודע, כי קרח בן יצהר, הוא מבחי' הרוח של קין מצד הרע שלו, כמו שנתבאר בפסוקים, ויקח קרח וע"ש, כי נתלבש זה הרוח הרע של קין בו, ולכן היה מקטרג להבל אחיו שהוא מרע"ה. משא"כ יתרו, כי גם הוא מן קין, כמש"ה וחבר הקיני נפרד מקין, אלא שהוא מבחי' הטוב של קין, ולכן נתן את צפורה בתו למשה, והטיב עמו, והאכילו לחם. משא"כ בקרח שהיה מצד הרע של קין כנזכר. וקרח חשב, כי בו יתוקן קין הבכור, ולכן נתגבר על משה שהוא הבל, וטעה בזה, כי אין תיקון קין בקרח, לפי שהוא מצד הרע שבו, אלא בזרע היוצא ממנו, והוא שמואל הנביא, שהוא מצד הטוב של קין. וז"ש רז"ל קורח ניבא ולא ידע, כי ראה אש יוצאה מאמתו, והבן זה. וז"ש ויראה את הקיני, כי קני הוא קין, ושמואל הוא מן קין. ונרמז בתיבת אוי מי יחיה משמו אל אותיות משמואל, פירוש, כי למעלה אמר וירא את עמלק וכו', שהוא מצד הרע של קין, כמו שנתבאר במקומו, ואמר כי אוי לו לעמלק כשיבא שמואל, שהוא זרז אשר לשאול על מלחמת עמלק, שנאמר וישסף שמואל את אגג:

And Moshe said, 'Thus you shall know that God has sent me to do all these works; for I have not done them of my own mind. If these men die the common death of all men, or if they are visited by the fate of all men, then God has not sent me. But if God creates a new thing, and the earth opens its mouth and swallows them up, with all that belongs to them, and they go down alive into Sheol; then you shall understand that these men have provoked God.' And it came to pass, as he finished speaking all these words, that the ground split beneath them; and the earth opened its mouth, and swallowed them up, and their houses, and all the men who belonged to Korah, and all their goods. (*Bamidbar* 16:32)

The only other appearance in the Torah of this terminology is when the earth swallowed the blood of Hevel.

בראשית פרק ד:י-יא
(י) וַיֹּאמֶר מֶה עָשִׂיתָ קוֹל דְּמֵי אָחִיךָ צֹעֲקִים אֵלַי מִן־הָאֲדָמָה: (יא) וְעַתָּה אָרוּר אָתָּה מִן־הָאֲדָמָה אֲשֶׁר פָּצְתָה אֶת־פִּיהָ לָקַחַת אֶת־דְּמֵי אָחִיךָ מִיָּדֶךָ:

And He said, 'What have you done? The voice of your brother's blood cries to me from the ground. And now you are cursed from the earth which has opened its mouth to receive your brother's blood from your hand. (*Bereishit* 4:10-11)

Korach, who follows in the footsteps of Kayin, receives the appropriate punishment. The earth "opens up its mouth" and swallows him.

The similarities between Korach and Kayin are not the only striking parallels among the *dramatis personae*; there is also a striking similarity between Moshe and Hevel. As we have seen, the name *Hevel* means nothingness; we are told elsewhere in the text that Moshe was the most modest of men.

במדבר פרק יב:ג

(ג) וְהָאִישׁ מֹשֶׁה עָנָו מְאֹד מִכֹּל הָאָדָם אֲשֶׁר עַל־פְּנֵי הָאֲדָמָה:

And the man Moses was very humble, more than any other man on the face of the earth. (*Bamidbar* 12:3)

We may assume that Moshe, like Hevel, did not think too much of himself. Moshe's position was not attained through political maneuvering; he was chosen directly by God. Although Moshe tried to decline, God impressed upon him that his destiny, his unique task, was to lead the Jewish people.

When Kayin argued with Hevel, Hevel did not respond. Similarly, *Pirkei Avot* describes the argument of Korach as "the argument of Korach and his followers," not as "the argument between Korach and Moshe."

משנה מסכת אבות פרק ה:יז

כָּל מַחֲלוֹקֶת שֶׁהִיא לְשֵׁם שָׁמַיִם, סוֹפָהּ לְהִתְקַיֵּם. וְשֶׁאֵינָהּ לְשֵׁם שָׁמַיִם, אֵין סוֹפָהּ לְהִתְקַיֵּם. אֵיזוֹ הִיא מַחֲלוֹקֶת שֶׁהִיא לְשֵׁם שָׁמַיִם, זוֹ מַחֲלוֹקֶת הִלֵּל וְשַׁמַּאי. וְשֶׁאֵינָהּ לְשֵׁם שָׁמַיִם, זוֹ מַחֲלוֹקֶת קֹרַח וְכָל עֲדָתוֹ:

Every controversy that is for the sake of Heaven is destined to endure; but one that is not for the sake of Heaven is not destined to endure. What is [an example of] a controversy that is for the sake of Heaven? The controversy between Hillel and Shammai. And what is [an example of] a controversy that is not for the sake Heaven? The controversy of Korach and his entire congregation. (Mishnah, *Avot* 5:17)[9]

---

9. The Zohar goes even further in highlighting the nature of dispute:

זוהר חלק א דף יז/ב

מַחֲלוֹקֶת דְּאִתְתַּקַּן כְּגַוְונָא דִּלְעֵילָא וְסָלִיק וְלָא נָחִית וְאִתְקַיָּים בְּאֹרַח מֵישָׁר, דָּא מַחֲלוֹקֶת דְּשַׁמַּאי וְהִלֵּל. וְקֻדְשָׁא בְּרִיךְ הוּא אַפְרִישׁ בֵּינַיְיהוּ וְאַסְכִּים לוֹן. וְדָא הֲוָה מַחֲלוֹקֶת לְשֵׁם שָׁמַיִם. וְשָׁמַיִם אַפְרִישׁ מַחֲלוֹקֶת. וְעַל דָּא אִתְקַיְּימוּ. וְדָא הֲוָה כְּגַוְונָא דְּעוֹבָדָא דִּבְרֵאשִׁית. וְקֹרַח בְּעוֹבָדָא דִבְרֵאשִׁית אַכְחִישׁ בְּכֹלָּא. וּפְלוּגְתָּא דְשָׁמַיִם הֲוָה. וּבָעָא לְאַכְחָשָׁא מִלֵּי דְאוֹרַיְיתָא. וַדַּאי בְּאִתְדַּבְּ־קוּתָא דְּגֵיהִנֹּם הֲוָה. וְעַל דָּא אִתְדַּבַּק בַּהֲדֵיהּ:

Moshe, the faithful shepherd,[10] cared for each member of his flock. He

וְרָזָא דָא בְּסִפְרָא דְאָדָם. חֲשׁוֹךְ כַּד אִתְעַר בְּתוּקְפֵּיהּ וּבָרָא בֵּיהּ גֵּיהִנֹּם וְאִתְדַּבַּק בַּהֲדֵיהּ בְּהַהוּא מַחְלוֹקֶת. כֵּיוָן דְּשָׁכִיךְ רוּגְזָא וְתוּקְפָּא, אִתְעַר מַחֲלוּקָה כְּגַוְונָא אָחֳרָא, מַחְלוֹקֶת דִּרְחִימוּ. וּתְרֵין מַחְלוֹקֶת הֲוו. חַד שֵׁירוּתָא וְחַד סִיּוּמָא. וְדָא אִיהוּ אָרְחֵהוֹן דְּצַדִּיקַיָּא שֵׁירוּתָא דִלְהוֹן בְּקִ־ שִׁיוּ וְסוֹפָא דִלְהוֹן בְּנַיְיחָא. קָרֵם הֲוָה שֵׁירוּתָא דְּמַחֲלוּקָה כְּפוּם רוּגְזָא וְתוּקְפָּא וְאִתְדַּבַּק בַּגֵּיהִנֹּם. שַׁמַּאי סוֹפָא דְּמַחְלוֹקֶת כַּד רוּגְזָא בְּנַיְיחָא אִצְטְרִיךְ לְאַתְעָרָא מַחֲלוּקָה דִּרְחִימוּ וּלְאַסְכָּמָא עַל יְדָא דִשְׁמַיִם : וְרָזָא דָא יְהִי רָקִיעַ בְּתוֹךְ הַמָּיִם וִיהִי מַבְדִּיל, דָּא מַחְלוֹקֶת קַדְמָאָה אִתְעָרוּ דְּרוּגְזָא וְתוּ־ קְפָּא בָּעָא לְאַפְרָשָׁא וְאִתְעַר גֵּיהִנֹּם עַד דְּרוּגְזָא וְתוּקְפָּא אִצְטָנַּן. וּכְדֵין וַיַּעַשׂ אֱלֹהִים אֶת הָרָקִיעַ וְגוֹ׳ אִתְעַר מַחְלוֹקֶת דִּרְחִימוּ וְחָבִיבוּ וְקִיּוּמָא דְעָלְמָא. וּבְרָזָא דָּא מַחְלוֹקֶת שַׁמַּאי וְהִלֵּל. דְּתוֹרָה שֶׁבְּעַל פֶּה עָאלַת בִּרְחִימוּ גַּבֵּי תּוֹרָה שֶׁבִּכְתָב וַהֲווּ בְקִיּוּמָא שְׁלִים:

The dispute between Shammai and Hillel was composed on the pattern of the supernal dispute, becoming more and not less worthy as it proceeded and perpetuating itself rightfully. The Holy One, blessed be he, approved of their dispute, because its motive was lofty and it therefore resembled [the dispute] which took place at the Creation. Hence, like the latter, the dispute between Shammai and Hillel has survived to this day.

Korach, on the other hand, denied the Creation, fought against Heaven itself and sought to confute the words of the Torah. He certainly was of the following of the Gehinnom, and therefore remained attached to it....

Shammai conducted his dispute in that spirit of calm which should follow the first burst of passion; it therefore became a quarrel of love and obtained the approval of Heaven. This is indicated by our text. It says first: "Let there be a firmament in the midst of the waters, and let it divide" (*Bereishit* 1:6). This refers to the beginning of quarrel, the outburst of passion and violence. There was a desire for reconciliation, but meanwhile the Gehinnom arose before the wrath and passion cooled down. Then "God made the firmament"; that is, there emerged a quarrel of love and affection which made for the permanence of the world. In this category is the dispute between Shammai and Hillel, which resulted in the Oral Law approaching the Written law with love, so that they mutually supported each other. (*Zohar, Bereishit* 17b)

The commentaries on this passage in the *Zohar* recount the tradition attributed to the Arizal that in the future the law will follow the rulings of Shammai. See *Mikdash Melech*, ad loc.

10. This appellation for Moshe is found in *Mechilta de-Rebbe Yishmael* 15:1, and numerous times in the *Zohar*.

מכילתא דרבי ישמעאל בשלח - מסכתא דויהי פרשה ו
בא זה ללמדך שכל מי שמאמין ברועה נאמן כאלו מאמין במאמר מי שאמר והיה העולם. כיוצא בדבר אתה אומר וידבר העם באלהים ובמשה (במדבר כא) אם באלהים דברו קל וחומר במשה אלא זה בא ללמדך שכל מי שמדבר ברועה נאמן כאלו מדבר במי שאמר והיה העולם:

Mechilta de-Rebbe Yishmael 15:1
We are hereby apprised that one who believes in the "faithful shepherd" believes in the pronouncement (i.e., the Torah) of Him who spoke and brought the world into being. Similarly, "And the people spoke against God and against Moshes"

was aware of the uniqueness of each individual. Korah, however, tried to blur the differences between people.

One of the profound teachings of Judaism is profound individualism: Each person certainly has an inalienable right to his or her dignity, but not all people have equal roles and destinies.

My revered teacher, Rav Yosef Dov Soloveitchik, *zt"l*, illustrated this idea with an insight regarding the verse, "*Shema Yisrael, Hashem Elokeinu, Hashem echad* — Hear, O Israel, God is the Lord, God is One." Rav Soloveitchik commented that he would prefer to translate the word *echad* (one) as "unique." Jewish monotheism does not differ from polytheism purely in numeric terms. We believe in one God, and we believe that He is unique. We also believe that man is created in the image of God, which means that each and every person is unique as well. The challenge is to discover that uniqueness and develop it—not to define ourselves in comparison with others, but to search within ourselves and find the unique image of God that each of us embodies.

The Torah commands us to love our neighbors as ourselves, yet we might well ask, how is it possible to love others this way? The secret to loving others is recognizing and appreciating their uniqueness. A mother loves all her children, and she appreciates the uniqueness of each child. We are commanded to find the uniqueness in each person and to love him or her for it. When a person identifies his own uniqueness and develops that uniqueness, the image of God within is manifest.[11]

Sefer Bereishit begins with one brother focusing only on the inequality he perceives between himself and his brother. Kayin is haunted by his brother's successes; he becomes depressed, and his depression turns to murderous rage. *Sefer Shemot,* on the other hand, begins with Moshe venturing out of Pharaoh's palace to help his brothers.

שמות פרק ב:יא
וַיְהִי׀ בַּיָּמִים הָהֵם וַיִּגְדַּל מֹשֶׁה וַיֵּצֵא אֶל־אֶחָיו וַיַּרְא בְּסִבְלֹתָם וַיַּרְא אִישׁ מִצְרִי מַכֶּה אִישׁ־עִבְרִי מֵאֶחָיו:

(*Bamidbar* 21:5). If they spoke against God, how much more so against Moshe! We are hereby apprised that one who speaks against the "faithful shepherd" speaks against Him who spoke and brought the world into being.
11. We will return to the idea of loving others in *Parashat Kedoshim*.

It came to pass in those days, when Moshe was grown, that he went out to his brothers and looked upon their burdens. He spied an Egyptian beating a Hebrew, one of his brothers. (*Shemot* 2:11)

Moshe seeks brotherhood; he leaves his comfort zone, going out to see his brothers' suffering. He is not jaded by his status as prince of Egypt. Quite the contrary, he recognizes the brotherhood that exists between all Jews.

שמות פרק ב:יב

וַיִּפֶן כֹּה וָכֹה וַיַּרְא כִּי אֵין אִישׁ וַיַּךְ אֶת־הַמִּצְרִי וַיִּטְמְנֵהוּ בַּחוֹל:

[Moshe] looked this way and that way, and when he saw that there was no man, he slew the Egyptian and hid him in the sand. (*Shemot* 2:12)

Although this scene ends in much the same way as the confrontation between Kayin and Hevel, with a dead body on the ground, Moshe's act is profoundly different: Kayin was motivated by jealousy of his brother, while Moshe's motivation was to protect his brother.

Above, we noted the teaching of the *Zohar* that the soul of Hevel transmigrated to Moshe; let us consider the larger character traits to which this brief statement alludes. First and foremost, Moshe never defined himself in terms of others. In fact, the first brothers that we find in the Torah who truly relate to one another with love and respect are Moshe and his brother Aharon.

שמות פרק ד, כז

(כז) וַיֹּאמֶר ה' אֶל־אַהֲרֹן לֵךְ לִקְרַאת מֹשֶׁה הַמִּדְבָּרָה וַיֵּלֶךְ וַיִּפְגְּשֵׁהוּ בְּהַר הָאֱלֹהִים וַיִּשַּׁק־לוֹ:

God said to Aharon, "Go into the wilderness to meet Moshe." He went and met him on the mountain of God, and he [Aharon] kissed him [Moshe]. (*Shemot* 4:27)

The Midrash stresses the importance of this kiss:

שמות רבה ה:י

וַיֵּלֶךְ וַיִּפְגְּשֵׁהוּ, הֲדָא הוּא דִכְתִיב (תהלים פה, יא): חֶסֶד וֶאֱמֶת נִפְגָּשׁוּ צֶדֶק וְשָׁלוֹם נָשָׁקוּ. חֶסֶד זֶה אַהֲרֹן, שֶׁנֶּאֱמַר (דברים לג, ח): וּלְלֵוִי אָמַר תֻּמֶּיךָ וְאוּרֶיךָ לְאִישׁ חֲסִידֶךָ. וֶאֱמֶת זֶה מֹשֶׁה, שֶׁנֶּאֱמַר (במדבר יב, ז): לֹא כֵן עַבְדִּי מֹשֶׁה וגו'. הֱוֵי חֶסֶד וֶאֱמֶת נִפְגָּשׁוּ, כְּמָה דְתֵימָא וַיֵּלֶךְ וַיִּפְגְּשֵׁהוּ בְּהַר הָאֱלֹהִים. צֶדֶק זֶה מֹשֶׁה, שֶׁנֶּאֱמַר (דברים לג, כא): צִדְקַת ה' עָשָׂה. וְשָׁלוֹם זֶה אַהֲרֹן, שֶׁנֶּאֱמַר (מלאכי ב, ו): בְּשָׁלוֹם וּבְמִישׁוֹר הָלַךְ אִתִּי. נָשָׁקוּ, וַיִּשַּׁק לוֹ. אָמְרוּ רַבּוֹתֵינוּ כָּל הַנְּשִׁיקוֹת שֶׁל תִּפְלוּת חוּץ מְשָׁלֹשׁ [כדכתיב לעיל], וַיִּשַּׁק לוֹ, מַהוּ וַיִּשַּׁק לוֹ, זֶה שָׂמַח בִּגְדֻלָּתוֹ שֶׁל זֶה וְזֶה שָׂמַח בִּגְדֻלָּתוֹ שֶׁל זֶה.

"He went and met him" — When it says "Kindness and truth met; righteousness and peace kissed" (*Tehillim* 85:11), "kindness" refers to Aharon, of whom it is said: "To Levi [Aharon's tribe] he said, 'Your *tumim* and *urim* will be with Your man of kindness'" (*Devarim* 33:8), while "truth" refers to Moshe, of whom it says: "My servant Moshe… is trusted in all My house" (*Bamidbar* 7:7). Hence "kindness and truth met" when "He went and met him on the mountain of God." "Righteousness" refers to Moshe, of whom it is said, "He carried out the righteousness of God" (*Devarim* 33:21), and "peace" refers to Aharon, of whom it says, "He walked with Me in peace and uprightness" (*Malachi* 2:6).… They "kissed," meaning that each of them rejoiced in the other's greatness. (*Shemot Rabbah* 5:10)

Throughout *Sefer Bereishit*, there is no harmony among brothers.[12] The

---

12. The exception, though not explicit in the text, are the sons of Rachel. According to the Midrash, Yosef and Binyamin did get along, as did Efraim and Menashe. Regarding Efraim and Menashe, even though the younger (Efraim) receives preferential treatment from his grandfather (*Bereishit* 48:13-14), we never find any expression of jealousy or hatred, and the absence of enmity, which was the default emotion between brothers throughout Bereishit, is striking.

מדרש רבה שמות - פרשה ה פסקה א

וַיֹּאמֶר ה' אֶל אַהֲרֹן לֵךְ לִקְרַאת מֹשֶׁה הַמִּדְבָּרָה, הֲדָא הוּא דִכְתִיב (שיר השירים ח, א): מִי יִתֶּנְךָ כְּאָח לִי, בְּאֵיזֶה אָח הַכָּתוּב מְדַבֵּר, אִם תֹּאמַר בְּקַיִן, וְהָא כְתִיב (בראשית ד, ח): וַיָּקָם קַיִן אֶל הֶבֶל

harmony, unity, and mutual respect between Moshe and Aharon is what enables them to lead the people out of Egypt to Mount Sinai, and enables them to accept the Torah. In order to leave Egypt, the Jewish people had to first become a nation. In order to receive the Torah they needed unity; the core of this unity was the love and mutual respect between Moshe and Aharon. For the first time, two brothers—Moshe and Aharon—understood that each of them, and every individual Jew, has a unique task. "Each rejoiced at the other's greatness," each appreciated the unique capabilities of the other—and when this is the basis of the relationship, there is no possible place for jealousy. Moshe and Aharon, in a very real sense, repaired the Kayin-Hevel rift,[13] and paved the way toward the unity that made the birth of the Jewish People possible.

אָחִיו וַיַּהַרְגֵהוּ. אִם תֹּאמַר כְּיִשְׁמָעֵאל לְיִצְחָק, הָא גָרְסִינַן יִשְׁמָעֵאל שׂוֹנֵא לְיִצְחָק. אִם תֹּאמַר כְּעֵשָׂו לְיַעֲקֹב, הָא כְּתִיב (בראשית כז, מא): וַיִּשְׂטֹם עֵשָׂו אֶת יַעֲקֹב. אִם תֹּאמַר כְּאַחֵי יוֹסֵף, וְהָכְתִיב (בראשית לז, ד): וַיִּשְׂנְאוּ אֹתוֹ, וּכְתִיב (בראשית כז, יא): וַיְקַנְאוּ בוֹ אֶחָיו. אֶלָּא כְּיוֹסֵף לְבִנְיָמִן, (שיר השירים ח, א): יוֹנֵק שְׁדֵי אִמִּי, כְּמשֶׁה לְאַהֲרֹן, שֶׁנֶּאֱמַר: וַיֵּלֶךְ וַיִּפְגְּשֵׁהוּ בְּהַר הָאֱלֹהִים וַיִּשַּׁק לוֹ,

"And God said to Aharon: Go into the wilderness to meet Moshe" (*Shemot* 4:27) — Thus it is written: Oh that you were as my brother' (*Shir Ha-Shirim* 8:1). To which brother does the verse refer? If you say Kayin, is it not written: And Kayin rose up against Hevel his brother, and slew him? (*Bereishit* 4:8) Should you say it refers to the relationship between Yishmael and Yitzchak, well, have we not learned that Yishmael hated Yitzchak? If you say it refers to Esav and Yaakov, does it not say, 'And Esav hated Yaakov' (*Bereishit* 27: 41). If you refer it to Yosef's brothers, does it not say: 'And they hated him (*Bereishit* 27:4)? and also, 'And his brothers envied him' (*Bereishit* 27: 2)? It can only refer to such a brother as Yosef was to Binyamin: 'That sucked the breasts of my mother" (*Shir Ha-Shirim* 8:1) or Moshe to Aharon, as it is said: 'And he went, and met him in the mountain of God, and kissed him' (*Shemot* 4:27). (*Shemot Rabbah* 5:1)

13. See my comments on *Parashat Kedoshim* in *Explorations*: The *Midrash Tanchuma* links the commandment of *shaatnez* with the fratricide perpetrated by Kayin. An expanded version of themes in this chapter will be treated at length in my forthcoming volume on Tisha B'Av, tentatively titled, "Like a Lion in Hiding."

מדרש תנחומא (ורשא) פרשת בראשית (ט) [ד, ג]

וַיְהִי מִקֵּץ יָמִים וַיָּבֵא קַיִן וְגוֹ׳. יֵשׁ מִקֵּץ שָׁנָה וְיֵשׁ מִקֵּץ שְׁנָתַיִם, וְיֵשׁ יָמִים, וְיֵשׁ אַרְבָּעִים שָׁנָה. אָמְרוּ חֲכָמֵינוּ זִכְרוֹנָם לִבְרָכָה, בְּנֵי אַרְבָּעִים שָׁנָה הָיוּ קַיִן וְהֶבֶל. וַיָּבֵא קַיִן מִפְּרִי הָאֲדָמָה, מַהוּ? מִן מוֹתַר מַאֲכָלוֹ. וְרַבָּנָן אָמְרֵי, זֶרַע פִּשְׁתָּן הָיָה, וְהֶבֶל הֵבִיא גַם הוּא מִבְּכֹרוֹת צֹאנוֹ וּמֵחֶלְבֵהֶן לְפִיכָךְ נֶאֱסַר צֶמֶר וּפִשְׁתִּים, שֶׁנֶּאֱמַר: לֹא תִלְבַּשׁ שַׁעַטְנֵז וְגוֹ׳ (דברים כב, יא). וְאָמַר הַקָּדוֹשׁ בָּרוּךְ הוּא, אֵינוֹ דִין שֶׁיִּתְעָרֵב מִנְחַת הַחוֹטֵא עִם מִנְחַת הַזַּכַּאי לְפִיכָךְ נֶאֱסַר.

The Missing 974 Generations and the Age of the World: The First Man and Evolution

תלמוד בבלי מסכת חגיגה יג:ב - יד:א

תַּנְיָא, רַבִּי אוֹמֵר מִשּׁוּם אַבָּא יוֹסִי בֶּן דּוֹסְתַּאי, "אֶלֶף אַלְפִין יְשַׁמְּשׁוּנֵיהּ", מִסְפַּר גְּדוּד אֶחָד, וְלִגְדוּדָיו - אֵין מִסְפָּר. וְרַב יִרְמְיָה בַּר אַבָּא אָמַר, "אֶלֶף אַלְפִין יְשַׁמְּשׁוּנֵיהּ" - לִנְהַר דִּינוּר, שֶׁנֶּאֱמַר, (דניאל ז) "נְהַר דִּינוּר נָגֵד וְנָפֵק מִן קֳדָמוֹהִי, אֶלֶף אַלְפִין יְשַׁמְּשׁוּנֵיהּ" וְגוֹ'. מֵהֵיכָן נָפֵק, מִזֵּיעָתָן שֶׁל חַיּוֹת, וּלְהֵיכָן שָׁפֵיךְ? אָמַר רַב, עַל רָאשֵׁי רְשָׁעִים יָחוּל בַּגֵּיהִנֹּם, שֶׁנֶּאֱמַר, (ירמיה כג) "הִנֵּה סַעֲרַת ה' חֵמָה יָצְאָה וְסַעַר מִתְחוֹלֵל, עַל רֹאשׁ רְשָׁעִים יָחוּל". וְרַב אַחָא בַּר יַעֲקֹב אָמַר, עַל אֲשֶׁר קֻמְּטוּ שֶׁנֶּאֱמַר, (איוב כב) "אֲשֶׁר קֻמְּטוּ וְלֹא עֵת, נָהָר יוּצַק יְסוֹדָם". תַּנְיָא, אָמַר רַבִּי שִׁמְעוֹן הֶחָסִיד, אֵלּוּ תֵּשַׁע מֵאוֹת וְשִׁבְעִים וְאַרְבַּע דּוֹרוֹת שֶׁקּוּמְטוּ לְהִבָּרְאוֹת קוֹדֶם שֶׁנִּבְרָא הָעוֹלָם, וְלֹא נִבְרָאוּ. עָמַד הַקָּדוֹשׁ בָּרוּךְ הוּא (וטרדן, איכא דאמרי,) וּשְׁתָלָן בְּכָל דּוֹר וָדוֹר, וְהֵן הֵן - עַזֵּי פָנִים שֶׁבַּדּוֹר.

It is taught: Rabbi said in the name of Abba Yosi ben Dostai: "A thousand thousands were serving Him" — This is the number of one troop; but of His troops there is no number. And Rav Yirmiyah bar Abba said, "A thousand thousands were serving Him" refers to the stream of fire, as it says, "A stream of fire was flowing forth before Him, a thousand thousands were serving Him [and a myriad myriads were standing before Him]" (*Daniel* 7). From where does [this stream of fire] emerge? From the perspiration of the *chayot*. And where does it empty? Rav Zuta bar Tuvia said in the name if Rav, 'Upon the heads of the wicked in hell, as it says, "Behold, a storm of God has gone forth in fury, a whirling storm; it shall whirl upon the head of the wicked" (Yirmiyah 23). And Rav Acha bar Yaakov said: The river flows over those who were snatched away, as it is stated, "Who were snatched away before their time, whose foundation was poured out as a stream" (*Iyov* 22:16). It is taught: Rabbi Shimon he-Chasid said: 'These are the nine hundred and seventy-four generations who were ordained to be created before the world was created, but were not created. The Holy One, blessed be He, arose and planted them in every generation, and it is they who are the insolent of each generation. (*Chagigah* 13b-14a)[1]

---

1. The Talmud in *Shabbat* 88b, and *Zevachim* 116a, also makes reference to these 974 generations:

תלמוד בבלי מסכת שבת דף פח עמוד ב

וְאָמַר רַבִּי יְהוֹשֻׁעַ בֶּן לֵוִי, בְּשָׁעָה שֶׁעָלָה מֹשֶׁה לַמָּרוֹם, אָמְרוּ מַלְאֲכֵי הַשָּׁרֵת לִפְנֵי הַקָּדוֹשׁ בָּרוּךְ הוּא, רִבּוֹנוֹ שֶׁל עוֹלָם, מַה לִּילוּד אִשָּׁה בֵּינֵינוּ? אָמַר לָהֶם, לְקַבֵּל הַתּוֹרָה בָּא. אָמְרוּ, לְפָנֶיךָ חֶמְדָּה גְנוּזָה, שֶׁגְּנוּזָה לָךְ תְּשַׁע מֵאוֹת שִׁבְעִים וְאַרְבָּעָה דוֹרוֹת קוֹדֶם שֶׁנִּבְרָא הָעוֹלָם, אַתָּה מְבַקֵּשׁ לִיתְּנָהּ לְבָשָׂר וָדָם"?

R. Yehoshua b. Levi also said: When Moshe ascended on high, the ministering angels spoke before the Holy One, blessed be He: "Sovereign of the Universe! What business has one born of woman amongst us?" "He has come to receive the Torah," He answered them. Said they to Him, "That secret treasure, which has been hidden by You for nine hundred and seventy-four generations before the world was created..?!" (*Shabbat* 88b)

תלמוד בבלי מסכת זבחים דף קטז עמוד א

רַבִּי אֶלְעָזָר הַמּוֹדָעִי אוֹמֵר, מַתַּן תּוֹרָה שָׁמַע וּבָא. שֶׁכְּשֶׁנִּיתְּנָה תּוֹרָה לְיִשְׂרָאֵל, הָיָה קוֹלוֹ הוֹלֵךְ מִסּוֹף הָעוֹלָם וְעַד סוֹפוֹ, וְכָל מַלְכֵי עוֹבְדֵי כּוֹכָבִים, אֲחָזָתַן רְעָדָה בְּהֵיכְלֵיהֶן, וְאָמְרוּ שִׁירָה. שֶׁנֶּאֱמַר, (תהלים כט) "וּבְהֵיכָלוֹ כֻּלּוֹ אוֹמֵר כָּבוֹד". נִתְקַבְּצוּ כֻּלָּם אֵצֶל בִּלְעָם הָרָשָׁע וְאָמְרוּ לוֹ, מַה קוֹל הֶהָמוֹן אֲשֶׁר שָׁמַעְנוּ? שֶׁמָּא מַבּוּל בָּא לָעוֹלָם? אָמַר לָהֶם "ה' לַמַּבּוּל יָשָׁב", אָמַר לָהֶם, "וַיֵּשֶׁב ה' מֶלֶךְ לְעוֹלָם" - כְּבָר נִשְׁבַּע הַקָּדוֹשׁ בָּרוּךְ הוּא שֶׁאֵינוֹ מֵבִיא מַבּוּל לָעוֹלָם. אָמְרוּ לוֹ, מַבּוּל שֶׁל מַיִם אֵינוֹ מֵבִיא, אֲבָל מַבּוּל שֶׁל אֵשׁ מֵבִיא, שֶׁנֶּאֱמַר, (שם סו) "כִּי הִנֵּה ... בָּאֵשׁ ה' נִשְׁפָּט וְגוֹ'." אָמַר לָהֶם כְּבָר נִשְׁבַּע שֶׁאֵינוֹ מַשְׁחִית כָּל בָּשָׂר. מַה קּוֹל הֶהָמוֹן הַזֶּה שֶׁשָּׁמַעְנוּ? אָמַר לָהֶם, חֶמְדָּה טוֹבָה יֵשׁ לוֹ בְּבֵית גְּנָזָיו, שֶׁהָיָה גְנוּזָה אֶצְלוֹ תתקע"ד [תְּשַׁע מֵאוֹת שִׁבְעִים וְאַרְבָּעָה] דוֹרוֹת קֹדֶם שֶׁנִּבְרָא הָעוֹלָם, וּבִקֵּשׁ לִתְּנָהּ לְבָנָיו, שֶׁנֶּאֱמַר, (תהלים כט) "ה' עֹז לְעַמּוֹ יִתֵּן". מִיָּד פָּתְחוּ כֻלָּם וְאָמְרוּ, "ה' יְבָרֵךְ אֶת עַמּוֹ בַשָּׁלוֹם".

R. Elazar of Modim said: He heard of the giving of the Torah and came. For when the Torah was given to Israel the sound travelled from one end of the earth to the other, and all the heathen kings were seized with trembling in their palaces, and they uttered song, as it is said, 'And in his place all say: 'Glory'. They all assembled by the wicked Bil'am and asked him: What is this tumultuous noise that we have heard? Perhaps a flood is coming upon the world, for it says, 'The Almighty sat enthroned at the flood, the Almighty sits as King forever.' [Bil'am] replied: 'The

This passage is difficult to understand—for numerous reasons. Rabbi Acha bar Yaakov speaks of people who were "ordained," "intended," or "meant to be," but instead were "wrinkled"—crushed, pressed, or contracted. As if this is not difficult enough to understand, the Talmud "clarifies" the passage by explaining that these were the members of a special "club" that existed (or did not exist[2]) for 974 generations prior to the creation of the world. The result is a teaching which seems impossible: They were created—yet not created; they were "pressed" or contracted and placed into future generations.[3] Did they exist or not? If not, why is their presence still felt?

Holy One, blessed be He, has already sworn that He will not bring [another] flood upon the world.' Perhaps, they ventured, He will not bring a flood of water, yet He will bring a flood of fire, as it is said, 'For by fire will the Lord contend'? 'He has already sworn that He will not destroy all flesh,' [Bil'am] assured them. 'Then what is the sound of this tumult that we have heard?' 'He has a precious treasure in His storehouse, which was hidden by Him nine hundred and seventy-four generations before the world was created, and He has desired to give it to His children, as it is said, 'The Lord will give strength unto His people.' Forthwith they all exclaimed, 'The Almighty will bless His people with peace.' (*Zevachim* 116a).

2. See *Midrash Tehillim* (Buber edition) section 90 for a *gematria* equation which points to the existence of these generations. *Midrash Tehillim* is an ancient midrash, sometimes referred to as *Aggadat Tehillim* or *Midrash Shocher Tov* and was first printed in Istanbul, 1512, and then again by Shlomo Buber in Vilna, 1891, based upon manuscripts.

מדרש תהלים (בובר) מזמור צ

זרמתם שנה יהיו. אלו תשע מאות ושבעים וארבעה דורות שהיו קודם לבריאת עולם ונשטפו כהרף עין בשביל שהיו רעים. ר׳ יוחנן אמר למה ב׳ של בראשית גדולה ביותר, לפי שהיא מצטרפת לשני ביתי״ן למלא ארבע, בראשית בגימטריא תתקע״ד הוו, כיצד תש״ר הרי תשע מאות, א׳ דבראשית מתחלף עם ל׳ דאלבם הרי שלשים, י׳ מתחלף עם מ׳ דאתב״ש הרי ארבעים, ב׳ שהיא גדולה כשני ביתי״ן מצטרפת לחשבון ארבעה, הרי תשע מאות ושבעים וארבעה, ואחר כך ברא אלהים את השמים ואת הארץ.

3. According to a mystical tradition recorded in the *Sefer ha-Bahir* section 195, the souls of the 974 wicked generations are transmigrated into new bodies, who are then judged for deeds performed in the previous life. This is the *Bahir*'s explanation for theodicy, because the wicked souls are being punished even though they currently inhabit righteous people. However, based on the *Bahir*'s context it sounds as if these people are presently righteous, while the Talmudic version makes these people sound presently wicked. See Rav Reuven Margoliot's notes on the *Sefer ha-Bahir* (Mosad Harav Kook edition) for other references to Kabbalistic treatment of this subject.

This strange Talmudic passage expounds upon on a Mishnah that places severe limits on certain subjects of study; there are, our Sages tell us, certain topics that cannot be completely explained or fully communicated in a normal classroom setting:

משנה מסכת חגיגה פרק ב משנה א

אֵין דּוֹרְשִׁין בָּעֲרָיוֹת בִּשְׁלשָׁה. וְלֹא בְמַעֲשֵׂה בְרֵאשִׁית בִּשְׁנַיִם. וְלֹא בַמֶּרְכָּבָה בְּיָחִיד, אֶלָּא אִם כֵּן הָיָה חָכָם וּמֵבִין מִדַּעְתּוֹ. כָּל הַמִּסְתַּכֵּל בְּאַרְבָּעָה דְבָרִים, רָאוּי לוֹ כְּאִלּוּ לֹא בָא לָעוֹלָם, מַה לְמַעְלָה, מַה לְמַטָּה, מַה לְפָנִים, וּמַה לְאָחוֹר. וְכָל שֶׁלֹּא חָס עַל כְּבוֹד קוֹנוֹ, רָאוּי לוֹ שֶׁלֹּא בָא לָעוֹלָם:

The [subject of] forbidden relations may not be expounded in the presence of three, nor the work of Creation in the presence of two, nor [the work of] the Chariot in the presence of one, unless he is a sage and understands of his own knowledge. Whosoever speculates upon [the following] four things, a pity for him! It is preferable that he had not come into the world: What is above, what is beneath, what came before, what after. And whoever takes the honor of his Maker lightly, it would have (been preferable had he not come into the world. (*Chagigah* 11b

Certain issues are meant to remain secret, obscure, unknown to all but the most capable and outstanding scholars. Other topics are to be given only slightly less limited exposure. The Mishnah dissuades even the most accomplished scholars from attempting to penetrate those areas deemed unfathomable. Although this list includes the mysteries of Creation, mainstream Jewish tradition and texts offer hints about the dawn and predawn of Creation—a period more appropriately termed "the twilight of Creation."[4] While it may be wise to avoid mystical content, the Torah offers us a peek at certain aspects of Creation that are readily accessible:

---

4. The Torah describes the creation as twilight: "And there was evening and there was morning, one day."

בראשית פרק א:א-ה

בְּרֵאשִׁית בָּרָא אֱלֹהִים אֵת הַשָּׁמַיִם וְאֵת הָאָרֶץ: וְהָאָרֶץ הָיְתָה תֹהוּ וָבֹהוּ וְחֹשֶׁךְ עַל־פְּנֵי תְהוֹם וְרוּחַ אֱלֹהִים מְרַחֶפֶת עַל־פְּנֵי הַמָּיִם: וַיֹּאמֶר אֱלֹהִים יְהִי אוֹר וַיְהִי־אוֹר: וַיַּרְא אֱלֹהִים אֶת־הָאוֹר כִּי־טוֹב וַיַּבְדֵּל אֱלֹהִים בֵּין הָאוֹר וּבֵין הַחֹשֶׁךְ: וַיִּקְרָא אֱלֹהִים׀ לָאוֹר יוֹם וְלַחֹשֶׁךְ קָרָא לָיְלָה וַיְהִי־עֶרֶב וַיְהִי־בֹקֶר יוֹם אֶחָד:

In the beginning, God created the heaven and the earth. And the earth was without form, and void; and darkness was upon the face of the deep. And the spirit of God hovered upon the face of the waters. And God said, 'Let there be light;' and there was light. And God saw the light, that it was good; and God differentiated between the light and the darkness. And God called the light Day, and the darkness he called Night. And there was evening and there was morning, one day. (*Bereishit* 1:1-5)

With these epic words, the Torah, and indeed the world, begins—but the beginning is clouded in mystery, allegory, allusion.

Returning to our passage about what may have existed before our present reality, Rashi explains by presenting a verse from *Tehillim*:[5]

תהלים פרק קה:ח-י

זָכַר לְעוֹלָם בְּרִיתוֹ דָּבָר צִוָּה לְאֶלֶף דּוֹר: אֲשֶׁר כָּרַת אֶת־אַבְרָהָם וּשְׁבוּעָתוֹ לְיִשְׂחָק[6]: וַיַּעֲמִידֶהָ לְיַעֲקֹב לְחֹק לְיִשְׂרָאֵל בְּרִית עוֹלָם:

He has remembered His covenant forever, the word He commanded to a thousand generations, the covenant which He made with Avraham, and his oath to Yitzchak and confirmed to Yaakov as law, and to Israel for an everlasting covenant. (*Tehillim* 105:8-10)

---
5. Rashi's comments are based on *Kohelet Rabbah* 1:35.
6. Regarding this variant spelling of Yitzchak, see Radak, *Yirmiyahu* 33:26.

רד"ק ירמיהו פרק לג:כו
ישחק - כתיב בשי"ן כמו בצד"י כי שני השרשים שוים בענין ושתי האותיות ממוצא אחד והוא אחד מד' הכתובים בשי"ן כנוי ליצחק:

"A thousand generations" were commanded into being by the Word of God. A cursory reading of this verse might lead to the understanding that the Torah's scope and efficacy are limited to a "mere" thousand generations. On the other hand, we might simply consider this a vernacular or metaphoric usage, citing other poetic uses of the "thousand years" or "thousand generations" to describe the futility of man's aspirations:

קהלת פרק ו:ו-ז

וְאִלּוּ חָיָה אֶלֶף שָׁנִים פַּעֲמַיִם וְטוֹבָה לֹא רָאָה הֲלֹא אֶל־מָקוֹם אֶחָד הַכֹּל הוֹלֵךְ: כָּל־עֲמַל הָאָדָם לְפִיהוּ וְגַם־הַנֶּפֶשׁ לֹא תִמָּלֵא:

And even if he lives one thousand years twice over, he has seen no good; do not all go to one place? All man's labor is for his mouth, and yet the appetite is not filled. (*Kohelet* 6:6-7)

While we know that God transcends time, the Psalmist nonetheless utilizes this same "thousand" expression to describe Divine time:

תהלים פרק צ:א-ד

תְּפִלָּה לְמֹשֶׁה אִישׁ הָאֱלֹהִים ה' מָעוֹן אַתָּה הָיִיתָ לָּנוּ בְּדֹר וָדֹר: בְּטֶרֶם הָרִים יֻלָּדוּ וַתְּחוֹלֵל אֶרֶץ וְתֵבֵל וּמֵעוֹלָם עַד עוֹלָם אַתָּה אֵ-ל: תָּשֵׁב אֱנוֹשׁ עַד דַּכָּא וַתֹּאמֶר שׁוּבוּ בְנֵי אָדָם: כִּי אֶלֶף שָׁנִים בְּעֵינֶיךָ כְּיוֹם אֶתְמוֹל כִּי יַעֲבֹר וְאַשְׁמוּרָה בַלָּיְלָה:

A Prayer of Moshe the man of God: Almighty God, you have been our dwelling place in all generations. Before the mountains were brought forth, before You had formed the earth and the world, forever and ever, You are God. You turn man back to dust; and say, 'Turn back, O children of men!' For a thousand years in your sight are but like yesterday when it is past, and like a watch in the night. (*Tehillim* 90:1-4)

Rashi, however, offers a very different explanation. Leaving no room for misinterpretation or misunderstanding of the Torah's eternal relevance, he explains that the verse does not mean "A thousand generations were commanded," but rather, "the Torah was commanded to the thousandth generation."[7] This interpretation is actually supported by the continuation of the verse itself: "…the word He commanded to a thousand generations … and to Israel <u>for an everlasting covenant</u>."

While this interpretation solves one problem, it creates another: The Torah is eternal, everlasting, and it was given to the thousandth generation—or was it? A straightforward count of the generations enumerated in the Torah from Adam to Moshe yields a number far short of one thousand. In fact, according to tradition, the Torah was given to the twenty-sixth generation.[8]

---

7. Rashi, *Chagigah* 14a, s.v. *kodem she-nivra ha-olam*; also see Rashi, *Shabbat* 88b, s.v. *tisha meot shivim v'arba dorot*, and Rashi's commentary to *Tehillim* 105:8, and Rashi, *Zevachim* 116a.

רש"י מסכת חגיגה דף יד עמוד א
קודם שנברא העולם - נגזר עליהם להבראות להיות קודם מתן תורה, לקיים מה שנאמר דבר צוה לאלף דור [תהלים קה] ראויה היתה תורה להינתן לסוף אלף דור, וכשראה שאין העולם מתקיים בלא תורה - עמד וטרדן, ונתנה לסוף עשרים וששה דורות מאדם הראשון עד משה רבינו.

רש"י מסכת שבת דף פח עמוד ב
תשע מאות ושבעים וארבעה דורות - באלפים שנה שקדמה תורה לעולם היו עתידין דורות הללו להבראות, שנאמר [תהלים קה] דבר צוה לאלף דור, וראה הקדוש ברוך הוא שאין העולם מתקיים בלא תורה - והעבירן, ולא בראן ונתנה לעשרים ושש דורות, הרי שחסרו תשע מאות ושבעים וארבעה דורות מאלף.

רש"י תהלים פרק קה פסוק ח
דבר צוה לאלף דור - התורה אשר צוה להודיעה בעולם לאחר אלף דור וראה שאין העולם מתקיים בלא תורה והעביר מהם תשע מאות ושבעים וארבעה דורות, ויש לפתו' כפשוטו זכר לישרא' את בריתו אשר צוה והבטיח לשמור להם לאלף דור כענין שומר הברית והחסד לאהביו ולשומרי מצוותיו לאלף דור:

8. See *Bereishit Rabbah* 1:4, 1:10, 21:9, *Vayikra Rabbah* 9:3, *Shir ha-Shirim Rabbah* 2:6, 5:13. The mystics saw great significance in the fact that the Torah being given to the twenty-sixth generation: The number 26 is the numerical equivalent of the Divine name: *yud* = 10, *heh* = 5, *vav* = 6, *heh* = 5, equaling 26.

תלמוד בבלי מסכת פסחים דף קיח עמוד א
אָמַר רַבִּי יְהוֹשֻׁעַ בֶּן לֵוִי, הַנֵּי עֶשְׂרִים וְשִׁשָּׁה "כִּי לְעוֹלָם חַסְדּוֹ", כְּנֶגֶד מִי? כְּנֶגֶד עֶשְׂרִים וְשִׁשָּׁה דּוֹרוֹת שֶׁבָּרָא הַקָּדוֹשׁ בָּרוּךְ הוּא בְּעוֹלָמוֹ, וְלֹא נָתַן לָהֶם תּוֹרָה, וְזָן אוֹתָם בְּחַסְדּוֹ:

R. Yehoshua b. Levi said: To what do the twenty-six [verses of] 'Give thanks' correspond? To the twenty-six generations which the Holy One, blessed be He, created in His world; though He did not give them the Torah, He sustained them by His love. (*Pesachim* 118a)

If the Torah was given to the thousandth generation, yet only twenty-six generations are discernible, nine hundred seventy-four generations are "missing." This, according to Rashi, is the lesson of the Talmud. According to this approach, both formulations are true: The Torah was given both to the thousandth generation and to the twenty-sixth generation. The solution lies in those who were "created, but not created" before our world came into existence.[9]

While this solution works mathematically, the theological implications are challenging. The passage that the Talmud offers as an "explanation" is difficult to understand.

---

9. Tosfot, *Chagigah* 14a explain that these 974 generations were planted in subsequent generations, which is consistent with the language of the Talmud. Rashi seems to understand that they were sentenced for their evil even though their behavior never came to fruition, but remained in the realm of potential. See the comments of the Maharsha, *Chagigah* 13b.

תוספות מסכת חגיגה דף יד עמוד א
וטרדן - ואיכא למ"ד ושתלן פרש"י לפי לשון ראשון נתן נשמתן בגיהנם ולא נבראו ותימה הוא וכי עביד דינא בלא דינא כי מה פשעו להיות בגיהנם ונראה לפרש לפרש שלא נבראו ביחד כי אם מעט לכל דור ודור כדי שלא יחריבו העולם ושני הלשונות בירושלמי שוה אך הלשון משונה ולכך לא חש למתני איכא דאמרי לה בהאי לישנא כיון שאינו משנה לה רק חדא תיבה.

מהרש"א חידושי אגדות מסכת חגיגה דף יג עמוד ב
על אשר קומטו פרש"י על תתקע"ד דורות שהעביר מן העולם כו' עכ"ל. אין רצונו שהעבירן מן העולם ממש דא"כ לא חטאו כלל ועל מה נדונו אלא שהעבירן אז קודם מתן תורה ושתלן בכל דור כו' ועל מה שעושין רשעה בכל דור ודור שפיר נדונו וכה"ג כתבו התוס' לפי גירסת הספרים:

Bereishit: The Missing 974 Generations | 41

תלמוד בבלי מסכת חגיגה דף יג עמוד ב
תַּנְיָא, אָמַר רַבִּי שִׁמְעוֹן הֶחָסִיד, אֵלּוּ תֵּשַׁע מֵאוֹת וְשִׁבְעִים וְאַרְבַּע דּוֹרוֹת שֶׁקּוּמְטוּ לְהִבָּרְאוֹת קוֹדֶם שֶׁנִּבְרָא הָעוֹלָם, וְלֹא נִבְרְאוּ. עָמַד הַקָּדוֹשׁ בָּרוּךְ הוּא וּשְׁתָלָן בְּכָל דּוֹר וָדוֹר, וְהֵן הֵן - עַזֵּי פָנִים שֶׁבַּדּוֹר.

These are the nine hundred and seventy-four generations who pressed themselves forward to be created before the world was created, but were not created. The Holy One, blessed be He, arose and planted them in every generation, and it is they who are the insolent of each generation. (*Chagigah* 13b-14a)

Were these people created or not? The entire passage seems paradoxical. An analysis of a series of teachings by Rav Abahu, recorded in the Midrash, may shed light on this paradox.

Rav Abahu analyzes a verse in the Torah which reflects upon Creation:

בראשית פרק ב:ד
(ד) אֵלֶּה תוֹלְדוֹת הַשָּׁמַיִם וְהָאָרֶץ בְּהִבָּרְאָם בְּיוֹם עֲשׂוֹת ה' אֱלֹהִים אֶרֶץ וְשָׁמָיִם:

These are the origins of the heavens and of the earth when they were created, on the day that the Almighty God made the earth and the heavens. (*Bereishit* 2:4)

Rav Abahu explains this verse with the following cryptic comment:

בראשית רבה פרשה יב ד"ה ג אלה תולדות
אֵלֶּה תוֹלְדוֹת הַשָּׁמַיִם וְגו', אָמַר רַבִּי אַבָּהוּ כָּל מָקוֹם שֶׁנֶּאֱמַר אֵלֶּה פָּסַל אֶת הָרִאשׁוֹנִים, וְאֵלֶּה מוֹסִיף עַל הָרִאשׁוֹנִים, כָּאן שֶׁנֶּאֱמַר אֵלֶּה פָּסַל אֶת הָרִאשׁוֹנִים, מַה פָּסַל תֹּהוּ וָבֹהוּ וְחשֶׁךְ.

'These are the generations of the heaven, etc.' Rabbi Abahu said: Wherever 'these are' [*elleh*] is written, it disqualifies [rejects] what came before it; 'and these are' [ve-elleh] adds to what came before. Here, where 'these are' is written, it disqualifies what preceded. What does it disqualify? 'Formlessness and void.' (*Bereishit Rabbah* 12:3)

In this context, the linguistic comment seems strange. What could possibly have preceded creation? Ostensibly, Creation is the beginning—nothing pre-existed Creation. Rav Abahu's answer is equally strange: *tohu va-vohu*", "formlessness and void," were disqualified; *tohu va-vohu* were rejected in favor of Creation. It is generally assumed that *tohu va-vohu* are non-entities, merely a description of a primordial state that existed prior to God's first act of creation, or perhaps before the completion of the world as we know it; *tohu va-vohu* is generally understood as the description of the world before the process of creation was complete, and not as an entity in and of itself.

בראשית פרק א :א-ב
(א) בְּרֵאשִׁית בָּרָא אֱלֹהִים אֵת הַשָּׁמַיִם וְאֵת הָאָרֶץ: (ב) וְהָאָרֶץ הָיְתָה תֹהוּ וָבֹהוּ וְחֹשֶׁךְ עַל־פְּנֵי תְהוֹם...

In the beginning God created the heavens and the earth. And the earth was without form, and void; and darkness was upon the face of the deep.... (*Bereishit* 1:1-2)

Apparently, Rabbi Abahu understands that *tohu va-vohu* does not describe an absence or void; rather, it describes an alternate reality, the result of a conscious act of creation, which was subsequently destroyed and replaced by the creation of our own reality.

Rather than speculating as to the meaning of *tohu va-vohu*, we can look to a second teaching of Rabbi Abahu, in which he explains the meaning of these words.

בראשית רבה פרשה ב ד״ה ה רבי אבהו

רַבִּי אַבָּהוּ וְרַבִּי חִיָּא רַבָּה, רַבִּי אַבָּהוּ אָמַר מִתְּחִלַּת בְּרִיָּתוֹ שֶׁל עוֹלָם צָפָה הַקָּדוֹשׁ בָּרוּךְ הוּא בְּמַעֲשֵׂיהֶן שֶׁל צַדִּיקִים וּמַעֲשֵׂיהֶן שֶׁל רְשָׁעִים, הֲדָא הוּא דִכְתִיב (תהלים א, ו): כִּי יוֹדֵעַ ה' דֶּרֶךְ צַדִּיקִים וְדֶרֶךְ רְשָׁעִים תֹּאבֵד. וְהָאָרֶץ הָיְתָה תֹהוּ וָבֹהוּ, אֵלּוּ מַעֲשֵׂיהֶן שֶׁל רְשָׁעִים, וַיֹּאמֶר אֱלֹהִים יְהִי אוֹר, אֵלּוּ מַעֲשֵׂיהֶן שֶׁל צַדִּיקִים, אֲבָל אֵינִי יוֹדֵעַ בְּאֵיזֶה מֵהֶם חָפֵץ, אִם בְּמַעֲשֵׂה אֵלּוּ אִם בְּמַעֲשֵׂה אֵלּוּ, כֵּיוָן דִּכְתִיב וַיַּרְא אֱלֹהִים אֶת הָאוֹר כִּי טוֹב, הֱוֵי בְּמַעֲשֵׂיהֶן שֶׁל צַדִּיקִים חָפֵץ, וְאֵינוֹ חָפֵץ בְּמַעֲשֵׂיהֶן שֶׁל רְשָׁעִים.

Rabbi Abahu and Rabbi Chiyya Rabbah were engaged in discussion. Rabbi Abahu said: From the very beginning of the world's creation the Holy One, blessed be He, foresaw the deeds of the righteous and the deeds of the wicked. Thus, "And the earth was formless and void [*tohu va-vohu*]" alludes to the deeds of the wicked. "And God said: Let there be light" [refers] to the actions of the righteous. I still might not know in which of these He delights, the former or the latter. But from what is written, "And God saw the light, that it was good," it follows that He desires the deeds of the righteous, and not the deeds of the wicked. (*Bereishit Rabbah* 2:5)

Here as Rabbi Abahu identifies the deeds of the wicked with *tohu va-vohu*, we also gain a sense of the passing of time, and a gradual process of Creation. The completed world is a monument to the rejected "pre-world" nothingness, which is now identified with the behavior of the wicked.

A third teaching by Rabbi Abahu links these first two teachings, and helps us form an organic whole of Rabbi Abahu's ideas:

בראשית רבה פרשה ג ד״ה ז אר״י בר

אָמַר רַבִּי יְהוּדָה בַּר סִימוֹן, יְהִי עֶרֶב אֵין כְּתִיב כָּאן, אֶלָּא וַיְהִי עֶרֶב, מִכָּאן שֶׁהָיָה סֵדֶר זְמַנִּים קֹדֶם לָכֵן. אָמַר רַבִּי אַבָּהוּ מְלַמֵּד שֶׁהָיָה בּוֹרֵא עוֹלָמוֹת וּמַחֲרִיבָן, עַד שֶׁבָּרָא אֶת אֵלּוּ, אָמַר דֵּין הַנְיָן לִי, יַתְהוֹן לָא הַנְיָן לִי. אָמַר

רַבִּי פִּנְחָס טַעְמֵיהּ דְּרַבִּי אַבָּהוּ (בראשית א, לא): וַיַּרְא אֱלֹהִים אֶת כָּל אֲשֶׁר עָשָׂה וְהִנֵּה טוֹב מְאֹד, דֵּין הֲנָיָין לִי יַתְהוֹן לָא הֲנָיָין לִי.

"And there was evening, etc."— Rabbi Yehudah b. Rabbi Simon said: "Let there be evening" is not written here, but "And there was evening," hence we know that a time-order existed before this. R. Abahu said: This proves that the Holy One, blessed be He, went on creating worlds and destroying them until He created this one, and declared, "This one pleases Me; those did not please Me." R. Pinchas said: This is Rabbi Abahu's reason: "And God saw everything that He had made, and, behold, it was very good" [*Bereishit* 1:31]: This pleases Me, but those did not please Me. (*Bereishit Rabbah* 3:7)[10]

In this third teaching, Rabbi Abahu's ideas are much more daring. The description of "worlds being created and destroyed" certainly dampens our egocentrism. More importantly, these ideas cannot be understood in a vacuum; all three teachings should be seen together: Creation as we know it replaced a pre-existing entity known as *tohu va-vohu* which was characterized by acts of wickedness.[11]

---

10. This idea may also be found in *Bereishit Rabbah* 9:2.
11. The Kabbalist Rav Shlomo Elyashiv in the *Leshem Shvo ve-Achalma, Sefer Ha-Deah* part 2 drush 2 section 1, identifies these missing generations with a world which existed in G-d's mind but not in actuality. This approach follows the Arizal and may be based on the Midrash in *Kohelet Rabbah* 1:35, where the missing generations are described as existing only in the "Divine plan."

קהלת רבה פרשה א ד"ה ב דבר אחר
וְכָךְ הוּא אוֹמֵר אֶלֶף דּוֹר עָלוּ בַּמַּחֲשָׁבָה לְהִבָּרְאוֹת, כַּמָּה נִמְחוּ מֵהֶם תְּשַׁע מֵאוֹת וְאַרְבָּעָה וְשִׁבְעִים דּוֹרוֹת, וּמַה טַּעַם (תהלים קה, ח): דָּבָר צִוָּה לְאֶלֶף דּוֹר, וְאֵיזֶה זֶה, זוֹ הַתּוֹרָה.

"A thousand generations were included in the Divine Plan [*alu ba-machshavah*] to be created, and how many of them were eliminated? Nine hundred and seventy-four. What is the proof? It is written, 'The word which He commanded to a thousand generations.' [*Tehillim* 105:8] To what does this allude? To the Torah." (*Kohelet Rabbah* 1:35; see my *Explorations, Parshat B'har*.)

Now perhaps we may understand our original passage from the Talmud: There were an additional 974 generations that existed, but did not exist. They existed in a different "world," a world not included in the account that begins with "Bereishit," a reality that preceded our own.[12]

It may be possible to discern the existence of this previous world and the wicked people who lived in it from the text of the Torah itself.[13] When the Torah describes man's creation, we are told of a merger of physical and spiritual attributes:

ספר לשם שבו ואחלמה - ספר הדע"ה חלק ב - דרוש ב ענף א

אמנם הנה המציאות הראשונים אשר יצא מהם מקודם ובתחלה. היה הכחות דמחצב הנשמות כי הוא המחצב הראשון מה"ד. מחצבים התחתונים. והוציא הוא את כל כחו לפועל מקודם ובתחלה. והנה יצא אז כל התתקע"ד דורות. שאמרו בחגיגה י"ג סע"ב. שעליהם נאמר אשר קומטו ולא עת כל נהר יוצק יסודם אלו תשע מאות ושבעים וארבעה דורות שקמטו להיבראות קודם שנברא העולם ולא נבראו ועמד הקב"ה ושתלן בכל דור ודור. ופי' רש"י ז"ל נגזר עליהם להיבראות כו' ע"ש. ומלשון זה משמע לכאורה שלא נבראו כלל. אמנם במדרש תהלים מזמור צ' בפסוק זרמתם שנה יהיו. אמרו שם אלו תשע מאות ושבעים וארבעה דורות שהיו קודם לבריאת עולם ונשטפו כהרף עין בשביל שהיו רעים. והם מרומזים במלת בראשית ע"ש. והרי לנו כי נבראו ויצאו במציאות ממש. אך הענין הוא כמו שאמרנו כי לא היו נשמות גמורים אלא רק בבחי' שרשים לבד וזהו שאמרו בגמרא ולא נבראו ר"ל שלא נבראו בשלימות וכן היה להם גופים ג"כ ולא היו כמו שלנו אלא ג"כ רק בבחי' שרשים לבד. וכן אמר בעמק המלך בשער עולם התוהו פי' ל' כי אלו התתקע"ד דורות היו נשמות מצד הגבורות והיה להם גופים ספיריים שלא היו כל כך חומריים כמו שלנו ע"ש. ואלו התתקע"ד דורות נודע הוא כי הם מחשבון אלף דור שהיו עתידין להיבראות קודם מתן תורה. וכמ"ש בבראשית רבה פ' כ"ח סימן ד'. אלף דור עלו במחשבה להיבראות וכמה נימוחו מהם תתקע"ד. ועם הכ"ו דורות אשר מאדה"ר עד משה רבע"ה. הם אלף דור שעל זה נאמר דבר צוה לאלף דור. וכן הוא ג"כ במדרש תהלים מזמור ק"ה ובכ"מ במדרש. כי התתקע"ד היו כולם רשעים שלא היה בהם טוב כלל מצד עצמם וכמו שיתבאר ולכן נימוחו כולם. אך הכ"ו דורות היו יותר מתוקנים הרבה ומזה היה כל היחידי סגולה אשר היה בכל דור ודור מאדה"ר עד משרבע"ה. וכמ"ש בפדר"א פ' כ"ב ובאבות דר' נתן ר"פ ל"ב וכן בזוה"ק בראשית ל"ח א' ונ"ו א' ובכ"מ. ולכן לא ניתן התורה אלא רק אחר שעברו כל אלו האלף דורות כולם משום שהיו רובן רשעים ולא היה אפשר ליתן להם התורה כלל:[אות ו]

12. Also see Rabbi Abahu's description of the creation of man and woman (*Berachot* 61a and *Eruvin* 18a):

תלמוד בבלי מסכת ברכות דף סא עמוד א

כְּדְרַבִּי אַבָּהוּ, דְּרַבִּי אַבָּהוּ רָמֵי, כְּתִיב "זָכָר וּנְקֵבָה בְּרָאָם", וּכְתִיב, (שם ט) "כִּי בְּצֶלֶם אֱלֹהִים עָשָׂה אֶת הָאָדָם", הָא כֵּיצַד? בִּתְחִלָּה עָלָה בְּמַחֲשָׁבָה לִבְרֹאת שְׁנַיִם, וּלְבַסּוֹף לֹא נִבְרָא אֶלָּא אֶחָד.

13. For further discussion of this topic see *Echoes of Eden: Bereishit*, pp. 1-18, "In Search of the Serpent."

בראשית פרק ב:ז-ח

(ז) וַיִּיצֶר ה' אֱלֹהִים אֶת־הָאָדָם עָפָר מִן־הָאֲדָמָה וַיִּפַּח בְּאַפָּיו נִשְׁמַת חַיִּים וַיְהִי הָאָדָם לְנֶפֶשׁ חַיָּה: (ח) וַיִּטַּע ה' אֱלֹהִים גַּן־בְּעֵדֶן מִקֶּדֶם וַיָּשֶׂם שָׁם אֶת־הָאָדָם אֲשֶׁר יָצָר:

And the Lord God formed man of the dust of the ground, and breathed into his nostrils the breath of life; and man became a living soul. And the Lord God planted a garden eastward in Eden; and there he put the man whom he had formed. (*Bereishit* 2:7-8)

The creation of Adam does not follow the pattern established for the creation of other aspects of the world; God does not simply say "Let there be man!"[14] Rather, man is formed by an amalgamation of two vastly disparate entities: the dust of the ground and the breath of God. The breath of God is ethereal, beyond human quantification. However, the dust of the earth is wholly of this world. On a conceptual level, we may say that the creation of man describes the merger of existing material with a Divine endowment. Perhaps this pre-existing material was an earlier form of man, a wicked version that lacked the 'breath of God' otherwise known as a soul. Such a man—of human form but lacking a *neshamah*—derived from the same word as "breath," *neshimah*, might be described as pure physicality, much like the dust of the earth itself.

This conceptual understanding may be found elsewhere in the Midrash. The Torah describes the birth of Shet (Seth) by saying that he was in the image of his father Adam who, in turn, was in the image of God:

בראשית פרק ה:א-ג

זֶה סֵפֶר תּוֹלְדֹת אָדָם בְּיוֹם בְּרֹא אֱלֹהִים אָדָם בִּדְמוּת אֱלֹהִים עָשָׂה אֹתוֹ: זָכָר וּנְקֵבָה בְּרָאָם וַיְבָרֶךְ אֹתָם וַיִּקְרָא אֶת־שְׁמָם אָדָם בְּיוֹם הִבָּרְאָם: וַיְחִי אָדָם שְׁלֹשִׁים וּמְאַת שָׁנָה וַיּוֹלֶד בִּדְמוּתוֹ כְּצַלְמוֹ וַיִּקְרָא אֶת־שְׁמוֹ שֵׁת:

---

14. The description of man's creation in the previous chapter is equally challenging, but beyond the scope of this essay: "And G-d said, 'Let us make man in our image, after our likeness; and let them have dominion over the fish of the sea, and over the birds of the air, and over the cattle, and over all the earth, and over every creeping thing that creeps upon the earth.' So G-d created man in His own image, in the image of G-d created He him; male and female He created them." (*Bereishit* 1:26-27)

Bereishit: The Missing 974 Generations | 47

This is the book of the generations of Adam. On the day God created man, in the likeness of God He made him; male and female He created them, and blessed them, and called their name Man, on the day they were created. And Adam lived a hundred and thirty years, and fathered a son in his own likeness, after his image, and called his name Shet. (*Bereishit* 5:1-3)

According to tradition, Adam was estranged from Eve during these one hundred and thirty years:

בראשית רבה (וילנא) פרשת בראשית פרשה כ סימן יא
רַבִּי סִימוֹן אָמַר אֵם כָּל חַי, אִמָּן שֶׁל כָּל הַחַיִּים, דְּאָמַר רַבִּי סִימוֹן כָּל מֵאָה וּשְׁלֹשִׁים שָׁנָה שֶׁפֵּרְשָׁה חַוָּה מֵאָדָם, הָיוּ רוּחוֹת הַזְּכָרִים מִתְחַמְּמִין מִמֶּנָּה וְהִיא יוֹלֶדֶת מֵהֶם, וְרוּחוֹת נְקֵבוֹת מִתְחַמְּמוֹת מֵאָדָם וּמוֹלִידוֹת מִמֶּנּוּ, הֲדָא הוּא דִכְתִיב (שמואל ב ז:יד): אֲשֶׁר בְּהַעֲוֹתוֹ וְהֹכַחְתִּיו בְּשֵׁבֶט אֲנָשִׁים וּבְנִגְעֵי בְּנֵי אָדָם, בְּנוֹי דְּאָדָם קַדְמָאָה.

Rabbi Simon said: "The mother of all living" means the mother of all life. For Rabbi Simon said: Throughout the entire one hundred and thirty years during which Adam was separated from Eve, the male demons were made ardent by her and she bore them offspring, while the female demons were inflamed by Adam and they bore his offspring, as it is written, "If he commit iniquity, I will chasten him with the rod of men, and with the afflictions of the children of man-Adam" (2 *Shmuel* 7:14), which means, the children of the first man. (*Bereishit Rabbah* 20:11)

This idea is further elaborated in the Midrash:

בראשית רבה (וילנא) פרשת בראשית פרשה כד:ו
דָּבָר אַחֵר, זֶה סֵפֶר תּוֹלְדֹת אָדָם, אֵלִין תּוֹלָדוֹת וְאֵין הָרִאשׁוֹנִים תּוֹלָדוֹת, וּמָה הֵן אֱלֹהוּת. בְּעוֹן קוֹמֵי אַבָּא כֹּהֵן בַּרְדְּלָא, אָדָם שֵׁת אֱנוֹשׁ, וְשָׁתַק, אָמַר לָהֶם עַד כָּאן בְּצֶלֶם אֱלֹהִים וכו' כִּדְכְתִיב לְעֵיל.

דָּבָר אַחֵר, אֵלּוּ תוֹלָדוֹת וְאֵין הָרִאשׁוֹנִים תוֹלָדוֹת, וּמָה הֵן רוּחוֹת, דְּאָמַר רַבִּי סִימוֹן כָּל מֵאָה וּשְׁלֹשִׁים שָׁנָה שֶׁפֵּרְשָׁה חַוָּה מֵאָדָם הָיוּ רוּחוֹת הַזְּכָרִים מִתְחַמְּמִים מִמֶּנָּה וְהָיוּ מוֹלִידִים מִמֶּנָּה, וְרוּחוֹת נְקֵבוֹת מִתְחַמְּמוֹת מֵאָדָם וּמוֹלִידִים מִמֶּנּוּ, הֲדָא הוּא דִכְתִיב (שמואל ב ז, יד): אֲשֶׁר בְּהַעֲוֹתוֹ וְהֹכַחְתִּיו בְּשֵׁבֶט אֲנָשִׁים וּבְנִגְעֵי בְּנֵי אָדָם, בְּנוֹי דְּאָדָם קַדְמָאָה מַאן דְּאָמַר דְּרוּחֵי דְּבֵיתָא טָבִין דְּרָבוּ עִמֵּיהּ, וּמַאן דְּאָמַר דְּאִינּוּן בִּישִׁין דְּחַכְּמִין יִצְרֵיהּ, מַאן דְּאָמַר דְּרוּחֵי דְחַקְלָא בִּישִׁין דְּלָא רָבִין עִמֵּיהּ, וּמַאן דְּאָמַר דְּאִינּוּן טָבִין דְּלָא חַכְּמִין יִצְרֵיהּ. דָּבָר אַחֵר, אֵלּוּ תוֹלָדוֹת וְאֵין הָרִאשׁוֹנִים תוֹלָדוֹת, לָמָּה שֶׁהֵן כָּלִין בַּמַּיִם,

"This is the book of the descendants of Adam." **These** were descendants, while the **earlier** ones were not descendants. What, then, were they? Divinities! [The answer is as] Abba Cohen Bardela was asked: [Why does Scripture enumerate] Adam, Shet, and Enosh, and then fall silent? To which he answered: Until this point, they were created in the likeness and image [of God], as was explained earlier (*Bereishit Rabbah* 23:6) Another interpretation: These are descendants, but the earlier ones were not [human] descendants. What, then, were they? **Demons**. For R. Simon said: Throughout the entire one hundred and thirty years during which Adam separated from Eve the male demons were made ardent by her and she bore their offspring, while the female demons were inflamed by Adam and they bore his offspring, as it is written, "If he commit iniquity, I will chasten him with the rod of men, and with the afflictions of the children of man-Adam" (2 *Shmuel* 7:14), which refers to the children of the first [primeval] man. (The reason for the view that house-spirits are benevolent is because they dwell with him [man], while the opinion that they are harmful is based on the fact that they understand man's evil inclinations. He who maintains that the spirits of the field are benevolent does so because they do not grow up with him; while as for the view that they are harmful, the reason is because they do not comprehend his evil inclinations.) These are the descendants of Adam, but the earlier ones were not descendants of Adam. Why? **Because they were destroyed by the flood**. (*Bereishit Rabbah* 24:6)

This Midrash cites an earlier teaching:

בראשית רבה (וילנא) פרשת בראשית פרשה כג
וּלְשֵׁת גַּם הוּא יֻלַּד בֵּן וַיִּקְרָא אֶת שְׁמוֹ אֱנוֹשׁ (בראשית ד, כו), בְּעוֹן קוֹמֵי אַבָּא כֹּהֵן בַּרְדְּלָא אָדָם שֵׁת אֱנוֹשׁ, וְשָׁתַק, אָמַר עַד כָּאן בְּצֶלֶם וּבִדְמוּת, מִכָּאן וָאֵילָךְ נִתְקַלְקְלוּ הַדּוֹרוֹת וְנִבְרְאוּ קַנְטוּרִין. אַרְבָּעָה דְּבָרִים נִשְׁתַּנּוּ בִּימֵי אֱנוֹשׁ בֶּן שֵׁת, הֶהָרִים נַעֲשׂוּ טְרָשִׁים, וְהִתְחִיל הַמֵּת מַרְחִישׁ, וְנַעֲשׂוּ פְּנֵיהֶם כְּקוֹפוֹת, וְנַעֲשׂוּ חֻלִּין לַמַּזִּיקִין. אָמַר רַבִּי יִצְחָק הֵן הֵן שֶׁגָּרְמוּ לְעַצְמָן לִהְיוֹת חֻלִּין לַמַּזִּיקִין, מַה בֵּין דְּגָחֵין לְצַלְמָא לְמַאן דְּגָחֵין לְבַר נָשׁ.

[...but from then onwards Centaurs were created. Four things changed in the days of Enosh: The mountains became [barren] rocks, the dead began to feel [the worms], men's faces became ape-like, and they became vulnerable (*chullin*) to demons. Said R. Yitzchak: They were themselves responsible for becoming vulnerable to demons, [for they argued]: What is the difference whether one worships an image or worships man? Hence, "Then man became degraded to call upon the name of the Lord" (*Bereishit* 4:26). (*Bereishit Rabbah* 23:6)]

In this amazing passage, we are told of other "offspring" of Adam and Chavah, offspring who did not possess the Divine image—children without souls. The Midrash describes these offspring as demons who were destroyed in the flood.[15]

In the *Guide for the Perplexed*, Rambam restates this Midrash, with one critical difference: According to Rambam, demons do not exist;

---

15. See the commentary to the Siddur of the Rokeach, *Hodu la-Hashem*, page 51.

פירושי סידור התפילה לרוקח [טו] הודו לה' עמוד נא
לכך מאלה תולדות השמים עד זה ספר תולדות אדם תתקע"ד דורות וכו"ו דורות מאדם ועד משה, הרי אלף דורות, לכך "לאלף דר'" בגמ' משה.

rather, the passage describes children of Adam who did not possess the Divine Image. They were human in form and animal in spirit, lacking the divine endowment their father possessed.

ספר מורה נבוכים - חלק א פרק ז

ובזאת ההשאלה נאמר ב'אדם': "ויחי אדם שלושים ומאת שנה, ויולד בדמותו כצלמו"; וכבר קדם לך ענין 'צלם אדם ודמותו' מה הוא; וכל מי שקדמו לו מן הבנים לא הגיעה אליהם הצורה האנושית באמת, אשר היא 'צלם אדם ודמותו', הנאמר עליה:

'בצלם אלוהים ובדמותו' אמנם 'שת', כאשר לימדהו והבינהו ונמצא שלם השלמות האנושי, נאמר בו: 'ויולד בדמותו כצלמו'. וכבר ידעת, כי כל מי שלא הגיעה לו זאת הצורה, אשר בארנו ענינה, הוא אינו איש, אבל בהמה על צורת איש ותבניתו, אבל יש לו יכולת על מיני ההזק וחידוש הרעות, מה שאין כן לשאר בעלי החיים; כי השכל והמחשבה שהיו מוכנים להגעת השלמות אשר לא הגיע, ישתמש בהם במיני התחבולות המביאות לרע והולד הנזקים, כאילו הוא דבר ידמה לאדם או יחקהו. וכן היו בני אדם הקודמים ל'שת'; ואמרו ב'מדרש': "כל אותן מאה ושלושים שנה שהיה אדם נזוף בהן היה מוליד רוחות" - רצונם לומר: 'שדים'; וכאשר רצהו האלוה, הוליד 'בדמותו כצלמו' - והוא אמרו: 'ויחי אדם שלושים ומאת שנה ויולד בדמותו כצלמו':

In this figurative sense, the verb *yalad* (to bear) is employed when it is said of Adam, "And Adam lived one hundred and thirty years, and begat [*va-yoled*] a son in his own likeness, in his form." [*Bereishit* 4: 3] As regards the words, "the form of Adam, and his likeness," we have already stated (Ch. 1) their meaning. Those sons of Adam who were born before that time were not human in the true sense of the word, they had not "the form of man." With reference to Shet who had been instructed, enlightened and brought to human perfection, it could rightly be said, "he (Adam) begat a son in his likeness, in his form." It is acknowledged that a man who does not possess this "form" (the nature of which has just been explained) is not human, but a mere animal in human shape and form. Yet such a creature has the power of causing harm and injury, a power which does not belong to other creatures. For those gifts of intelligence and judgment with which he has been endowed for the purpose of acquiring perfection, but which he has failed to apply to their proper aim, are used by him for wicked and mischievous ends; he begets evil things, as though he merely resembled man, or simulated his outward appearance. Such was the condition of those sons of Adam who preceded Shet. In reference to this subject the Midrash says: "During the 130 years when Adam was chastised, he fathered 'spirits,'" i.e., "demons"; when, however, he was again restored to Divine favor "he fathered in his likeness, in his form." This is the sense of the passage, "Adam lived one hundred and thirty years, and he fathered in his likeness, in his form" [*Bereishit* 5:3]. (*Guide for the Perplexed* 1:7)[16]

The question is, if Adam had progeny who did not possess a Divine soul,[17] could he have had ancestors who also were similarly spiritually challenged?[18]

---

16. See *Pirkei de-Rabbi Eliezer*, chapter 22:

פרקי דרבי אליעזר פרק כב

כְּתִיב [בראשית ה, ג] וַיְחִי אָדָם שְׁלֹשִׁים וּמְאַת שָׁנָה וַיּוֹלֶד בִּדְמוּתוֹ כְּצַלְמוֹ, מִכָּאן אַתָּה לָמֵד שֶׁלֹּא הָיָה קַיִן מִזַּרְעוֹ וְלֹא מִדְּמוּתוֹ וְלֹא מִצַּלְמוֹ שֶׁל אָדָם, וְלֹא מַעֲשָׂיו דּוֹמִין לְמַעֲשֵׂה הֶבֶל אָחִיו, עַד שֶׁנּוֹלַד שֵׁת שֶׁהָיָה מִזַּרְעוֹ וּדְמוּתוֹ, וּמַעֲשָׂיו דּוֹמִין לְמַעֲשֵׂה הֶבֶל אָחִיו, שֶׁנֶּאֱמַר וַיּוֹלֶד בִּדְמוּתוֹ כְּצַלְמוֹ. רַבִּי יִשְׁמָעֵאל אוֹמֵר מִשֵּׁת עָלוּ וְנִתְיַחֲסוּ כָּל הַבְּרִיּוֹת וְכָל דּוֹרוֹת הַצַּדִּיקִים, וּמִקַּיִן עָלוּ וְנִתְיַחֲסוּ כָּל דּוֹרוֹת הָרְשָׁעִים הַפּוֹשְׁעִים וְהַמּוֹרְדִים שֶׁמָּרְדוּ בַּמָּקוֹם, וְאָמְרוּ אֵין אָנוּ צְרִיכִין לְטִפַּת גְּשָׁמֶיךָ וְלֹא לָדַעַת אֶת דְּרָכֶיךָ, שֶׁנֶּאֱמַר [איוב כא, יד] וַיֹּאמְרוּ לָאֵל סוּר מִמֶּנּוּ. רַבִּי מֵאִיר אוֹמֵר גְּלוּיֵי בָשָׂר עֶרְוָה הָיוּ הוֹלְכִין דּוֹרוֹת שֶׁל קַיִן הָאֲנָשִׁים וְהַנָּשִׁים, כַּבְּהֵמָה, וּמִטַּמְּאִין בְּכָל זְנוּת, אִישׁ בְּאִמּוֹ וּבִבִתּוֹ וּבְאֵשֶׁת אָחִיו, בַּגָּלוּי וּבָרְחוֹבוֹת, בְּיֵצֶר הָרָע וּבְמַחְשְׁבוֹת לִבָּם, שֶׁנֶּאֱמַר [בראשית ו, ה] וַיַּרְא ה' כִּי רַבָּה רָעַת הָאָדָם בָּאָרֶץ. רַבִּי אוֹמֵר רָאוּ הַמַּלְאָכִים שֶׁנָּפְלוּ מִמְּקוֹם קְדֻשָּׁתָן מִן הַשָּׁמַיִם אֶת בְּנוֹת קַיִן מְהַלְּכוֹת גְּלוּיוֹת בְּשַׂר עֶרְוָה, וּמְכַחֲלוֹת עֵינֵיהֶן כְּזוֹנוֹת, וַתָּעוּ אַחֲרֵיהֶן וְלָקְחוּ מֵהֶן נָשִׁים, שֶׁנֶּאֱמַר [שם ב] וַיִּרְאוּ בְנֵי הָאֱלֹהִים אֶת בְּנוֹת הָאָדָם וְגוֹ'.

17. Mystical literature speaks of the possibility of a person losing their divinity, their image of God, their soul. See *Zohar, Bereishit* 94a.

18. I once asked this question to Rav Yaakov Weinberg, Rosh Yeshiva of Ner Yisrael, who responded that such a possibility is "*hashkafically*" acceptable, so long as there is a qualitative spiritual distinction between Adam and his predecessors.

When the Torah describes a part of Adam's core as the dust of the earth, could this refer to people, a people who "existed yet never existed"? Could it describe an existence that may have had a physical impact on this world but no spiritual impact? Could Adam have physically had a mother while spiritually the breath of God served as an impetus for a new world?[19]

There is a least one opinion in the Talmud that may reject such a possibility:

תלמוד בבלי מסכת חולין דף ס עמוד א

אָמַר רַבִּי יְהוּדָה, שׁוֹר שֶׁהִקְרִיב אָדָם הָרִאשׁוֹן - קַרְנָיו קוֹדְמוֹת לְפַרְסוֹתָיו, שֶׁנֶּאֱמַר, "וְתִיטַב לַה' מִשּׁוֹר פָּר מַקְרִן מַפְרִיס". "מַקְרִן" בְּרֵישָׁא, וְהָדַר "מַפְרִיס". מְסַיְּיעָא לֵיהּ לְרַבִּי יְהוֹשֻׁעַ בֶּן לֵוִי, דְּאָמַר רַבִּי יְהוֹשֻׁעַ בֶּן לֵוִי, כָּל מַעֲשֵׂה בְרֵאשִׁית בְּקוֹמָתָן נִבְרְאוּ. בְּדַעְתָּם נִבְרְאוּ. בְּצִבְיוֹנָם נִבְרְאוּ. שֶׁנֶּאֱמַר, (בראשית ב) "וַיְכֻלּוּ הַשָּׁמַיִם וְהָאָרֶץ וְכָל צְבָאָם", אַל תִּקְרֵי "צְבָאָם", אֶלָּא, "צִבְיוֹנָם":

Rabbi Yehudah further said: The bullock which Adam sacrificed had fully developed horns before it had hoofs, as it is said: "And it shall please the Lord better than a bullock that has horns and hooves"; the verse first says: "that has horns" and then "hooves." This supports Rabbi Yehoshua ben Levi, who said: All the animals of the creation were created in their full-grown stature, with their full cognitive abilities, and with their own unique character, for it is written: "And the heaven and the earth were finished, and all the host of them [*tzeva'am*]." Read not *tzeva'am* but *tzivyonam* [their character]. (*Chullin* 60a)

This distinction is imparted by God, as described in the verses of *Bereishit*. This does not necessarily mean that Rav Yaakov accepted this idea, though he agreed that it is a valid opinion. I did not press him as to his understanding. My precise formulation was, "Is it possible that Adam had parents and grandparents who did not possess a soul?"

19. When modern people speak about such ideas they are often motivated by polemical or apologetical considerations, but could such a charge be waged against Rabbi Abahu or Rambam, who predate Darwin by millennia?

If man is to be included in this statement, then man, too, was created as a fully-grown being. Alternatively, one could explain that this source need not contradict our thesis. Adam, too, was "created" by virtue of receiving his soul, after he was physically full-grown.

If there were previous generations, which "existed yet did not exist"—existed physically yet not spiritually—what happened to them? Are there any references to their existence?

The Torah apparently refers to different species of man coexisting—but just barely:[20]

---

20. The Mishnah, *Kil'ayim* 8:5, makes an obscure reference to something called *Adnei Ha-Sadeh,* or in some sources *Avnei Ha-Sadeh* (based on *Iyov* 5:23). See Jerusalem Talmud, Venice and Vila editions, for the two versions. *Avnei Ha-Sadeh* is an ape-like being that walks upright, looks like man, but is a beast. See the commentaries to this Mishnah, and Rashi, *Iyov* 5:23.

איוב פרק ה:כג
כִּי עִם־אַבְנֵי הַשָּׂדֶה בְרִיתֶךָ וְחַיַּת הַשָּׂדֶה הָשְׁלְמָה־לָךְ:

רש״י איוב פרק:כג
אבני השדה - מין אדם הן:

משנה מסכת כלאים פרק ח:ה
הַפְּרוּטִיּוֹת אֲסוּרוֹת, וְהָרָמָךְ מֻתָּר. וְאַדְנֵי הַשָּׂדֶה, חַיָּה. רַבִּי יוֹסֵי אוֹמֵר, מְטַמְּאוֹת בָּאֹהֶל כָּאָדָם.

…Wild man-like creatures are deemed as belonging to the category of *chayah*. R. Yose said: [When dead], they [or part of their corpses] transmit uncleanness [to men and to objects susceptible thereto which are] under the same roof, as does [the corpse of] a human being.

תלמוד ירושלמי (ונציה) מסכת כלאים פרק ח דף ג ה״ד
אבני השדה חיה ייסי ערקי בר נש דטור הוא והוא חיי מן טיבורייה איפסק טיבורייה לא חיי..

תלמוד ירושלמי (וילנא) מסכת כלאים פרק ח הלכה ד
אַדְנֵי הַשָּׂדֶה חַיָּה. יְיסֵי עָרְקִי בַּר נָשׁ דְטוּר הוּא וְהוּא חַיִּי מִן טִיבּוּרְיָיה אִפְסָק טִיבּוּרְיָה, לֹא חַיַּי. רַבִּי חָמָא בַּר עוּקְבָא בְּשֵׁם רַבִּי יוֹסֵי בֶּן חֲנִינָה, טַעְמָא דְרַבִּי יוֹסֵי וְכֹל אֲשֶׁר יִגַּע עַל פְּנֵי הַשָּׂדֶה ודורש בגדל על פני השדה.

ספרא שמיני פרשה ד תחילת פרק ו
(ה) כל ההולך על כפיו זה הקוף הולך להביא את הקופד ואת חולדת הסנאים, ואת אבני השדה ואת כלב הים זו חיה טהורה, חיה טמאה מנין תלמוד לומר ההולכת על ארבע, כל חיה להביא את הפיל.

בראשית פרק ו:א-ד

וַיְהִי כִּי־הֵחֵל הָאָדָם לָרֹב עַל־פְּנֵי הָאֲדָמָה וּבָנוֹת יֻלְּדוּ לָהֶם: וַיִּרְאוּ בְנֵי־הָאֱלֹהִים אֶת־בְּנוֹת הָאָדָם כִּי טֹבֹת הֵנָּה וַיִּקְחוּ לָהֶם נָשִׁים מִכֹּל אֲשֶׁר בָּחָרוּ: וַיֹּאמֶר ה' לֹא־יָדוֹן רוּחִי בָאָדָם לְעֹלָם בְּשַׁגַּם הוּא בָשָׂר וְהָיוּ יָמָיו מֵאָה וְעֶשְׂרִים שָׁנָה: הַנְּפִלִים הָיוּ בָאָרֶץ בַּיָּמִים הָהֵם וְגַם אַחֲרֵי־כֵן אֲשֶׁר יָבֹאוּ בְּנֵי הָאֱלֹהִים אֶל־בְּנוֹת הָאָדָם וְיָלְדוּ לָהֶם הֵמָּה הַגִּבֹּרִים אֲשֶׁר מֵעוֹלָם אַנְשֵׁי הַשֵּׁם:

And it came to pass, when men began to multiply on the face of the earth, and daughters were born to them, that the sons of the powerful[21] (*elohim*) saw the daughters of men, that they were pretty; and they took as wives all those whom they chose. And God said, "My spirit shall not always strive with man, for he also is flesh; yet his days shall be a hundred and twenty years." There were *Nefilim* on the earth in those days; and also after that, when the sons of the *elohim* copulated with the daughters of men, and they bore children to them, these became the mighty men of old, men of renown. (*Bereishit* 6:1-4)

The introduction to the flood story includes a description of the forced relations between the sons of the *elohim* and the daughters of man-Adam: Powerful brutes took innocent, refined women by force. The result was the flood, and the eradication of this brutal species. The only

---

ספרי דברים פרשת עקב פיסקא נ

(כג) והוריש ה', ה' מוריש ואין בשר ודם מוריש. את כל הגוים, שומע אני כמשמעו תלמוד לומר האלה, אין לי אלא אלה מנין לרבות את מסייעיהם תלמוד לומר את כל הגוים האלה מלפניכם שתהו אתם רבים והולכים והם מתמעטים והולכים וכן הוא אומר [שמות כג:כ] מעט מעט אגרשנו מפניך ואומר [שמות כג:כט] לא אגרשנו מפניך בשנה אחת [פן תהיה הארץ שממה ורבה עליך חית השדה] דברי רבי יעקב אמר לו רבי אלעזר בן עזריה או לפי שישראל צדיקים הם למה יראים מן החיה והלא אם צדיקים הם אין יראים מן החיה שכן הוא אומר [איוב ה:כג] כי עם אבני השדה בריתך אם תאמר מפני מה יגע יהושע כל היגיעה ההיא אלא לפי שחטאו ישראל נגזר עליהם מעט מעט אגרשנו מפניך.

---

21. It is unlikely that the term "*elohim*" implies divinity in this context; rather, it means "powerful." In other cases in the Torah the word *elohim* is used to refer to judges (*Shemot* 22:27); see Onkelos and Rashi on *Bereishit* 6:2.

survivors of the flood were Noach and his descendants.[22] These verses clearly outline the strained co-existence of two types of people. Were these other "men" descendants of Adam, or vestiges of an earlier world?

The Torah is a book of truth, not merely a history book; only ideas that are spiritually relevant to us are recorded. Our world begins with Adam; whether or not Adam had physical precursors does not impact the new world that begins when God endows him with a soul.[23] Our story begins with Adam, the first man with the capacity to relate to and emulate God; this is our legacy. *Bereishit* thus alludes to a reality that preceded our own—one that was devoid of morality, whose inhabitants lacked the Divine Image with which Adam was endowed. The Torah concerns itself with the moral and ethical point of origin of the species known as Man; the Torah's account of Creation distinguishes our reality from the moral and ethical void that preceded it. Nonetheless, the Torah contains vestigial references to the generations that preceded Adam, and the Talmud traces the effects of these earlier generations: "The Holy One, blessed be He, planted them in every generation, and it is they who are the insolent of each generation."[24] The question we are left to ponder is whether they existed in fact or in thought alone.

---

22. For a more extensive discussion of this topic, see *Echoes of Eden: Bereishit*, pp. 37-50, "Parashat Noach: Na'ama."
23. For a discussion of the time issue, namely, how can the world be older than the nearly-6000 years which Judaism so often speaks of, see my *Explorations* on *Parashat B'har*, and the discussion of the concept of "cosmic Jubilees."
24. The Talmud (*Yoma* 38b) likewise teaches that the righteous of previous generations effect subsequent generations: "R. Chiya b. Abba said in the name of R. Yohanan: No righteous man dies out of this world, before another, like himself, is created, as it is said: 'The sun also rises, and the sun goes down', — before the sun of Eli set, the sun of Shmuel of Ramataim rose.' R. Hiyya b. Abba also said in the name of R. Yohanan: 'The Holy One, blessed be He, saw that the righteous are but few, therefore He planted them throughout all generations, as it is said: 'For the pillars of the earth are the Lord's, and He has set the world upon them.'"

Parashat Noach

Was Noach a *Tzaddik*?

בראשית פרק ו:ט
אֵלֶּה תּוֹלְדֹת נֹחַ נֹחַ אִישׁ צַדִּיק תָּמִים הָיָה בְּדֹרֹתָיו אֶת־הָאֱלֹהִים הִתְהַלֶּךְ־נֹחַ:

These are the generations of Noah; Noah was a righteous man. He was perfect in his generations. Noah walked with God. (*Bereishit* 6:9)

The saga of Noach is well known, but Noach himself remains an elusive personality. The phrase "He was perfect in his generations" sounds like a back-handed compliment: Why is his stature limited, made into a relative statement that compares him to others in "his generations"? How does this qualification reflect upon the nature of his righteousness? Rashi records two conflicting opinions:[1]

---

[1] Rashi treats the verse as if it says Noach was righteous in his generation, even though the verse actually states that Noah was "righteous"—without any qualification—and only qualifies the word *tamim*, "perfect," with the phrase, "in his generations." Moreover, the passage in the Talmud (*Sanhedrin* 108a) which is apparently Rashi's source, does not speak of righteousness *per se*; see below. Rashi may have been influenced by a reference to the righteousness of Noach in *Bereishit* 7:1:

בראשית פרק ז:א
(א) וַיֹּאמֶר ה' לְנֹחַ בֹּא־אַתָּה וְכָל־בֵּיתְךָ אֶל־הַתֵּבָה כִּי־אֹתְךָ רָאִיתִי צַדִּיק לְפָנַי בַּדּוֹר הַזֶּה:

Then God said to Noah, "Go into the ark, with all your household, for you alone have I found to be *tzadik* before Me in this generation.

In general, the proper translation of *tzaddik* may be "innocent" rather than "righteous," refering to a legal status; see *Bereishit* 18:23-25:

רש"י בראשית פרק ו פסוק ט

בְּדֹרֹתָיו - יֵשׁ מֵרַבּוֹתֵינוּ דּוֹרְשִׁים אוֹתוֹ לְשֶׁבַח, כָּל שֶׁכֵּן אִלּוּ הָיָה בְדוֹר צַדִּיקִים הָיָה צַדִּיק יוֹתֵר; וְיֵשׁ שֶׁדּוֹרְשִׁים אוֹתוֹ לִגְנַאי, לְפִי דוֹרוֹ הָיָה צַדִּיק וְאִלּוּ הָיָה בְדוֹרוֹ שֶׁל אַבְרָהָם לֹא הָיָה נֶחְשָׁב לִכְלוּם:

Some of the sages expound this positively: Certainly, if he had been in a generation of righteous people, he would have been more righteous. Others expound it negatively: In his generation he was righteous, but if he had lived in the generation of Avraham, he would have been considered worthless. (Rashi, *Bereishit* 6:9)

There is a lack of symmetry in Rashi's comment on this verse: On the one hand, Noach is compared to "a generation of righteous people," while on the other hand he is compared to "the generation of Avraham." Could Avraham's generation not have served as the model for both opinions? Perhaps we might better understand Noah's righteousness if we first examine the generation in which he lived.

בראשית פרק ו:א-יג

וַיְהִי כִּי־הֵחֵל הָאָדָם לָרֹב עַל־פְּנֵי הָאֲדָמָה וּבָנוֹת יֻלְּדוּ לָהֶם: וַיִּרְאוּ בְנֵי־הָאֱלֹהִים אֶת־בְּנוֹת הָאָדָם כִּי טֹבֹת הֵנָּה וַיִּקְחוּ לָהֶם נָשִׁים מִכֹּל אֲשֶׁר בָּחָרוּ: ...וַתִּשָּׁחֵת הָאָרֶץ לִפְנֵי הָאֱלֹהִים וַתִּמָּלֵא הָאָרֶץ חָמָס: וַיַּרְא אֱלֹהִים אֶת־הָאָרֶץ וְהִנֵּה נִשְׁחָתָה כִּי־הִשְׁחִית כָּל־בָּשָׂר אֶת־דַּרְכּוֹ עַל־הָאָרֶץ: וַיֹּאמֶר אֱלֹהִים לְנֹחַ קֵץ כָּל־בָּשָׂר בָּא לְפָנַי כִּי־מָלְאָה הָאָרֶץ חָמָס מִפְּנֵיהֶם וְהִנְנִי מַשְׁחִיתָם אֶת־הָאָרֶץ:

בראשית פרק יח, כג-כה

(כג) וַיִּגַּשׁ אַבְרָהָם וַיֹּאמַר הַאַף תִּסְפֶּה צַדִּיק עִם־רָשָׁע: (כד) אוּלַי יֵשׁ חֲמִשִּׁים צַדִּיקִם בְּתוֹךְ הָעִיר הַאַף תִּסְפֶּה וְלֹא־תִשָּׂא לַמָּקוֹם לְמַעַן חֲמִשִּׁים הַצַּדִּיקִם אֲשֶׁר בְּקִרְבָּהּ: (כה) חָלִלָה לְּךָ מֵעֲשֹׂת כַּדָּבָר הַזֶּה לְהָמִית צַדִּיק עִם־רָשָׁע וְהָיָה כַצַּדִּיק כָּרָשָׁע חָלִלָה לָּךְ הֲשֹׁפֵט כָּל־הָאָרֶץ לֹא יַעֲשֶׂה מִשְׁפָּט:

Avraham came forward and said, "Will You sweep away the innocent along with the guilty? What if there should be fifty innocent people within the city; will You then wipe out the place and not forgive it for the sake of the innocent fifty who are in it? Far be it from You to do such a thing, to bring death upon the innocent as well as the guilty, so that innocent and guilty fare alike. Far be it from You! Shall not the Judge of all the earth do justice?"

> When men began to multiply on the face of the earth and daughters were born to them, the sons of the powerful ones saw the daughters of man, that they were desirable, and they took for themselves whatever women they chose.... The earth became corrupt before God, and the earth was filled with violence. God looked upon the earth, and, behold, it was corrupt; for all flesh had corrupted its way upon the earth. God said to Noah, "The end of all flesh has come before Me, for the earth is filled with violence through them; I will eradicate them from the earth." (*Bereishit* 6:1-2, 11-13)

The people of Noach's generation were guilty of corruption and thievery.[2] It was a generation in which moral boundaries were broken down; the fabric of society, the social contract, was torn beyond repair. Powerful men took women by force, creating an atmosphere of chaos and injustice.

What was the nature of Noach's righteousness? Apparently, Noach did not take part in the sexual immorality and thievery of his generation; he did not commit the crimes of which those around him were guilty. On the other hand, the text does not inform us of any acts of righteousness on is part, nor good deeds of any kind. This is the greatness—and the tragedy—of Noach.

The *Zohar* recounts a conversation between Noach and God after the flood:

---

2. See the comments of Ibn Ezra, and Rashi, *Bereishit* 6:11:

אבן עזרא בראשית פרק ו פסוק יא
חמס בגזל ועשק, וקחת גם הנשים בחזקה.

רש"י בראשית פרק ו פסוק יא
ותשחת לשון עֶרְוָה וַעֲ"זָ (סנה' נ"ז) כְּמוֹ פֶּן תַּשְׁחִיתוּן (דב' ד'), כִּי הִשְׁחִית כָּל בָּשָׂר וְגוֹ':

"[The earth] was corrupt" refers to lewdness and idolatry, as in the verse "lest you behave corruptly" (*Devarim* 4:16) as in "for all flesh had corrupted...."

זוהר - השמטות כרך א [בראשית] דף רנד עמוד ב[3]

תָּנוּ רַבָּנָן, מָה הֵשִׁיב הַקָּדוֹשׁ בָּרוּךְ הוּא לְנֹחַ, כְּשֶׁיָּצָא מִן הַתֵּיבָה וְרָאָה כָּל הָעוֹלָם חָרֵב, וְהִתְחִיל לִבְכּוֹת עָלָיו, וְאָמַר, רִבּוֹנוֹ שֶׁל עוֹלָם, נִקְרֵאתָ רַחוּם, הָיָה לְךָ לְרַחֵם עַל בְּרִיּוֹתֶיךָ. הֵשִׁיבוֹ הַקָּדוֹשׁ בָּרוּךְ הוּא, רַעְיָא שַׁטְיָא, כְּעַן אֲמַרְתְּ דָּא, וְלָא בְּזִמְנָא דַּאֲמָרִית לָךְ בְּלִישָׁנָא רְכִיכָא, דִּכְתִיב (שם ו) עֲשֵׂה לְךָ תֵּבַת עֲצֵי גֹפֶר כו', וַאֲנִי הִנְנִי מֵבִיא אֶת הַמַּבּוּל כו', לְשַׁחֵת כָּל בָּשָׂר כו', וַיֹּאמֶר ה' לְנֹחַ כו', כִּי אֹתְךָ רָאִיתִי צַדִּיק לְפָנַי בַּדּוֹר הַזֶּה, כּוֹלֵי הַאי אִתְעַכַּבִית עִמָּךְ, וַאֲמָרִית לָךְ, בְּדִיל דְּתִבְעֵי רַחֲמִין עַל עָלְמָא. וּמִכְּדֵין דְּשָׁמַעְתְּ דְּתִשְׁתֵּיזִיב אַתְּ בְּתֵיבוּתָא, לָא עָאל בְּלִבָּךְ בִּישׁוּתָא דְּעָלְמָא, וַעֲבַדְתְּ תֵּיבוּתָא וְאִשְׁתְּזֵבְתָּא. וּכְעַן דְּאִתְאֲבֵיד עָלְמָא, פָּתַחְתְּ פּוּמָךְ לְמַלָּלָא קֳדָמַי בָּעְיָין וְתַחֲנוּנִין.

Our Rabbis taught: How did God respond when Noach left the ark and saw the world had been destroyed and began to mourn, and cried before God, "Master of the Universe, You are called compassionate. You should have had compassion for Your creation."

God responded, "You are a foolish shepherd. **Now** you say this?! Why did you not say it when I told you that I saw you were righteous among your generation, or afterward when I said that I would bring a flood upon the people, or afterward when I instructed you to build an ark? I constantly procrastinated and said, 'When is [Noach] going to pray for mercy for the world?'... And now that the world is destroyed, you open your mouth to cry before Me and to ask for supplication?" (*Zohar Hashmatot*, Margoliot edition, *Bereishit* 254b)

Noach, as the leader of the generation, had responsibilities. He was given the task of building the ark, yet he did not save even one person outside his immediate family. Noach was an island—neither hurting others nor helping them. As a shepherd of God's flock, Noach had the responsibility to teach, to enlighten, to lead the people back to the path

---

3. This passage is also found, with slight variations, in *Zohar Chadash, Parashat Noah*.

of righteousness. Failing that, he was given the opportunity to plead for mercy on their behalf, to defend his charges before the heavenly court, but he made no such attempt. God compares him to a shepherd who sees his flock straying from the proper path and wandering in the proximity of dangerous wolves, only to conclude that the sheep deserve to be devoured because they have strayed. Rather than trying to save them, he mourns their loss after they are killed. God reprimands Noach for acting like a "foolish shepherd" who is guilty of malpractice.

The *Zohar* continues:

זוהר - השמטות כרך א [בראשית] דף רנד עמוד ב

אָמַר רַבִּי יוֹחָנָן, בֹּא וּרְאֵה מַה בֵּין הַצַּדִּיקִים שֶׁהָיוּ לְיִשְׂרָאֵל אַחַר כָּךְ, וּבֵין נֹחַ. נֹחַ לֹא הֵגִין עַל דּוֹרוֹ, וְלֹא הִתְפַּלֵּל עָלָיו כְּאַבְרָהָם. דְּכֵיוָן דְּאָמַר הַקָּדוֹשׁ בָּרוּךְ הוּא לְאַבְרָהָם, זַעֲקַת סְדוֹם וַעֲמוֹרָה כִּי רָבָּה, מִיָּד וַיִּגַּשׁ אַבְרָהָם וַיֹּאמַר. וְהִרְבָּה דְבָרִים כְּנֶגֶד הַקָּדוֹשׁ בָּרוּךְ הוּא, עַד שֶׁשָּׁאַל שֶׁאִם יִמְצָא שָׁם עֲשָׂרָה צַדִּיקִים, שֶׁיְכַפֵּר לְכָל הַדּוֹר בִּשְׁבִילָם, וְחָשַׁב אַבְרָהָם שֶׁהָיוּ י' בָּעִיר, עִם לוֹט וְאִשְׁתּוֹ וּבָנָיו וּבְנוֹתָיו, וַחֲתָנָיו, וְלָכֵן לֹא הִתְפַּלֵּל יוֹתֵר:

בָּא מֹשֶׁה וְהֵגִין עַל כָּל הַדּוֹר, כֵּיוָן שֶׁאָמַר הַקָּדוֹשׁ בָּרוּךְ הוּא לְמֹשֶׁה, יִשְׂרָאֵל חָטָאוּ, סָרוּ מַהֵר מִן הַדֶּרֶךְ. מַה כְּתִיב בֵּיהּ, (שמות לב) וַיְחַל מֹשֶׁה. מַהוּ וַיְחַל. מְלַמֵּד שֶׁהִתְפַּלֵּל עַד שֶׁאֲחָזַתּוּ חַלְחָלָה. רַבָּנָן אָמְרֵי, לֹא הִנִּיחַ מֹשֶׁה לְהַקָּדוֹשׁ בָּרוּךְ הוּא, עַד שֶׁנָּתַן נַפְשׁוֹ עֲלֵיהֶם מִן הָעוֹלָם הַזֶּה וּמִן הָעוֹלָם הַבָּא. דִּכְתִיב, (שם) וְעַתָּה אִם תִּשָּׂא חַטָּאתָם וְאִם אַיִן מְחֵנִי נָא מִסִּפְרְךָ אֲשֶׁר כָּתַבְתָּ: אָמַר רַבִּי יוֹסֵי מֵהָכָא, (תהלים קו) וַיֹּאמֶר לְהַשְׁמִידָם לוּלֵי מֹשֶׁה בְחִירוֹ עָמַד בַּפֶּרֶץ לְפָנָיו. וְכֵן כָּל הַצַּדִּיקִים הֵגִינוּ עַל דּוֹרָם, וְלֹא הִנִּיחוּ מִדַּת הַדִּין לִשְׁלוֹט בָּהֶם: וְנֹחַ הִתְעַכֵּב עִמּוֹ הַקָּדוֹשׁ בָּרוּךְ הוּא, וְאָמַר לֵיהּ רִבּוּי דְבָרִים, שֶׁמָּא יְבַקֵּשׁ עֲלֵיהֶם רַחֲמִים, וְלֹא הִשְׁגִּיחַ, וְלֹא בִּיקֵּשׁ עֲלֵיהֶם רַחֲמִים, וְעָשָׂה הַתֵּיבָה וְנֶאֱבַד כָּל הָעוֹלָם: מַה רָאָה נֹחַ שֶׁלֹּא בִקֵּשׁ רַחֲמִים עַל דּוֹרוֹ. אָמַר לוֹ, אֲפִילוּ הוּא לֹא חָשַׁב בְּלִבּוֹ שֶׁיִּמָּלֵט.

Rabbi Yochanan said: Come and see the difference between the righteous among the Jews after Noach, and Noach. Noach did not defend his generation, nor did he pray for them, as Avraham did. When God told Avraham that the outcry of Sodom and

Amorah had become great [i.e., they deserved destruction], Avraham immediately began to pray before God until he asked God if He would forgive the entire city if ten righteous people were found [in it]. Avraham was certain that in the city in which Lot and his wife and children lived, there must have been ten righteous people. Therefore, Avraham did not pray any further.

Afterwards, Moshe came, and he prayed for and protected his generation when God said to him, "They have turned away quickly from the way in which I commanded them" (*Shemot* 32:8). It is said that Moshe did not leave God alone until [He] forgave the Jewish People. Moshe was willing to give his soul for the people in both this world and the next. As it is written, "And now, if You will, forgive their sin; and if You will not [forgive them], expunge me, I pray, from Your book that You have written" (*Shemot* 32). Rabbi Yosi said, '[We learn this] from the verse, "He would have destroyed them had not Moshe, His chosen one, confronted Him in the breach to avert His destructive wrath" (*Tehillim* 106:23). Likewise, all the righteous ones defended their respective generations and would not allow the Attribute of Judgement to reign over them. God procrastinated with Noach, and said many things to him, so that he could beg for mercy on their behalf, but Noach paid no mind and did not ask for mercy on their behalf. He built the ark, and the world was lost.'

What was Noach thinking, that he did not ask for mercy for his generation? He said to himself, "Perhaps even I won't escape." (*Zohar Hashmatot*, Margoliot edition, *Bereishit* 254b)

The next great religious leader after Noach was Avraham, who pleaded with God on behalf of the people of Sodom and Amorah.[4] Generations

---

4. See *Bereishit* 18, especially verses 23-25:

בראשית פרק יח:כג-כו

וַיִּגַּשׁ אַבְרָהָם וַיֹּאמַר הַאַף תִּסְפֶּה צַדִּיק עִם רָשָׁע: אוּלַי יֵשׁ חֲמִשִּׁים צַדִּיקִם בְּתוֹךְ הָעִיר הַאַף תִּסְפֶּה וְלֹא־תִשָּׂא לַמָּקוֹם לְמַעַן חֲמִשִּׁים הַצַּדִּיקִם אֲשֶׁר בְּקִרְבָּהּ: חָלִלָה לְךָ מֵעֲשֹׂת כַּדָּבָר הַזֶּה לְהָמִית צַדִּיק עִם רָשָׁע וְהָיָה כַצַּדִּיק כָּרָשָׁע חָלִלָה לָּךְ הֲשֹׁפֵט כָּל־הָאָרֶץ לֹא יַעֲשֶׂה מִשְׁפָּט:

later, Moshe went even further out on a limb than Avraham: After the Jewish people committed the unfathomable sin of worshiping the golden calf at the foot of Mount Sinai, God informed Moshe that He intended to destroy the entire nation. Despite the people's guilt, Moshe pleaded with God to have mercy on them, since they had just left Egypt and had not yet had time to develop spiritually. He even had the audacity to tell God that if He would wipe out the entire nation, He should wipe Moshe out as well.[5] Moshe is referred to in the *Zohar* as a "faithful shepherd."[6]

Noach never engaged God in similar dialogue. While Avraham tried to spare the wicked cities from annihilation, or at the very least to save some of the people living there, Noach accepted God's decree in silence. The people of his generation were guilty; there was no argument, and he left them to suffer their fate. Moshe, despite the unquestioned guilt of his people, was prepared to sacrifice himself to save them. We can easily imagine that if Moshe had been in Noach's place, he would have refused to board the ark, demanding that if God did not have mercy on the people, he, Moshe, should be washed away along with them. To be fair, perhaps the example of Noach is what informed and inspired Avraham to do more, and the example of Avraham is what informed and inspired Moshe to do more. Nonetheless, Noach's efforts pale in comparison.

According to tradition, Noach built the ark over a period of 120 years. How is it possible that this "righteous" man did not manage to influence even one person in all that time? Perhaps his name is meant to give us a clue: Noach means "comfortable:" He was comfortable and self-satisfied in his own righteousness.

The sad truth is that Noach was a spiritual misanthrope. The comparison between this failed shepherd and the ultimate leader of a wayward flock—Moshe, the only other person in the Torah who was saved in an ark—is inescapable:

שמות פרק ב:א-ה
וַיֵּלֶךְ אִישׁ מִבֵּית לֵוִי וַיִּקַּח אֶת־בַּת־לֵוִי: וַתַּהַר הָאִשָּׁה וַתֵּלֶד בֵּן וַתֵּרֶא אֹתוֹ כִּי־טוֹב הוּא וַתִּצְפְּנֵהוּ שְׁלֹשָׁה יְרָחִים: וְלֹא־יָכְלָה עוֹד הַצְּפִינוֹ וַתִּקַּח־לוֹ תֵּבַת

---

5. *Shemot* 32:32; see below.
6. See footnote 11, above.

גֹּמֶא וַתַּחְמְרָה בַחֵמָר וּבַזָּפֶת וַתָּשֶׂם בָּהּ אֶת־הַיֶּלֶד וַתָּשֶׂם בַּסּוּף עַל־שְׂפַת הַיְאֹר: וַתֵּתַצַּב אֲחֹתוֹ מֵרָחֹק לְדֵעָה מַה־יֵּעָשֶׂה לוֹ: וַתֵּרֶד בַּת־פַּרְעֹה לִרְחֹץ עַל־הַיְאֹר וְנַעֲרֹתֶיהָ הֹלְכֹת עַל־יַד הַיְאֹר וַתֵּרֶא אֶת־הַתֵּבָה בְּתוֹךְ הַסּוּף וַתִּשְׁלַח אֶת־אֲמָתָהּ וַתִּקָּחֶהָ:

A man of the house of Levi went and took as his wife a daughter of Levi. The woman conceived and bore a son. When she saw that he was good, she hid him for three months. And when she could no longer hide him, she took for him an ark made of reeds and daubed it with loam and with pitch. She put the child in it, and she laid it in the rushes by the bank of the river. His sister stood at a distance to see what would be done to him. The daughter of Pharaoh came to wash herself at the river, and her maidens walked along by the side of the river. When she saw the ark among the reeds, she sent her maid to fetch it (*Shemot* 2:1–5).

Moshe, as an infant floating in an ark on the Nile, began his mission where Noach had ended his own. Moshe's entire career would be filled with self-sacrifice for his flock; the 120 years of his life would rectify Noach's failure to reach out to others over the course of the 120 years he spent building the ark. Moshe was the "faithful shepherd.

According to the Arizal, Moshe was chosen to complete the task which Noach, the "foolish shepherd" had failed to see through. This idea is borne out by a verse in Yeshayahu, the *haftarah* associated with *Parashat Noach*:

ישעיהו פרק נד:ט
כִּי־מֵי נֹחַ זֹאת לִי אֲשֶׁר נִשְׁבַּעְתִּי מֵעֲבֹר מֵי־נֹחַ עוֹד עַל־הָאָרֶץ כֵּן נִשְׁבַּעְתִּי מִקְּצֹף עָלַיִךְ וּמִגְּעָר־בָּךְ:

For this is like the waters of Noach to Me; for just as I have sworn that the waters of Noach should no more go over the earth, so have I sworn that I will not be angry with you [the Jewish people] or rebuke you. (*Yeshayahu* 54:9)

The *Zohar* focuses on the prophet Yeshayahu's use of the term *mei Noach*, "waters of Noach":

זוהר ויקרא יד:-טו.

רִבִּי יוֹסֵי אָמַר, (ישעיה נד) כִּי מֵי נֹחַ זֹאת לִי אֲשֶׁר נִשְׁבַּעְתִּי מֵעֲבוֹר מֵי נֹחַ. הַאי קְרָא קַשְׁיָא, כְּתִיב (בראשית ז) וּמֵי הַמַּבּוּל הָיוּ עַל הָאָרֶץ. וּכְתִיב (בראשית ט) וְלֹא יִכָּרֵת כָּל בָּשָׂר עוֹד מִמֵּי הַמַּבּוּל. מֵי הַמַּבּוּל כְּתִיב, וְלָא מֵי נֹחַ, וְהָכָא כְּתִיב כִּי מֵי נֹחַ זֹאת לִי...

אֶלָּא הָכִי תָּאנָא, כַּד זַכָּאִין סַגִּיאוּ בְּעָלְמָא, קוּדְשָׁא בְּרִיךְ הוּא חַדֵּי וּמִשְׁתַּבַּח בְּהוּ. דְּתָנֵינָן כַּד שָׁארֵי זַכָּאָה בְּעָלְמָא, וְאִשְׁתְּכַח בֵּיהּ, כִּבְיָכוֹל אַטִּיל שְׁלָמָא בְּעָלְמָא, וְכָל עָלְמָא מִתְבָּרְכָא בְּגִינֵיהּ, וְאַטִּיל שְׁלָמָא בְּפָמַלְיָא שֶׁל מַעֲלָה... תַּנְיָא אָמַר רִבִּי יוֹסֵי, בְּזִמְנָא דִּבְנֵי עָלְמָא אִשְׁתְּכָחוּ חַיָּיבִין קַמֵּי קוּדְשָׁא בְּרִיךְ הוּא, הַהוּא זַכָּאָה דְּאִשְׁתְּכַח בְּעָלְמָא, (בעי) קוּדְשָׁא בְּרִיךְ הוּא אִשְׁתְּעֵי בַּהֲדֵיהּ, בְּגִין דְּיִבְעֵי רַחֲמִין עַל עָלְמָא, וְיִתְפַּיֵּיס בַּהֲדַיְיהוּ. מַה עֲבַד קוּדְשָׁא בְּרִיךְ הוּא, אִשְׁתְּעֵי בַּהֲדֵיהּ עַל אִינוּן חַיָּיבֵי עָלְמָא. אָמַר לֵיהּ לְאוֹטָבָא לֵיהּ בִּלְחוֹדוֹי, וּלְשֵׁיצָאָה לְכֻלְּהוּ. מַה אָרְחֵיהּ דְּהַהוּא בַּר נַשׁ זַכָּאָה. שָׁבִיק דִּידֵיהּ, וְנָסִיב לְדְכוּלֵּי עָלְמָא בְּדִיל דְּיִתְפַּיֵּיס קוּדְשָׁא בְּרִיךְ הוּא בַּהֲדַיְיהוּ:

מְנָא לָן. מִמֹּשֶׁה... וְאִלּוּ בְּנֹחַ כְּתִיב, (בראשית ו) וַיֹּאמֶר אֱלֹהִים לְנֹחַ קֵץ כָּל בָּשָׂר בָּא (דף ט"ו ע"א) לְפָנַי וְגוֹ'. אָמַר לֵיהּ נֹחַ, וְלִי מַה אַתְּ עָבִיד. אָמַר לֵיהּ וַהֲקִימוֹתִי אֶת בְּרִיתִי אִתָּךְ וְגוֹ' עֲשֵׂה לְךָ תֵּבַת עֲצֵי גֹפֶר. וְלָא בָּעָא רַחֲמֵי עַל עָלְמָא, וְנָחִיתוּ מַיָּא, וְאוֹבִידוּ בְּנֵי עָלְמָא, וּבְגִין כַּךְ מֵי נֹחַ כְּתִיב. מֵי נֹחַ וַדַּאי, דְּבֵיהּ הֲווֹ תַּלְיָין, דְּלָא בָּעָא רַחֲמֵי עַל עָלְמָא:

R. Yosi said: 'It is written, "For this is as the waters of Noach unto me" [*Yeshayahu* 54:9]. This verse is difficult: [In other places] the Torah states, "And the waters of the flood were upon the earth," and "all living things will never again be wiped out by the waters of the flood." The waters are referred to as "waters of the flood," and here the expression used is "waters of Noach...."

We have been taught: R. Yosi said that when mankind is guilty before God, God engages a righteous man so that the latter may pray for mankind and obtain forgiveness for them. God first promises to save him alone and destroy the rest. The proper thing for a righteous man to do at such a time is to forget himself and espouse the cause of the whole world in order to appease God's wrath against them, as Moshe did when Israel sinned… However, when God said to Noach, "The end of all flesh has come before me," Noach replied, "And what will You do to me?", to which God replied, "I will establish My covenant with you; make for yourself an ark of gopher wood." So Noach did not pray for the world, and the waters came down and destroyed mankind, and therefore they are called "the waters of Noach" and they are indeed the waters of Noach, because he was responsible; he did not pray for the world.' (*Zohar, Vayikra*, 14b-15a)

The *Zohar* points out that in the prophecy of Yeshayahu, the flood is referred to as *mei Noach*, "the waters of Noach." The blame for the flood is placed squarely on Noach's shoulders, because he failed to intercede on behalf of his generation. This approach may be contrasted with an even more pointed and poignant turn of phrase Moshe uses in defense of his People. As we have noted, Moshe's devotion to his flock knew no bounds; he valiantly offered his own life for the Jewish People:

שמות פרק לב:לב
וְעַתָּה אִם־תִּשָּׂא חַטָּאתָם וְאִם־אַיִן מְחֵנִי נָא מִסִּפְרְךָ אֲשֶׁר כָּתָבְתָּ:

Now, if You will, forgive their sin; and if you do not, I beg You to expunge [*m'cheini*, מְחֵנִי] me from Your book which You have written. (*Shemot* 32:32)

The Hebrew word *m'cheini* (מחני) is composed of the same letters as "*mei Noah*" (מי נח): This, says the *Zohar*, is the defining moment: Moshe prayed on behalf of the sinners[7] and offered his own life in

---

7. See *Likkutei Halachot* (Breslov): "Noach was the type of *tzaddik* who never imagined repentance was even possible. Therefore, he secluded himself in his ark." Also see *Yismach Moshe, Parashat Noach* 29b, where Noach is compared to Rabbi Shimon bar Yochai, who hid in his cave and had no influence on this world:

their defense—specifically by using the word *m'cheini*—and in this way, Noach's failure was corrected.[8]

ספר ליקוטי הלכות או"ח - הלכות שבת הלכה ה-ז

כִּי עַתָּה אֵין הַשֵּׁם יִתְבָּרֵךְ רוֹצֶה מֵאִתָּנוּ כִּי אִם הִתְעוֹרְרוּת מְעַט, כַּמְבֹאָר בְּדִבְרֵי רַבּוֹתֵינוּ זַ"ל שֶׁהַשֵּׁם יִתְבָּרֵךְ מְבַקֵּשׁ מִיִּשְׂרָאֵל שֶׁיִּפְתְּחוּ בִּתְשׁוּבָה כְּעֵינָא דְּמַחְטָא וַאֲנָא אֶפְתַּח לְהוֹן תַּרְעִין רַבְרְבִין וְכוּ', אֲבָל גַּם זֶה הַמְּעַט דִּמְעַט קָשֶׁה מְאֹד לְהַתְחִיל כִּי אִם בְּכֹחַ הַצַּדִּיקִים הַגְּדוֹלִים שֶׁמַּמְשִׁיכִין דַּרְכֵי הַתְּשׁוּבָה הַנַּ"ל לְחַזֵּק אֶת כָּל הָרוֹצֶה לָשׁוּב בְּכָל מָקוֹם שֶׁהוּא וְכוּ':

וְכָל זֶה מְרֻמָּז בַּזֹּהַר חָדָשׁ בְּעִנְיָן תֵּבַת נֹחַ (עַיֵּן שָׁם בְּפָרָשַׁת נֹחַ בְּדַף כַּד כֹּה דְּפוּס סְלַאוִיטָא), מַה שֶּׁכָּתוּב שָׁם שֶׁלֹּא בִקֵּשׁ עַל דּוֹרוֹ, וְהָשִׁיבוֹ הַקָּדוֹשׁ-בָּרוּךְ-הוּא וְאַחַר שֶׁיָּצָא מֵהַתֵּבָה וְרָאָה כָּל הָעוֹלָם חָרֵב הִתְחִיל לִבְכּוֹת עָלָיו וְכוּ', וְהָשִׁיבוֹ הַקָּדוֹשׁ-בָּרוּךְ-הוּא:

רַעְיָא שַׁטְיָא כְּעָן אֲמַרְתְּ דָּא וְלֹא מִקֹּדֶם וְכוּ', כֵּיוָן דַּחֲזָא נֹחַ זֹאת כַּף הִקְרִיב עָלָוָן וְקָרְבָּנִין וְכוּ', עַיֵּן שָׁם מַה שֶּׁמְּבֹאָר שָׁם מַעֲלַת מֹשֶׁה רַבֵּנוּ שֶׁמָּסַר נַפְשׁוֹ עַל יִשְׂרָאֵל וְהִצִּילָם וְכוּ' וּמְבֹאָר שָׁם שֶׁבִּשְׁבִיל זֶה לֹא בִקֵּשׁ נֹחַ רַחֲמִים עַל דּוֹרוֹ כִּי אֲפִלּוּ הוּא לֹא חָשַׁב בְּלִבּוֹ שֶׁיִּמָּלֵט וְכוּ', עַיֵּן שָׁם שֶׁמַּאֲרִיךְ כַּמָּה הַקָּדוֹשׁ-בָּרוּךְ-הוּא רוֹצֶה שֶׁיְּבַקְּשׁוּ רַחֲמִים עַל יִשְׂרָאֵל וְכוּ', אֲפִלּוּ אִם הֵם כְּמוֹ שֶׁהֵם וְכוּ', וְעַיֵּן שָׁם מַה שֶּׁכָּתוּב עַל פָּסוּק (בְּרֵאשִׁית ח) וַיְשַׁלַּח אֶת הָעוֹרֵב זֶה דָּוִד שֶׁהָיָה קוֹרֵא תָּמִיד כְּעוֹרֵב וְכוּ', וּמַה שֶּׁכָּתוּב שָׁם עַל פָּסוּק (שָׁם) וַיְשַׁלַּח אֶת הַיּוֹנָה עַד וְלֹא יָסְפָה שׁוּב אֵלָיו עוֹד וְכוּ' עַיֵּן שָׁם. וְכָל הַפְּגָם שֶׁל נֹחַ וְתִקּוּנוֹ הַכֹּל הוּא בְּעִנְיָן בְּקִיאוּת הַנַּ"ל שֶׁלֹּא הָיָה בָּקִי בַּהֲלִיכָה זֹאת שֶׁל דַּרְכֵי הַתְּשׁוּבָה כְּמוֹ מֹשֶׁה וְהַצַּדִּיקִים הַגְּדוֹלִים שֶׁמַּמְשִׁיכִין דַּרְכֵי הַתְּשׁוּבָה הַנַּ"ל בִּבְקִיאוּת נִפְלָא מְאֹד, כִּי נֹחַ הָיָה צַדִּיק תָּמִים, אֲבָל לֹא הִשִּׂיג שֶׁאֶפְשָׁר לָצֵאת וּלְהוֹרִיד עַצְמוֹ לְהִסְתַּכֵּל עַל רְשָׁעִים כָּאֵלּוּ לַעֲסֹק עִמָּהֶם לִמְצֹא בָּהֶם אֵיזֶה זְכוּת וּלְהִתְפַּלֵּל עֲלֵיהֶם וּלְעוֹרְרָם בְּאֵיזֶה נְקֻדָּה טוֹבָה וְכוּ' שֶׁבְּכָל זֶה עָסַק מֹשֶׁה וְהַצַּדִּיקִים הַגְּדוֹלִים שֶׁאַחֲרָיו בִּיגִיעוֹת עֲצוּמוֹת, שֶׁכָּל זֶה כָּלוּל בִּבְחִינַת בְּקִיאוּת הַנַּ"ל בָּעֵיל וְנָפִיק, וְעַל-כֵּן סָבַר הַלְוַאי שֶׁיַּצִּיל אֶת עַצְמוֹ וְכוּ' כִּי לֹא הִשִּׂיג רַחֲמָיו יִתְבָּרֵךְ עַד הֵיכָן הֵם מַגִּיעִים, וְעַל-כֵּן הֻכְרַח לִכְנֹס אֶל הַתֵּבָה לְהִתְחַבֵּא שָׁם לְהִנָּצֵל עַצְמוֹ כִּי תֵּבַת נֹחַ נִבְנָה וְנַעֲשָׂה בְּחָכְמָה וּקְדֻשָּׁה גְּבוֹהַּ מְאֹד, כִּי הָיָה כַּוָּנוֹת עֲמוּקוֹת בְּגָבְהָהּ וְאָרְכָּהּ וְרָחְבָּהּ, וּבְכָל בִּנְיָנָהּ כַּמְבֹאָר בַּתּוֹרָה כָּל פְּרָטֵי עֲשִׂיָּתָהּ, וְהִיא מְרֻמֶּזֶת עַל תְּשׁוּבָה שֶׁעוֹשִׂין בְּיוֹם כִּפּוּר, כְּמוֹ שֶׁכָּתוּב בַּזֹּהַר הַקָּדוֹשׁ (תִּקּוּן כא דַף נד) תֵּבַת נֹחַ דָּא יוֹם כִּפּוּר, וְכֵן אִיתָא שָׁם:

ספר ישמח משה - פרשת נח דף כט/ב

וא"ל רבש"ע נקראת רחום (שמות לד ו), היה לך לרחם על בריותיך. השיבו הקב"ה רעיא שטיא, כען אמרת דא, ולא בזמנא דאמרת לך ואני הנני מביא מבול וגו' (בראשית ו יז) וכו', ואכדין דשמעית דתשתתזיב את בתיבותא, לא עלה בלבד בישובא דעלמא וכו', עיין שם. והנה בעונש רבי שמעון בן יוחאי לי"ב חדש הואיל ולא חס על העולם, הכי נמי לנח מדה כנגד מדה אינו חס על העולם, לא יראה העולם זה אסור במערה וזה בתיבה כנ"ל. ובזה נראה לי לפרש הא דאיתא במדרש רבה (ב"ר פל"א יד) בפסוק (שם שם בראשית י"ד) קינים תעשה את התיבה, מה הקן הזה מטהר את המצוער, כך תיבתך מטהרתך. דהנה כמו שנקרא מי נח, הואיל ולא המליץ הוי כאילו הביאו, כך כיון דלא המליץ והסכים למקטרג הוי כאילו קטרג, דאם לא כן למה נקרא מי נח, וזה ברור.

8. Arizal, *Shaar Pesukim Bereishit*, drush 4. *Sefer Ha-Likkutim, Parashat Noach*:

שער הפסוקים - פרשת בראשית - דרוש ד'

ודע, כי נח היה משה, ולא רצה להתפלל על בני דורו, כמ"ש חז"ל על פסוק (ישעיהו נ"ד ט') כי מי נח זאת לי וגו'. כי הוא גרם שיבאו מי המבול, ולכן נקראו על שמו מי נח. ואמנם אעפ"י שלא התפלל עליהם, עכ"ז בזכותו נתלה להם ק"ך שנה, אולי יחזרו בתשובה כמנין שנותיו של מרע"ה. וז"ש, בשגם הוא בשר, והיו ימיו ק"ך שנה. ובשגם זה הבל, וזה משה, כנודע.

After Noach left the ark, he saw the destruction of the world and recognized that he and his family were the only survivors. How did he cope with this? The Torah tells us that one of the first things Noach did was plant a vineyard; he made wine and become intoxicated.

בראשית פרק ט: כ-כא
וַיָּחֶל נֹחַ אִישׁ הָאֲדָמָה וַיִּטַּע כָּרֶם: וַיֵּשְׁתְּ מִן־הַיַּיִן וַיִּשְׁכָּר וַיִּתְגַּל בְּתוֹךְ אָהֳלֹה:

Noach began to work the land, and he planted a vineyard. He drank of the wine and became drunk, and he lay uncovered inside his tent. (*Bereishit* 9:20–21)

Noach could not cope with the enormity of the destruction around him. Apparently only when he saw the cataclysmic results of the flood, did he begin to grasp his own failure to prevent it. Only then, he finally understood that his passivity had resulted in the destruction of an entire civilization.

Noach's personal story begins to devolve rapidly from this moment of clarity; one of his sons, Ham, discovers Noach's nakedness and takes advantage of while his intoxicated state.[9]

ספר הליקוטים - פרשת נח - פסוק א

ודע, כי נח הוא יסוד המקבל כולם, והוא יסוד אבא, היורד עד יסוד ז"א, ומשקה לבינה הוא הגן העליון, ולמלכיות שהוא הגן תחתון, ולזה נק' מעיין גנים. ונח הוא בחינה זאת של יסוד אבא הנכנס בתוך ז"א, ולזה נקרא נח, מלשון מנוחה. ודע, כי מרע"ה הוא בחינת יסוד אבא, מראשו ועד סופו. ונח נתעלה ביסוד זה בבחינותו למטה, ולזה נכנסו שניהם בתיבה. בתיבת נח בדור המבול זפת, ובתיבת משה חמר וזפת. חמר כנגד דור הפלגה, וזפת כנגד דור המבול, שבא לתקן השני פגמות.. ולזה מהם היו משליכים ביאור, (שמות י"ד כ"ט) והמים להם חומה שהיו מדור המבול ועדיין עבדו ע"ז, ומה היו בונים אותם בבנין במקום לבנים. וזמ"ש פרעה (שם ה' י"ח) ותוכן לבנים לבנים תתנו, קרי בה לבנים, לפי שהיו נגד דור הפלגה. ולפי שנח פגם על שלא התפלל על בני דורו, בא מרע"ה לתקן ומסר נפשו עליהם. ואמר (שם ל"ב ל"ב) אם תשא חטאתם ואם אין מחני נא, בסוד (בראשית ז' כ"ג) וימח את כל היקום. וזהו ג"כ מ"ש (שמות ל"ג י"ב) ואתה אמרת ידעתיך בשם וגם מצאת ח"ן בעיני, בסוד (בראשית ו' ח') ונח מצא ח"ן. לזה השיב הקב"ה למשה ואמר (דברים ט' י"ד) הרף ממני ואשמידם ואעשה אותך לגוי גדול, כדמיון נח. אמנם יוסף הוא יסוד זעיר, לבוש ליסוד אבא, ומשה יסוד אבא. ולזה נאמר (שמות י"ג י"ט) ויקח משה את עצמות יוסף עמו, לפי שמגיע יסוד אבא עד תשלום יסוד זעיר, וזמ"ש בזוהר משה ויוסף כחדא אזלין:

---

9. See my *Explorations, Parashat Shemini*, for a Kabbalistic understanding of the wine Noach drank.

בראשית פרק ט: כב-כד

וַיַּרְא חָם אֲבִי כְנַעַן אֵת עֶרְוַת אָבִיו וַיַּגֵּד לִשְׁנֵי־אֶחָיו בַּחוּץ: וַיִּקַּח שֵׁם וָיֶפֶת אֶת־הַשִּׂמְלָה וַיָּשִׂימוּ עַל־שְׁכֶם שְׁנֵיהֶם וַיֵּלְכוּ אֲחֹרַנִּית וַיְכַסּוּ אֵת עֶרְוַת אֲבִיהֶם וּפְנֵיהֶם אֲחֹרַנִּית וְעֶרְוַת אֲבִיהֶם לֹא רָאוּ: וַיִּיקֶץ נֹחַ מִיֵּינוֹ וַיֵּדַע אֵת אֲשֶׁר־עָשָׂה־לוֹ בְּנוֹ הַקָּטָן:

Ham, the father of Canaan, saw the nakedness of his father, and he told his two brothers outside. Shem and Yefet took a garment and laid it upon both their shoulders. They went backward and covered the nakedness of their father [with] their faces backward, and they did not see their father's nakedness. Noach awoke from his wine and knew what his youngest son had done to him. (*Bereishit* 9:22–24)

The Sages offer two opinions of what occurred when Ham revealed his father's nakedness:

תלמוד בבלי סנהדרין ע.

וַיִּיקֶץ נֹחַ מִיֵּינוֹ, וַיֵּדַע אֵת אֲשֶׁר עָשָׂה לוֹ בְּנוֹ הַקָּטָן". רַב וּשְׁמוּאֵל, חַד אָמַר, סֵרְסוֹ. וְחַד אָמַר, רְבָעוֹ.

"And Noach awoke from his wine and knew what his youngest son had done to him" — Rav and Shmuel [differ]; one says that he castrated him, while the other contends that he sexually abused him. (*Sanhedrin* 70a)

Noach's children were not saved from the flood on the merit of their own righteousness, but in their father's merit—but this did not prevent Ham from committing a terrible outrage against his father. Apparently, Noach not only failed to educate the people of his generation, he failed to educate even his own children. Ham was as guilty as those who were eradicated by the flood; he shared their culture of violence, sexual licentiousness, and inflated sense of entitlement. Noach's passivity had brought about the destruction of Ham's world, and the Talmudic opinions that Ham raped or castrated his father are an expression of Ham's disdain for that passivity.

Noach lived for 350 years after the flood, witnessing the birth of countless descendants, numerous new generations. What message did Noach impart to his descendants? What insight had he gained from having survived the cataclysm? What wisdom did he share with his children, grandchildren, and great-grandchildren? Noach remained as silent after the flood as he had been before it. He remained passive; he had nothing to say. In a sense, we may say that he remained "naked," silently wallowing in a hazy state of intoxication. He had no influence on people or events after the flood.

בראשית פרק יא: א-ו

וַיְהִי כָל־הָאָרֶץ שָׂפָה אֶחָת וּדְבָרִים אֲחָדִים: וַיְהִי בְּנָסְעָם מִקֶּדֶם וַיִּמְצְאוּ בִקְעָה בְּאֶרֶץ שִׁנְעָר וַיֵּשְׁבוּ שָׁם: וַיֹּאמְרוּ אִישׁ אֶל־רֵעֵהוּ הָבָה נִלְבְּנָה לְבֵנִים וְנִשְׂרְפָה לִשְׂרֵפָה וַתְּהִי לָהֶם הַלְּבֵנָה לְאָבֶן וְהַחֵמָר הָיָה לָהֶם לַחֹמֶר: וַיֹּאמְרוּ הָבָה| נִבְנֶה־לָּנוּ עִיר וּמִגְדָּל וְרֹאשׁוֹ בַשָּׁמַיִם וְנַעֲשֶׂה־לָּנוּ שֵׁם פֶּן־נָפוּץ עַל־פְּנֵי כָל־הָאָרֶץ: וַיֵּרֶד ה' לִרְאֹת אֶת־הָעִיר וְאֶת־הַמִּגְדָּל אֲשֶׁר בָּנוּ בְּנֵי הָאָדָם: וַיֹּאמֶר ה' הֵן עַם אֶחָד וְשָׂפָה אַחַת לְכֻלָּם וְזֶה הַחִלָּם לַעֲשׂוֹת וְעַתָּה לֹא־יִבָּצֵר מֵהֶם כֹּל אֲשֶׁר יָזְמוּ לַעֲשׂוֹת:

The whole earth was of one language and one speech. It came to pass as [the people] journeyed from the east that they found a plain in the land of Shinar, and they lived there. They said one to another, "Come, let us make bricks and burn them thoroughly." They had brick for stone and loam for mortar. They said, "Come, let us build us a city and a tower whose top may reach to Heaven, and let us make for ourselves a name, lest we be scattered upon the face of the whole earth." God came down to see the city and the tower that the sons of man built. God said, "Behold, the people are one, and they have all one language, and **this** is what they begin to do? Now should nothing be withheld from them, all that they have schemed to do?" (*Bereishit* 11:1–6)

All the people of the world were gathered in Shinar, building the Tower of Bavel; rabbinic tradition tells us that Noach was among them:

> **סדר עולם רבה [ליינר] פרק א ד"ה מאדם עד המבול**
> נמצא נח חיה אחר הפלגה עשר שנים.
>
> We find that Noach lived for ten years after the dispersion [which resulted from the Tower of Bavel]. (*Seder Olam Rabbah* [Leiner edition], Chapter 1)

Noach was still alive, but he was silent. Not only did he fail to protect or educate his contemporaries, but even his own children and grandchildren were deprived of guidance from this "righteous" man. Noach should have learned from the pain and tragedy he had seen, should have become a teacher and leader, sharing his hard-earned insights and teaching moral conviction and religious commitment to the generations after the flood—but once again, he said nothing, in stark contrast to another prominent individual who lived in the generation that built the Tower of Bavel.

> **סדר עולם רבה [ליינר] פרק א ד"ה מאדם עד המבול**
> אבינו אברהם היה בפלגה בין מ"ח שנה
>
> Our forefather Avraham was forty-eight years old at the dispersion [which resulted from the Tower of Bavel]. (*Seder Olam Rabbah* [Leiner edition], Chapter 1)

Noach and Avraham, two spiritual giants, met at the tower where all the people of the world had gathered. Yet it appears that Noach had no words of wisdom to share with Avraham. Whatever greatness Avraham would achieve, he would do so without the benefit of Noach's tutelage.

Some commentaries see this meeting of Noach and Avraham as a potential watershed in human history. The Torah hints at the opportunity:

בראשית פרק יא:ה-ו

וַיֵּרֶד ה' לִרְאֹת אֶת־הָעִיר וְאֶת־הַמִּגְדָּל אֲשֶׁר בָּנוּ בְּנֵי הָאָדָם: וַיֹּאמֶר ה' הֵן עַם אֶחָד וְשָׂפָה אַחַת לְכֻלָּם וְזֶה הַחִלָּם לַעֲשׂוֹת וְעַתָּה לֹא־יִבָּצֵר מֵהֶם כֹּל אֲשֶׁר יָזְמוּ לַעֲשׂוֹת:

God came down to see the city and the tower that the sons of man built. God said, "Behold, the people are one, and they have all one language, and **this** is what they begin to do? Now, nothing that they propose to do will bebeyond their reach." (*Bereishit* 11:5–6)

A spirit of unity swept the people assembled in the plains of Shinar;[10] Noach was there with his experience, and Avraham was there with his idealism. The time and place were ripe for a religious renaissance. With the right leadership, the world could have been elevated and redeemed. The people could have reached up to Heaven even without the aid of a tower. But alas, Noach was silent, and Avraham was forced to face the challenge alone.

When Noach died, Avraham took on the role of teacher, leader, and protector of his generation at age 58—the numerical equivalent of Noach's name, נ״ח—and assumed the responsibilities that Noach had left untended.[11]

This missed opportunity is precisely what Rashi alludes to in his comments on the verse describing Noach's righteousness. The lack of symmetry we noted at the outset is not a careless use of words or a lopsided analogy; Rashi carefully crafted his comments on the verse, drawing from the two sources we have examined:

---

10. See the comments of Alshich, *Bereishit* 11:6:

אלשיך בראשית פרק יא

(ו) ויאמר ה' להליץ בעדם הן עם אחד ושפה אחת לכולם, לומר גם כי לעשות הפך רצונו ית־ברך כיוונו, עם כל זה אחדות היה ביניהם כי בקשו להדמות אל הקדושה. וזה החילם לעשות, ואף על פי שסופם לרעה, כיון שהחילם הוא אחדות שהוא חדא לטיבותא ראוי לרחם עליהם. אך לעומת זה חדא לריעותא, כי ועתה לא יבצר מהם כל אשר יזמו לעשות, על ידי האחדות והכנתם להרע כנזכר, ונמצא העולם אבד בהגביה הטומאה:

11. As noted in *Seder Olam Rabbah*, chapter 1 (cited above): Avraham was forty-eight at the building of the Tower, and Noah died ten years later.

רש"י בראשית פרק ו:ט

בְּדֹרֹתָיו – יֵשׁ מֵרַבּוֹתֵינוּ דּוֹרְשִׁים אוֹתוֹ לְשֶׁבַח, כָּל שֶׁכֵּן אִלּוּ הָיָה בְדוֹר צַדִּיקִים הָיָה צַדִּיק יוֹתֵר; וְיֵשׁ שֶׁדּוֹרְשִׁים אוֹתוֹ לִגְנַאי, לְפִי דוֹרוֹ הָיָה צַדִּיק וְאִלּוּ הָיָה בְדוֹרוֹ שֶׁל אַבְרָהָם לֹא הָיָה נֶחְשָׁב לִכְלוּם:

Some of the sages expound this positively: Certainly, if he had been in a generation of righteous people, he would have been more righteous. Other sages expound it negatively: In his generations he was righteous, but if he had lived in the generation of Avraham, he would have been considered worthless. (Rashi, *Bereishit* 6:9)

The Talmudic passage that serves as Rashi's source makes no mention of Avraham; it refers to "another generation" in general terms:[12]

תלמוד בבלי סנהדרין קח עמוד א

אֵלֶּה תּוֹלְדֹת נֹחַ, נֹחַ אִישׁ צַדִּיק תָּמִים הָיָה בְּדֹרֹתָיו" (בראשית ו), אָמַר רַבִּי יוֹחָנָן, בְּדוֹרוֹתָיו, וְלֹא בְּדוֹרוֹת אֲחֵרִים. וְרֵישׁ לָקִישׁ אָמַר, בְּדוֹרוֹתָיו, כָּל שֶׁכֵּן בְּדוֹרוֹת אֲחֵרִים.

"Noach was a righteous man. He was perfect in his generations" — Rabbi Yochanan said: In his generations, but not in other generations. Resh Lakish[13] maintained: [Even] in his generations—how much more so in other generations. (*Sanhedrin* 108a)

The Midrashic passage that serves as Rashi's second source also addresses Noach's righteousness:

---

12. This passage, while speaking of the greatness of Noah, does not necessarily address his tzidkut. It may be defining Noah's perfectness (tamim), which would be more in line with the phrase being explained.

13. It is interesting that Resh Lakish, a reformed criminal who became a great rabbi, insisted that Noah would have been greater in a more conducive environment. For more on the transformation of Resh Lakish, see *The Crowns on the Letters* (forthcoming).

מדרש בראשית רבה ל:ט

בְּדֹרֹתָיו, רַבִּי יְהוּדָה וְרַבִּי נְחֶמְיָה, רַבִּי יְהוּדָה אָמַר בְּדֹרֹתָיו הָיָה צַדִּיק, הָא אִלּוּ הָיָה בְּדוֹרוֹ שֶׁל מֹשֶׁה אוֹ בְּדוֹרוֹ שֶׁל שְׁמוּאֵל לֹא הָיָה צַדִּיק. בְּשׁוּק סָמַיָּא צָוְחִין לַעֲוִירָא סַגִּי נְהוֹר, מָשָׁל לְאֶחָד שֶׁהָיָה לוֹ מַרְתֵּף אֶחָד שֶׁל יַיִן, פָּתַח חָבִית אַחַת וּמְצָאָהּ שֶׁל חֹמֶץ, שְׁנִיָּה כֵּן, שְׁלִישִׁית וּמְצָאָהּ קוֹסֵס, אָמְרִין לֵיהּ קוֹסֵס הוּא, אָמַר לְהוֹן וְאִית הָכָא טַב מִינָהּ, אָמְרוּ לֵיהּ לָא. כָּךְ בְּדֹרֹתָיו הָיָה צַדִּיק הָא אִלּוּ הָיָה בְּדוֹרוֹ שֶׁל מֹשֶׁה אוֹ בְּדוֹרוֹ שֶׁל שְׁמוּאֵל לֹא הָיָה צַדִּיק. רַבִּי נְחֶמְיָה אָמַר וּמָה אִם בְּדֹרֹתָיו הָיָה צַדִּיק, אִלּוּ הָיָה בְּדוֹרוֹ שֶׁל מֹשֶׁה אוֹ בְּדוֹרוֹ שֶׁל שְׁמוּאֵל עַל אַחַת כַּמָּה וְכַמָּה, מָשָׁל לִצְלוֹחִית שֶׁל אֲפַרְסְמוֹן מֻקֶּפֶת צָמִיד פָּתִיל, וּמֻנַּחַת בֵּין הַקְּבָרוֹת, וְהָיָה רֵיחָהּ נוֹדֵף, וְאִלּוּ הָיָה חוּץ לַקְּבָרוֹת עַל אַחַת כַּמָּה וְכַמָּה, מָשָׁל לִבְתוּלָה שֶׁהָיְתָה שְׁרוּיָה בְּשׁוּק שֶׁל זוֹנוֹת וְלֹא יָצָא עָלֶיהָ שֵׁם רָע, אִלּוּ הָיְתָה בְּשׁוּקָן שֶׁל כְּשֵׁרוֹת עַל אַחַת כַּמָּה וְכַמָּה, כָּךְ, וּמָה אִם בְּדֹרֹתָיו הָיָה צַדִּיק אִלּוּ הָיָה בְּדוֹרוֹ אוֹ בְּדוֹרוֹ שֶׁל שְׁמוּאֵל עַל אַחַת כַּמָּה וְכַמָּה...

Rabbi Yehudah said: Only in his generations was he a righteous man [by comparison]; had he flourished in the generation of **Moshe** or **Shmuel**, he would not have been called "righteous." In the street of the totally blind, a one-eyed man is called clear-sighted, and an infant is called a scholar. It is like a man who had a wine vault. He opened one barrel and found it vinegar, [and opened] another and found it [also] vinegar. But the third [he opened], he found turning sour. "It is turning," people said to him. "Is there any better here?" he retorted. Similarly, **in his generations** [Noah] was a righteous man…

Rabbi Nechemiah said: If he was righteous even in his generation, how much more righteous he would have been [had he lived] in the age of Moshe. (*Bereishit Rabbah* 30:9)

The reference to Moshe is understood: Moshe became the ultimate leader, taking responsibility to the point of self-sacrifice, whereas Noah failed — not once, in the generation of the flood; not twice, with his own children; but again and again, over hundreds of years. By why did Rabbi Yehudah choose to compare Noah to Shmuel, above all the other prophets or leaders of Israel? The message seems to be that there is more than one model of leadership: Shmuel was neither a king nor a political leader; he was the moral compass of the nation. It was Shmuel who admonished King Shaul, and it was Shmuel who anointed King David. If Noach could not lead as Moshe had, he should have assumed an auxiliary or supporting role—teaching Avraham, supporting his leadership, encouraging his own descendants to follow Avraham's moral path, publicly anointing Avraham as the leader of the next generation. Once again, Noach failed; he remained silent. Had he communicated with Avraham—or with any of his own descendants—he could have changed the world; the Torah would surely have recorded any such an attempt.

By making two minor "edits," Rashi changed the complexion of the sources, and revealed his own interpretation of the verses that describe Noach's character. While each of the rabbinic sources was built symmetrically—one recording the disagreement between Rav Yochanan and Resh Lakish regarding Noach's stature relative to his surroundings in general terms, and the other comparing Noach to two archetypical leaders (Moshe and Shmuel), Rashi inserts another biblical character (Avraham), and only on one side of the equation.[14] Rashi's comments use the general terms of the Talmudic discussion on one side of the equation, and a specific comparison, as in the Midrashic discussion—but with a twist—on the other side of the equation. There is a powerful message in this subtle shift: Both sides of the equation weigh alternative scenarios that might have influenced Noach, for better or worse. Rashi's formulation points out that the two sides of the equation do not contradict one another. Had Noach lived in a more righteous generation, he himself would have achieved greater spiritual and moral heights. On the other hand, in the generation of Avraham, he would have been considered worthless. In fact, Rashi seems to be reminding us

---

14. There is also a lack of symmetry in the manner in which Rashi presents the two sides of the argument: One is presented as the opinion of "some of the Sages," while the other is presented without attribution. In both the Talmudic and Midrashic source material, both sides of the argument are attributed to illustrious rabbis.

that Noach did live in Avraham's generation,[15] and, despite his greatness as an individual, he remained silent, and was, therefore, worthless.

The image of Noach conveyed by the verses is of a righteous man who remained calm in the face of turbulent waters, withstanding incredible social pressures. Anyone who has been faced with peer pressure can appreciate Noach's greatness: The corruption of his entire generation did not cause him to shift from his moral center.

Yet Noach's righteousness was a double-edged sword. While his ability to reject the seductive depravity of the world is commendable, his morality was built around isolationism. He saw no connection between his own future and the future of those around him. Noach is therefore remembered as a righteous person in his generation, but one who was neither proactive nor influential. He remained alone, floating in his ark, forming no relationships and affecting no change. In a world teeming with people and ideas, both before and after the flood, he remained silent and alone.

---

15. See Rav Yonatan Eibeshitz in *Tiferet Yonatan*, *Bereishit* 6:9, p. 14 (*Parashat Noach*), for a similar observation:

ספר תפארת יהונתן על בראשית פרק ו פסוק ט

איש צדיק תמים היה בדורותיו. אמרו חז"ל יש דורשין לשבח ויש דורשין לגנאי <u>ואבאר דאלו ואלו דברי אלקים חיים</u>. דהנה נח היה ראוי לחשוב לו לחטא ולהענש שלא הוכיח לאנשי דורו כפי הצורך שיחזרו למוטב אך הי' לו לזה תירוץ מספיק דרשאי אדם לומר מי אנכי איש כסיל ונבער מדעת לבא במזור ותרופה למכת חביירי ועדיין לא הגעתי לרואי ביקור חביריי. רק זהו דוקא במקום שנמצאים שם אנשים חשובים יותר ממנו אבל במקום שאין איש השתדל להיות איש וא"כ באמת חטא במה דלא הוכיח לאנשי דורו וזהו שאמרו לשבח. <u>כי אלו היה בדורו של אברהם באמת דיקולא מצוארי' הוי נחית על אברהם הגדול ממנו בחכמה להוכיח לאנשי דורו ולא חטא כלל.</u> אבל עכשיו חטא או איפכא דבאמת היה לו תירוץ דמוטב שיהיה שוגגין ולא יהיה מזידין. אבל אם כבר אחרים מיחו בזה. ואומרים שדבר זה הוא עבירה אין לו תירוץ זה וזה שדורשין לגנאי אלו היה בדורו של אברהם ולא היה לו באמת תירוץ זה. מוטב שיהיה שוגגין ואעפ"כ לא הוכיח לאנשי דורו כל הצורך היה נחשב לו לחטא. משא"כ עתה שהיה לו תירוץ הנ"ל:

Parashat Lech Lecha

Avraham's Discovery

בראשית פרק יב, א
וַיֹּאמֶר ה' אֶל־אַבְרָם לֶךְ־לְךָ מֵאַרְצְךָ וּמִמּוֹלַדְתְּךָ וּמִבֵּית אָבִיךָ אֶל־הָאָרֶץ אֲשֶׁר אַרְאֶךָּ:

God said to Avram, "Go, for yourself, from your country, from your birthplace, from your father's home, to the land which I will show you...." (*Bereishit* 12:1)

Parashat Lech Lecha begins with God's command to Avraham (Avram) to leave behind everything with which he is familiar and to set out for an unknown destination. The Torah, however, does not tell us why God chose Avraham. What was special about him? Why was he destined to become the first of the patriarchs, the founder of a nation? Who was Avraham? What were his accomplishments? What would his resume look like? Regarding all these questions, the Torah is silent.

Midrashic literature ably fills in the gaps, recounting Avraham's trials, his lonely explorations, and his eventual discovery of God.[1] While

---

1. See *Shabbat* 156a, which discusses Avraham's mastery of astrology. *Avodah Zarah* 14b recounts how Avraham had 400 chapters of Idolatry. Also see Rambam's statement, cited in note 2, below, that Avraham worshiped idols:

תלמוד בבלי מסכת שבת דף קנו עמוד א
וְאַף רַב סָבַר, אֵין מַזָּל לְיִשְׂרָאֵל, דְּאָמַר רַב יְהוּדָה, אָמַר רַב, מִנַּיִן שֶׁאֵין מַזָּל לְיִשְׂרָאֵל? שֶׁנֶּאֱמַר, (בראשית טו) "וַיּוֹצֵא אוֹתוֹ הַחוּצָה", אָמַר אַבְרָהָם לִפְנֵי הַקָּדוֹשׁ בָּרוּךְ הוּא, רִבּוֹנוֹ שֶׁל עוֹלָם, (שם) "בֶּן בֵּיתִי יוֹרֵשׁ אוֹתִי". אָמַר לוֹ, לָאו, כִּי אִם אֲשֶׁר יֵצֵא מִמֵּעֶיךָ. אָמַר לְפָנָיו, רִבּוֹנוֹ שֶׁל עוֹלָם, נִסְתַּכַּלְתִּי בְּאִצְטַגְנִינוּת שֶׁלִּי, וְאֵינִי רָאוּי לְהוֹלִיד בֵּן. אָמַר לוֹ, צֵא מֵאִצְטַגְנִינוּת שֶׁלְּךָ - שֶׁאֵין מַזָּל לְיִשְׂרָאֵל...

Rav, too, holds that Israel is immune from planetary influence. For Rav Yehudah said in Rav's name: "How do we know that Israel is immune from planetary influence? Because it is said, '…and he brought him out.' Avraham pleaded

we have no question about the authenticity of our Oral Tradition, we might well ask: If the stories of Avraham's youth are to be taken literally, why does the Torah itself not share them with us?[2] Why was it left to our

before the Holy One, blessed be He, 'Sovereign of the Universe! A member of my household (staff) will be my heir.' 'Not so,' He replied, 'but he that shall come forth out of your own loins.' 'Sovereign of the Universe!' cried [Avraham], 'I have looked at my constellation and find that I am not fated to beget a child.' 'Go out of [i.e., cease] your constellation [gazing], for Israel is free from planetary influence....'"

תלמוד בבלי מסכת עבודה זרה דף יד עמוד ב
א"ל רב חסדא לאבימי: גמירי, דעבודת כוכבים דאברהם אבינו ד' מאה פירקי הוויין,...

Said R. Chisda to Abimi: There is a tradition that the [tractate] *Avodah Zarah* of our father Avraham consisted of four hundred chapters....

2. Rambam cites these Midrashim in the *Hilchot Avodah Zarah* (Idolatry) 1:2-3:

רמב"ם הלכות עבודה זרה פרק א
הלכה ב...-וְעַל דֶּרֶךְ זֶה הָיָה זֶה הָעוֹלָם הוֹלֵךְ וּמִתְגַּלְגֵּל עַד שֶׁנּוֹלַד עַמּוּדוֹ שֶׁל עוֹלָם וְהוּא אַבְרָהָם אָבִינוּ:
הלכה ג - כֵּיוָן שֶׁנִּגְמַל אֵיתָן זֶה הִתְחִיל לְשׁוֹטֵט בְּדַעְתּוֹ וְהוּא קָטָן וְהִתְחִיל לַחֲשֹׁב בַּיּוֹם וּבַלַּיְלָה וְהָיָה תָּמֵהַּ הֵיאַךְ אֶפְשָׁר שֶׁיִּהְיֶה הַגַּלְגַּל הַזֶּה נוֹהֵג תָּמִיד וְלֹא יִהְיֶה לוֹ מַנְהִיג וּמִי יְסַבֵּב אוֹתוֹ. כִּי אִי אֶפְשָׁר שֶׁיְּסַבֵּב אֶת עַצְמוֹ. וְלֹא הָיָה לוֹ מְלַמֵּד וְלֹא מוֹדִיעַ דָּבָר אֶלָּא מֻשְׁקָע בְּאוּר כַּשְׂדִּים בֵּין עוֹבְדֵי כּוֹכָבִים הַטִּפְּשִׁים וְאָבִיו וְאִמּוֹ וְכָל הָעָם עוֹבְדֵי כּוֹכָבִים וְהוּא עוֹבֵד עִמָּהֶם וְלִבּוֹ מְשׁוֹטֵט וּמֵבִין עַד שֶׁהִשִּׂיג דֶּרֶךְ הָאֱמֶת וְהֵבִין קַו הַצֶּדֶק מִתְּבוּנָתוֹ הַנְּכוֹנָה. וְיָדַע שֶׁיֵּשׁ שָׁם אֱלוֹהַּ אֶחָד וְהוּא מַנְהִיג הַגַּלְגַּל וְהוּא בָּרָא הַכּל וְאֵין בְּכָל הַנִּמְצָא אֱלוֹהַּ חוּץ מִמֶּנּוּ. וְיָדַע שֶׁכָּל הָעוֹלָם טוֹעִים וְדָבָר שֶׁגָּרַם לָהֶם לִטְעוֹת זֶה שֶׁעוֹבְדִים אֶת הַכּוֹכָבִים וְאֶת הַצּוּרוֹת עַד שֶׁאָבַד הָאֱמֶת מִדַּעְתָּם. וּבֶן אַרְבָּעִים שָׁנָה הִכִּיר אַבְרָהָם אֶת בּוֹרְאוֹ. כֵּיוָן שֶׁהִכִּיר וְיָדַע הִתְחִיל לְהָשִׁיב תְּשׁוּבוֹת עַל בְּנֵי אוּר כַּשְׂדִּים וְלַעֲרֹךְ דִּין עִמָּהֶם וְלוֹמַר שֶׁאֵין זוֹ דֶּרֶךְ הָאֱמֶת שֶׁאַתֶּם הוֹלְכִים בָּהּ וְשִׁבֵּר הַצְּלָמִים וְהִתְחִיל לְהוֹדִיעַ לָעָם שֶׁאֵין רָאוּי לַעֲבֹד אֶלָּא לֶאֱלוֹהַּ הָעוֹלָם וְלוֹ רָאוּי לְהִשְׁתַּחֲווֹת וּלְהַקְרִיב וּלְנַסֵּךְ כְּדֵי שֶׁיַּכִּירוּהוּ כָּל הַבְּרוּאִים הַבָּאִים. וְרָאוּי לְאַבֵּד וּלְשַׁבֵּר כָּל הַצּוּרוֹת כְּדֵי שֶׁלֹּא יִטְעוּ בָּהֶן כָּל הָעָם כְּמוֹ אֵלּוּ שֶׁהֵם מְדַמִּים שֶׁאֵין שָׁם אֱלוֹהַּ אֶלָּא אֵלּוּ. כֵּיוָן שֶׁגָּבַר עֲלֵיהֶם בִּרְאָיוֹתָיו בִּקֵּשׁ הַמֶּלֶךְ לְהָרְגוֹ וְנַעֲשָׂה לוֹ נֵס וְיָצָא לְחָרָן. וְהִתְחִיל לַעֲמֹד וְלִקְרֹא בְּקוֹל גָּדוֹל לְכָל הָעוֹלָם וּלְהוֹדִיעָם שֶׁיֵּשׁ שָׁם אֱלוֹהַּ אֶחָד לְכָל הָעוֹלָם וְלוֹ רָאוּי לַעֲבֹד. וְהָיָה מְהַלֵּךְ וְקוֹרֵא וּמְקַבֵּץ הָעָם מֵעִיר לְעִיר וּמִמַּמְלָכָה לְמַמְלָכָה עַד שֶׁהִגִּיעַ לְאֶרֶץ כְּנַעַן וְהוּא קוֹרֵא שֶׁנֶּאֱמַר (בראשית כא לג) "וַיִּקְרָא שָׁם בְּשֵׁם ה' אֵל עוֹלָם«. וְכֵיוָן שֶׁהָיוּ הָעָם מִתְקַבְּצִין אֵלָיו וְשׁוֹאֲלִין לוֹ עַל דְּבָרָיו הָיָה מוֹדִיעַ לְכָל אֶחָד וְאֶחָד כְּפִי דַּעְתּוֹ עַד שֶׁיַּחֲזִירֵהוּ לְדֶרֶךְ הָאֱמֶת עַד שֶׁנִּתְקַבְּצוּ אֵלָיו אֲלָפִים וּרְבָבוֹת וְהֵם אַנְשֵׁי בֵית אַבְרָהָם וְשָׁתַל בְּלִבָּם הָעִקָּר הַגָּדוֹל הַזֶּה וְחִבֵּר בּוֹ סְפָרִים וְהוֹדִיעוֹ לְיִצְחָק בְּנוֹ....

(1:2) ... The world continued in this fashion until the pillar of the world—the Patriarch Avraham—was born. (1:3) After this great man was weaned, he began to explore and to think. Though he was a child, he began to think [incessantly], throughout the day and night, wondering: How is it possible for the sphere to continue to revolve without having anyone controlling it? Who is causing it to revolve? Surely, it does not cause itself to revolve.

Sages to inform us of Avraham's past? While these questions could be posed about any section of Midrash, in this instance the complete lack of explanation of Avraham's special status leaves us with no apparent reason for God's decision to reveal Himself—to this man, or to anyone at all. Why is this information found exclusively in the Oral Tradition?

Let us consider the picture of Avraham that is painted by our Sages: Avraham was born into a world of polytheism. His father, Terach, is described as a sculptor and purveyor of idols. When Avraham is asked to mind the store, he engages the customers in theological debate.

He had no teacher, nor was there anyone to inform him. Rather, he was mired in Ur Kasdim among the foolish idolaters. His father, mother, and all the people [around him] were idol worshipers, and he would worship with them. [However,] his heart was exploring and [gaining] understanding. Ultimately, he appreciated the way of truth and understood the path of righteousness through his accurate comprehension. He realized that there is one God who controls the sphere, that He created everything, and that there is no other God among all the other entities. He knew that the entire world was mistaken. What caused them to err was their worship of the stars and graven images, which made them lose awareness of the truth. Avraham was forty years old when he became aware of his Creator. When he recognized and knew Him, he began to formulate replies to the inhabitants of Ur Kasdim and debate with them, telling them that they were not following a proper path. He broke their idols and began to teach the people that it is fitting to serve only the Master of the Universe. To Him [alone] is it fitting to bow down, sacrifice, and offer libations, so that the people of future [generations] would recognize Him. [Conversely,] it is fitting to destroy and break all the images, lest all the people err concerning them, like those people who thought that there are no other gods besides these [images]. When he overcame them through the strength of his arguments, the king desired to kill him. He was [saved through] a miracle and left for Charan. [There,] he began to call in a loud voice to all people and inform them that there is one God in the entire world and it is proper to serve Him. He would go out and call to the people, gathering them in city after city and country after country, until he came to the land of Canaan—proclaiming [God's existence the entire time], as it says, "And He called there in the name of the Lord, the eternal God" (*Bereishit* 21:33). When the people would gather around him and ask him about his statements, he would explain to each one of them according to their understanding, until they turned to the path of truth. Ultimately, thousands and myriads gathered around him. These are the men of the house of Avraham. He planted in their hearts this great fundamental principle, composed texts about it, and taught it to Yitzchak, his son.

בראשית רבה (וילנא) פרשת נח פרשה לח סימן יג

רַבִּי חִיָּא בַּר בְּרֵיהּ דְּרַב אַדָּא אַדְּיָפוֹ, תֶּרַח עוֹבֵד צְלָמִים הָיָה, חַד זְמַן נְפֵיק לַאֲתַר, הוֹשִׁיב לְאַבְרָהָם מוֹכֵר תַּחְתָּיו. הֲוָה אָתֵי בַּר אֵינַשׁ בָּעֵי דְיִזְבַּן, וַהֲוָה אָמַר לֵהּ בַּר כַּמָּה שְׁנִין אַתְּ, וַהֲוָה אָמַר לֵיהּ בַּר חַמְשִׁין אוֹ שִׁתִּין, וַהֲוָה אָמַר לֵיהּ וַי לֵיהּ לְהַהוּא גַבְרָא דַּהֲוָה בַּר שִׁתִּין וּבָעֵי לְמִסְגַּד לְבַר יוֹמֵי, וַהֲוָה מִתְבַּיֵּשׁ וְהוֹלֵךְ לוֹ. חַד זְמַן אֲתָא חַד אִתְּתָא טְעִינָא בִּידָהּ חָדָא פִּינָךְ דְּסֹלֶת, אָמְרָה לֵיהּ הֵא לָךְ קָרֵב קֳדָמֵיהוֹן, קָם נְסֵיב בּוּקְלָסָא בִּידֵיהּ, וְתַבְרִינוּן לְכָלְּהוֹן פְּסִילַיָּא, וִיהַב בּוּקְלָסָא בִּידָא דְרַבָּה דַּהֲוָה בֵּינֵיהוֹן. כֵּיוָן דַּאֲתָא אֲבוּהּ אֲמַר לֵיהּ מַאן עָבֵיד לְהוֹן כְּדֵין, אֲמַר לֵיהּ מָה נִכְפּוּר מִינָךְ אֲתַת חָדָא אִתְּתָא טְעִינָא לָהּ חָדָא פִּינָךְ דְּסֹלֶת, וַאֲמָרַת לִי הֵא לָךְ קָרֵיב קֳדָמֵיהוֹן, קָרֵיבִת לְקֳדָמֵיהוֹן הֲוָה דֵּין אֲמַר אֲנָא אֵיכוֹל קַדְמָאי, וְדֵין אֲמַר אֲנָא אֵיכוֹל קַדְמָאי, קָם הָדֵין רַבָּה דַּהֲוָה בֵּינֵיהוֹן נָסַב בּוּקְלָסָא וְתַבְרִינוֹן. אֲמַר לֵיהּ מָה אַתָּה מַפְלֶה בִּי, וְיָדְעִין אִינּוּן. אֲמַר לֵיהּ וְלֹא יִשְׁמְעוּ אָזְנֶיךָ מַה שֶׁפִּיךָ אוֹמֵר.

Terach was a manufacturer of idols. He once went away and left Avraham to sell them in his place. A man entered and wished to buy one. "How old are you?" Avraham asked him. "Fifty years," was the reply. "Woe to such a man!" [Avraham] exclaimed. "You are fifty years old and would worship a day-old object!" At this, [the man] became ashamed and departed.

On another occasion, a woman came in with a plateful of flour and requested of him, "Take this and offer it to [the idols]." [Avraham] took a stick, broke [all the idols], and put the stick in the hand of the largest. When his father returned, he demanded, "What have you done?" "I cannot hide it from you," [Avraham] replied. "A woman came with a plateful of fine flour and requested that I offer it to them. One idol claimed, 'I must eat first,' while another claimed, 'I must eat first.' Thereupon the largest arose, took the stick, and broke the others." "Why do you mock me?" [Terach] cried out. "Have they any knowledge?" "Do your ears hear what your mouth is saying?" [Avraham] retorted. (*Bereishit Rabbah* 38:13)

Avraham's theological challenge was most certainly the result of many long hours of painstaking inquiry and analysis: We are told that Avraham considered the various forms of worship practiced in his region, rejecting one after the other through the use of critical thinking. Through the application of pure logic, Avraham concluded that the world must have had a beginning:

בראשית רבה (וילנא) פרשת לך לך פרשה לט: ג

וַיֹּאמֶר ה' אֶל אַבְרָם (בראשית יב, א): רַבִּי בֶּרֶכְיָה פָּתַח (שיר השירים ח, ח): אָחוֹת לָנוּ קְטַנָּה וְשָׁדַיִם אֵין לָהּ וגו', אָחוֹת לָנוּ קְטַנָּה, זֶה אַבְרָהָם שֶׁאִיחָה אֶת כָּל בָּאֵי הָעוֹלָם. בַּר קַפָּרָא אָמַר כְּזֶה שֶׁהוּא מְאַחֶה אֶת הַקֶּרַע, קְטַנָּה, שֶׁעַד שֶׁהוּא קָטָן הָיָה מְסַגֵּל מִצְווֹת וּמַעֲשִׂים טוֹבִים. וְשָׁדַיִם אֵין לָהּ, לֹא הֱנִיקוּהוּ לֹא לְמִצְווֹת וּמַעֲשִׂים טוֹבִים. (שיר השירים ח, ח):

"God said to Avram"— Rabbi Birchiya expounded upon the verse, "We have a little sister, and she has not yet developed breasts" (*Shir ha-Shirim* 8:8). This refers to Avraham, who made himself like a brother to the entire world; Bar Kapparah said, [Avraham] healed the rift [that had come into the world]. "A little sister" — even when Avraham was a young person he collected good deeds and pious acts. "She has no breasts" — Avraham's piety was not nurtured by anyone else.

"Little" — even as a young person he stored up pious acts and good deeds. (*Bereishit Rabbah* 39:3)

בראשית רבה (וילנא) פרשת ויגש פרשה צה

וּמֵהֵיכָן לָמַד אַבְרָהָם אֶת הַתּוֹרָה, רַבָּן שִׁמְעוֹן אוֹמֵר נַעֲשׂוּ שְׁתֵּי כִלְיוֹתָיו כִּשְׁתֵּי כַדִּים שֶׁל מַיִם וְהָיוּ נוֹבְעוֹת תּוֹרָה, וּמִנַּיִן שֶׁכֵּן הוּא, שֶׁנֶּאֱמַר (תהלים טז, ז): אַף לֵילוֹת יִסְּרוּנִי וגו'. רַבִּי לֵוִי אָמַר מֵעַצְמוֹ לָמַד תּוֹרָה, שֶׁנֶּאֱמַר (משלי יד, יד): מִדְּרָכָיו יִשְׂבַּע סוּג לֵב וּמֵעָלָיו אִישׁ טוֹב:

From where did Avraham learn Torah? Said Rabbi Shimon bar Yochai: His two kidneys became like two full pitchers from which Torah gushed forth. How do we know that it is so? Because it says, "I will bless God who has given me counsel [in the night-seasons my reins [kidneys] instruct me" (*Tehillim* 16:7). R. Levi said: He learned Torah of himself, for it says, 'The dissembler in his heart shall have his fill, from his own ways; and a good man shall be satisfied from himself." (*Mishlei* 14:14) (*Bereishit Rabbah* 95:3)

These obscure Midrashim describe Avraham's theological development, stressing that he arrived at his conclusions on his own; he had no teacher. He reasoned that there must be some great force that created and sustains this world; there must be a First Cause, there must be a God. After shattering his father's idols, Avraham argued with Terach, "If you recognize that the idols do not have the power to help or harm one another, how can you possibly base all of your dreams, hopes, and aspirations on the power of these impotent stones?"

Avraham was persecuted for his beliefs. After he out-reasoned his father, Terach handed him over to Nimrod, a wicked tyrant who was determined to "re-educate" Avraham, attempting to convince him to worship idols or the forces of nature—anything concrete.

בראשית רבה (וילנא) פרשת נח פרשה לח סימן יג

נַסְבֵיהּ וּמְסָרֵיהּ לְנִמְרוֹד. אָמַר לֵיהּ נִסְגּוֹד לְנוּרָא, אָמַר לֵיהּ אַבְרָהָם וְנִסְגּוֹד לְמַיָּא דְּמַטְפִין נוּרָא. אָמַר לֵיהּ נִמְרוֹד נִסְגּוֹד לְמַיָּא, אָמַר לֵיהּ אִם כֵּן נִסְגּוֹד לַעֲנָנָא דִטְעִין מַיָּא. אָמַר לֵיהּ נִסְגּוֹד לַעֲנָנָא. אָמַר לֵיהּ אִם כֵּן נִסְגּוֹד לְרוּחָא דִמְבַדַּר עֲנָנָא. אָמַר לֵיהּ נִסְגּוֹד לְרוּחָא. אָמַר לֵיהּ וְנִסְגּוֹד לְבַר אֵינָשָׁא דְסָבֵיל רוּחָא. אָמַר לֵיהּ מִלִּין אַתְּ מִשְׁתָּעֵי, אֲנִי אֵינִי מִשְׁתַּחֲוֶה אֶלָּא לָאוּר, הֲרֵי אֲנִי מַשְׁלִיכְךָ בְּתוֹכוֹ, וְיָבוֹא אֱלוֹהַּ שֶׁאַתָּה מִשְׁתַּחֲוֶה לוֹ וְיַצִּילְךָ הֵימֶנּוּ. הֲוָה תַּמָּן הָרָן קָאֵים פְּלוּג, אָמַר מַה נַּפְשָׁךְ אִם נָצַח אַבְרָהָם אֲנָא אָמַר מִן דְּאַבְרָהָם אֲנָא וְאִם נָצַח נִמְרוֹד אֲנָא אָמַר דְּנִמְרוֹד אֲנָא. כֵּיוָן שֶׁיָּרַד אַבְרָהָם לְכִבְשַׁן הָאֵשׁ וְנִצַּל, אָמְרִין לֵיהּ דְּמַאן אַתְּ, אָמַר לְהוֹן מִן אַבְרָהָם אֲנָא, נְטָלוּהוּ וְהִשְׁלִיכוּהוּ לָאוּר וְנֶחְמְרוּ בְּנֵי מֵעָיו, וְיָצָא וּמֵת עַל פְּנֵי תֶּרַח אָבִיו, הֲדָא הוּא דִכְתִיב: וַיָּמָת הָרָן עַל פְּנֵי תֶּרַח וגו'.

Thereupon [Terach] seized [Avraham] and delivered him to Nimrod. "Let us worship the fire!" [Nimrod] proposed.

"Let us rather worship water, which extinguishes the fire," replied [Avraham].

"Then let us worship water!"

"Let us rather worship the clouds which bear the water."

"Then let us worship the clouds!"

"Let us rather worship the winds which disperse the clouds."

"Then let us worship the wind!"

"Let us rather worship human beings, who withstand the wind."

"You are just bandying words," [Nimrod] exclaimed. "We will worship naught but the fire. Behold, I will cast you into it, and let your God whom you adore come and save you from it." (*Bereishit Rabbah* 38:13)

With each suggestion, Avraham forces Nimrod to recognize that the object of his worship can be reduced to a previous form or vanquished by something more powerful. This dialogue illustrates Avraham's underlying philosophical position: There must be an all-powerful and perfect God.

Avraham was unwilling to back down, even when facing the most powerful man of his time. Avraham had no illusions about the dangerous ground he was treading, and the Midrashic account of his confrontation with Nimrod illustrates Avraham's heroism: He was willing to sacrifice everything for the ideas and ideals in which he had come to believe. Eventually, Nimrod cast Avraham into the fire, but Avraham was saved; miraculously, he escaped from the furnace unscathed.[3] Why does the

---

3. This may be the meaning of the verse in which God forges a covenant with Avraham and his descendants (*Bereishit* 15:7), as it is rendered in the translation of the Targum [Pseudo]-Yonatan:

בראשית פרק טו:ז
וַיֹּאמֶר אֵלָיו אֲנִי ה' אֲשֶׁר הוֹצֵאתִיךָ מֵאוּר כַּשְׂדִּים לָתֶת לְךָ אֶת־הָאָרֶץ הַזֹּאת לְרִשְׁתָּהּ:

Torah omit these impressive stories of religious searching and discovery, persecution and heroism? Surely the image of Avraham withstanding the torments of his persecutor would have served as an important example for future generations.

Apparently, God preferred to begin Avraham's story with revelation: God speaks to Avraham, commands him, and the structure of the biblical narrative implies that nothing that came before this revelation is relevant:

בראשית פרק יב:א
וַיֹּאמֶר ה' אֶל־אַבְרָם לֶךְ־לְךָ מֵאַרְצְךָ וּמִמּוֹלַדְתְּךָ וּמִבֵּית אָבִיךָ אֶל־הָאָרֶץ אֲשֶׁר אַרְאֶךָּ:

God said to Avram, "Go for yourself from your country, from your birthplace, from your father's home, to the land which I will show you...." (*Bereishit* 12:1)

For all of Avraham's genius, his decisions and behavior are based on logic—wonderful logic, compelling logic, but nevertheless human logic. There are limits to the human mind, to man's understanding. When man analyzes the world around him, he is limited by his subjectivity.[4] Did

---

תרגום יונתן על בראשית ט״ו:ז'
וַאֲמַר לֵיהּ אֲנָא יְיָ דְאַפֵּיקְתָּךְ מֵאַתּוּן נוּרָא דְכַשְׂדָּאֵי לְמִתַּן לָךְ יַת אַרְעָא הֲדָא לְמֵירְתָהּ:

כתר יונתן בראשית פרשת לך לך פרק טו פסוק ז
ויאמר לו אני יי שהוצאתיך מכבשן האש של כשדים לתת לך את הארץ הזאת לרשתה:

And He said to him, "I am God who brought you out of the fiery furnace [the Aramaic word for 'fire' is *ur*] of Kasdim, to give you this land to inherit it.'" (Targum Yonatan, *Bereishit* 15:7)

4. See *Kuzari* 4:27:

ספר הכוזרי - מאמר רביעי
(כז) אמר החבר: יפה אמרת מלך הכוזרים וכחך לאלוה זוהי האמת וזוהי האמונה באמת ועזיבת כל מותר ויתכן כי העיון הזה שמצאנו בספר יצירה היה עיונו של אברהם אבינו שעה שכבר נתבררו לו אחדות האלוה ורבונותו אך טרם זכה להתגלות אולם לאחר שזכה להתגלות עזב את כל ההקשים ולא בקש מעם האלוה כי אם להיות לו לרצון אחרי אשר למדו האלוה מה הוא הרצון במה ישב ובאיזה מקום וכבר דרשו החכמים על מאמר הכתוב ויוצא אותו החוצה צא מאצטגנינות שלך כלומר עזב חכמת הכוכבים וכל חכמת טבע מספקת וכל ספר

Lech Lecha: Avraham's Discovery | 91

Avraham know that he was right? All the logic he could muster pointed in the direction of the truth of his conclusions. Clearly, he felt that he had uncovered the truth, and that he had found God. Avraham was so

אפלטון על נביא אחד בדורו של מרינוס שאמר על פי חזון שהיה אליו מאת האלוה לפילוסוף אחד שהשתדל מאד לזכות להתגלות האלוה על ידי עיון בפילוסופיה לא בדרך הזאת תגיע אלי כי אם על ידי אותם ששמתים מתוכים ביני ובין יצירי רצונו לומר הנביאים וחקי האמת וכבר נרמז ענין זה בספר יצירה בסוד ספירת העשרה ספירה זו הסכם עליה במזרח ובמערב אם כי אין לכך יסוד בחכמה טבעית ולא הכרעה מצד הקש שכלי כי אם סוד אלוהי הלא הוא אמרו עשר ספירות בלימה בלם פיך מלדבר בלם לבך מלהרהר ואם רץ לבך שוב למקום שלכך נאמר רצוא ושוב ועל דבר זה נכרתה ברית ומדתן עשר אשר אין להן סוף נעוץ סופן בתחלתן ותחלתן בסופן כשלהבת קשורה בגחלת דע וחשב וצור שהיוצר אחד ואין בלעדיו ולפני אחד מה אתה סופר וחתימת הספר היא וכשהבין אברהם אבינו וצר (וחקק וצרף ויצר) וחקר וחשב ועלתה בידו נגלה עליו אדון הכל וקראו אוהבי וכרת לו ברית בין עשר אצבעות ידיו והוא ברית לשון ובין עשר אצבעות רגליו והוא ברית מילה וקרא עליו בטרם אצרך בבטן ידעתיך:

The Rabbi: Just so, O King of the Khazars, by God! This is the truth, the real faith, and everything else may be abandoned. Perhaps this was Avraham's point of view when divine power and unity dawned upon him prior to the revelation accorded to him. As soon as this took place, he gave up all his speculations and only strove to gain God's favor, having ascertained what this was, and how and where it could be obtained. The Sages explain the words: 'And he brought him outside' (*Bereishit* 15), thus: Give up your horoscopy! This means: Forsake astrology as well as any other doubtful study of nature. Plato relates that a prophet, who lived at the time of the king Morinus, said prophetically to a philosopher who was zealously devoted to his art: You cannot reach me on this road, but only those whom I have placed as intermediaries between me and mankind, meaning the prophets and the true law. The Book of *Yetzirah* is constructed on the mystery of ten units equally acknowledged in east and west, but neither from natural causes, nor rational conviction. The following sentences are a Divine mystery, "Ten *Sefirot* without anything else; close your mouth from speaking, close your heart from thinking. If your heart runs away, return to God" (*Sefer Yetzirah* 1:8); for with reference to this [the prophet] says, "Running and returning" (*Yechezkel* 1:15). On this basis the covenant was made: Their measure is ten in endless progression, (*Yechezkel* 1:7) the end being linked to the beginning, and the beginning to the end just as a flame which is attached to the coal. You must know, think, and reflect that the Creator is one, without another, and there is no number which you can count before "one" (*Yechezkel* 6:4). The book concludes as follows: As soon as Avraham had understood, meditated, discerned and clearly grasped, the Lord of the universe revealed Himself to him, called him His friend and made a covenant with him between the ten fingers of his hand, which is the covenant of the tongue; and between the ten toes of his feet, which is the covenant of circumcision, and He pronounced upon him the word: "Before I formed you in your mother's womb I knew you" (*Yirmiyahu* 1:5).

convinced of the merit of his argument that he was literally prepared to die defending it. He was not satisfied with merely embracing his new *weltanschauung*; he endeavored to teach and inspire others to follow the same path. The Midrashic portrait of Avraham is of a spiritual giant who arrived at a conclusion based on careful, compelling logic, a man who is so intellectually honest that he is willing to die for his convictions. But could he know with complete certainty that he was, indeed, correct?

The answer may explain why the Torah begins the saga of Avraham with revelation: The Torah is not primarily a history book; it is a document that describes the covenant between God and His people, between the People and their God. A covenant of this kind, a commitment of this kind, can only be based on revelation. While human logic has its limits, revelation goes beyond logic. The Torah is replete with commandments, yet such commandments can only exist if there is a command, and, by definition, a Commander. Revelation is the vehicle through which God commands us.

Let us consider: When Avraham chose to be thrown into the furnace rather than renounce his belief, did he know that this was the right choice? Before God spoke to him, did Avraham know the proper response for each situation, or was he merely drawing the most logical conclusions he was capable of reaching? In hindsight, we know that each of Avraham's decisions was correct; Avraham was so spiritually sensitive that he was able to discern God's will; this is the reason our Sages recorded and preserved the account of Avraham's early life in Midrashic literature. The belief in monotheism is eminently logical, and Avraham was the ultimate champion of monotheism. He behaved with conviction and heroism, but in the absence of a Divine command—of any Divine communication—Avraham's behavior took on a subjective element. Although he was correct, the story of the Jewish people begins only with meta-logical revelation, at the moment when subjective human intuition is set aside and the responsibility that is born of recognizing the Commander begins.

בראשית רבה (וילנא) פרשת לך לך פרשה לט:א

וַיֹּאמֶר ה' אֶל אַבְרָם לֶךְ לְךָ מֵאַרְצְךָ וגו' (בראשית יב, א), רַבִּי יִצְחָק פָּתַח (תהלים מה, יא): שִׁמְעִי בַת וּרְאִי וְהַטִּי אָזְנֵךְ וְשִׁכְחִי עַמֵּךְ וּבֵית אָבִיךְ, אָמַר רַבִּי יִצְחָק מָשָׁל לְאֶחָד שֶׁהָיָה עוֹבֵר מִמָּקוֹם לְמָקוֹם, וְרָאָה בִּירָה אַחַת דּוֹלֶקֶת, אָמַר תֹּאמַר שֶׁהַבִּירָה הַזּוֹ בְּלֹא מַנְהִיג, הֵצִיץ עָלָיו בַּעַל הַבִּירָה, אָמַר לוֹ אֲנִי הוּא בַּעַל הַבִּירָה. כָּךְ לְפִי שֶׁהָיָה אָבִינוּ אַבְרָהָם אוֹמֵר תֹּאמַר שֶׁהָעוֹלָם הַזֶּה בְּלֹא מַנְהִיג, הֵצִיץ עָלָיו הַקָּדוֹשׁ בָּרוּךְ הוּא וְאָמַר לוֹ אֲנִי הוּא בַּעַל הָעוֹלָם. (תהלים מה, יב): וְיִתְאָו הַמֶּלֶךְ יָפְיֵךְ כִּי הוּא אֲדֹנָיִךְ. וְיִתְאָו הַמֶּלֶךְ יָפְיֵךְ, לְיַפּוֹתֵךְ בָּעוֹלָם, (תהלים מה, יב): וְהִשְׁתַּחֲוִי לוֹ, הֱוֵי וַיֹּאמֶר ה' אֶל אַבְרָם.

[Avraham] may be compared to a man who was traveling from place to place when he saw a castle fully illuminated. "Is it possible that this castle has no master?" he wondered. The owner of the castle looked out and said, "I am the owner of the castle."

Similarly, because our father Avraham said, "Is it conceivable that the world is without a master?" The Holy One, blessed be He, looked out and said to him, "I am the Master, the Sovereign of the Universe".... Hence, "God said to Avram, 'Go, for your own benefit, from your country, from your birthplace, from your father's home, to the land which I will show you....'" (*Bereishit Rabbah* 39:1)

Avraham believed in God—a God who is involved in human history, a God who controls human destiny. What led Avraham to his discovery? Perhaps the Torah's message is that belief in One God is ultimately such a simple concept that anyone, even a child, can conceive of it.[5]

---

5. Rav Elchanan Wasserman, in his *Kovetz Maamarim* (p. 11), raises a question which is related to our present query: How can the Torah expect a twelve- year-old girl or thirteen-year-old boy to be capable of belief in or knowledge of God, when some of the greatest philosophers in the world, who possessed keen, trained minds, have stumbled terribly in pursuit of intellectual truth? Reb Elchanan answered quite simply that knowledge of God is not as difficult as we might think: Were it not for the evil inclination, all mankind would be able to clearly see and

Nonetheless, deep spiritual sensitivity and understanding do not necessarily exist in a vacuum, nor are they born *ex nihilo*. The Torah hints at the source of Avraham's inspiration: None other than his father Terach, the pagan purveyor of idols.

There is something unique about Terach:

בראשית פרק יא:כד-כו

וַיְחִי נָחוֹר תֵּשַׁע וְעֶשְׂרִים שָׁנָה וַיּוֹלֶד אֶת־תָּרַח: וַיְחִי נָחוֹר אַחֲרֵי הוֹלִידוֹ אֶת־תֶּרַח תְּשַׁע־עֶשְׂרֵה שָׁנָה וּמְאַת שָׁנָה וַיּוֹלֶד בָּנִים וּבָנוֹת: וַיְחִי־תֶרַח שִׁבְעִים שָׁנָה וַיּוֹלֶד אֶת־אַבְרָם אֶת־נָחוֹר וְאֶת־הָרָן:

Nachor lived twenty-nine years, and fathered **Terach**. **Nachor** lived after he fathered Terach 119 years, and fathered [more] sons and daughters. And **Terach** lived seventy years, and fathered Avram, **Nachor**, and Charan. (*Bereishit* 11:24–26)

Terach, son of Nachor, named one of his sons after his father; he is the first person recorded in the Torah to do so. And so, every day of Avraham's youth, when he looked at his brother Nachor he was reminded of his roots, and of his father's roots. Perhaps this is what started Avraham wondering about the origins of other things. This approach, taken to its extreme, eventually led Avraham to break out of the pagan mindset and to embrace monotheism.

If this is so, we might be tempted to ascribe to Terach the nascent belief in One God. However, Terach was unable to take the idea to its conclusion; apparently, Terach was "derailed" somewhere along the way. Another instance of this same phenomenon is to be found at the end of *Parashat Noach*:

---

understand truth. It is not the belief in God per se which people find difficult. Rather, the implications of this belief are what make it difficult. If the ramifications of belief were removed or disconnected from belief itself, belief would indeed be attainable by all those who seek truth, even a bar- or bat-mitzvah, or a three-year-old like Avraham. See my *Explorations: Devarim*, "Parashat Ki Teizei -Going to War." See *Sanhedrin* 63b.

Lech Lecha: Avraham's Discovery

בראשית פרק יא, לא

וַיִּקַּח תֶּרַח אֶת־אַבְרָם בְּנוֹ וְאֶת־לוֹט בֶּן־הָרָן בֶּן־בְּנוֹ וְאֵת שָׂרַי כַּלָּתוֹ אֵשֶׁת אַבְרָם בְּנוֹ וַיֵּצְאוּ אִתָּם מֵאוּר כַּשְׂדִּים לָלֶכֶת אַרְצָה כְּנַעַן וַיָּבֹאוּ עַד־חָרָן וַיֵּשְׁבוּ שָׁם:

Terach took Avram, his son, and Lot the son of Charan (his son's son), and Sarai, his daughter-in-law (his son Avram's wife), and went out with them from Ur Kasdim to go to the land of Canaan. They came to Charan and dwelt there. (*Bereishit* 11:31)

Terach was on his way to Canaan—the Land of Israel—but he never arrived.[6] Instead, he settled in Charan. Terach knew that he must leave the place of his birth, his homeland, his people; he knew that his destination was the Land of Israel, but he never quite completed his mission. The revelation with which our *parashah* opens commands Avraham, in a sense, to continue what his father began but did not complete.

בראשית פרק יב, א

וַיֹּאמֶר ה' אֶל־אַבְרָם לֶךְ־לְךָ מֵאַרְצְךָ וּמִמּוֹלַדְתְּךָ וּמִבֵּית אָבִיךָ אֶל־הָאָרֶץ אֲשֶׁר אַרְאֶךָּ:

God said to Avram, "Go, for yourself, from your country, from your birthplace, from your father's home, to the land which I will show you...." (*Bereishit* 12:1)

---

6. Perhaps Terach also heard a voice calling him to go to the Land of Israel (Canaan) see *Sefat Emet Lech Lecha* 5672. Also see *Ha'amek Davar Bereishit* 11:31.

ספר שפת אמת - בראשית - פרשת לך - שנת תרל"ב

רמב"ן הקשה שנאמר לך לך בלי שנזכר מקודם חיבתו. ובזוה"ק נראה כי זה עצמו השבח ששמע זה המאמר לך לך שנאמר מהש"ת לכל האנשים תמיד כמ"ש וי לאינון דשינתא בחוריהון ואאע"ה שמע וקיבל. וממילא נקרא רק הדיבור אליו כי הלא לא נמצא מיוחד לשומעו. רק הוא אבל בודאי זה השבח בעצמו שהי' מוכן לקבל המאמר:

העמק דבר בראשית פרק יא :לא

ויקח תרח את אברם בנו וגו' ללכת ארצה כנען. אף על גב שלא היה עוד מאמר ה' לאברהם אבינו, מכ"מ כבר היה הערה מן השמים וראה מרחוק קדושת הארץ, וכמש"כ להלן ט"ו ז'. והא דכתיב ויקח תרח וגו', אף על גב דעיקר רצון אותה יציאה היה אברם ובעצתו, מכ"מ כיון שהיה אברם שקוע ברעיונות אלקיות או חכמות, ולא יכול להנהיג נסיעה הוא וביתו, על כן נמסר הנסיעה לאביו והוא לקח את אברם וכל הכבודה על ידו:

Based on logic, Avraham understood that there must be something beyond logic, something beyond nature. Avraham sought an elusive, higher wisdom. God's revelation was his answer—confirmation that Avraham's logical conclusions were correct. Both the medium and the message were revelation: The fact that God communicated directly with man, as well as the content of that communication, shaped Avraham's personal destiny.[7]

The closing section of the *parashah* is equally instructive, for it is here that Avraham is given the commandment of circumcision:

בראשית פרק יז:ט-יב

וַיֹּאמֶר אֱלֹהִים אֶל־אַבְרָהָם וְאַתָּה אֶת־בְּרִיתִי תִשְׁמֹר אַתָּה וְזַרְעֲךָ אַחֲרֶיךָ לְדֹרֹתָם: זֹאת בְּרִיתִי אֲשֶׁר תִּשְׁמְרוּ בֵּינִי וּבֵינֵיכֶם וּבֵין זַרְעֲךָ אַחֲרֶיךָ הִמּוֹל לָכֶם כָּל־זָכָר: וּנְמַלְתֶּם אֵת בְּשַׂר עָרְלַתְכֶם וְהָיָה לְאוֹת בְּרִית בֵּינִי וּבֵינֵיכֶם: וּבֶן־שְׁמֹנַת יָמִים יִמּוֹל לָכֶם כָּל־זָכָר לְדֹרֹתֵיכֶם יְלִיד בָּיִת וּמִקְנַת־כֶּסֶף מִכֹּל בֶּן־נֵכָר אֲשֶׁר לֹא מִזַּרְעֲךָ הוּא:

The Almighty said to Avraham, "You shall keep My covenant, you and your descendants after you throughout the generations. This is My covenant which you shall keep between Me and you, and your descendants after you: Every male child among you shall be circumcised. You shall circumcise the flesh of your foreskin, and it shall be a sign of the covenant between Me and

---

7. The progression of Avraham's spiritual growth is described in the *Zohar*, *Bereishit* 80a.

זהר מנוקד/תרגום/ חלק א דף פ/א

כָּלְהוּ דַּרְגִּין דְּנָטְעִין בְּהַאי אֲתָר. וַיִּטַּע אֹהֶלֹה בְּהָ"א כְּתִיב. פָּרִישׁ פְּרִישׂוּ וְקַבִּיל מַלְכוּ שְׁמַיָּא בְּכֻלְּהוּ דַּרְגִּין דְּאָחִידָן בֵּיהּ. וּכְדֵין יָדַע דְּקוּדְשָׁא בְּרִיךְ הוּא שַׁלִּיט עַל כֹּלָּא. וּכְדֵין בָּנָה מִזְבֵּחַ. וּתְרֵין מַדְבְּחָן הָווּ, בְּגִין דְּהָכָא אִתְגְּלִי לֵיהּ דְּהָא קוּדְשָׁא בְּרִיךְ הוּא שַׁלִּיט עַל כֹּלָּא וְיָדַע חָכְמָה עִלָּאָה, מַה דְּלָא הֲוָה יָדַע מִקַּדְמַת דְּנָא. וּבָנָה תְּרֵין מַדְבְּחָן חַד לְדַרְגָּא דְאִתְגַּלְיָא וְחַד לְדַרְגָּא דְאִתְכַּסְּיָא.

[וַיַּעְתֵּק מִשָּׁם הָהָרָה. מִשָּׁם יָדַע הַר ה', וְכָל הַדַּרְגוֹת הַנְּטוּעוֹת בַּמָּקוֹם הַזֶּה. וַיֵּט אָהֳלֹה, כָּתוּב בְּהָ"א. פָּרַשׂ פְּרִישָׂה וְקִבֵּל מַלְכוּת שָׁמַיִם בְּכָל הַדְּרָגוֹת שֶׁאֲחוּזוֹת בּוֹ, וְאָז יָדַע שֶׁהַקָּדוֹשׁ בָּרוּךְ הוּא שׁוֹלֵט עַל הַכֹּל, וְאָז בָּנָה מִזְבֵּחַ. וּשְׁנֵי מִזְבְּחוֹת הָיוּ, מִשּׁוּם שֶׁכָּאן הִתְגַּלָּה לוֹ שֶׁהֲרֵי הַקָּדוֹשׁ בָּרוּךְ הוּא שׁוֹלֵט עַל הַכֹּל, וְיָדַע הַחָכְמָה הָעֶלְיוֹנָה מַה שֶּׁלֹּא הָיָה יוֹדֵעַ מִלְּפָנֵי כֵן. וּבָנָה שְׁנֵי מִזְבְּחוֹת - אֶחָד לַדַּרְגָּה הַגְּלוּיָה, וְאֶחָד לַדַּרְגָּה הַנִּסְתֶּרֶת.]

you. Every eight-day-old male shall be circumcised among you, every male child for all generations, whether he is born in your house or bought with money from any stranger who is not of your descendants." (*Bereishit* 17:9–12)

The basic message of circumcision is that nature is not enough; nature is not perfect. Man can and must "improve" nature. Circumcision is a symbolic declaration that man can rise above nature, that we strive to go beyond nature by controlling our natural sexuality. As a concept, though, circumcision could only be the result of revelation. It is the next step, the step beyond the logical conclusions of which man is capable; we may say that it is the meta-logical conclusion that Terach and his generation were unable to find. After Avraham's lonely, logical search led him to realize that there was something beyond human logic, beyond the forces of nature, God revealed Himself to Avraham. The bond between God and Avraham was forged specifically with the commandment of circumcision—precisely because this commandment, above all others, allows us to go beyond nature, to rise above nature in a way that could never have been possible through human logic alone.

Parashat Vayeira

The Trial

Parashat Vayeira recounts the tenth and last of Avraham's trials: "The Binding of Yitzchak." Avraham is commanded to sacrifice his beloved son, his long-awaited heir. Avraham does not complain, nor does he engage God in dialogue. Unlike on other occasions, he does not attempt to negotiate. It seems that Avraham senses that this is something he must do. We, on the other hand, are faced with an obvious question: What is the purpose of this test?

Countless scholars, Jewish and non-Jewish alike, over generations, have studied this text and attempted to penetrate its lesson. The Danish philosopher Soren Kierkegaard, in *Fear and Trembling*, describes Avraham as a "knight of faith," and concludes that the Binding of Yitzchak was a "leap of faith," a term that has taken a central place in the lexicon of virtually every contemporary religious thinker since. Interestingly, in Jewish sources, Avraham is not described as one who excelled in faith, *per se*, as much as he is described as one who loved God.

זוהר חלק א דף עז/א

תָּא חֲזֵי, אַבְרָהָם בָּעֵי לְקָרְבָא לְקוּדְשָׁא בְּרִיךְ הוּא וְאִתְקָרַב. הֲדָא הוּא דִכְתִיב, (תהלים מה) אָהַבְתָּ צֶדֶק וַתִּשְׂנָא רֶשַׁע. בְּגִין דְּאָהַב צֶדֶק וְשָׂנֵא רֶשַׁע אִתְקָרַב לִצְדָקָה, וְעַל דָּא כְּתִיב, (ישעיה מא) אַבְרָהָם אוֹהֲבִי. מַאי טַעְמָא אוֹהֲבִי, בְּגִין דִּכְתִיב אָהַבְתָּ צֶדֶק. רְחִימוּתָא דְּקוּדְשָׁא בְּרִיךְ הוּא דְּרָחִים אַבְרָהָם מִכָּל בְּנֵי דָרֵיהּ דַּהֲווּ אַבִּירֵי לֵב וְאִנּוּן רְחוֹקִים מִצְּדָקָה כְּמָה דְאִתְּמָר:

Come and see: Avraham wished to come close to God, and he (succeeded) in coming close, as it is written, "You loved righteousness and hated wickedness" [*Tehillim* 45:8], and it is further written, "Avraham who loves me" [*Yeshayahu* 41:8]. What is the meaning of Avraham's love of God? He loved righteousness; this was Avraham's love of God in which he excelled over all his contemporaries. (*Zohar, Bereishit* 76b)

Based on Jewish sources, then, perhaps we should label Avraham's response to God's command a "leap of love," rather than a "leap of faith." It was love of God that allowed Avraham to behave as he did when called upon to perform this superhuman task.

Let us consider the *Akeidah* (binding): What is the essence of this challenge? At first glance, the question seems absurd: Avraham was being asked to sacrifice his son, and the very notion of child sacrifice is abhorrent to modern man.[1] However, on a conceptual level, the idea of an individual who is willing to sacrifice his child for his own ideals may not be completely alien to us. Even enlightened, modern society is often prepared to sacrifice children for its ideals; if this were not so, there would be no war. As difficult as sacrificing one's child is, it seems that it may be justifiable when it is done for the sake of one's beliefs.

Perhaps, then, the challenge of the *Akeidah* lay in the paradoxical nature of God's commandment. After all, God Himself had previously informed Avraham that Yitzchak would be his spiritual heir. If Yitzchak is to be sacrificed, how will he inherit Avraham's position, his possessions, his land? A dead Yitzchak cannot lead, nor can he sire any descendants. The challenge of the *Akeidah*, then, falls within the realm of logical inconsistency—but it is more than a technical problem: Yitzchak's death would indicate that God is fickle, and His word cannot be trusted.

The theological problem is compounded by the personal pain Avraham must have felt. Philo of Alexandria suggested that the sacrifice of Yitzchak would mean the eradication of all laughter from the world,

---

1. We should keep in mind that, in a sense, Avraham himself had been the victim of "child sacrifice." His own father had a hand in casting Avraham into Nimrod's furnace in Ur Kasdim. Moreover, this same tradition describes how Avraham was miraculously saved, and may explain Avraham's confidence that his own son would somehow be saved as well.

for the name *Yitzchak* means "laughter." While Avraham would not abort his mission, his life's work would lose its luster, its very meaning, with Yitzchak's demise. Certainly, for Avraham, the death of his beloved son would mark the death of his relationship with his God.

Midrashic and kabbalistic sources offer a deeper understanding of the dilemma: In these sources, Avraham is described as the individual who excelled in the trait of *chesed* (compassion or kindness).[2] Avraham,

---

2. The association of Avraham with the attribute of *chesed* is based on a verse in Micha 7:20. While it is referenced in Midrashic sources, Avraham's identification with *chesed* is stronger in mystical sources, Chasidic and even some non-Chasidic literature. See *Zohar, Bereishit* 213b; *Sefer ha-Bahir* section 135. Also see Rashi, 2 *Shmuel* 21:2; *Mesillat Yesharim* 19:26:

מיכה פרק ז פסוק כ
תִּתֵּן אֱמֶת לְיַעֲקֹב חֶסֶד לְאַבְרָהָם אֲשֶׁר־נִשְׁבַּעְתָּ לַאֲבֹתֵינוּ מִימֵי קֶדֶם:

מסכתות קטנות מסכת כלה רבתי פרק ט
דרש רבא, כל מי שיש בו שלש מדות הללו, בידוע שהוא מזרעו של אברהם, רחמן ובישן וגומל חסדים; בשלמא גומל חסדים, שנאמר תתן אמת ליעקב חסד לאברהם; בישן נמי כדדרש רבא, דדרש רבא הנה נא ידעתי כי אשה יפת מראה את, ולא עד עכשיו; אלא רחמן, הא אברהם לא רחים על בריה, היינו רבותיה דאברהם, להודיעך חיבתו בהקדוש ברוך הוא.

בראשית רבה (וילנא) פרשת חיי שרה פרשה נח:ט
וְאַחֲרֵי כֵן קָבַר אַבְרָהָם (בראשית כג, יט), הֲדָא הוּא דִכְתִיב (משלי כא, כא): רֹדֵף צְדָקָה וָחֶסֶד יִמְצָא חַיִּים צְדָקָה וְכָבוֹד. רֹדֵף צְדָקָה, זֶה אַבְרָהָם, שֶׁנֶּאֱמַר (בראשית יח, יט): וְשָׁמְרוּ דֶּרֶךְ ה' לַעֲשׂוֹת צְדָקָה. וָחֶסֶד, שֶׁגָּמַל חֶסֶד לְשָׂרָה. יִמְצָא חַיִּים, (בראשית כה, ז): וּשְׁנֵי חַיֵּי אַבְרָהָם מְאַת שָׁנָה וְשִׁבְעִים שָׁנָה וְחָמֵשׁ שָׁנִים. צְדָקָה וְכָבוֹד, אָמַר רַבִּי שְׁמוּאֵל בַּר יִצְחָק, אָמַר לוֹ הַקָּדוֹשׁ בָּרוּךְ הוּא אֲנִי אֻמָּנוּתִי גּוֹמֵל חֲסָדִים, תָּפַשְׂתָּ אֻמָּנוּתִי בּוֹא לְבַשׁ לְבוּשִׁי (בראשית כד, א): וְאַבְרָהָם זָקֵן בָּא בַּיָּמִים.

בראשית רבה (וילנא) פרשת חיי שרה פרשה ס:ב
וַיֹּאמַר ה' אֱלֹהֵי אֲדֹנִי אַבְרָהָם וגו'. (בראשית כד, יב). וַעֲשֵׂה חֶסֶד עִם אֲדֹנִי אַבְרָהָם, הִתְחַלְתָּ גְּמֹר. רַבִּי חַגַּי בְּשֵׁם רַבִּי יִצְחָק אָמַר הַכֹּל צְרִיכִין לְחֶסֶד אֲפִלּוּ אַבְרָהָם שֶׁהַחֶסֶד מִתְגַּלְגֵּל בָּעוֹלָם בִּשְׁבִילוֹ, נִצְרַךְ לְחֶסֶד, שֶׁנֶּאֱמַר: וַעֲשֵׂה חֶסֶד עִם אֲדֹנִי אַבְרָהָם, הִתְחַלְתָּ גְּמֹר.

מדרש תנחומא (בובר) פרשת חיי שרה
עמד אברהם ודיבק במדת חסד, א"ל הקדוש ברוך הוא שלי היתה המדה הזאת, ואתה אחזתה בה, חייך שאני עושה אותך כיוצא בי, מנין שנאמר חזה הוית עד די כרסוון רמיו ועתיק יומין יתב לבושיה כתלג חיור וגו' (דניאל ז ט), מה כתיב למעלה מן הענין, ואחרי כן קבר אברהם את שרה אשתו (בראשית כג יט), עמד ונטפל בה, א"ל הקדוש ברוך הוא ראוי אתה לעטרה, שנאמר ואברהם זקן.

in his understanding of monotheism, knew that God is all-powerful, and thus has no needs. Therefore, there is absolutely nothing that human beings can do for God. What is left for man is to try to emulate God. Thus, Avraham tried to impress upon his pagan neighbors that God has no need for their sacrifices; what we can do is to treat one another with kindness, just as God created the world as an act of incredible kindness and love.[3]

זוהר כרך ג (דברים) פרשת ואתחנן [דף רסב עמוד ב]

תָּנִינָן, וְאָהֲבָתָּ מַאן דְּרָחִים לֵיהּ לְמַלְכָּא, עָבִיד לֵיהּ טִיבוּ חֶסֶד עִם כֹּלָּא. וְחֶסֶד יַתִּירָא, הַהוּא דְּאִקְרֵי חֶסֶד דֶּאֱמֶת, דְּלָא בָּעֵי אֲגַר עֲלֵיהּ, אֶלָּא בְּגִין רְחִימוּתָא דְּמַלְכָּא, דְּרָחִים לֵיהּ יַתִּיר, וּבְרָחִימוּתָא דְּמַלְכָּא תַּלְיָא חֶסֶד. וְעַל דָּא אִקְרֵי (ישעיה מא) אַבְרָהָם אוֹהֲבִי. וּבְגִין דְּרָחִים לֵיהּ יַתִּיר, אַסְגֵּי חֶסֶד בְּעָלְמָא. וְעַל דָּא, הָכָא וְאָהֲבָתָּ. וּבִרְחִימוּתָא תַּלְיָא חֶסֶד, וְדָא הִיא בֵּיתָא תְּלִיתָאָה.

זוהר חלק א דף ריג/ב

תָּא חֲזֵי, מִנַּיִן שֶׁקָּרָא קוּדְשָׁא בְּרִיךְ הוּא לְיַעֲקֹב אֵ"ל, אַתְּ בְּעֶלְיוֹנָא, וַאֲנָא אֱהֵא בְּתַתָּאָה, (נ"א את תהא בתתאה, ואנא אהא אלהא בעלאה). מַאי קָא מַיְירֵי. (בראשית יז) וַיַּעַל אֱלֹהִים מֵעַל אַבְרָהָם, אֲבָהָתָן אִינּוּן רְתִיכָאן דְּקוּדְשָׁא בְּרִיךְ הוּא. תָּנָא, (מיכה ז) תִּתֵּן אֱמֶת לְיַעֲקֹב חֶסֶד לְאַבְרָהָם, הָא תְּרֵין סְפִירָן, בִּתְרֵין רְתִיכָן, רַבְרְבָן עִלָּאִין: תְּלִיתָאָה יִצְחָק, מַאי (בראשית לא) וַיִּשָּׁבַע יַעֲקֹב בְּפַחַד אָבִיו יִצְחָק. וּבְגִין פַּחַד יִצְחָק דְּהַוָה סְפִירָה, וְקוּדְשָׁא בְּרִיךְ הוּא דְּהוּא כָּרְסֵי יְקָרָא רְתִיכָא עִלָּאָה, וּסְפִירָה דְיִצְחָק הִיא מֵעֶלְיָיא, מְפָרְשָׁא יַתִּיר מִכָּל סְפִירָן דַּאֲבָהָתָא, הָדָא הוּא דִכְתִיב וַיִּשָּׁבַע יַעֲקֹב בְּפַחַד אָבִיו יִצְחָק:

ספר הבהיר - המיוחס לרבי נחוניא בן הקנה ז"ל

קלה. אמר ר' יוחנן מאי דכתיב (שמות י"ז יא) והיה כאשר ירים משה ידו וגבר ישראל (שמות י"ג יא) וכאשר יניח ידו וגבר עמלק, מלמד שהעולם מתקיים בשביל נשיאת כפים, מאי טעמא, משום דאותו כח שניתנו ליעקב אבינו שמו ישראל, לאברהם ליצחק וליעקב ניתנו כוחות, אחד לכל אחד ואחד, ובמדה שהלך כל אחד ואחד דוגמתה ניתן לו, אברהם גמל חסד לעולם שהיה מזמין לכל באי עולם ועוברי דרכים מזון וגומל חסד ויוצא לקראתם דכתיב (בראשית י"ח ב) וירץ לקראתם, ועוד וישתחו ארצה (שם) זאת היתה גמילות חסד שלימה, והקב"ה מדד לו במדתו ונתן לו מדת החסד דכתיב (מיכה ז' כ) תתן אמת ליעקב חסד לאברהם, אשר נשבעת לאבותינו מימי קדם, מאי מימי קדם, מלמד שאם לא היה אברהם גומל חסד וזוכה למדת חסד לא היה יעקב זוכה למדת אמת, שבזכות שזכה אברהם למדת חסד זכה יצחק למדת פחד דכתיב (בראשית ל"א נג) וישבע יעקב בפחד אביו יצחק, אטו יש איש שישבע כך באמונת פחד אביו, אלא עד כאן לא ניתן ליעקב כח, ונשבע בכח שניתן לאביו שנאמר וישבע יעקב בפחד אבי יצחק, ומאי ניהו, מאי ניהו, תהו שממנו יוצא הרע המתהא את בני אדם, הוא דכתיב (מ"א י"ח לח) ותפול אש ותאכל את העולה ואת העצים ואת האבנים ואת העפר ואת המים אשר בתעלה לחכה, וכתיב (דברים ד כד) כי ה' אלהיך אש אוכלה הוא אל קנא:

---

3. See *Tehillim* 89, which begins with a reference to *Eitan ha-Ezrachi*, which the Talmud (*Bava Batra* 15a) understands as another name for Avraham:

Chesed was Avraham's credo. Now, God was calling upon Avraham to go against the most basic principle of his life's work. Viktor Frankl, in his classic work *Man's Search for Meaning*, describes the need for meaning as one of the most profound needs in the hierarchy of human existence. What God was asking of Avraham was not merely to sacrifice his son Yitzchak, but to sacrifice his own life's meaning and mission. We can easily appreciate that had the test been to entertain fifty, one hundred, even two hundred guests for dinner, Avraham would have risen to the challenge heroically, with a smile on his face and gladness in his heart. That would not have been a challenge; that sort of "test" would have fit neatly into Avraham's worldview of *chesed*. Instead, God asked Avraham to perform an act which was the very antithesis of *chesed*. Perhaps this was the most difficult aspect of the *Akeidah*: With one stroke of the knife, Avraham would concede to his pagan neighbors that their human sacrifices had been correct after all, and that he himself had been wrong about God's true nature.[4]

And yet, with this understanding comes an even greater insight into the challenge of the *Akeidah*: The pagan world in which Avraham

---

תהלים פרק פט, א-ג
מַשְׂכִּיל לְאֵיתָן הָאֶזְרָחִי: חַסְדֵי ה' עוֹלָם אָשִׁירָה לְדֹר וָדֹר| אוֹדִיעַ אֱמוּנָתְךָ בְּפִי: כִּי־אָמַרְתִּי עוֹלָם חֶסֶד יִבָּנֶה שָׁמַיִם| תָּכִן אֱמוּנָתְךָ בָהֶם:

A maskil of Eitan ha-Ezrachi: I will sing of God's *chesed* forever; with my mouth I will make known Your faithfulness to all generations. For I have said, The world is built by love [*chesed*]; your faithfulness shall you establish in the very heavens."

תלמוד בבלי מסכת בבא בתרא דף טו עמוד א
אָמַר רַב, אֵיתָן הָאֶזְרָחִי זֶה הוּא אַבְרָהָם. כְּתִיב הָכָא, (תהלים פט) "אֵיתָן הָאֶזְרָחִי", וּכְתִיב הָתָם, (ישעיה מא) "מִי הֵעִיר מִמִּזְרָח צֶדֶק יִקְרָאֵהוּ לְרַגְלוֹ".

Rav said, "Eitan ha-Ezrachi is Avraham. Here [in *Tehillim*, he is called] Eitan ha-Ezrachi, and elsewhere, [*Yeshayahu* 41] he is referred to as 'He who raised up righteousness from the East.'"

4. We may well imagine that when commanded to perform circumcision, Avraham was convinced that this would be the most extreme pain he would ever cause his child, the most extreme situation in which he would take a knife to his offspring. Little did he realize that circumcision paled in comparison to what was yet to come at the *Akeidah*.

was raised was one in which gods were created in the image of man. Judaism teaches that man is created in the image of God, and Avraham had spent years attempting to refine that divine image within himself through acts of *chesed*, in emulation of God. Perhaps, after all the years he had spent spreading the idea of a compassionate, all-powerful God, the very basis of Avraham's faith was being put to the test: Was he, or was he not, different from the pagans who surrounded him? They might easily have claimed that Avraham, too, had created a god in his own image—a "kinder, gentler" god than theirs, but a god of Avraham's creation nonetheless. If called upon by God to perform an act which was the antithesis of *chesed*, would Avraham obey? Would Avraham be capable of subservience even when the commandment disrupted his own understanding of the nature of God's relationship with mankind?

When God calls upon Avraham and demands the sacrifice of Yitzchak, Avraham immediately sets out to obey. Only when we understand that the greatness of Avraham was his *chesed* are we able to fully appreciate the significance of this test: The first step toward religious development is to utilize one's capabilities, one's natural gifts, in the service of God—but God wanted Avraham to go even further. The *Akeidah* taught Avraham, and all of us, that man can go beyond his innate tendencies and skills. Therefore, He called upon Avraham to perform an act which is the complete opposite of his natural instinct. Avraham excelled in *chesed*; this was his natural tendency, the most basic feature of his religious personality—but could he perform an act of *din* (justice or judgment)?

This understanding is borne out by a close reading of the verses, with particular attention to the particular name of God used in this passage.

בראשית פרק כב, א-ב
וַיְהִי אַחַר הַדְּבָרִים הָאֵלֶּה וְהָאֱלֹהִים נִסָּה אֶת־אַבְרָהָם וַיֹּאמֶר אֵלָיו אַבְרָהָם וַיֹּאמֶר הִנֵּנִי: (ב) וַיֹּאמֶר קַח־נָא אֶת־בִּנְךָ אֶת־יְחִידְךָ אֲשֶׁר־אָהַבְתָּ אֶת־יִצְחָק וְלֶךְ־לְךָ אֶל־אֶרֶץ הַמֹּרִיָּה וְהַעֲלֵהוּ שָׁם לְעֹלָה עַל אַחַד הֶהָרִים אֲשֶׁר אֹמַר אֵלֶיךָ:

> It came to pass after these things, that God [Elokim] tested Avraham. He said to him, "Avraham." And he said, "Here I am." He [Elokim] said, "Take your son, your only son, your beloved Yitzchak, and go to the land of Moriah. Lift him up there as an offering upon one of the mountains which I will tell you." (*Bereishit* 22:1–2)

The Name of God that appears in this passage is *Elokim*, which denotes the aspect of God of Judgment. The concluding verse of the account of *Akeiah* is even more pointed:

בראשית פרק כב, יא-יב

וַיִּקְרָא אֵלָיו מַלְאַךְ ה' מִן־הַשָּׁמַיִם וַיֹּאמֶר אַבְרָהָם| אַבְרָהָם וַיֹּאמֶר הִנֵּנִי:
וַיֹּאמֶר אַל־תִּשְׁלַח יָדְךָ אֶל־הַנַּעַר וְאַל־תַּעַשׂ לוֹ מְאוּמָה כִּי| עַתָּה יָדַעְתִּי כִּי־
יְרֵא אֱלֹהִים אַתָּה וְלֹא חָשַׂכְתָּ אֶת־בִּנְךָ אֶת־יְחִידְךָ מִמֶּנִּי:

> An angel of God [*mal'ach Hashem*] called to him from Heaven, and said, "Avraham, Avraham." [Avraham] said, "Here I am." [The angel] said, "Do not lay your hand upon the lad, and do not do anything to him; for now I know that you fear *Elokim*, seeing that you did not withhold your son, your only son, from Me." (*Bereishit* 22:11–12)

The angel is an angel of Hashem, and the verse uses the four-letter name of God, which represents *chesed*. The angel, speaking in terms of *chesed*, states that Avraham has proven to be one who also reveres *Elokim*, which represents *din* (justice or judgment). Avraham has proven his ability to relate to God in both His attribute of *chesed* (love) and *din* (judgment). Avraham's tenth test, then, was to relate to God in a manner contrary to his personal instincts.

Greatness is found not only in using ones' skills in the service of God, but in developing new skills for the service of God. When Avraham achieved this, when he was prepared to sacrifice his son, the sacrifice itself became unnecessary.

We may say that this test was an act of kindness on God's part: He was fully aware of Avraham's capabilities and devotion, and had no need to test Avraham's love. The *Akeidah* allowed Avraham to relate to God in a new way, to achieve a level of worship he had not previously imagined. In an act of kindness and love, God allowed Avraham to develop another aspect of the divine image within himself—an aspect that Avraham did not come to easily, but which he achieved through sheer faith. If we judge this last test according to the well-known rabbinic principle, "According to the difficulty is the reward,"[5] Avraham most probably received a greater reward for the *Akeidah* than for any of his other accomplishments or acts of kindness or heroism.[6]

---

5. Mishnah, *Avot* 5:23:

משנה מסכת אבות פרק ה
בֶּן הֵא הֵא אוֹמֵר, לְפוּם צַעֲרָא אַגְרָא:

Ben Heh-Heh said: According to the difficulty is the reward.

6. According to *Vayikra Rabbah* 29:9, the *Akeidah* was assigned as the Torah reading for Rosh Hashanah because it serves as a defense of the Jewish People:

מדרש רבה ויקרא - פרשה כט פסקה ט
דָּבָר אַחֵר, בַּחֹדֶשׁ הַשְּׁבִיעִי, רַבִּי בֶּרֶכְיָה הָיָה קָרֵי לֵיהּ יַרְחָא דִּשְׁבוּעָתָא, שֶׁבּוֹ נִשְׁבַּע הַקָּדוֹשׁ בָּרוּךְ הוּא לְאַבְרָהָם אָבִינוּ עָלָיו הַשָּׁלוֹם, הֲדָא הוּא דִכְתִיב (בראשית כב, טז): וַיֹּאמֶר בִּי נִשְׁבַּעְתִּי נְאֻם ה', מַה צֹּרֶךְ הָיָה לִשְׁבוּעָה, רַבִּי בִּיבֵי בַּר אַבָּא בְּשֵׁם רַבִּי יוֹחָנָן אָמַר אַבְרָהָם עָמַד בִּתְפִלָּה וְתַחֲנוּנִים לִפְנֵי הַקָּדוֹשׁ בָּרוּךְ הוּא וְאָמַר לְפָנָיו רִבּוֹנוֹ שֶׁל עוֹלָם גָּלוּי וְיָדוּעַ לְפָנֶיךָ בְּשָׁעָה שֶׁאָמַרְתָּ לִי (בראשית כב, ב): קַח נָא אֶת בִּנְךָ אֶת יְחִידְךָ, הָיָה בְּלִבִּי מַה לַהֲשִׁיבָךְ, וְהָיָה בְּלִבִּי מַה לֵּאמַר, אֶתְמוֹל אָמַרְתָּ לִי (בראשית כא, יב): כִּי בְיִצְחָק יִקָּרֵא לְךָ זָרַע, וְעַכְשָׁיו אַתָּה אוֹמֵר לִי (בראשית כב, ב): וְהַעֲלֵהוּ שָׁם לְעֹלָה, אֶלָּא כְּשֵׁם שֶׁהָיָה לִי מַה לַהֲשִׁיבָךְ וְכָבַשְׁתִּי אֶת יִצְרִי וְלֹא הֱשִׁיבוֹתִיךְ (תהלים לח, עד): כְּחֵרֵשׁ לֹא אֶשְׁמָע וּכְאִלֵּם לֹא יִפְתַּח פִּיו, כָּךְ כְּשֶׁיִּהְיוּ בָּנָיו שֶׁל יִצְחָק בָּאִים לִידֵי עֲבֵרוֹת וּמַעֲשִׂים רָעִים תְּהֵא מַזְכִּיר לָהֶם עֲקֵדַת יִצְחָק אֲבִיהֶם וְעָמַד מִכִּסֵּא הַדִּין לְכִסֵּא רַחֲמִים וּמִתְמַלֵּא עֲלֵיהֶם רַחֲמִים, וּתְרַחֵם עֲלֵיהֶם וְתַהֲפֹךְ לָהֶם מִדַּת הַדִּין לְמִדַּת רַחֲמִים, אֵימָתַי בַּחֹדֶשׁ הַשְּׁבִיעִי.

Another exposition of the phrase "In the seventh month [*shevi'i*]" [*Vayikra* 23:20]: R. Berachiah used to call it the month of the oath [*shevu'ata*], for on that month the Holy One, blessed be He, made an oath to our forefather Avraham, peace be upon him, as it says, "By My self have I sworn, said the Almighty" [*Bereishit* 22:16]. What need was there for the oath? R. Bibi b. Abba in the name of R. Yochanan explained: Our forefather Avraham stood before the Holy One, blessed be He, in prayer and supplication, and said to Him: "Sovereign of the Universe! It was manifest and known to You, when You said to me, 'Take your son, your only son,' that there was in my mind an answer I could have given You and that there was in

Vayeira: The Trial

Lest we forget, there was another player in the *Akeidah*, and that was Yitzchak. According to tradition, Yitzchak was thirty-seven years old at the time;[7] what was Yitzchak's role in the *Akeidah*?

בראשית פרק כב,ג,ו

וַיַּשְׁכֵּם אַבְרָהָם בַּבֹּקֶר וַיַּחֲבֹשׁ אֶת־חֲמֹרוֹ וַיִּקַּח אֶת־שְׁנֵי נְעָרָיו אִתּוֹ וְאֵת יִצְחָק בְּנוֹ וַיְבַקַּע עֲצֵי עֹלָה וַיָּקָם וַיֵּלֶךְ אֶל־הַמָּקוֹם אֲשֶׁר־אָמַר־לוֹ הָאֱלֹהִים: ... וַיִּקַּח אַבְרָהָם אֶת־עֲצֵי הָעֹלָה וַיָּשֶׂם עַל־יִצְחָק בְּנוֹ וַיִּקַּח בְּיָדוֹ אֶת־הָאֵשׁ וְאֶת־הַמַּאֲכֶלֶת וַיֵּלְכוּ שְׁנֵיהֶם יַחְדָּו:

Avraham rose early in the morning; he saddled his donkey, and took two of his young men with him, as well as his son Yitzchak.... Avraham took the wood for the kindling and placed it on [the

---

my mind something I could have said: Only yesterday You promised me that "It is through Yitzchak that you shall gain posterity' [*Bereishit* 21:12], and now You tell me, 'Offer him there for a burnt-offering!' (ibid. 22:2). However, just as I had an answer to give You but controlled my inclination and did not reply, "As a deaf man, I hear not and... as a dumb man that did not open his mouth" [*Tehillim* 38:14], so when the children of Yitzchak succumb to transgressions and evil deeds, You must recollect for them the binding of their forefather Yitzchak and rise from the Throne of Judgment and take Your seat upon the Throne of Mercy, and being filled with compassion for them, have mercy upon them and change the Attribute of Justice into the Attribute of Mercy for their sake! When? 'In the seventh month.'"

7. There are two variants of *Bereishit Rabbah* 56:8; one suggests that Yitzchak was thirty-seven years old at the time of the *Akeidah*, and the other suggests that he was twenty-six years old.

בראשית רבה (וילנא) פרשת וירא פרשה נו:ח

דָּבָר אַחֵר, אָמַר רַבִּי יִצְחָק בְּשָׁעָה שֶׁבִּקֵּשׁ אַבְרָהָם לַעֲקֹד יִצְחָק בְּנוֹ, אָמַר לוֹ אַבָּא בָּחוּר אֲנִי וְחוֹשְׁשַׁנִי שֶׁמָּא יִזְדַּעֲזַע גּוּפִי מִפַּחְדָּהּ שֶׁל סַכִּין וַאֲצַעֲרֶךָ, וְשֶׁמָּא תִּפָּסֵל הַשְּׁחִיטָה וְלֹא תַעֲלֶה לְךָ לְקָרְבָּן, אֶלָּא כָּפְתֵנִי יָפֶה יָפֶה, מִיָּד וַיַּעֲקֹד אֶת יִצְחָק, כְּלוּם יָכוֹל אָדָם לִכְפּוֹת בֶּן שְׁלשִׁים וְשֶׁבַע [נסח אחר: בן עשרים ושש שנה] אֶלָּא לְדַעְתּוֹ.

Another comment: R. Yitzchak said: When Avraham wished to sacrifice his son Yitzchak, [the latter] said to [the former]: 'Father, I am a young man and am afraid that my body may tremble for fear of the knife, and I will distract you, whereby the slaughter may be rendered unfit and this will not count as a real sacrifice; therefore bind me very firmly.' Forthwith, "[Avraham] bound Yitzchak." Can one bind a thirty-seven-year old (another version: twenty-six-year old) man without his consent?

shoulders of] his son Yitzchak, and he took in his hand the fire and the knife, and they both went together. (*Bereishit* 22:3-6)

Avraham and Yitzchak, we are told, traveled together. The text seems to stress that their "togetherness" denotes more than mere traveling companions. They were "in on it together,"[8] partners in this mission.

בראשית רבה (וילנא) פרשת וירא פרשה נו:ג
וַיֵּלְכוּ שְׁנֵיהֶם יַחְדָּו, זֶה לַעֲקֹד וְזֶה לֵעָקֵד, זֶה לִשְׁחֹט וְזֶה לִשָּׁחֵט.

"And they both went together" — one to bind and the other to be bound, one to slaughter and the other to be slaughtered. (*Bereishit Rabbah* 56:3)

What follows is a unique dialogue. It is the only recorded conversation between Avraham and Yitzchak in the entire Torah:

בראשית פרק כב:ז-ח
וַיֹּאמֶר יִצְחָק אֶל אַבְרָהָם אָבִיו וַיֹּאמֶר אָבִי וַיֹּאמֶר הִנֶּנִּי בְנִי וַיֹּאמֶר הִנֵּה הָאֵשׁ וְהָעֵצִים וְאַיֵּה הַשֶּׂה לְעֹלָה: וַיֹּאמֶר אַבְרָהָם אֱלֹהִים יִרְאֶה לּוֹ הַשֶּׂה לְעֹלָה בְּנִי וַיֵּלְכוּ שְׁנֵיהֶם יַחְדָּו:

Yitzchak spoke to his father Avraham and said, "My father." [Avraham] said, "Here I am, my son." [Yitzchak] said, "Here is the kindling and the wood; but where is the lamb for the offering?" Avraham said, "God will see to a lamb for an offering, my son." And both of them walked on together. (*Bereishit* 22:7–8)

---

8. See Rabbenu Bachya, *Bereishit* 18:33:

רבנו בחיי, בראשית יח:לג
ועל דרך הקבלה ... ואין למדת הדין פעולה עד שתמסרם מדת החסד בדין, ואז מדת הדין פועלת בנידונים. וזהו סוד הכתוב (בראשית כב, ו) ויקח בידו את האש ואת המאכלת, כלומר שמדת החסד לוקחת כוחותיו של יצחק ומוסרת בדין, וזהו וילכו שניהם יחדיו, ויצחק הולך אחר אברהם ברשותו ובהסכמתו. והנה מדת הדין עקורה לפני מדת החסד שאלמלא כן תחרב העולם, וזהו סוד ויעקוד את יצחק בנו (שם, ט). וזהו ביאור לשון ורב חסד שהחסד מתרבה על הדין, וזה מבואר:

Yitzchak was an adult when he set out on this journey with Avraham. He was well aware of the pagan practices of the surrounding society, yet he walked together with his father, completely dedicated to his father's purpose. Yitzchak embodies *din*; he follows the law, as set down by his father. Yitzchak's relationship with God is through his father's teachings, and father and son walk together, two people sharing one mission.

On the third day of their journey, Avraham lifts up his eyes and sees the mountain from afar. He tells the two young men who are accompanying them to wait with the donkey while he and Yitzchak go to make the sacrifice.

בראשית פרק כב:ד-ה
בַּיּוֹם הַשְּׁלִישִׁי וַיִּשָּׂא אַבְרָהָם אֶת־עֵינָיו וַיַּרְא אֶת־הַמָּקוֹם מֵרָחֹק: וַיֹּאמֶר אַבְרָהָם אֶל־נְעָרָיו שְׁבוּ־לָכֶם פֹּה עִם־הַחֲמוֹר וַאֲנִי וְהַנַּעַר נֵלְכָה עַד־כֹּה וְנִשְׁתַּחֲוֶה וְנָשׁוּבָה אֲלֵיכֶם:

On the third day Avraham looked up, and saw the place from afar. Avraham said to his young men, 'Stay here with the donkey; and I and the boy will go to the place and worship, and return to you. (*Bereishit* 22:4–5)

God initially told Avraham, "Take your son… and bring him up him as an offering upon one of the mountains which I will tell you." He did not tell Avraham which specific mountain to seek out; that information would follow. Later, though, "Avraham looked up and saw the place from afar" (*Bereishit* 22:4). The Midrash expounds on this:

בראשית רבה (וילנא) פרשת וירא פרשה נו:א,ב
.... וַיַּרְא אֶת הַמָּקוֹם מֵרָחֹק, מָה רָאָה רָאָה עָנָן קָשׁוּר בָּהָר, אָמַר דּוֹמֶה שָׁאוֹתוֹ מָקוֹם שֶׁאָמַר לִי הַקָּדוֹשׁ בָּרוּךְ הוּא לְהַקְרִיב אֶת בְּנִי שָׁם. אָמַר לְיִצְחָק, בְּנִי, רוֹאֶה אַתָּה מַה שֶּׁאֲנִי רוֹאֶה, אָמַר לוֹ הֵן. אָמַר לִשְׁנֵי נְעָרָיו, רוֹאִים אַתֶּם מַה שֶּׁאֲנִי רוֹאֶה, אָמְרוּ לוֹ לָאו. אָמַר הוֹאִיל וַחֲמוֹר אֵינוֹ רוֹאֶה וְאַתֶּם אֵין אַתֶּם רוֹאִים (בראשית כב, ה): שְׁבוּ לָכֶם פֹּה עִם הַחֲמוֹר.

"…And he saw the place from afar" — What did [Avraham] see? He saw a cloud enveloping the mountain, and said, "It appears that that is the place where the Holy One, blessed be He, told me to sacrifice my son." He then said to [Yitzchak], "Yitzchak, my son, do you see what I see?" "Yes," he replied. Then he said to his two servants, "Do you see what I see?" "No," they answered. [Avraham told them,] "Since you do not see it, stay here with the donkey." (*Bereishit Rabbah* 56:1–2)

Only Avraham and Yitzchak see the cloud, the physical manifestation of spirituality, hovering above the mountain; Avraham's two servants (his "young men") see nothing. For this reason, Avraham instructs them to stay behind with the donkey—specifically with the "*chamor*," which is related to the word *chomer*, the Hebrew word for physical matter—as if to say, "If you cannot see the spiritual cloud hovering over the mountain, if your perception is exclusively of the physical, your place is here, in the physical realm."[9]

When Avraham and Yitzchak reach the designated spot, Yitzchak is tied to the altar. It is important that we note that at no point was Avraham commanded to tie Yitzchak, to bind or constrain him in any way. And yet, throughout the ages, this entire episode has been referred to as *Akeidat Yitzchak*, the binding of Yitzchak. Why, in fact, did Avraham bind Yitzchak if God had never asked him to do so?

Again, the Sages fill in the missing information: According to Midrashic and kabbalistic sources, Yitzchak represents *din*.[10] He is a

---

9. The *Zohar* and Maharal treat this topic. We will return to this concept in our discussion of *Chayei Sarah*, below.

10. While the association of Yitzchak with the attribute of *din* is considered a "given" in many later sources, an explicit statement of this association is not easily found in Talmudic or Midrashic sources. In my opinion, though, this association is implied in *Vayikra Rabbah* 29:9; see note 42, above. Also see *Zohar, Bereishit* 72a, *Zohar, Bereishit* 213b, (cited in note 37, above, which refers to "Pachad Yitzchak") and *Tikkunei Zohar* 139a:

זוהר כרך א (בראשית) פרשת נח עב
יִצְחָק אַתְקִין צְלוֹתָא דְמִנְחָה וְאוֹדַע בְּעָלְמָא דְּאִית דִּין וְאִית דַּיָּין דְּיָכוֹל לְשֵׁזָבָא וּלְמֵידַן עָלְמָא.

willing, enthusiastic participant in the *Akeidah*. He lies down on the altar, stretches out his neck, and says to his father:

מדרש תנחומא פרשת וירא סימן מו ד"ה מו ולך לך
... אָמַר לוֹ: אַבָּא, אָסְרֵנִי יָדַי וְרַגְלַי, מִפְּנֵי שֶׁהַנֶּפֶשׁ חֲצוּפָה הִיא וּכְשֶׁאֶרְאֶה אֶת הַמַּאֲכֶלֶת שֶׁמָּא אֶזְדַּעְזֵעַ וְיִפָּסֵל הַקָּרְבָּן, בְּבַקָּשָׁה מִמְּךָ אַל תַּעַשׂ בִּי מוּם.

[Yitzchak] said, 'Father, tie my hands and feet, for the soul is weak (impudent?) and when I see the blade I fear I will shudder and I will become disqualified as an offering. Please, father, in order that I not become unworthy.' (*Tanchuma Bereishit* 46)[11]

According to the Midrash, the actual binding was Yitzchak's idea. Perhaps this is why, throughout history, this episode has been called *Akeidat Yitzchak*, and not "Avraham's tenth test."

As the knife is about to make its mark on Yitzchak, a voice calls out from Heaven, instructing Avraham to desist. Yitzchak is to be spared; there will be no human sacrifice that day, or any other day. A ram is sacrificed in Yitzchak's stead.

God's emissary bestows a blessing on Avraham, and the account of the *Akeidah* comes to a close:

בראשית פרק כב:יט-כ
וַיָּשָׁב אַבְרָהָם אֶל־נְעָרָיו וַיָּקֻמוּ וַיֵּלְכוּ יַחְדָּו אֶל־בְּאֵר שָׁבַע וַיֵּשֶׁב אַבְרָהָם בִּבְאֵר שָׁבַע:

תיקוני זוהר נספח (מעמ' קלט) דף קלט עמוד א (זהו תקון כ"ב וכ"ג):
בְּרֵאשִׁית בָּרָא אלהי"ם, בְּרֵאשִׁית בָּ"ר, תַּ"שׁ, דָּא אֵילוֹ דְיִצְחָק. בְּרֵאשִׁית תַּמָּן אֵ"שׁ לְעוֹלָה דְיִצְחָק, וְרָזָא דְמִלָּה, (וְעַל אִלֵּין תְּלַת גִּלְגּוּלִין אִתְמַר (שיר ז ב) מה יפו פעמיך בנעלים בת נדיב, (רות ד ד) וְזֹאת לְפָנִים דָּא אִימָא עִלָּאָה עָלְמָא דְאָתֵי, ד"א לגביה צריך חליצה, והדא הוא דכתיב (שמות ג ה) של נעליך וגומר, ואם לאו לית לון רשו לרווחא רמתאה (נ"א לרוחא דמיתא) לסלקא לעלמא דאתי, ובגין דאיהי יום הכפורים אסיר בנעילת הסנדל, (בראשית כב ז) הִנֵּה הָאֵשׁ וְהָעֵצִים וְאַיֵּה הַשֶּׂה לְעוֹלָה, נָפַק קָלָא וְאָמַר מֵשִׁית יוֹמֵי בְרֵאשִׁית אִתְבְּרֵי לַעֲקֵדָה דְיִצְחָק: בְּגִין דְּלָא אִית קָרְבָּן דְּבָטִיל מוֹתָנָא כַּעֲקֵדָה דְיִצְחָק, דְּאִתְּמַר בֵּיהּ (שם) וַיַּעֲקֹד אֶת יִצְחָק בְּנוֹ, אִתְקַשַּׁר מִדַּת הַדִּין (מלאך המות) וְאִתְעַקַּד לְעֵילָא, וְלָא הֲוָה לֵיהּ רְשׁוּ לְקָרְבָא לְגַבֵּי דִינָא רַבְרְבָא דְאִיהוּ גְבוּרָה, לְתַבְעָא דִינָא, וַעֲקֵדָה דָּא מוֹעִילָה לְגָלוּתָא, דַּהֲוָה עָתִיד לְאִתְקַטְלָא מָשִׁיחַ בֶּן יוֹסֵף, וְקָלָא נָפִיק מֵהַהוּא זִמְנָא (שם) אַל תַּעַשׂ לוֹ מְאוּמָה (שם יב), בְּגִין דְּאִתְגַּבְּרוּ רַחֲמֵי עַל דִּינָא, וְרָזָא דְמִלָּה (תהלים צח א) הוֹשִׁיעָה לּוֹ יְמִינוֹ, וּלְבָתַר זְרוֹעַ קָדְשׁוֹ, דְּגַבַּר יְמִינָא עַל שְׂמָאלָא:

---

11. See a close parallel in *Vayikra Rabbah* 29:9, cited in note 42, above.

Avraham returned to his young men, and they rose and went together to Be'er Sheva. (*Bereishit* 22:19)

The Torah records Avraham's movements—but what about Yitzchak? Why does the Torah not tell us about his descent from the mountain? Did Yitzchak, in fact, come down?[12] What was his frame of mind? Did he leave the scene willingly, anxiously, joyously? In fact, the next time Yitzchak is mentioned in the text, three years have elapsed. He is standing in a field, eyes gazing heavenward, praying to God.

בראשית פרק כד:סג
וַיֵּצֵא יִצְחָק לָשׂוּחַ בַּשָּׂדֶה לִפְנוֹת עָרֶב וַיִּשָּׂא עֵינָיו וַיַּרְא וְהִנֵּה גְמַלִּים בָּאִים:

Yitzchak went out to pray in the field toward evening. He lifted up his eyes and saw, and behold—the camels were coming. (*Bereishit* 24:63)

Later in his life, Yitzchak became blind (*Bereishit* 27:1). The Sages explain that his blindness was caused by the tears shed by the angels during those moments on the mountain when it appeared that his father's knife would kill him.[13] Evidently, Yitzchak's sight, his perception, was forever altered by the events of the *Akeidah*. The experience on the mountain changed him, permanently.

---

12. See the remarkable comments of Ibn Ezra on this verse, particularly regarding the premise he rejects —that Yitzchak may have actually died at the *Akeidah*:

אבן עזרא בראשית פרק כב:יט
וישב אברהם ולא הזכיר יצחק, כי הוא ברשותו. והאומר ששחטו ועזבו, ואח"כ חיה אמר הפך הכתוב:

13. Rashi, *Bereishit* 27:1, based on *Bereishit Rabbah* 65:10; however, in *Bereishit Rabbah* 56:8, the tears are said to be from the eyes of Avraham. Another suggestion is that because the Sages consider blindness a sort of "living death," in a sense Yitzchak may be said to have died as a result of the *Akeidah*. See *Pirkei de-Rabbi Eliezer*, chapter 32:

רש"י, בראשית כז:א
דָּבָר אַחֵר כְּשֶׁנֶּעֱקַד עַל גַּבֵּי הַמִּזְבֵּחַ וְהָיָה אָבִיו רוֹצֶה לְשָׁחֳטוֹ, בְּאוֹתָהּ שָׁעָה נִפְתְּחוּ הַשָּׁמַיִם, וְרָאוּ מַלְאֲכֵי הַשָּׁרֵת וְהָיוּ בּוֹכִים, וְיָרְדוּ דִמְעוֹתֵיהֶם וְנָפְלוּ עַל עֵינָיו, לְפִיכָךְ כָּהוּ עֵינָיו:

Another explanation: When Yitzchak was bound on the altar, and his father was about to slaughter him, the heavens opened, and the ministering angels saw and wept, and their tears fell upon Yitzchak's eyes. As a result, "his eyes became dim."

בראשית רבה (וילנא) פרשת תולדות פרשה סה:י
וַיְהִי כִּי זָקֵן יִצְחָק וַתִּכְהֶיןָ עֵינָיו. דָּבָר אַחֵר, מֵרָאֹת, מִכֹּחַ אוֹתָהּ רְאִיָּה, שֶׁבְּשָׁעָה שֶׁעָקַד אַבְרָהָם אָבִינוּ אֶת בְּנוֹ עַל גַּבֵּי הַמִּזְבֵּחַ בָּכוּ מַלְאֲכֵי הַשָּׁרֵת, הֲדָא הוּא דִכְתִיב (ישעיה לג, ז): הֵן אֶרְאֶלָּם צָעֲקוּ חֻצָה וגו', וְנָשְׁרוּ דְּמָעוֹת מֵעֵינֵיהֶם לְתוֹךְ עֵינָיו, וְהָיוּ רְשׁוּמוֹת בְּתוֹךְ עֵינָיו, וְכֵיוָן שֶׁהִזְקִין כָּהוּ עֵינָיו, הֲדָא הוּא דִכְתִיב: וַיְהִי כִּי זָקֵן יִצְחָק, וגו' דָּבָר אַחֵר, מֵרָאֹת, מִכֹּחַ אוֹתָהּ הָרְאִיָּה, שֶׁבְּשָׁעָה שֶׁעָקַד אַבְרָהָם אָבִינוּ אֶת יִצְחָק בְּנוֹ עַל גַּבֵּי הַמִּזְבֵּחַ, תָּלָה עֵינָיו בַּמָּרוֹם וְהִבִּיט בַּשְּׁכִינָה. מוֹשְׁלִים אוֹתוֹ מָשָׁל לְמָה הַדָּבָר דּוֹמֶה, לְמֶלֶךְ שֶׁהָיָה מְטַיֵּל בְּפֶתַח פָּלָטִין שֶׁלּוֹ וְתָלָה עֵינָיו וְרָאָה בְּנוֹ שֶׁל אוֹהֲבוֹ מֵצִיץ עָלָיו בְּעַד הַחַלּוֹן, אָמַר אִם הוֹרְגוֹ אֲנִי עַכְשָׁו מַכְרִיעַ אֲנִי אֶת אוֹהֲבִי, אֶלָּא גּוֹזְרַנִי שֶׁיִּסְתְּמוּ חַלּוֹנוֹתָיו. כָּךְ בְּשָׁעָה שֶׁהֶעֱקִיד אַבְרָהָם אָבִינוּ אֶת בְּנוֹ עַל גַּבֵּי הַמִּזְבֵּחַ תָּלָה עֵינָיו וְהִבִּיט בַּשְּׁכִינָה, אָמַר הַקָּדוֹשׁ בָּרוּךְ הוּא אִם הוֹרְגוֹ אֲנִי עַכְשָׁו אֲנִי מַכְרִיעַ אֶת אַבְרָהָם אוֹהֲבִי, אֶלָּא גּוֹזֵר אֲנִי שֶׁיִּכְהוּ עֵינָיו, וְכֵיוָן שֶׁהִזְקִין כָּהוּ עֵינָיו, וַיְהִי כִּי זָקֵן יִצְחָק וגו'.

"[Yitzchak's] eyes became dim of sight" (*Bereishit* 27:1) — as a result of that sight, for when our father Avraham bound his son Yitzchak, the ministering angels wept, as it says, "Behold, their valiant ones cry without, the angels of peace weep bitterly" (*Yeshayahu* 33:7): Tears dropped from their eyes into his, and left their mark upon them, and so when he became old his eyes dimmed, as it is written, "And it came to pass, that when Yitzchak was old, [his eyes became dim of sight" (*Bereishit* 27:1). Another interpretation [of the words "dim of sight"] is: through that sight. For when our father Avraham bound Yitzchak on the altar, [Yitzchak] lifted up his eyes heavenward and gazed at the Shechinah. This may be illustrated by the case of a king who was taking a stroll by his palace gates, when looking up he saw his friend's son peering at him through a window. He said, "If I execute him now [for his disrespect] I will make my friend suffer; therefore I will rather order that his windows be sealed up." Thus, when our father Avraham bound his son on the altar, [Yitzchak] looked up and gazed at the Shechinah. Said the Holy One, blessed be He: If I slay him now, "I will make Avraham, My friend, suffer; therefore, I rather decree that his eyes should be dimmed."; Thus it is written, "And it came to pass, when Yitzchak was old...."

בראשית רבה (וילנא) פרשת וירא פרשה נו
מִיָּד וַיִּשְׁלַח אַבְרָהָם אֶת יָדוֹ, הוּא שׁוֹלֵחַ יָד לִטֹּל אֶת הַסַּכִּין וְעֵינָיו מוֹרִידוֹת דְּמָעוֹת וְנוֹפְלוֹת דְּמָעוֹת לְעֵינָיו שֶׁל יִצְחָק מֵרַחֲמָנוּתוֹ שֶׁל אַבָּא, וְאַף עַל פִּי כֵן הַלֵּב שָׂמֵחַ לַעֲשׂוֹת רְצוֹן יוֹצְרוֹ,

Immediately, "Avraham stretched forth his hand" — he stretched forth his hand to take the knife while the tears streamed from his eyes, and these tears, prompted by a father's compassion, dropped into Yitzchak's eyes. Yet even so, his heart rejoiced to obey the will of his Creator.

Avraham's test was to perform an act that went against his own basic nature of *chesed*, and he passed that test flawlessly. Was the *Akeidah* a test for Yitzchak as well? What was the intended lesson for him? As we have seen, Yitzchak's personality is identified with the concept of *din*, the deep-seated trait of judgment. Perhaps, then, his test began where Avraham's test ended: Yitzchak was willing, even anxious, to be sacrificed, to give his life in obedience to God's command; this was completely in line with a *din*-oriented view of the world. The real test for Yitzchak was coming down the mountain, re-joining the rest of the world, relating to God through the attribute of *chesed*. His test, like his father's, involved worshipping and obeying God outside of his comfort zone, going beyond his natural inclination. The challenge posed to Yitzchak was, therefore, the mirror image of the challenge posed to Avraham.

Did Yitzchak pass this test? Our Sages answer this question by describing a scene that will unfold in the future:

תלמוד בבלי מסכת שבת דף פט עמוד ב

אָמַר רַבִּי שְׁמוּאֵל בַּר נַחְמָנִי, אָמַר רַבִּי יוֹנָתָן, מַאי דִּכְתִיב, (ישעיה סג) "כִּי אַתָּה אָבִינוּ, כִּי אַבְרָהָם לֹא יְדָעָנוּ, וְיִשְׂרָאֵל לֹא יַכִּירָנוּ, אַתָּה ה' אָבִינוּ גּוֹאֲלֵנוּ" וְגוֹ'. לְעָתִיד לָבוֹא אוֹמֵר לוֹ הַקָּדוֹשׁ בָּרוּךְ הוּא לְאַבְרָהָם, בָּנֶיךָ חָטְאוּ לִי, אוֹמֵר לְפָנָיו, רִבּוֹנוֹ שֶׁל עוֹלָם, יִמָּחוּ עַל קְדוּשַׁת שְׁמֶךָ. אָמַר, אֵימָא לֵיהּ לְיַעֲקֹב, דַּהֲוָה לֵיהּ צַעַר גִּדּוּל בָּנִים, אֶפְשָׁר דְּבָעֵי רַחֲמֵי עֲלַיְיהוּ. אָמַר לֵיהּ, בָּנֶיךָ חָטְאוּ, אָמַר לְפָנָיו, רִבּוֹנוֹ שֶׁל עוֹלָם, יִמָּחוּ עַל קְדוּשַׁת שְׁמֶךָ. אָמַר, לָא בְּסָבֵי טַעְמָא, וְלָא בְּדַרְדְּקֵי עֵצָה. אָמַר לֵיהּ לְיִצְחָק, בָּנֶיךָ חָטְאוּ לִי. אָמַר לְפָנָיו, רִבּוֹנוֹ שֶׁל עוֹלָם - בָּנַי וְלֹא בָּנֶיךָ? בְּשָׁעָה שֶׁהִקְדִּימוּ לְפָנֶיךָ "נַעֲשֶׂה" לְ"נִשְׁמַע", קָרָאתָ לָהֶם, (שמות ד) "בְּנִי בְכֹרִי". עַכְשָׁיו - בָּנַי וְלֹא בָּנֶיךָ? וְעוֹד, כַּמָּה חָטְאוּ? כַּמָּה שְׁנוֹתָיו שֶׁל אָדָם - שִׁבְעִים שָׁנָה. דַּל עֶשְׂרִים דְּלָא עָנַשְׁתְּ עֲלַיְיהוּ, פָּשׁוּ לְהוּ חַמְשִׁין. דַּל עֶשְׂרִים וַחֲמִשָּׁה דְּלֵילְוָותָא, פָּשׁוּ לְהוּ עֶשְׂרִים וַחֲמִשָּׁה, דַּל תַּרְתֵּי סְרֵי וּפַלְגָּא דְצַלּוּיֵי, וּמֵיכַל, וּדְבֵית הַכִּסֵּא. פָּשׁוּ לְהוּ תַּרְתֵּי סְרֵי וּפַלְגָּא. אִם אַתָּה סוֹבֵל אֶת כֻּלָּם, מוּטָב. וְאִם לָאו

פרקי דרבי אליעזר פרק לב

רַבִּי שִׁמְעוֹן אוֹמֵר בְּשָׁעָה שֶׁנֶּעֱקַד יִצְחָק נָשָׂא אֶת עֵינָיו לְמַעְלָה וְרָאָה אֶת הַשְּׁכִינָה, וּכְתִיב [שמות לג, כ] כִּי לֹא יִרְאַנִי הָאָדָם וָחָי. אֶלָּא תַּחַת הַמִּיתָה כָּהוּ עֵינָיו לְעֵת זִקְנָתוֹ, שֶׁנֶּאֱמַר [בראשית כז, א] וַיְהִי כִּי זָקֵן יִצְחָק וַתִּכְהֶיןָ עֵינָיו מֵרְאֹת. מִכָּאן אַתָּה לָמֵד שֶׁהַסּוּמָא חָשׁוּב כַּמֵּת.

Vayeira: The Trial

‎- פַּלְגָּא עֲלַי וּפַלְגָּא עֲלָךְ. וְאִם תֹּאמַר, כּוּלְּהוּ עֲלַי, הָא קְרֵיבִית נַפְשִׁי קַמָּךְ. פָּתְחוּ וְאָמְרוּ, "אַתָּה אָבִינוּ". אוֹמֵר לָהֶם יִצְחָק, עַד שֶׁאַתֶּם מְקַלְּסִין לִי, קַלְּסוּ לְהַקָּדוֹשׁ בָּרוּךְ הוּא, וּמַחְוֵי לְהוֹן יִצְחָק קוּדְשָׁא בְּרִיךְ הוּא בְּעֵינַיְיהוּ. מִיָּד נוֹשְׂאִים עֵינֵיהֶם לַמָּרוֹם וְאוֹמְרִים, (ישעיה סג) "אַתָּה ה' אָבִינוּ גּוֹאֲלֵנוּ מֵעוֹלָם שְׁמֶךָ".

Rav Shmuel bar Nachmani said in the name of Rav Yochanan: What is the meaning of the verse, "You are our father, for Avraham did not know us and Yisrael did not recognize us. You, God, are our Father, our Redeemer; forever is Your Name" [*Yeshayahu* 63:16]? In the future, God will say to Avraham, "Your children have sinned against Me." Avraham will say to Him, "Master of the Universe, wipe them out for the sake of the sanctification of Your Name." God will say, "Perhaps Yaakov, who experienced difficulty raising his children, will ask for mercy for the Jewish People." God will say to him, "Your children have sinned against Me." [Yaakov] will say to Him, "Master of the universe, wipe them out for the sake of the sanctification of Your Name." God... will then say to Yitzchak, "Your children have sinned against Me." [Yitzchak] will say to Him, "Master of the universe, my children? My children, and not Your children? When the Jews said, 'We will do and we will listen,' You called them 'My firstborn son,' and now You call them my children, and not Your children? Besides, how much did they sin? How many years are the years of a man's life—seventy? Subtract twenty, for a person is not punished for the sins of the first twenty years of his life; You are left with fifty. Subtract twenty-five, which are [spent in sleep], and You are left with twenty-five. Subtract twelve and a half which a person uses to pray, eat, and answer nature's call, and You are left with twelve and a half. If You can tolerate all of this, then good; if not, then let us split it, half for You and half for me. If you want to say that all of the years of their sins are on me, remember that I sacrificed my soul for You." [Thereupon,] they shall commence and say, "For you [Yitzchak] are our father." Then Yitzchak shall say to them, "Instead of praising me, praise the Holy One, blessed be He," and Yitzchak shall show them the Holy One, blessed be He, with their own eyes. Immediately they shall lift up their eyes on high and exclaim, "You, God, are our Father, our Redeemer; forever is Your Name." (*Shabbat* 89b)

In this amazing passage, we are told that in the future, Avraham and Yaakov will not come to the defense of the Jews who have sinned. Their response to God is one of *din*, of judgment: "Wipe them out." Yitzchak, however, engages God in negotiations that are reminiscent of Avraham's conversation with God regarding the fate of the cities of Sodom and Amorah. Yitzchak will not tolerate the Jews' being punished. He argues, he negotiates, and finally plays a trump card: In the merit of his own willingness to be sacrificed, God must forgive his descendants. Yitzchak is credited with a level of empathy, compassion and *chesed* that surpasses even that of Avraham, whose nature was the essence and the paragon of *chesed*. Apparently, the *chesed* that Yitzchak acquired is stronger than the trait of *chesed* that came naturally to Avraham. Yitzchak becomes a *baal teshuvah* (penitent) vis-à-vis *chesed*, with the elevated stance ascribed to *baalei teshuvah* by our Sages:[14] A trait acquired through experience and personal effort is stronger than a natural inclination.

In the final analysis, Yitzchak does descend the mountain. He learns to serve God through an attribute that does not come naturally to him, just as Avraham did: The crucible of the *Akeidah* enabled Avraham to acquire and refine the attribute of *din*, while at the same time it enabled Yitzchak to refine the attribute of *chesed*. It is not Avraham's natural-born *chesed*, but Yitzchak's acquired *chesed*—attained through the unimaginable trial of the *Akeidah*—that will ultimately save the entire Jewish people.[15]

---

14. See *Berachot* 34b and *Sanhedrin* 99a.
15. The implications of the *Akeidah* impact not only Yitzchak's character, but also the relationship between *din* (judgment) and *chesed* or *rachamim* (kindness or compassion). See R. Avraham Sabah, *Tzror Hamor, Bereishit* 22:1:

צרור המור על בראשית פרק כב פסוק א
והאלהים נסה את אברהם, ובזה השמן של אפרסמון מעורבים ריח שמניך טובים גנוזים בסתר החכמה. שכל זה היה לכלול מדת הדין עם רחמים, בענין שלא תוכל להזיק. כי יצחק סוד הפחד והדין, כאומרו בענין ופחד יצחק היה לי (לק' לא, מב), ולולי שגברו רחמי אברהם על פחד יצחק היה משחית העולם. ולכן אמר והאלהים שהוא מדת הדין, נסה את אברהם ורוממהו והעלהו לכלול את יצחק עם הרחמים. וזהו שאמרו נסה את אברהם, לרבות את יצחק. כי ג"כ נתנסה יצחק בהיותו בן שלשים ושבעה שנים, ואם היה רוצה היה בועט באביו הזקן ומשליכו על אחד ההרים. אבל קבל הדבר בשמחה וברצון נפשו נעקד והושם על גבי מזבח להיותו סימן לבניו, שבזכות זה יעקור השם כל מדות הדין ויכפה אותם ויכבשו רחמיו את כעסו. כדכתיב ישוב ירחמנו יכבוש עונותינו (מיכה ז, יט), וזהו ענין נסיון אברהם ועקידת יצחק, שעקדו אברהם וקשרו במדת רחמיו כדי שלא יצא להשחית העולם. ולכן יצחק הוא אמצעי בן אברהם ויעקב, רחמים מכאן ורחמים מכאן, בענין שלא יצא לקטרג. וכאן נתבשר ביעקב, דכתיב ביום השלישי וישא אברהם את עיניו (לק' פס' ד), הוא יעקב משולש בזכות החוט המשולש. ולכן בר"ה אנו אומרים ועקידת יצחק היום לזרעו תזכור, כמו שהוא נעקד ונקשר כן תקשור ותכפה כל מיני מדות הדין. וזהו סוד תקיעה תרועה תקיעה, יצחק באמצע. וכן בכאן סוד ויסע ויבא ויט, כנגד אברהם יצחק ויעקב. וזהו סוד ובכן ובכן ובכן. כמו שפי' רשתי בספר צרור הכסף בהלכות ראש השנה, הנה הוא נמצא בפא"ס היא העיר הגדולה. וכל זה ברחמי השם על בניו, ונתן לנו עצות טובות איך נהיה נצולים מכל מיני זעם ועברה, אחר שמדת הדין ודרך המשפט טובה שאלמלא מוראה איש את רעהו חיים בלעו (ע"ז ד.):

Parashat Chayei Sarah

The First Matriarch

Parashat Chayei Sarah marks the transition of the matriarchy from Sarah to Rivkah. A great deal of the narrative is devoted to the death and burial of Sarah on the one hand, and the search for a wife for Yitzchak on the other. Rabbi Yosef Dov Soloveitchik, *zt"l*, once noted that with the death of Sarah, "[Avraham] walks off the covenantal stage."[1] Despite his relative longevity, Avraham seems to disappear after Sarah's passing: He ceases to be a major player, and the mantle of leadership passes to Yitzchak—and Rivkah. Apparently, the partnership between Avraham and Sarah was such that the death of one causes the focus to shift away from the other. Theirs was a complete, total partnership, and Avraham was keenly aware of the nature and importance of this partnership. Therefore, as soon as the burial and mourning period ended, he set out to find a woman who could partner with Yitzchak in the same way.

The centrality of this partnership in the mission Avraham had taken upon himself, the mission that Yitzchak would soon inherit, is clear from the very outset: In *Parashat Lech Lecha*, we were told that when Avraham and Sarah headed toward the Land of Canaan, they brought with them "the *nefesh* they had made[2] in Charan."[3] This is understood as

---

1. See R. Avraham Besdin, *Man of Faith in the Modern World — Reflections of the Rav*, vol. 2, p. 86.
2. For an alternative interpretation, see the comments of the Radak *ad loc.*, who understands this phrase as referring to the work of Avraham and Lot:

רד"ק בראשית פרק יב:ה

ואת הנפש אשר עשו בחרן - העבדים והשפחות שקנו בחרן, ויהיה עשו כמו "עשה לי את החיל הזה" (דברים ח׳) ודעת אונקלוס על אותם האנשים שהחזירו לאמונה טובה היא אמונת אברהם אבינו, <u>כי לוט היה מאמונתו לפיכך נתחבר עמו, והוא גם כן היה קורא לאנשים ומראה להם טעמים שיאמינו בה' ויעבדו אותו לבדו ולא הגלולים לפיכך אמר אשר עשו ולא אשר עשה.</u> ורז"ל (ב"ר ל"ט) דרשו אשר עשו על אברהם ושרי, הוא מגייר את האנשים והיא הנשים, אשר עשו, כמו "אשר עשה את משה ואת אהרן" (שמואל א' י"ב ו') שגדלם ולמדם. ויצאו ללכת וגו' כלם היה בלבם נכון ללכת ארצה כנען עם אברהם וכן עשו.

3. *Bereishit* 12:6.

a reference to their followers, to the people whom they had converted to monotheism. Rashi explains:

רש"י בראשית פרק יב:ה

אֲשֶׁר־עָשׂוּ בְחָרָן ‑שֶׁהִכְנִיסָן תַּחַת כַּנְפֵי הַשְּׁכִינָה; אַבְרָהָם מְגַיֵּר אֶת הָאֲנָשִׁים וְשָׂרָה מְגַיֶּרֶת הַנָּשִׁים, וּמַעֲלֶה עֲלֵיהֶם הַכָּתוּב כְּאִלּוּ עֲשָׂאוּם.

"The souls they had made in Haran" — The souls which he had brought beneath the sheltering wings of the Shechinah. Avraham converted the men and Sarah converted the women and Scripture accounts it to their credit as if they had made them.[4] (Rashi, *Bereishit* 12:5)

Avraham and Sarah shared their mission—as equals, each of them working in their own sphere of influence. This observation gives us some insight into the spiritual greatness of the patriarchs and the matriarchs. In his eulogy for Sarah, Avraham explains to the world who she was and what had been lost with her passing. Sarah was more than

---

בראשית פרק יב:ה

וַיִּקַּח אַבְרָם אֶת־שָׂרַי אִשְׁתּוֹ וְאֶת־לוֹט בֶּן־אָחִיו וְאֶת־כָּל־רְכוּשָׁם אֲשֶׁר רָכָשׁוּ וְאֶת־הַנֶּפֶשׁ אֲשֶׁר־עָשׂוּ בְחָרָן וַיֵּצְאוּ לָלֶכֶת אַרְצָה כְּנַעַן וַיָּבֹאוּ אַרְצָה כְּנָעַן:

4. Based on *Bereishit Rabbah* 39:14. It should be noted that Rashi does not suggest this interpretation is *peshuto shel mikra* (the straightforward understanding of the text); rather, he explains, the straightforward reading of the verse refers to slaves, servants, and other members of the household staff:

רש"י בראשית פרק יב

אשר עשו בחרן שהכניסן תחת כנפי השכינה; אברהם מגייר את האנשים ושרה מגיירת הנשים, ומעלה עליהם הכתוב כאילו עשאום; ופשוטו של מקרא עבדים ושפחות שקנו להם, כמו עשה את כל הכבוד הזה (שם ל"א), וישראל עשה חיל (במדבר כד יח), לשון קונה וכונס.

The souls that they had "made" in Charan — The souls which he had brought beneath the sheltering wings of the *Shechinah*. Avraham converted the men and Sarah converted the women, and Scripture accounts it unto them as if they had made them (*Bereishit Rabbah* 39:14). However, the simple meaning of the text is that it refers to the men-servants and to the maidservants whom they had acquired for themselves. The word *asah* is used here as, "he has acquired [*asah*] all this wealth" (*Bereishit* 31:1), and (Numbers 24:8), "And Israel acquires (עושה) wealth" — an expression for acquiring and amassing.

just the woman who prepared food for Avraham's guests;[5] she took a proactive role in educating and inspiring other women.

Of all her students, one stands out in particular: Hagar.[6] When she is introduced in *Bereishit* 16, Hagar is described only as Sarah's Egyptian servant,[7] but Midrashic literature (cited by Rashi) provides some biographical information:

בראשית רבה (וילנא) פרשת לך לך פרשה מה סימן א
אָמַר רַבִּי שִׁמְעוֹן בֶּן יוֹחָאי הָגָר בִּתּוֹ שֶׁל פַּרְעֹה הָיְתָה, וְכֵיוָן שֶׁרָאָה פַּרְעֹה מַעֲשִׂים שֶׁנַּעֲשׂוּ לְשָׂרָה בְּבֵיתוֹ, נָטַל בִּתּוֹ וּנְתָנָהּ לוֹ, אָמַר מוּטָב שֶׁתְּהֵא בִּתִּי שִׁפְחָה בְּבַיִת זֶה וְלֹא גְבִירָה בְּבַיִת אַחֵר, הֲדָא הוּא דִכְתִיב: וְלָהּ שִׁפְחָה מִצְרִית וּשְׁמָהּ הָגָר, הָא אַגְרִיךְ.

Rabbi Shimon ben Yochai taught: Hagar was Pharaoh's daughter. When Pharaoh saw what was done on Sarah's behalf in his house, he took his daughter and gave her to [Avraham], saying, "Better that my daughter should be a handmaid in such a house than a mistress in another house." Thus, the verse, "And she had an Egyptian handmaid, whose name was Hagar," as if Pharaoh said, "Here is your reward." (*Bereishit Rabbah* 45:1)[8]

---

5. See *Bereishit* 18:6:

בראשית פרק יח, ו-ז
וַיְמַהֵר אַבְרָהָם הָאֹהֱלָה אֶל־שָׂרָה וַיֹּאמֶר מַהֲרִי שְׁלֹשׁ סְאִים קֶמַח סֹלֶת לוּשִׁי וַעֲשִׂי עֻגוֹת׃

6. The name "Hagar" may be rooted in the Hebrew word for "the stranger" or "the convert."

7. *Bereishit* 16:1:

בראשית פרק טז, א
וְשָׂרַי אֵשֶׁת אַבְרָם לֹא יָלְדָה לוֹ וְלָהּ שִׁפְחָה מִצְרִית וּשְׁמָהּ הָגָר׃

Now Sarai, Avram's wife, bore him no children; and she had an Egyptian maidservant whose name was Hagar.

8. The Midrash goes on to relate that Avimelech, too, encouraged his daughter to join Avraham and Sarah.

Hagar seems to be the "prototype" of a daughter of a later Pharaoh, known as Bitya (or Batya, both meaning "daughter of God") who saved Moshe, raised him as her own son in the Pharaoh's palace, and joined the Israelites when they were liberated from Egypt; see *Divrei ha-Yamim* I 4:18-19 and *Megillah* 13a, *Sanhedrin*

When it became apparent to Sarah that she would be unable to bear children, she sought an appropriate partner for Avraham, one with the most illustrious lineage she could find. A lesser woman than Sarah might have been afraid to bring in such "competition," but Sarah felt that if Avraham was to have a child, that child must be the greatest child possible. In an act of complete self-sacrifice, Sarah invites her protégé, the erstwhile Egyptian princess, to bear a child for Avraham.

בראשית רבה (וילנא) פרשת לך לך פרשה מה סימן ג
וַתִּקַּח שָׂרַי אֵשֶׁת אַבְרָם אֶת הָגָר הַמִּצְרִית שִׁפְחָתָהּ (בראשית טז, ג), לְקָחַתָּהּ בִּדְבָרִים, אָמְרָה לָהּ אַשְׁרַיִךְ שֶׁאַתְּ מִדַּבֶּקֶת לַגּוּף הַקָּדוֹשׁ הַזֶּה.

"Sarai, Avram's wife, took Hagar the Egyptian..." (Bereishit 16:3)
— She took [persuaded] her with words: "Fortunate are you to be united with so holy a man." (*Bereishit Rabbah* 45:3)

Hagar, who had been Sarah's primary disciple, became pregnant. She concluded from this that God now favored her, and not Sarah, and that Sarah was an unworthy partner for Avraham. As a result, she began to conduct herself as the head of the household.[9]

בראשית רבה (וילנא) פרשת לך לך פרשה מה סימן ד
...וְהָיְתָה הָגָר אוֹמֶרֶת לָהֶם שָׂרַי גְּבִרְתִּי אֵין סִתְרָהּ כְּגִלּוּיָהּ, נִרְאֵית צַדֶּקֶת וְאֵינָהּ צַדֶּקֶת, אִלּוּ הָיְתָה צַדֶּקֶת רְאוּ כַּמָּה שָׁנִים שֶׁלֹּא נִתְעַבְּרָה וַאֲנִי בְּלַיְלָה אֶחָד נִתְעַבַּרְתִּי...

...Hagar would say, "My mistress Sarah is not inwardly what she is outwardly; she appears to be a righteous woman, but she

---

19b, *Shemot Rabbah* 1:26 and 1:30. Hagar, who had the potential to be like Bitya and play a vital secondary role in Jewish history, instead demanded the central, starring role:

דברי הימים א פרק ד:יח-יט
וְאִשְׁתּוֹ הַיְהֻדִיָּה יָלְדָה אֶת יֶרֶד אֲבִי גְדוֹר וְאֶת חֶבֶר אֲבִי שׂוֹכוֹ וְאֶת יְקוּתִיאֵל אֲבִי זָנוֹחַ וְאֵלֶּה בְּנֵי בִּתְיָה בַת פַּרְעֹה אֲשֶׁר לָקַח מָרֶד:

9. Hagar's status is unresolved; she is referred to both as the servant of Sarah and as a wife of Avraham (Avram).

is not. She has not merited to conceive all these years, whereas I conceived in one night." ... (*Bereishit Rabbah* 45:4)

It is not difficult to understand or perhaps even sympathize with Hagar. She had been born into the aristocracy, but a serendipitous event led her away from her father's pagan world.[10] Perhaps Avraham's genius

---

10. According to the Targum (Pseudo) Yonatan (*Bereishit* 16:5), Hagar was the granddaughter of Nimrod, the man who tried to kill Avraham by throwing him into a fiery furnace. Similarly, the Targum (Pseudo) Yonatan (*Bereishit* 14:14) reports that Avraham's servant Eliezer was a son of Nimrod, which may explain his great military prowess:

תרגום יונתן על בראשית ט״ז:ה׳

וַאֲמֶרֶת שָׂרַי לְאַבְרָם כָּל עוּלְבָּנִי מִינָךְ דַהֲוִינָא רְחִיצָא דְּתֶעֱבַד דִּינִי דַאֲנָא שַׁבְקִית אֲרַע וּבֵית אַבָּא וְעָלִית עִמָּךְ לְאַרַע נוּכְרַיְתָא וּכְדוֹן בְּגִין דְּלָא הֲוֵינָא יַלְדָא חֲרָרִית אַמְתִי וִיהַבְתָּהּ לְמִשְׁכּוּב בְּעִיטְפָךְ וַחֲמַת אֲרוּם עֲבַרְיָנִית וְיִתַּבֵּז אִיקְרִי בְּאַנְפָּהָא יִתְגְּלֵי יְיָ קֳדָם יְיָ עוּלְבָּנִי וְיִפְרוֹס שְׁלָמֵיהּ בֵּינִי וּבֵינָךְ וְתִתְמְלֵי אַרְעָא מִינָן וְלָא נִצְטָרֵךְ לִבְנָהָא דְּהָגָר בְּרַת פַּרְעֹה בַּר נִמְרוֹד דְּטַלְקָךְ לְאַתּוּנָא דְּנוּרָא

כתר יונתן בראשית פרשת לך פרק טז:ה

ותאמר שרי לאברם כל עלבוני ממך שהייתי בטוחה שתעשה דיני שאני עזבתי ארץ ובית אבא ובאתי עמך לארץ נכריה ועתה בעבור שלא הייתי יולדת שחררתי שפחתי ונתתיה בחיקיך ותרא כי הרתה ויתבזה כבודי בפניה ועתה יתגלה לפני יי עלבוני ויפרוס שלום ביני ובינך ותתמלא הארץ ממנו ולא נצטרך לבניה של הגר בת פרעה בן נמרוד שהטילך לכבשן האש.

Targum Yonatan on *Bereishit* 16:5

And Sarah said to Avram, "All my affliction is from you. Being secure that you would do me justice, I left the land and house of my father, and came up with you to a foreign land; and when as I was not able to become a mother, I set free my handmaid, and gave her to you; and she sees that she has conceived, and my honour is despised before her. But now my affliction is manifest before God, who will make peace between me and you, and the land shall be replenished from us, nor shall we need the help of the progeny of Hagar the daughter of Pharoh, son of Nimrod, who threw you into the furnace of fire.

תרגום יונתן על בראשית י״ד:י״ד

וְכַד שְׁמַע אַבְרָם אֲרוּם אִשְׁתְּבִי אֲחוּי וְחוֵי וְזַיַין יַת עוּלֵימוֹי דַּחֲנִיךְ לִקְרָבָא מְרַבְּיָנֵי בֵּיתֵיהּ וְלָא צְבוֹ לְמֵהַלְכָא עִימֵיהּ וּבָחַר מִנְּהוֹן יַת אֱלִיעֶזֶר בַּר נִמְרוֹד דַּהֲוָה מְתִיל בִּגְבוּרְתֵּיהּ כְּכֻלְּהוֹן תְּלַת מְאָה וְתַמְנְסַר וּרְדַף עַד דָּן

כתר יונתן בראשית פרשת לך פרק יד:יד

וכאשר שמע אברם כי נשבה אחיו חימש את בחוריו שחינך למלחמה מגידולי ביתו ולא רצו ללכת עמו ויבחר מהם את אליעזר בן נמרוד שהיה דומה בגבורתו ככולם שלש מאות ושמונה עשר וירדוף עד דן.

captivated her, and she came to believe that it was better for her to serve in his house than to rule Egypt. But now, after many years of service, the opportunity to rule in Avraham's house unexpectedly landed in her lap, as it were. She believed that she had received a Divine sign that she, who was born to be queen, would, indeed be the queen—of Avraham's nascent movement.

Hagar's mistake was in assuming that Avraham alone led the people, that he alone was a spiritual giant. She failed to recognize that it was a partnership, the combination of Avraham and Sarah, that was the basis for the great spiritual movement she herself had joined.

Sarah understood very well what Hagar had missed, and Sarah responded—but not out of selfishness or jealousy. Sarah understood that she and Avraham were partners and equals. The moment Hagar overstepped the boundaries of her role, Sarah made those boundaries clear, and insisted that Avraham do the same. Although Hagar was offended, even aggrieved, her pain was not the result of some petty squabble with her "boss." Hagar was crestfallen when she was made to understand that she would not be replacing Sarah as Avraham's partner. Later, when Hagar's son Yishmael exhibited the same desire to usurp Yitzchak's position as heir to Avraham's spiritual legacy, Sarah informed Avraham that it was time to send Hagar and Yishmael away. Avraham was upset and conflicted, and God Himself had to help Avraham put things into perspective:

בראשית פרק כא, יב-יג
וַיֹּאמֶר אֱלֹהִים אֶל־אַבְרָהָם אַל־יֵרַע בְּעֵינֶיךָ עַל־הַנַּעַר וְעַל־אֲמָתֶךָ כֹּל אֲשֶׁר תֹּאמַר אֵלֶיךָ שָׂרָה שְׁמַע בְּקֹלָהּ כִּי בְיִצְחָק יִקָּרֵא לְךָ זָרַע:

But God said to Avraham, "Do not be troubled because of the boy and your slave. Do everything that Sarah tells you, for it is through Yitzchak that you will gain posterity." (*Bereishit* 21:12)

Targum *Yonatan* on *Bereishit* 14:14
And when Avram heard that his brother was taken captive, he armed his young men who were trained for war, who had grown up in his house; but they did not agree to go with him. And he chose from them Eliezer the son of Nimrod, who was equal in strength to all the three hundred and eighteen; and he pursued unto Dan.

To make this point even stronger, Rashi explains that Sarah's prophetic abilities surpassed Avraham's; her decision to banish Hagar was the result of superior prophetic[11] perception.[12] And yet, they were partners; there could be no replacements, neither for Sarah nor for Avraham. Without Sarah, there is no Avraham. The covenantal community requires two leaders, a man and a woman, Avraham and Sarah.

Our Sages find other intimations of Sarah's greatness in the text: Commenting on a verse at the end of our *parashah*, Rashi records an oral tradition preserved in the Midrash:[13]

---

11. Rashi, *Bereishit* 21:12:

רש"י בראשית פרק כא:יב
שְׁמַע בְּקֹלָהּ - לָמַדְנוּ, שֶׁהָיָה אַבְרָהָם טָפֵל לְשָׂרָה בִּנְבִיאוּת:

"Do everything that Sarah tells you" — we may infer that Avraham was inferior to Sarah in respect of prophecy (*Exodus Rabbah* 1:1).

12. Rabbi Soloveitchik once commented that when it came to the question "Who is a Jew," the matriarchs had greater insight than the patriarchs: Sarah understood that Yitzchak alone should inherit (and not Yishmael), and Rivkah understood (prophetically) that Yaakov, and not Esav, would be the one to continue the family legacy. (Additionally, the arrangements between Rachel and Leah, which circumvented Yaakov's wishes, produce the twelve tribes). Rabbi Soloveitchik concluded that as a result of the matriarchs' insight, Judaism is determined by matrilineal descent.

13. *Bereishit Rabbah* 60:16, *Zohar Bereishit* 133a:

בראשית רבה (וילנא) פרשת חיי שרה פרשה ס:טז
וַיְבִאֶהָ יִצְחָק הָאֹהֱלָה שָׂרָה אִמּוֹ (בראשית כד, סז), כָּל יָמִים שֶׁהָיְתָה שָׂרָה קַיֶּמֶת הָיָה עָנָן קָשׁוּר עַל פֶּתַח אָהֳלָהּ, כֵּיוָן שֶׁמֵּתָה פָּסַק אוֹתוֹ עָנָן, וְכֵיוָן שֶׁבָּאת רִבְקָה חָזַר אוֹתוֹ עָנָן. כָּל יָמִים שֶׁהָיְתָה שָׂרָה קַיֶּמֶת הָיוּ דְּלָתוֹת פְּתוּחוֹת לִרְוָחָה, וְכֵיוָן שֶׁמֵּתָה שָׂרָה פָּסְקָה אוֹתָהּ הָרְוָחָה, וְכֵיוָן שֶׁבָּאת רִבְקָה חָזְרָה אוֹתָהּ הָרְוָחָה. וְכָל יָמִים שֶׁהָיְתָה שָׂרָה קַיֶּמֶת הָיָה בְּרָכָה מְשֻׁלַּחַת בָּעִסָּה, וְכֵיוָן שֶׁמֵּתָה שָׂרָה פָּסְקָה אוֹתָהּ הַבְּרָכָה, כֵּיוָן שֶׁבָּאת רִבְקָה חָזְרָה. כָּל יָמִים שֶׁהָיְתָה שָׂרָה קַיֶּמֶת הָיָה נֵר דּוֹלֵק מִלֵּילֵי שַׁבָּת וְעַד לֵילֵי שַׁבָּת, וְכֵיוָן שֶׁמֵּתָה פָּסַק אוֹתוֹ הַנֵּר, וְכֵיוָן שֶׁבָּאת רִבְקָה חָזַר. וְכֵיוָן שֶׁרָאָה אוֹתָהּ שֶׁהִיא עוֹשָׂה כְּמַעֲשֵׂה אִמּוֹ, קוֹצָה חַלָּתָהּ בְּטָהֳרָה וְקוֹצָה עִסָּתָהּ בְּטָהֳרָה, מִיָּד וַיְבִאֶהָ יִצְחָק הָאֹהֱלָה.

"And Yitzchak brought her into his mother Sarah's tent." (*Bereishit* 24:67) —You find that as long as Sarah lived, a cloud hung over her tent; when she died, that cloud disappeared, but when Rivkah came, it returned. As long as Sarah lived, her doors were wide open; at her death that liberality ceased; but when Rivkah came, that openhandedness returned. As long as Sarah lived, there was a blessing on her dough, and the lamp used to burn from the evening of the Sabbath until the

The reference to "a cloud tied to her tent" is a very particular, and also a very uncommon image[14] which appears in Midrashic literature evening of the following Sabbath; when she died, these ceased, but when Rivkah came, they returned. And so when he saw her following in his mother's footsteps, separating her *challah* in purity and handling her dough in purity, straightway, "Yitzchak brought her into the tent…."

זוהר כרך א בראשית פרשת חיי שרה דף קלג עמוד א
וַיְבִיאֶהָ יִצְחָק הָאֹהֱלָה שָׂרָה אִמּוֹ. אָמַר רַבִּי יוֹסֵי הַאי קְרָא קַשְׁיָא. הָאֹהֱלָה. לְאֹהֶל שָׂרָה אִמּוֹ מִבָּעֵי לֵיהּ, מַאי הָאֹהֱלָה. דַּאֲהַדְּרַת תַּמָּן שְׁכִינְתָּא, בְּגִין דְּכָל זִמְנָא דְּשָׂרָה קָיְימָא בְּעָלְמָא שְׁכִינְתָּא לָא אַעֲדֵי מִינָהּ, וּשְׁרָגָּא הֲוָה דְּלִיקַת מֵעֶרֶב שַׁבָּת לְעֶרֶב שַׁבָּת וַהֲוָה נָהִיר כָּל אִינּוּן יוֹמֵי דְּשַׁבַּתָּא, בָּתַר דְּמִיתַת, כָּבְתָה הַהִיא שְׁרָגָא. כֵּיוָן דְּאָתַת רִבְקָה אַהֲדְרַת שְׁכִינְתָּא וּשְׁרָגָא אַדְלִיקַת. שָׂרָה אִמּוֹ, דְּדָמְיָא לְשָׂרָה בְּכָל עוֹבָדָהָא. רַבִּי יְהוּדָה אָמַר כַּמָּה דִּדְיוּקְנֵיהּ דְּיִצְחָק הֲוָה כְּדִיוּקְנֵיהּ דְּאַבְרָהָם, וְכָל מַאן דְּחָמֵי לְיִצְחָק אָמַר דָּא אַבְרָהָם, וַדַּאי אַבְרָהָם הוֹלִיד אֶת יִצְחָק, הָכִי נָמֵי רִבְקָה דִּיוּקְנָהּ מַמָּשׁ הֲוַת דִּיוּקְנָא דְּשָׂרָה, וּבְגִין כַּךְ שָׂרָה אִמּוֹ וַדַּאי. אָמַר רִבִּי אֶלְעָזָר בְּכֹלָּא הָכִי הוּא, אֲבָל תָּא חֲזֵי, רָזָא אִיהוּ דְּאַף עַל גַּב דְּשָׂרָה מִיתַת, דִּיּוּקְנָהּ לָא אַעֲדֵי מִן בֵּיתָא, וְלָא אִתְחֲזֵי תַּמָּן מִיּוֹמָא דְּמִיתַת עַד דְּאָתַת רִבְקָה, כֵּיוָן דְּעָאלַת רִבְקָה אִתְחֲזִיאַת דִּיּוּקְנָא דְּשָׂרָה, דִּכְתִיב וַיְבִיאֶהָ יִצְחָק הָאֹהֱלָה וְגוֹ' מִיָּד שָׂרָה אִמּוֹ אִתְחֲזִיאַת תַּמָּן, וְלָא הֲוָה חָמֵי לָהּ בַּר יִצְחָק בִּלְחוֹדוֹי כַּד עָיֵיל תַּמָּן, וְעַל דָּא וַיִּנָּחֵם יִצְחָק אַחֲרֵי אִמּוֹ (ס"א מַאי אַחֲרֵי אִמּוֹ, אַחֲרֵי) דְּאִמּוֹ אִתְחֲזִיאַת וְאִזְדַּמְּנָא בְּבֵיתָא, וְעַל דָּא לָא כְּתִיב אַחֲרֵי מִיתַת אִמּוֹ, אֶלָּא אַחֲרֵי אִמּוֹ.

"And Yitzchak brought her into his mother Sarah's tent." — R. Yosi remarked: "The letter *heh* at the end of the word *ha'ohelah* [into the tent] is a reference to the *Shechinah*, which now returned to the tent. For during the whole of Sarah's life the *Shechinah* did not depart from it, and a light used to burn there from one Sabbath eve to the other; once lit, it lasted all the days of the week. After her death the light was extinguished, but when Rivkah came the *Shechinah* returned and the light was rekindled. Thus the verse reads literally, 'And he brought her into the tent, Sarah his mother,' the last phrase implying that Rivkah was in all her works a replica of Sarah his mother."

R. Yehudah said: "Just as Yitzchak was the very image of Avraham, so that whoever looked at Yitzchak said, 'There is Avraham' and knew at once that 'Avraham begat Yitzchak,' so was Rivkah the very image of Sarah. She was thus, so to say, in the phrase of our text, 'Sarah his mother.'"

R. Eleazar said: "All this is truly said. But observe a deeper mystery here. For, in fact, although Sarah died, her image did not depart from the house. It was not, however, visible for a time, but as soon as Rivkah came it became visible again, as it is written, 'and he brought her into the tent, Sarah his mother,' as if to say, 'and forthwith Sarah his mother made her appearance.' No one, however, saw her save Yitzchak, and thus we understand the words, 'and Yitzchak was comforted after his mother,' that is, after his mother became visible and was installed in the house again.' [*Zohar* 133a]

14. For additional instances of the cloud "tied" to a particular place, see *Midrash Tanchuma* (Buber) *Parashat Chukat* (22), and Targum (Pseudo) Yonatan, *Shemot* 19:16:

only very rarely. Of particular interest is the occurrence involving Avraham and Yitzchak: As Avraham headed toward the *Akeidah*, he lifted his gaze and saw something that was at once both physical and spiritual: He was able to identify the place he sought because he saw a

---

מדרש תנחומא (בובר) פרשת חקת

[כב] [קוראים אל ה' והוא יענם (תהלים צט ו). זה קורא וענינה, וזה קורא וענינה. בעמוד ענן (תהלים צ"ט: ז), הרי שמענו במשה שנדבר עמו בעמוד ענן, שנאמר וירד ה' בענן ויתיצב עמו שם (שמות לד ה), ובאהרן נדבר עמו בענן, שנאמר וירד ה' בענן ויעמוד פתח האהל (במדבר יב ה), אבל בשמואל לא שמענו, והיכן שמענו מן הדין קרא, ותעננה אותם ותאמרנה יש הנה לפניך (שמואל א' ט:יב), ר' יודן בשם ר' מרי בר יעקב, אמרו להם הנשים, אי אתם רואים ענן קשור למעלה מחצירו, ואין יש אלא ענן, כמה דתימר ויש אשר יהיה הענן (במדבר ט:כ). ושמואל בקוראי שמו, שמענו במשה שנכתבה תורה לשמו, שנאמר זכרו תורת משה עבדי (מלאכי ג כב), ובשמואל נכתב לו ספר, שנאמר ויכתב בספר וינח לפני ה' (שמואל א' י:כה), אבל באהרן לא שמענו, אלא מלמד שניתנה לו הפרשה הזו, שלא תזוז ממנו ולא מבניו, עד סוף כל הדורות, ואיזו זו זאת חוקת התורה].

"They (i.e., Moshe, Aharon, and Shmuel) cried unto God and He answered them." (*Tehillim* 99:6) — The first cried out and was answered; the second also cried out and was answered: "He spoke to them in a pillar of cloud" (v. 7). We have been told that Moshe conversed with God in a pillar of cloud, as stated "God descended in the cloud and stood with [Moshe] there" (*Shemot* 34:5).. So, too, with Aharon, he conversed with God in the cloud, as it is stated, "God descended in pillar of cloud, stood at the entrance of the tent, and called Aharon and Miriam" (*Bamidbar* 12:5). About Shmuel, however, we have not explicitly heard any such thing. So where did we hear it indirectly? From the verse, "And they [the young women] answered them and said: See, [Shmuel] is just ahead of you.' (I *Shmuel* 9:12). R. Yudan said in the name of R. Mari bar Yaakov: The women really said to them: Do you not see a cloud fixed above his courtyard? Now *yeish* can only be a cloud, just as it is said, "And it would happen [*yeish*) that tht cloud would be [a few days over the tabernacle] (*Bamidbar* 9:20).

And Shmuel was among those who call upon his name (*Tehillim* 99:6). We have heard of Moshe that Torah was written for his name, as stated, "Remember the Torah of My servant Moshe" (*Malachi* 3:22). So also in the case of Shmuel, a book was written for him, as stated, "[Then Shmuel told the people the rules of kingship], wrote them in a book, and placed it before the Lord(I *Shmuel* 10:25). In the case of Aharon, however, I have not heard [of his book]. It is simply that there is a teaching that this *parashah* was granted to him, so that it would never budge, neither from him nor from his children, till the end of all the generations. And which [*parashah*] was this? "This is the statute of the Torah" (*Bamidbar* 19:2).

כתר יונתן שמות פרשת יתרו פרק יט:טז

ויהי ביום השלישי בששי בחודש בעת הבוקר ויהי קולות של רעמים וברקים וענן כבד קשור על ההר וקול שופר חזק מאוד ויזועזע כל העם אשר במחנה:

mountain with a peculiar cloud "tied" to its summit. Yitzchak shared this vision; the other young men who accompanied them did not.

בראשית פרק כב:ד-ה
בַּיּוֹם הַשְּׁלִישִׁי וַיִּשָּׂא אַבְרָהָם אֶת־עֵינָיו וַיַּרְא אֶת־הַמָּקוֹם מֵרָחֹק: וַיֹּאמֶר אַבְרָהָם אֶל־נְעָרָיו שְׁבוּ־לָכֶם פֹּה עִם־הַחֲמוֹר וַאֲנִי וְהַנַּעַר נֵלְכָה עַד־כֹּה וְנִשְׁתַּחֲוֶה וְנָשׁוּבָה אֲלֵיכֶם:

On the third day Avraham lifted up his eyes and saw the place from afar. And Avraham said to his young men, "Stay here with the donkey; and I and the lad will go yonder and worship, and come back to you." (*Bereishit* 22:4-5)

מדרש רבה בראשית פרשה נו סימן א,ב
ביום השלישי וירא את המקום מרחוק מה ראה ראה ענן קשור בהר אמר דומה שאותו מקום שאמר לי הקב"ה להקריב את בני שם:
אמר ליצחק בני רואה את מה שאני רואה א"ל הין אמר לשני נעריו רואים אתם מה שאני רואה אמרו לו לאו אמר הואיל וחמור אינו רואה ואתם אין אתם רואים שבו לכם פה עם החמור...

"On the third day…he saw the place from afar." — What did he see? He saw a cloud tied the mountain, and said: "It appears that that is the place where the Holy One, blessed be He, told me to sacrifice my son." He then said to him [Yitzchak]: "Yitzchak, my son, do you see what I see?" "Yes," he replied. [Avraham] then said to his two servants: "Do you see what I see?" "No," they answered. "Since you do not see it, 'Stay here with the donkey….' (*Bereishit Rabbah* 56:1-2)

The two young servants saw only the mountain, the physical reality devoid of the spiritual component expressed by the cloud. Therefore, Avraham instructed them to remain with the *chamor*, the donkey. As we noted in *Parashat Vayeira*, the root of this word is *chomer*, denoting physicality. Avraham and Yitzchak are able to see both the physical and spiritual, but the others are limited to the physical plane. They do not see the cloud; they are, therefore, unworthy of continuing the spiritual journey that Avraham and Yitzchak share.

Interestingly, Avraham is described in the Midrash as one of three people who rides on a *chamor*; the other two are Moshe and the Messiah (Mashiach).

The prophet Zecharyah describes Mashiach as a poor man riding on a donkey.[15] Citing this verse, the Gemara teaches that there are two possible scenarios for the final redemption and the onset of the Messianic Age:

תלמוד בבלי מסכת סנהדרין דף צח עמוד א

אָמַר רַבִּי אֲלֶכְסַנְדְּרָאִי, רַבִּי יְהוֹשֻׁעַ בֶּן לֵוִי רָמֵי, כְּתִיב, [דניאל ז] "וַאֲרוּ עִם עֲנָנֵי שְׁמַיָּא כְּבַר אֱנָשׁ אָתֵה", וּכְתִיב, [זכריה ט] "עָנִי וְרֹכֵב עַל חֲמוֹר". זָכוּ - "עִם עֲנָנֵי שְׁמַיָּא", לֹא זָכוּ "עָנִי וְרֹכֵב עַל חֲמוֹר".

Rabbi Alexanderi taught: Rabbi Yehoshua ben Levi contrasted two verses: It is written, "Behold, one resembling a son of man came with the clouds of heaven" (*Daniel* 7:13), and it is written, "[Behold, your king will come to you] lowly, and riding upon a donkey" (*Zecharyah* 9:9). If [the Jewish people] are meritorious, [Mashiach will come] with the clouds of Heaven; if not, [he will be] lowly and riding upon a donkey. (*Sanhedrin* 98a)

The denouement of history is in our hands. The Mashiach will be revealed in clouds of glory if we are worthy; if we are unworthy, our redemption

---

15. *Zecharyah* 9:9:

זכריה פרק ט:ט

גִּילִי מְאֹד בַּת־צִיּוֹן הָרִיעִי בַּת יְרוּשָׁלִַם הִנֵּה מַלְכֵּךְ יָבוֹא לָךְ צַדִּיק וְנוֹשָׁע הוּא עָנִי וְרֹכֵב עַל־חֲמוֹר וְעַל־עַיִר בֶּן־אֲתֹנוֹת:

Rejoice greatly, O daughter of Zion; shout, O daughter of Jerusalem; behold, your King comes to you; he is just, and victorious; humble and riding on a donkey, on a colt the foal of a donkey.

will be of a far less exalted nature. If we are deserving, the clouds will be revealed sooner; if not, the redemption will take longer, and the process will be slow and plodding—but the redemption will surely come. And just as the clouds are an image that is laden with meaning, representing man's ability to recognize and connect to the metaphysical plane, so, too, the image of the Messiah as a poor man riding on his donkey is no mere literary device: According to mystical sources, this metaphor holds the key to the redemption itself: The *Zohar*[16] explains that the role of Mashiach is to ride on the *chamor*, to subdue the physical.[17]

In Jewish thought, there is no ideological tension between the physical world and the spiritual world. The physical world was created for our benefit, and we are entrusted with its care and proper use. The physical world is a means to an end; we are charged with elevating and perfecting our physical selves and the physical world around us by utilizing them in spiritual contexts. So many individuals, movements, philosophies and nations have made (and continue to make) the tragic error of worshipping the physical as an end unto itself. In this vein, Jewish mysticism describes the Messiah as one who rides on top of the *chamor*, utilizes and subdues the physical world, and ushers in an age of

---

16. *Zohar, Bamidbar* 207a:

זוהר חלק ג דף רז/א

אָמַר רַבִּי יוֹסֵי, אִינּוּן דִּימִינָא כְּלִילָן כֻּלְּהוּ בְּחַד, דְּאִקְרֵי חֲמוֹ״ר. וְהַאי הוּא הַהוּא חֲמוֹר, דִּכְתִיב, (דברים כב) לֹא תַחֲרוֹשׁ בְּשׁוֹר וּבַחֲמוֹ״ר יַחְדָּיו. וְהַאי הוּא חֲמוֹר, דְּזַמִּין מַלְכָּא מְשִׁיחָא לְמִשְׁלַט עֲלֵיהּ...

Those of the right are all merged in one called "donkey," and that is the donkey of which it is written, "You shall not plow with an ox and a donkey together" [*Devarim* 22:10]. That is also the donkey which the King Mashiach shall control. (*Zohar, Bamidbar* 207a)

17. See comments of the Maharal in *Netzach Yisrael* chapter 40:

ספר נצח ישראל עמוד קסט - פרק מ

ועוד מדברי חכמים אשר העמיקו בחכמתם גלו ענין מעלתו של המשיח, א״ר אלכסנדרי ריב״ל רמי כתיב וארו עם ענני שמיא כבר אינש וכתיב עני רוכב על החמור זכו עם עננא שמיא לא זכו עני רוכב על החמור...ור״ל כי מה שאנו אומרים שהמשיח אתי על חמרא דבר זה מורה על מעלת המשיח, מפני שהחמור הוא פשוט יותר מכל ב״ח שהוא בריה פשוטה שאין לו דעת וחכמה, וכאשר רוכב הוא על דבר פשוט מורה שהוא נבדל במעלתו לגמרי ואל תשגיח.

enlightenment in which all of humanity is able to rise up and connect with the spiritual plane.

This, then, is the greatness that Avraham displayed throughout his life: He knew how to master the physical world around him. He understood that man-made idols are meaningless. He was willing to commit himself and his offspring to the covenant of circumcision in order to perfect his body and to symbolize the goal of controlling his physical nature. He and Yitzchak were able to see the cloud, to transcend the shackles of the physical plane, and ascend the mountain. He and Yitzchak were uniquely capable of overcoming their own physical limitations as they willingly submitted to the test of the *Akeidah*.

The matriarchs, too, shared this unique vision. Sarah, and then Rivkah, had "a cloud tied to her tent"—the same cloud that was "tied" to the place of the *Akeidah,* the holiest place in the world according to Jewish tradition. Despite the fact that they lived in the physical world, they were connected to the spiritual world.[18]

---

18. The description of the tent of the matriarchs is strikingly similar to the *Mishkan* and the *Beit ha-Mikdash*: The matriarch's tents, with the miraculous candles, dough and cloud, immediately bring to mind three of the major elements of the Mishkan and Beit HaMikdash: The candelabra with its perpetual flame, the *shulchan* that held the *lechem ha-panim*, and the clouds of glory that symbolized God's presence. See Ramban's comments in his introduction to the book of *Shemot*, where he states that the end of the exile in Egypt was achieved only when the people returned to the level of the patriarchs (and, presumably, the matriarchs) through the building the *Mishkan*. In other words, the creation of the *Mishkan* enabled the Children of Israel to recreate the level of holiness and spirituality of the tent of their matriarch Sarah.

רמב"ן שמות הקדמה

השלים הכתוב ספר בראשית שהוא ספר היצירה בחדוש העולם ויצירת כל נוצר ובמקרי האבות שהם כעניין יצירה לזרעם מפני שכל מקריהם ציורי דברים לרמוז ולהודיע כל עתיד לבא להם ואחרי שהשלים היצירה התחיל ספר אחר בעניין המעשה הבא מן הרמזים ההם ונתייחד ספר ואלה שמות בעניין הגלות הראשון הנגזר בפי' ובגאולה ממנו ולכן חזר והתחיל בשמות יורדי מצרים ומספרם אף על פי שכבר נכתב זה בעבור כי ירידתם שם הוא ראשית הגלות כי מאז הוחל. והנה הגלות איננו נשלם עד יום שובם אל מקומם ואל מעלת אבותם ישובו. וכשיצאו ממצרים אף על פי שיצאו מבית עבדים עדיין יחשבו גולים כי היו בארץ לא להם נבוכים במדבר וכשבאו אל הר סיני ועשו המשכן ושב הקדוש ברוך הוא והשרה שכינתו ביניהם אז שבו אל מעלות אבותם שהיה סוד אלוה עלי אהליהם והם הם המרכבה ואז נחשבו גאולים ולכן נשלם הספר הזה בהשלימו עניין המשכן ובהיות כבוד ה' מלא אותו תמיד:

Avraham and Sarah, Yitzchak and Rivkah were equals—all of them, spiritual giants.[19] However, Avraham saw the cloud only when he was on the way to offer his beloved son as an offering. Only when he was willing to surrender everything he loved to the Almighty, did he merit this spiritual vision. Yitzchak saw the cloud when he prepared to give his life for the service of God. And yet, we are told, this vision was a constant in the tent of Sarah, and then Rivkah. The spiritual apex Avraham and Yitzchak achieved at the *Akeidah* was the spiritual norm that Sarah and Rivkah experienced (and shared with others) in their personal lives, in their tents, each and every day.

How did Sarah achieve this exalted level of spirituality? We are told that Sarah died at the age of 127. Rashi, drawing on the Midrash, explains that when she was one hundred years old, she was like a twenty-year-old regarding sin: Until twenty years of age, we are not held responsible for our actions. Thus, we are all completely free of sin at the age of twenty. At the age of one hundred, Sarah was equally clean of sin.[20]

---

19. See *Zohar, Bereishit* 129a:

זוהר חלק א דף קכט/א

אָמַר רַבִּי אַבָּהוּ בַּתְּחִלָּה נִקְרֵאת הַנְּשָׁמָה אַבְרָהָם וְהַגּוּף שָׂרָה, עַכְשָׁיו נִקְרֵאת הַנְּשָׁמָה יִצְחָק וְהַגּוּף רִבְקָה. תְּנַן בְּמַתְנִיתִין, אָמַר רַבִּי שִׁמְעוֹן אַרְבָּעִים שָׁנָה קוֹדֶם קִיּוּם הַגּוּף מַמְתֶּנֶת הַנְּשָׁמָה לַגּוּף בְּאֶרֶץ יִשְׂרָאֵל. בְּאֵיזֶה מָקוֹם בְּמָקוֹם הַמִּקְדָּשׁ.

20. Rashi, *Bereishit* 23:1:

רש"י בראשית פרק כג:א

ויהיו חיי שרה מאה שנה ועשרים שנה ושבע שנים - לְכָךְ נִכְתַּב שָׁנָה בְּכָל כְּלָל וּכְלָל, לוֹמַר לְךָ שֶׁכָּל אֶחָד נִדְרָשׁ לְעַצְמוֹ בַּת ק' כְּבַת כ' לַחֵטְא, מַה בַּת כ' לֹא חָטְאָה, שֶׁהֲרֵי אֵינָהּ בַּת עוֹנָשִׁין, אַף בַּת ק' בְּלֹא חֵטְא, וּבַת כ' כְּבַת ז' לְיוֹפִי:

שני חיי שרה - כֻּלָּן שָׁוִין לְטוֹבָה:

"and the life of Sarah was 100 years, 20 years, and 7 years" — The reason the word *shanah* is written at every term is to tell you that each term must be explained by itself as a complete number: At the age of one hundred she was as a woman of twenty as regards sin—for just as at the age of twenty one may regard her as having never sinned, since she had not then reached the age when she was subject to punishment, so, too, when she was one hundred years old she was sinless—and when she was twenty she was as beautiful as when she was seven. "[T]he years of Sarah's life" — The word "years" is repeated, without a number, to indicate that they were all equally good.

When she was twenty, the Midrash continues, she was as beautiful as a seven-year-old. Here, the Midrash is somewhat difficult to understand; in fact, we might have reversed the two analogies, comparing her innocence to that of a seven-year-old, and her beauty to that of a twenty-year-old. Rabbi Shimshon Raphael Hirsch explains that, in truth, a seven-year-old is quite beautiful—perhaps not in a sexual or sensual sense, but with the beauty of a child. We would think that the idea of sinlessness would be more appropriate for a seven-year-old than for a twenty-year-old, but Rabbi Hirsch points out that a seven-year-old lacks the opportunity and capability to sin.[21] Sarah's purity, then, was not that of a seven-year-old child who has neither the inclination nor

---

21. R. Samson Raphael Hirsch, *Bereishit* 23:1:

רש"ר הירש בראשית פרק כג:א

ידועים דברי חז"ל לפסוק זה, ששנות החיים מתחלקות בו לשלש קבוצות (עי' בראשית רבה נח, א). אם נקרא אותו כפשוטו, הרי נאמר ששרה חיה לא מאה - ועשרים - ושבע שנים, אלא מאה שנה ועשרים שנה ושבע שנים. שלשה מספרים אלה מעמידים לפנינו את מהלך התפתחותם של חיי אדם: גיל הילדות, גיל הנעורים המבוגרים וגיל הזיקנה המושלמת. אין ביטוי טוב יותר לחיים שלמים ברוח ובמוסר מאשר שאותו אדם היה בימי זיקנותו, בוגר בימי בגרותו, ילד בימי ילדותו. יתירה מזו: חז"ל מעירים עוד (שם) שאדם, החי חיי אמת, נוטל מכל תקופת גיל של חייו את התכונה המפארת אותה - אל תקופת חייו המאוחרת יותר. מכאן גם הביטוי "בא בימים" (להלן כד, א): הוא בא בעיצומם של הימים, הוא אינו נטמע ואינו שוקע בריבוי הימים, אלא עובר דרכם. הוא נוטל את ההישגים הרוחניים והמוסריים של הימים שעברו ומעבירם אל הימים שיבואו, ושום דבר מן הימים, שנעשה "שלו" באמת, לא יתן לקחת מידיו.

"שרה לקחה את יופיה של בת השבע לגיל העשרים, ואת נקיותה של בת העשרים מחטא לקחה אתה אלי קבר" מה רחוקה ההשקפה זו של חז"ל מן ההשקפה השכיחה בינינו כיום, ולאו דוקא לאושרנו! הם מבקשים את היופי לא בבת העשרים, כי אם בבת השבע, את הנקיות מחטא לא בבת השבע, כי אם בגיל הנעורים המבוגרים. רגילים אנחנו לדבר דרך שיגרה על "תמימות של ילד", אך יהיה זה מעציב אם עלינו לקנא בילד בשל תמימותו. תמימות, נקיות מחטא, מניחוח את האפשרות של אשמה; נקיות מחטא פירושה שקדמו לה לבטים עם החזר שניות והתאוות, והיא התגברה עליהן. אולם רק הבת הבוגרת ונעשית אשה, ורק הבן הבוגר ונעשה גבר רק הם מסוגלים להגיע אל מדרגת הנקיות מחטא.

כל השנים האלה גם יחד קרויות חיי שרה, היא חיה בכולן, וכל מאה ועשרים ושבע שנות חייה היו חיי חיים, חיי חיוניות ושמחה, חיים טובים ובעלי משמעות, ולא היה בהם אף רגע, שמוטב היה לה שלא לחיות אותו. ואף - על - פי - כן, כך סיומו של סיפור זה - לא היו "חיי שרה" אלא "שני חיי שרה", שנים מתוך חיי שרה, לא היו אלא פרק - זמן, קטע מתוך חייה. שכן אין שיעור החיים נמדד במידת הזמן, הניתנת לנו בעולם הזה: "צדיקים אפילו במיתתן קרויין חיים" (עי' ברכות יח ע"א), "ילכו מחיל אל חיל" (תהלים פד, ח) - לקראת התפתחות הולכת ונמשכת לעדי עד. ואמרו חז"ל בחכמתם: "יודע ה' ימי תמימם" (תהלים לז, יח) - החיים בתמימות ובשלמות עם ה', "כשם שהן תמימים כך שנותם תמימים", אין בהן אף רגע, אף יום, שלא נכתב בספר הזכרון אשר לפני ה'; אין אף יום אחד במאה - עשרים - ושבע שנות חיים כאלה בעולם הזה שאין בו חשיבות; אולם "ונחלתם לעולם תהיה": נחלת אמת טמונה "ביום שכולו ארוך", שכן נאמר "שני חיי שרה" (עי' בראשית רבה נח, א).

occasion to sin, but rather of the twenty-year-old who makes conscious choices and refuses to sin.

Rabbi Soloveitchik, *zt"l*, explained the eulogy that Avraham shared[22] that the greatness of Sarah and her role within the covenantal community may be culled from the words of Rashi: She was one hundred, she was twenty, she was seven: Whereas most people pass from one stage of life to the next, leaving the previous stage behind and taking with them nothing more than fond memories, Sarah retained the essence of each stage of her life even after she had moved on to the next stage.[23] Each of these ages—one hundred, twenty, seven—has unique qualities. A seven-year-old has innocence; a twenty-year-old has strength; a hundred-year-old has wisdom. The secret of Sarah's greatness was that throughout her entire life she was one hundred and twenty and seven. Rashi explains the words, "the years of the life of Sarah" — All were equally good. At every point in her life, Sarah remained the same. She was always as innocent as a seven-year-old, with the strength, determination, and idealism of a twenty-year-old, and the wisdom of a one-hundred-year-old.

While each of these traits is certainly desirable, their importance to the religious character is even greater:[24] Innocence is a quality necessary for prayer; in order for a person to pray, he or she must feel that God is really listening. The cynicism that so many of us accrue as we move through life eats away at this innocence, and we lose the ability to stand before God and verbalize our innermost thoughts, fears, and aspirations. A child, on the other hand, is not weighed down by cynicism and still possesses the ability to relate directly and honestly to a loving parent. When we pray, we should feel that God is our Father in Heaven and we are His children; Sarah never lost that innocence.

---

22. See Rabbi Avraham Besdin, *Man of Faith in the Modern World — Reflections of the Rav*, vol. 2, p. 83ff.
23. This is based on the phrase in Rashi, *Bereshit* 23:1 "…they were all equally good."
24. These ideas are presented, albeit in a somewhat truncated form, by Rabbi Avraham Besdin, in *Man of Faith in the Modern World — Reflections of the Rav*, vol. 2; a recording of the orginal lecture can be heard at YuTorah.org. http://www.yutorah.org/lectures/lecture.cfm/751379/rabbi-joseph-b-soloveitchik/chayei-sarah/ .

The greatness of a twenty-year-old is physical strength and idealism. A twenty-year-old feels that he or she can change the world, that anything is possible. There are no limits, no rules—only potential. Twenty-year olds feel that they are not limited by the mistakes and failings of the previous generation. They believe they can build a better world. This is how Sarah retained the strength of a twenty-year-old—by always remaining idealistic, never feeling limited.

A one-hundred-year-old possesses wisdom, born of the perspective that only experience can give. Great sages are almost always older people whose skills have not diminished over the years. Quite the opposite: they possess insight and sensitivity that transcends "book knowledge." Sarah always had this wisdom. Similarly, even at a tender age, Sarah's spiritual heir, Rivkah, was able to transcend her station and relate to others as a person far beyond her years.

Sarah was always one hundred, and twenty, and seven.[25] Throughout her life she possessed all these skills. This is the greatness of Sarah, the greatness which made her our first matriarch—and the perfect match for Avraham.

---

25. The Talmud (*Bava Kamma* 97b) speaks of a "coin of Avraham the patriarch:"

תלמוד בבלי מסכת בבא קמא דף צז עמוד ב
וְאֵיזֶהוּ מַטְבֵּעַ שֶׁל אַבְרָהָם אָבִינוּ? זָקֵן וּזְקֵינָה מִצַּד אֶחָד, וּבָחוּר וּבְתוּלָה מִצַּד אַחֵר:

"And what is the coin of Avraham our Patriarch? An elderly man and woman on one side, and a young man and woman on the other side."

Rashi understands that the two sides of the coin represent the two first couples, Avraham and Sarah, and Yitzchak and Rivkah. This would be consistent with the comments with which we began: Avraham and Sarah were a team, a partnership that would be replaced by the new, younger team of Yitzchak and Rivkah. The Maharsha, however, understands that the two sides of the coin represent Avraham and Sarah as young and old, reflecting the miracle they experienced of regaining their youth (and parenting a child at an advanced age). We may posit that this is consistent with the view of Rashi (as interpreted by Rabbi Soloveitchik): Sarah (and Avraham) were always young and vibrant, yet always elderly and wise.

רש"י מסכת בבא קמא דף צז עמוד ב
בחור ובתולה - יצחק ורבקה. זקן וזקינה - אברהם ושרה.

מהרש"א חידושי אגדות מסכת בבא קמא דף צז עמוד ב
מטבע של אברהם זקן וזקינה מצד א' בחור ובתולה מצד ב' עיין פרש"י ויותר נראה לפרש כולם ע"ש הנס שאחר שנעשו זקנים כמ"ש ואדוני זקן ואני זקנתי חזרו לימי נעורים דהיינו שנעשו הם בחור ובתולה כמ"ש אחרי בלותי היתה לי עדנה וק"ל:

Parashat Toldot

Yaakov and Esav

In *Parashat Toldot* we meet a dysfunctional family. The family is our own, or to be more precise, that of our ancestors. There seems to be a lack of communication and a state of tension between the two sons, Yaakov and Esav. To add to the dysfunctionality, each parent seems to have a favorite son: Yitzchak loves Esav, while Rivkah loves Yaakov. Since we are descendants of Yaakov, we know which brother we are supposed to be "rooting" for, yet our identification with Yaakov raises some questions: The Torah tells us that Yitzchak loved Esav, which is very difficult for us to understand or accept. Why would Yitzchak love Esav? We are told that God Himself hated Esav![1]

מלאכי פרק א:ב-ג
(ב) אָהַבְתִּי אֶתְכֶם אָמַר ה' וַאֲמַרְתֶּם בַּמָּה אֲהַבְתָּנוּ הֲלוֹא־אָח עֵשָׂו לְיַעֲקֹב נְאֻם־ה' וָאֹהַב אֶת־יַעֲקֹב: (ג) וְאֶת־עֵשָׂו שָׂנֵאתִי וָאָשִׂים אֶת־הָרָיו שְׁמָמָה וְאֶת־נַחֲלָתוֹ לְתַנּוֹת מִדְבָּר:

"I have loved you," says God, yet you say, "How have you loved us?" "Was not Esav Yaakov's brother?" says God, "yet I loved Yaakov, and I hated Esav, and laid waste his mountains and gave his heritage to the jackals of the wilderness." (*Malachi* 1:2–3)

When Yitzchak grew older, why did he wish to bless Esav—the son whom even God did not love? We would have thought (and certainly preferred) that Yaakov would have been the sole beneficiary of Yitzchak's blessing.

---
1. One needs to use caution when utilizing later sources referring to Esav, some of these sources refer to the individual Esav, yet others to either the nation which later emerged, or even Rome and Christianity which are at times described as "Esav or Edom" in rabbinic literature.

The key to understanding the relationship between Yitzchak and Esav, as well as the relationship between Yaakov and Esav, may be found in the beginning of the *parashah*—before the two sons were born.

Rivkah was pregnant, and she was experiencing extreme, perhaps unnatural, pain. She sought Divine counsel,[2] and asked God to explain the inner turmoil she was experiencing:[3]

בראשית פרק כה, כג

(כג) וַיֹּאמֶר ה' לָהּ שְׁנֵי גוֹיִם בְּבִטְנֵךְ וּשְׁנֵי לְאֻמִּים מִמֵּעַיִךְ יִפָּרֵדוּ וּלְאֹם מִלְאֹם יֶאֱמָץ וְרַב יַעֲבֹד צָעִיר:

---

2. *Bereishit* 25:22: "She went to seek out God."

בראשית פרק כה, כב

וַיִּתְרֹצֲצוּ הַבָּנִים בְּקִרְבָּהּ וַתֹּאמֶר אִם כֵּן לָמָּה זֶּה אָנֹכִי וַתֵּלֶךְ לִדְרֹשׁ אֶת ה':

3. The Midrash (*Bereishit Rabbah* 63:6) beautifully describes the turmoil, as one son wishing to "get out" when she passed a place of worship of monotheism, while the other was attracted to places of worship of idolatry. Presumably Rivkah did not know at that point that she was carrying twins, and felt that this fetus was exhibiting "schizophrenic" behavior. The word of God which came to her, informed her, that she was carrying two children, who would become two nations, who were in fact headed in radically different directions. See Rashi, *Bereishit* 25:22.

רש"י בראשית פרק כה פסוק כב

(כב) וַיִּתְרֹצֲצוּ - על כרחך המקרא הזה אומר דרשני, שסתם מה היא רציצה זו וכתב אם כן למה זה אנכי? רבותינו דרשוהו לשון ריצה; כשהיתה עוברת על פתחי תורה של שם ועבר, יעקב רץ ומפרכס לצאת, עוברת על פתח עבודת אלילים, עשו מפרכס לצאת. דבר אחר מתרוצצים זה עם זה ומריבים בנחלת שני עולמות:

"And [the children] struggled" — You must admit that this verse calls for a Midrashic interpretation since it leaves unexplained what this struggling was about and it states that she exclaimed, "If it be so, wherefore did I desire this" [i.e., she asked whether this was the normal course of child-bearing, feeling that something extraordinary was happening]. Our Rabbis explain that the word [*va-yitrotzetzu*] has the meaning of running, moving quickly [*ritzah*]: whenever she passed by the doors of Torah [i. e., the Schools of Shem and Ever], Yaakov moved convulsively in his efforts to be born, but whenever she passed by the gate of a pagan temple Esav moved convulsively in his efforts to be born. Another explanation is: they struggled with one another and quarreled as to how they should divide the two worlds as their inheritance.

God said to her, "Two nations are in your womb, and two peoples shall be separated from your bowels. One people shall be stronger than the other people, and the elder shall serve the younger." (*Bereishit* 25:23)

Rivkah alone was informed of the divergent paths her children's destinies would take; apparently, Yitzchak was unaware that they would father two separate nations, that each had their own mission. We might well wonder whether having this information would have benn a blessing or a curse.[4] While some people like to peek at the last page of a novel to see how the story ends, do we really want this kind of knowledge about our children's lives? Once Rivkah knows her younger son will be successful, does this then become a self-fulfilling prophecy? Does Yitzchak sense his wife's ambivalence toward their older son, and does he then try to over-compensate? Does Rivkah choose not to share the prophecy she has received with her husband, in order to assure that he would nurture Esav, without prejudice or the burden of foregone conclusions?

The verses go on to describe the birth of the twins:

בראשית פרק כה:כה-כו

(כה) וַיֵּצֵא הָרִאשׁוֹן אַדְמוֹנִי כֻּלּוֹ כְּאַדֶּרֶת שֵׂעָר וַיִּקְרְאוּ שְׁמוֹ עֵשָׂו: (כו) וְאַחֲרֵי־כֵן יָצָא אָחִיו וְיָדוֹ אֹחֶזֶת בַּעֲקֵב עֵשָׂו וַיִּקְרָא שְׁמוֹ יַעֲקֹב וְיִצְחָק בֶּן־שִׁשִּׁים שָׁנָה בְּלֶדֶת אֹתָם:

The first [baby] came out red all over like a hairy garment; and they called his name "Esav." After that his brother came out, his hand grasping Esav's heel, and he [Yitzchak] named him Yaakov. (*Bereishit* 25: 25–26)

Both parents name the firstborn son, together, while only the father names the second. In fact, nowhere in the Torah does Rivkah refer

---

4. The verses from the prophecy of Malachi quoted above, regarding God's hatred of Esav, reflect this problem; the chapter begins with a description of prophecy as a *massa*, a burden.

to her second son as Yaakov. She always calls him "my son." Perhaps this is because she knows that his identity is not determined by his relationship with his brother. Perhaps she realizes that he will one day receive a different name.

בראשית פרק כה:כז

(כז) וַיִּגְדְּלוּ֙ הַנְּעָרִ֔ים וַיְהִ֣י עֵשָׂ֗ו אִ֛ישׁ יֹדֵ֥עַ צַ֖יִד אִ֣ישׁ שָׂדֶ֑ה וְיַעֲקֹב֙ אִ֣ישׁ תָּ֔ם יֹשֵׁ֖ב אֹהָלִֽים:

The boys grew, and Esav became a skillful hunter, a man of the field, while Yaakov was a pure man who dwelled in the tents. (*Bereishit* 25:27)

We would have thought that Yitzchak, one of the founding fathers of the Jewish People, would have preferred the man of the tents to the hunter. After all, of the two sons, Yaakov was the one who should have reminded Yitzchak of his own saintly father Avraham, who was famed for his tent, his hospitality, his unique methods of spreading monotheism among those whom he welcomed to his home. Why, then, did Yitzchak favor Esav?

The Torah provides an answer:

בראשית פרק כה:כח

וַיֶּאֱהַ֥ב יִצְחָ֛ק אֶת־עֵשָׂ֖ו כִּי־צַ֣יִד בְּפִ֑יו וְרִבְקָ֖ה אֹהֶ֥בֶת אֶֽת־יַעֲקֹֽב:

Yitzchak loved Esav, because he ate of his venison; but Rivkah loved Yaakov. (*Bereishit* 25:28)

This short verse is striking, for two reasons: Once again, it points up the dysfunctionality of this family, in which each parent favors a different child. Additionally, we are struck by the assymetry of the parents' favoritism: Yitzchak's love for Esav seems conditional; it is "*talui be-davar.*" Yitzchak loved his son Esav "*ki tzayid be-fiv*" (literally, "for the hunt was in his mouth"), while Rivkah's love for Yaakov was unconditional. Yitzchak's relationship with Esav is most perplexing;

can it be that the father simply loved to eat the meat his son brought him? Was he perhaps enchanted by Esav's daring and adventurous personality? Can this be the whole story?

The story of Yaakov's surreptitious acquisition of the blessings his father intended for Esav is well known. This episode, coupled with the Torah's declaration of Yitzchak's love for Esav, leads many readers to misinterpret Yitzchak's feelings for each of his sons. While some assume that Yitzchak loved Esav more than he loved Yaakov, the text does not bear this out. Additionally, it is incorrect to assume that Yitzchak intended to bequeath Avraham's legacy to Esav; this is certainly not the case. Yitzchak knew exactly who Yaakov and Esav were, what their respective strengths and weaknesses were. Nonetheless, unlike his wife who possessed "inside information" regarding their destinies, Yitzchak dared to dream that his son Esav, the hunter, might yet be part of God's plan. While Rivkah knew that the two sons would become separate nations, Yitzchak continued to believe, or at least to hope, that they would remain one family. A careful reading of the blessings he intends for each son illustrates Yitzchak's mindset.

In *Parashat Toldot*, Yitzchak imparts three blessings upon his two sons. The first was intended for Esav, but was surreptitiously taken by Yaakov. The second was bestowed upon Esav; Yitzchak was fully aware that it was Esav who stood before him when he gave this blessing. The third and final blessing was given to Yaakov; Yitzchak knew he was addressing Yaakov, and he also knew that Yaakov had already taken the first blessing by guile.

The first blessing, intended for Esav but taken by Yaakov, is certainly a beautiful one.

בראשית פרק כז:כח-כט
וְיִתֶּן־לְךָ הָאֱלֹהִים מִטַּל הַשָּׁמַיִם וּמִשְׁמַנֵּי הָאָרֶץ וְרֹב דָּגָן וְתִירֹשׁ: יַעַבְדוּךָ עַמִּים וְיִשְׁתַּחֲווּ לְךָ לְאֻמִּים הֱוֵה גְבִיר לְאַחֶיךָ וְיִשְׁתַּחֲווּ לְךָ בְּנֵי אִמֶּךָ אֹרְרֶיךָ אָרוּר וּמְבָרֲכֶיךָ בָּרוּךְ:

May God give you from the dew of the heavens and the fat of the earth, and the fullness of grain and wine. Nations will be subservient to you, and peoples will bow to you. You will be your brother's master, and the sons of your mother will bow to you. Those you curse shall be accursed and those you bless shall be blessed. (*Bereishit* 27:28–29)

When Esav stands before his father and understands that his brother has taken the blessing intended for him, Esav cries to Yitzchak, "Bless me as well, Father!" But Yitzchak is very clear:

בראשית פרק כז:לד-לה

... וַיֹּאמֶר לְאָבִיו בָּרֲכֵנִי גַם־אָנִי אָבִי: וַיֹּאמֶר בָּא אָחִיךָ בְּמִרְמָה וַיִּקַּח בִּרְכָתֶךָ:

"Your brother came in deception and took *your* blessing." (*Bereishit* 27:34-35)

The blessing intended for Esav but taken by Yaakov speaks of wealth and power. What it neglects to mention is a spiritual mission or message. It was never Yitzchak's intention to leave these spiritual gifts to his elder son. After bestowing the blessing for prosperity and plenty on Yaakov, Yitzchak seems to have "run out" of blessings; he is unable to give Esav the spiritual blessing that has not yet been bestowed on Yaakov. This becomes even more obvious when Yaakov is about to leave home, and Yitzchak summons him and blesses him:

בראשית פרק כח:ג-ד

(ג) וְאֵל שַׁדַּי יְבָרֵךְ אֹתְךָ וְיַפְרְךָ וְיַרְבֶּךָ וְהָיִיתָ לִקְהַל עַמִּים: (ד) וְיִתֶּן־לְךָ אֶת־בִּרְכַּת אַבְרָהָם לְךָ וּלְזַרְעֲךָ אִתָּךְ לְרִשְׁתְּךָ אֶת־אֶרֶץ מְגֻרֶיךָ אֲשֶׁר־נָתַן אֱלֹהִים לְאַבְרָהָם:

The Almighty God will bless you and make you fruitful and numerous, and you will become a great nation. He will grant you the blessing of Avraham, for you and your descendants, to inherit the land of your sojournings which the Almighty gave to Avraham. (*Bereishit* 28:3–4)

Evidently, Yitzchak did have another blessing to give. This "blessing of Avraham," which included the inheritance of the Land of Israel, was a spiritual blessing, and it was always intended for Yaakov; Yitzchak could not and would not give it to Esav. The blessing of power and wealth which Yaakov took had always been intended for Esav; only through Rivkah's intervention, Yaakov received both the spiritual and the physical blessings.[5]

Yitzchak apparently felt that the son who was devoted to spiritual pursuits should receive only spiritual blessings, while the son who was was devoted to physical pursuits should only be given blessings involving the physical realm. Rivkah's understanding was quite different; she felt that her spiritual son would not survive without the physical blessing as well. Apparently, God agreed with Rivkah.

Perhaps Yitzchak pitied Esav; perhaps he felt that if Esav would be a hunter, dedicating his life to physical pursuits, he would be better off

---

5. There is also a fourth blessing: The blessing given by God to Yaakov after he leaves home (*Bereishit* 28:12-16), which echoes Yitzchak's blessing to Yaakov. It is a blessing for the Land of Israel and for numerous descendents; the elements that make up the blessing Yaakov took from Esav are noticeably absent, which might make us wonder if blessings can actually be "stolen." Would Yaakov ever benefit from the "stolen" blessings? Perhaps the point of the entire ruse was not to procure the blessings for Yaakov, but to prevent Esav from receiving them.

בראשית פרק כח:יב-טז

(יב) וַיַּחֲלֹם וְהִנֵּה סֻלָּם מֻצָּב אַרְצָה וְרֹאשׁוֹ מַגִּיעַ הַשָּׁמָיְמָה וְהִנֵּה מַלְאֲכֵי אֱלֹהִים עֹלִים וְיֹרְדִים בּוֹ: (יג) וְהִנֵּה ה' נִצָּב עָלָיו וַיֹּאמַר אֲנִי ה' אֱלֹהֵי אַבְרָהָם אָבִיךָ וֵאלֹהֵי יִצְחָק הָאָרֶץ אֲשֶׁר אַתָּה שֹׁכֵב עָלֶיהָ לְךָ אֶתְּנֶנָּה וּלְזַרְעֶךָ: (יד) וְהָיָה זַרְעֲךָ כַּעֲפַר הָאָרֶץ וּפָרַצְתָּ יָמָּה וָקֵדְמָה וְצָפֹנָה וָנֶגְבָּה וְנִבְרְכוּ בְךָ כָּל מִשְׁפְּחֹת הָאֲדָמָה וּבְזַרְעֶךָ: (טו) וְהִנֵּה אָנֹכִי עִמָּךְ וּשְׁמַרְתִּיךָ בְּכֹל אֲשֶׁר תֵּלֵךְ וַהֲשִׁבֹתִיךָ אֶל הָאֲדָמָה הַזֹּאת כִּי לֹא אֶעֱזָבְךָ עַד אֲשֶׁר אִם עָשִׂיתִי אֵת אֲשֶׁר דִּבַּרְתִּי לָךְ:

And he dreamed, and beheld a ladder set up on the earth, and the top of it reached to heaven; and behold, angels of God were ascending and descending on it. And, behold, the Lord stood above it [or, above him], and said, "I am the Almighty, God of Avraham your father, and the God of Yitzchak; the land on which you lie, to you will I give it, and to your descendants; And your descendants shall be [numerous] as the dust of the earth, and you shall surge forth to the west, and to the east, and to the north, and to the south; and in you and in your descendants shall all the families of the earth be blessed. And, behold, I am with you, and I will protect you everywhere you go, and I will bring you back to this land; for I will not leave you until I have done that about which I have spoken to you."

prospering by God's hand than by utilizing his own unsavory tactics to succeed. Whatever his rationale might have been, it is clear from the text that Yitzchak's love for Esav was, indeed, conditional, and therefore limited. It seems, though, that Yitzchak was fully aware of the different capabilities of his two sons:[6] Yaakov reminded him of his own father, and Esav reminded him of his father's adversary and would-be executioner, Nimrod. Esav is described as a hunter; the only other person described in this way was Nimrod.[7] Yitzchak had no doubt about Yaakov's capabilities; he knew that his younger son would live a life imbued with spirituality. The other child, Esav, was far more challenging: Yitzchak loved him for his hunting, and was intrigued with the idea of bringing those capabilities under control, of harnessing Esav's wild power and bringing him in as a partner for Yaakov. In his mind's eye, Yitzchak

---

6. See comments of Rav Hirsch, *Bereishit* 27:1:

רש״ר הירש בראשית פרק כז:א

שני בניו של יצחק ייצגו שני יסודות בביתו; עשו - את הכוח החומרי, יעקב - את הכוח הרוחני. יודע היה יצחק, כי האומה זקוקה לשני הכיוונים. אף הוא כנראה ידע את הנבואה, כי הרב בכוחו החומרי יעבוד לצעיר ולחלש ממנו: "ורב יעבד צעיר". אך כסבור היה יצחק, שעשו ויעקב יקיימו את תעודת אברהם בכוחות משותפים, בלב אחים ומתוך השלמה הדדית; לפיכך הועיד לעשו ברכה בעלת תוכן חומרי, וברכה רוחנית היתה שמורה עמו ליעקב. ברכה זו, שנר עדה ליעקב, היתה חסרת כל ערך לעשו, שכן מטבעו לא היתה לו כל הבנה לצד הרוחני של בית אברהם. אולם, מבית לבן ידעה רבקה כי הקללה שבפיצול זה, ידעה מנסיונה, שהחומר יהיה לברכה וישועה רק בבית שרוח אברהם מפעמת בו, רק בידו של זה שרוחו של אברהם מדריכה אותו. היא היטיבה לראות: החומר שאין עמו רוח, היה בעיניה קללה, את הברכה ראתה רק בלתי מחולקת, יורדת על ראשו של אחד. שיקולים אלה יסבירו לנו את מעשי שניהם,

7. *Bereishit* 1:8,9. Also see 1 *Divrei ha-Yamim* 1:10, where Nimrod is described as a warrior, but not as a hunter.

בראשית פרק י:ח-ט

(ח) וְכוּשׁ יָלַד אֶת־נִמְרֹד הוּא הֵחֵל לִהְיוֹת גִּבֹּר בָּאָרֶץ: (ט) הוּא־הָיָה גִבֹּר־צַיִד לִפְנֵי ה' עַל־כֵּן יֵאָמַר כְּנִמְרֹד גִּבּוֹר צַיִד לִפְנֵי ה':

And Cush begot Nimrod, who was the first man of might on earth. He was a mighty hunter before God; hence the saying, "Like Nimrod a mighty hunter before God.

דברי הימים א פרק א:י

(י) וְכוּשׁ יָלַד אֶת־נִמְרוֹד הוּא הֵחֵל לִהְיוֹת גִּבּוֹר בָּאָרֶץ: ס

And Cush begot Nimrod; he was the first man of might on earth.

imagined what might have been if Avraham and Nimrod had joined forces: Perhaps their combined talents could have ushered in the Messianic Age. Now, Yitzchak hoped to realize this potential through Esav and Yaakov, and sought to engineer this historic union.

In a sense, it was easy for Yitzchak to imagine the spiritual life Yaakov would lead; the thought of Esav, his wild son, being involved in spirituality by partnering with Yaakov, was irresistible to Yitzchak.[8] Esav, for his part, never wanted to disappoint his father, and he did his best to show Yitzchak his positive side,[9] giving his father hope that this plan could work.

---

8. See *Sfat Emet, Bereshit, Parashat Toldot* 5651:

שפת אמת ספר בראשית - פרשת תולדות - שנת [תרנ"א]

בענין ברכת יצחק שרצה ליתנה לעשו. ובפי' נראה כי ברכת יעקב היתה מיוחדת אליו כמו שברכו לבסוף ברכת אברהם שהוא עיקר הברית שכרת השי"ת לזרעו אחריו. אבל זו הברכה היא להיות גביר לאחיו כו'. כי יעקב ועשו היו מיוחדין לב' עולמות כמ"ש עשו איש שדה ויעקב יושב אהלים ואם הי' עשו מתקן מעשיו הי' הוא כמו זבולון עם יששכר והוא הי' מושל על כל האומות להכין הכל לקרב אל הקדושה. ולא הי' נצרך ליעקב רק לעסוק בתורת ה' בלי מלחמות. כי הרי כתיב ראשית גוים עמלק. והוא איש שדה. דיש מדבר שדה בית כמ"ש האר"י ז"ל בקבלת שבת נעשה ממדבר שדה ע"ש. ושבת עצמו הוא בחי' אהל ובית. והנה יעקב הוא בחי' השבת יושב אהלים כמ"ש בשבת אל יצא איש ממקומו. וכמא' חז"ל יעקב כתוב בו שמירת שבת כו'. אבל התקונים שצריך בימי המעשה לעשות ממדבר שדה. והוא הכנה אל השבת דרך זה רצה יצחק להנחיל לעשו. אך כי לא זכה עשו לזה. והוצרך לקבל יעקב גם זאת על שכמו לתקן עוה"ז.

9. Rashi (*Bereishit* 25:27) states that Esav deceived his father as to his true nature by asking him questions on matters of religious observance; we might wonder, though, what Esav's motivation was: Was he trying to mislead or mock his father, or was he simply trying (but failing) to be the type of son he thought his father wanted him to be?

רש"י בראשית פרשת תולדות פרק כה פסוק כז

יֹדֵעַ צַיִד - לָצוּד וּלְרַמּוֹת אֶת אָבִיו בְּפִיו וְשׁוֹאֲלוֹ אַבָּא, הֵיאַךְ מְעַשְּׂרִין אֶת הַמֶּלַח וְאֶת הַתֶּבֶן? כְּסָבוּר אָבִיו שֶׁהוּא מְדַקְדֵּק בְּמִצְוֹת:

"A cunning hunter" (literally, one who knows hunting) — [Esav] understandood how to entrap and deceive his father with his mouth. He would ask him, "Father how should salt and straw be tithed" (although he knew full well that these are not subject to the law of tithes)? Consequently, his father believed him to be scrupulous in his observance of the commandments.

Yitzchak knew that Esav was a hunter; by commanding him to bring him food, he turned the hunt into a mitzvah.[10] Yitzchak's goal was to bring spirituality to the son who immersed himself in physical pursuits. If we listen carefully we can hear Yitzchak's excitement when his son comes to him for his blessing:

בראשית פרק כז, יח-כב

(יח) וַיָּבֹא אֶל־אָבִיו וַיֹּאמֶר אָבִי וַיֹּאמֶר הִנֶּנִּי מִי אַתָּה בְּנִי: (יט) וַיֹּאמֶר יַעֲקֹב אֶל־אָבִיו אָנֹכִי עֵשָׂו בְּכֹרֶךָ עָשִׂיתִי כַּאֲשֶׁר דִּבַּרְתָּ אֵלָי קוּם־נָא שְׁבָה וְאָכְלָה מִצֵּידִי בַּעֲבוּר תְּבָרֲכַנִּי נַפְשֶׁךָ: (כ) וַיֹּאמֶר יִצְחָק אֶל־בְּנוֹ מַה־זֶּה מִהַרְתָּ לִמְצֹא בְּנִי וַיֹּאמֶר כִּי הִקְרָה ה' אֱלֹהֶיךָ לְפָנָי: (כא) וַיֹּאמֶר יִצְחָק אֶל־יַעֲקֹב גְּשָׁה־נָּא וַאֲמֻשְׁךָ בְּנִי הַאַתָּה זֶה בְּנִי עֵשָׂו אִם־לֹא: (כב) וַיִּגַּשׁ יַעֲקֹב אֶל־יִצְחָק אָבִיו וַיְמֻשֵּׁהוּ וַיֹּאמֶר הַקֹּל קוֹל יַעֲקֹב וְהַיָּדַיִם יְדֵי עֵשָׂו:

He went to his father and said, "Father." And he said, "Yes, which of my sons are you?" Yaakov said to his father, "I am Esav, your firstborn; I have done as you told me. Pray sit up and eat of my game, that you may give me your heartfelt blessing." Yitzchak said to his son, "How did you succeed so quickly, my son?" And he said, "Because the Almighty your God granted me good fortune." Yitzchak said to Yaakov, "Come closer that I may feel you, my son—whether you are really my son Esav or

---

10. See comments of Rav Hirsch, *Bereishit* 27:2-4:

רש"ר הירש בראשית פרק כז:ב-ד

לפי זה ברור הדבר גם כאן. יצחק רצה לברך את עשו ברוח ייעודו שלעתיד. כדרך שהוא קיווה, שנטיותיו עתידות להיות לברכה למטרות נעלות, כן ביקש לראותו בשעת הברכה. יש להעלות את מלאכת הציד האכזרית, ולעשותה כלי שרת למטרה אנושית נעלה. ואכן נראה, שלא היה עשו רגיל אצל הציד, כדי להביא תבשיל מבריא לאביו הזקן והחלוש. נפשו חשקה בציד, בדם המהביל, בהתגברות על כוח החיה. אך לא היה זה ממידותיו של עשו לצוד ציד עבור חולה שנחלש, למען יסעד בו הלה את לבו. "שא נא כליך, וצודה לי ציד, ועשה לי מטעמים" - אתה עצמך, השתמש הפעם בכלי אומנותך, כדי לעשות חסד עם אדם, כדי לסעוד את לבבו של זקן; תחוש גם אתה בסיפוק הבא לו לאדם, בשעה שהוא מהנה את זולתו. משום כך, בברכה שהוא נותן למי שנדמה לו כעשו, הוא מכוון אותו ממלאכת הציד אל "השדה אשר ברכו ה'", אל החקלאות, אל שמירת העושר של חיי האומה היהודית. סעד הלב והברכה הבאה בעקבותיו רמוזים במליצה: "בעבור תברכך נפשי". משום כך בפסוק ה: הפעם הלך עשו לצוד ציד במטרה להביא הביתה.

not." So Yaakov drew close to his father Yitzchak, who felt him, and declared: "The voice is the voice of Yaakov, yet the hands are the hands of Esav." (Bereishit 27:18-22)

Yitzchak was elated by what he heard: Esav had begun to speak like Yaakov! The voice—the kindness, the gentleness, the respect, and the reference to God's involvement in his successful hunting expedition—all of these were the voice of Yaakov. Yitzchak was not confused or wary; he did not wonder why he heard "the voice of the voice of Yaakov" coupled with "the hands of Esav;" had he been in doubt, he would have stopped to investigate further before bestowing the blessing on his son. No, Yitzchak was not confused, he was overjoyed; he believed that his plan to unite his two sons had come to fruition. He heard precisely what he had always hoped to hear—the fusion of the very different capabilities of each of his sons. Little did he realize that in fact it was Yaakov who had taken on Esav's hands, and not Esav who had taken on Yaakov's voice. Later, when Yitzchak is confronted with his error, he nonetheless Yitzchak confirms that the blessing which he bestowed upon Yaakov would not be rescinded:

בראשית פרק כז:לג
(לג) וַיֶּחֱרַד יִצְחָק חֲרָדָה גְּדֹלָה עַד־מְאֹד וַיֹּאמֶר מִי־אֵפוֹא הוּא הַצָּד־צַיִד וַיָּבֵא לִי וָאֹכַל מִכֹּל בְּטֶרֶם תָּבוֹא וָאֲבָרֲכֵהוּ גַּם־בָּרוּךְ יִהְיֶה:

And Yitzchak was seized with great dread and he said, 'Who, then, was the hunter who brought me food, which I consumed before you arrived, and whom I blessed? He, nonetheless is blessed.'" (Bereishit 27:33)

When the real Esav enters, he is less respectful, even somewhat gruff:

בראשית פרק כז:לא
(לא) וַיַּעַשׂ גַּם־הוּא מַטְעַמִּים וַיָּבֵא לְאָבִיו וַיֹּאמֶר לְאָבִיו יָקֻם אָבִי וְיֹאכַל מִצֵּיד בְּנוֹ בַּעֲבוּר תְּבָרֲכַנִּי נַפְשֶׁךָ:

He too prepared a dish and brought it to his father. And he said to his father, "Let my father sit up and eat of his son's game, so that you may give me your heartfelt blessing." (*Bereishit* 27:31)

The Sages hint at a deeper understanding of the text, which will shed light on the perspective of Yitzchak. When Yaakov stands before his father to receive the blessing, Yitzchak is under the impression that he is Esav.

בראשית פרק כז, כז

וַיִּגַּשׁ וַיִּשַּׁק־לוֹ וַיָּרַח אֶת־רֵיחַ בְּגָדָיו וַיְבָרֲכֵהוּ וַיֹּאמֶר רְאֵה רֵיחַ בְּנִי כְּרֵיחַ שָׂדֶה אֲשֶׁר בֵּרֲכוֹ ה':

[Yaakov] came near and kissed [his father], and [Yitzchak] smelled the scent of his clothes and blessed him. He [Yitzchak] said, "Behold the scent of my son is like the scent of a *field* that is blessed by God." (*Bereishit* 27:27)

What is Yitzchak smelling?

בראשית רבה [וילנא] פרשה סה ד"ה כב ולא הכירו

(בראשית כז, כז): וַיִּגַּשׁ וַיִּשַּׁק לוֹ וַיָּרַח אֶת רֵיחַ בְּגָדָיו, אָמַר רַבִּי יוֹחָנָן אֵין לְךָ דָּבָר שֶׁרֵיחוֹ קָשֶׁה מִן הַשֶּׁטֶף הַזֶּה שֶׁל עִזִּים וְאַתְּ אָמַרְתְּ וַיָּרַח אֶת רֵיחַ בְּגָדָיו וַיְבָרֲכֵהוּ, אֶלָּא בְּשָׁעָה שֶׁנִּכְנַס יַעֲקֹב אָבִינוּ אֵצֶל אָבִיו נִכְנְסָה עִמּוֹ גַּן עֵדֶן, הֲדָא הוּא דַּאֲמַר לֵיהּ (בראשית כז, כז): רְאֵה רֵיחַ בְּנִי כְּרֵיחַ שָׂדֶה, וּבְשָׁעָה שֶׁנִּכְנַס עֵשָׂו אֵצֶל אָבִיו נִכְנְסָה עִמּוֹ גֵּיהִנֹּם,

R. Yochanan said: There is no harsher scent than the stench of goats that was on his clothing, yet the text says he "smells the scent of his clothes and blesses him!" Rather, when the Patriarch Yaakov entered to his father, Gan Eden entered with him.... And when Esav entered to his father, Gehinom [Hell] entered with him. (*Bereishit Rabbah* 65:22)

The observation of the Midrash is striking: Yaakov enters in clothing saturated with blood and sweat, and Yitzchak speaks of "the scent of a field that is blessed by God," referring to the Garden of Eden. We noted earlier that Yitzchak's spiritual identity is somehow related to "the field." After the *Akeidah*, the text does not describe the descent of Yitzchak from the mountain. We do not see Yitzchak in the next number of sections in the Torah. He is absent from the description of the death and burial of Sarah. Even when Avraham's servant searches for a bride for him, Yitzchak is absent. The next time we see Yitzchak is when we find him in a *field*:

בראשית פרק כד:סג
וַיֵּצֵא יִצְחָק לָשׂוּחַ בַּשָּׂדֶה לִפְנוֹת עָרֶב וַיִּשָּׂא עֵינָיו וַיַּרְא וְהִנֵּה גְמַלִּים בָּאִים:

Yitzchak went out to pray in the field toward evening. (*Bereishit* 24:63)

Yitzchak, who was last seen on an altar, ready and willing to be sacrificed to God, now stands in a *field* and gazes heavenward. Specifically from the field, Yitzchak searches for God. What was Yitzchak trying to accomplish there? The answer lies in the scent of Eden, a scent that was associated with a time prior to the sin of Adam, before man is cursed to work the field. It is possible that Esav was attracted to the field, in part, because of his father, Yitzchak. Esav knew of his father's attraction to the field.

If the physical realm can be elevated in the service of God, then the sin of Adam can be rectified. When Yaakov enters and Yitzchak smells Paradise, Yitzchak believes that his son has succeeded in mending the world, returning that scent of Gan Eden to the world. Of course, when the real Esav enters, the gates of Hell are opened, and Yitzchak sadly realizes how far the world is from perfection. Yaakov, who sat and learned in the tents, and not Esav, who hunted, had the scent of Paradise on him. Perfection will not come from the man of the fields; it will come from the *ish tam*, the "complete man," Yaakov.

Bringing perfection to the world will not be an easy task. Yaakov's odyssey will take him on a circuitous route far from the tents which he has called home. He is forced now to leave the tents, to quite ironically become a man of the field. Just as Avraham had to grow in a trait against his nature, so too, Yaakov will have to leave his natural habitat and become a worldly man—a man of the field. As we have seen, the greatness of the patriarchs was in creating new aspects of self, new avenues toward the worship of God.

בראשית פרק ל:טז
וַיָּבֹא יַעֲקֹב מִן הַשָּׂדֶה בָּעֶרֶב וַתֵּצֵא לֵאָה לִקְרָאתוֹ...

Yaakov came out of the field in the evening, and Leah went out to meet him.... (*Bereishit* 30:16)

Things have now come full circle; Yaakov, the pure man of the tents, has now become a man of the field. He has taken the responsibility of Esav, in addition to his own mission.[11]

---

11. Some kabbalists explain that Yaakov is in a sense now leading two lives: his own life, and the life of Esav. This explains why Yaakov had two wives: Rachel, who was always destined for Yaakov, and Leah, who was destined for Esav. See Leshem, *Hakdamot u-Shearim*, shaar 7, chapter 5.

ספר לשם שבו ואחלמה - הקדמות ושערים - שער ז פרק ה
והנה באם שהיינו זוכים שיתגלה האור הפנימי דכל המלכות הכללי ושייצאו הנשמות דהי"ב שבטים מהמלכות הכללי כתיקונן הנה היה ראוי שיוצא ממנה נשמת יעקב וישראל מצד החד סדים שבה ונשמת רחל ולאה כלולה מבלהה וזלפה באחוריהם והם כולן מצד הגבורות שבה שיהיו כל אלו הד' נשים כולן רק גוף אחד לבד כמו יעקב וישראל והיתה נקראת כולה רק בשם רחל לבד שהיא עיקרה של בית המנהגת את כל העולמות בי"ע ור"ל שכל גילויו ית"ש בהנהגת הבי"ע הוא רק בה ולכן היו נקראות כולן על שם רחל ומהם שניהם שהוא מישראל ורחל היה ראוי שיוצאים כל הי"ב שבטים כולם אשר הם מושרשים בהפנימיות דרחל הכללי דאצילות וכנז' והנה זה היה אז האמהות ג"כ רק ג'.כמו האבות וכן יעקב וישראל היה נקרא מאז רק בשם ישראל לבד ע"ד שהוא באברהם שהנקורא לאברהם אברם עובר בלאו ועשה כמ"ש בברכות ספ"ק כי שם ישראל וכן שורש לאה הנה הוא בשכינתא עלאה שהוא בחי' המוחין והדעת אשר במלכות הכללי וכאשר היה משתתף ומתפשט כל המלכות הכללי כולה בה-עולמות בי"ע ביחודה כהראוי הרי לא היה בחי' חלוקות כלל בין שכינתא עלאה לתתאה כי היה כולה מתגלית בבי"ע ביחודה שלמעלה ולכן היה נקרא יעקב רק בשם ישראל שהוא אור הדעת שבה שהיה מתפשט ומתגלה ג"כ למטה וכן לאה ורחל היו לגוף אחד שהוא בחי' המוחין המתייחדים ומאירים בהגוף והיו נקרא על שם רחל משום שהיא הגילוי העיקרי אשר בבחי'

As a result of this meeting with Leah in the field, two children enter the world—Yissachar and Zevulun. These two sons will have a different type of relationship: They will succeed where Yaakov and Esav failed.[12]

בראשית רבה [וילנא] פרשה צט ד"ה ט זבולן לחוף

זְבוּלֻן לְחוֹף יַמִּים יִשְׁכֹּן (בראשית מט: יג), הֲרֵי זְבוּלוּן קָדַם לְיִשָּׂשכָר שֶׁכֵּן מְיַחֲסָן יִשָּׂשכָר זְבוּלוּן, וְלָמָּה כֵן, אֶלָּא שֶׁהָיָה זְבוּלוּן עוֹסֵק בִּפְרַקְמַטְיָא וְיִשָּׂשכָר עוֹסֵק בַּתּוֹרָה, וּזְבוּלוּן בָּא וּמַאֲכִילוֹ, לְפִיכָךְ קְדָמוֹ, עָלָיו אָמַר הַכָּתוּב (משלי ג, יח): עֵץ חַיִּים הִיא לַמַּחֲזִיקִים בָּהּ. יִשָּׂשכָר כּוֹנֵס וּזְבוּלוּן מֵבִיא בָּאֳנִיּוֹת וּמוֹכֵר וּמֵבִיא לוֹ כָּל צָרְכּוֹ, וְכֵן משֶׁה אוֹמֵר (דברים לג, יח): שְׂמַח זְבוּלֻן בְּצֵאתֶךָ, לָמָּה שֶׁיִּשָּׂשכָר בְּאֹהָלֶיךָ שֶׁלְּךָ הֵן שֶׁאַתְּ מַסִּיעוֹ לֵישֵׁב בָּהֶן.

"Zevulun will resides on the shores of the sea" [*Bereishit* 49:13] — Zevulun comes before Yissachar, though surely Yissachar was older than Zevulun, since their birth is thus recorded: Yissachar,

---

פרצוף ממש משא"כ לאה שהיא רק הארת הבינה לבד דהמוחין ולכן היה נכלל לאה ברחל שהוא הארת המוחין אשר בהפרצוף ועי"ז היתה כלולה פרצו' רחל מלמעלה למטה וכן ישראל שהיא מהמוחין והוא הדעת ממש המתפשט בת"ת שהוא יעקב הנה הוא נקרא על שם ישראל לחוד כי הוא נשמתו ממש והוא פנימית הפרצו' ועיקרו...

12. See *Sefat Emet*, Toldot 5651:

ספר שפת אמת - בראשית - פרשת תולדות - שנת [תרנ"א]

בענין ברכת יצחק שרצה ליתנה לעשו. ובפי' נראה כי ברכת יעקב היתה מיוחדת אליו כמו שברכו לבסוף ברכת אברהם שהוא עיקר הברית שכרת השי"ת לזרעו אחריו. אבל זו הברכה היא להיות גביר לאחיו כו'. כי יעקב ועשו היו מיוחדין לב' עולמות כמ"ש עשו איש שדה ויעקב יושב אהלים ואם הי' עשו מתקן מעשיו הי' הוא כמו זבולון עם יששכר והוא הי' מושל על כל האומות להכין הכל לקרב אל הקדושה. ולא הי' נצרך ליעקב רק לעסוק בתורת ה' בלי מלחמות. כי הרי כתיב ראשית גוים עמלק. דיש מדבר שדה ובית כמ"ש האר"י ז"ל בקבלת שבת נעשה ממדבר שדה ע"ש. ושבת עצמו הוא בחי' אהל ובית. והנה יעקב הוא בחי' השבת יושב אהלים כמ"ש בשבת אל יצא איש ממקומו. וכמא' חז"ל יעקב כתוב בו שמירת שבת כו'. אבל התקונין שצריך בימי המעשה לעשות ממדבר שדה. והוא הכנה אל השבת דרך זה רצה יצחק להנחיל לעשו. אך כי לא זכה עשו לזה. והוצרך לקבל יעקב גם זאת על שכמו לתקן עוה"ז. ובמדרש שובי השולמית כו' ע"ש שהוא התאספות שצריכין בנ"י לאסוף בכל הד' מלכיות להוציא בלעם מפיהם ולהעלות עוה"ז להיות מוכן לקבל השפעת הקדושה. [ויתכן לומר שהוא בחי' המלבושים שהי' עשו ונמסרו ליעקב שהוא תיקון החיצוניות. בשל"ה הוא מלבו"ש. ואיתא כי עשו גי' שלום. אך שהרע את מעשיו וניתן ליעקב]. וז"ש אני שלום וכי אדבר המה למלחמה כידוע שסתם מלחמה הוא עשו ועמלק. וכמ"ש במדרש אין לך מלחמה שנוצחת שלא יהי' בה מזרע עשו. והי' מוכן שיהי' נלחם מלחמת מצוה. הכנה ליעקב. אם הי' מתקן מעשיו לטוב:

Zevulun. Why is it so? Because Zevulun engaged in commerce, while Yissachar studied Torah, and Zevulun came and provided him with sustenance. Therefore he is given precedence. Of him [Scripture says], "It [Torah] is a tree of life to them that uphold it" [*Mishlei* 3:18]. Yissachar gathered [knowledge] while Zevulun brought [merchandise] in ships, sold it, and provided him with all his needs. And thus too said Moshe: "Rejoice, Zevulun, in your travels" [*Devarim* 33:18]. Why? Because "Yissachar [is] in your tents": they are *your* [Zevulun's] tents, since you enable [Zevulun] to sit in them [and study]. (*Bereishit Rabbah* 99:9)

Despite their differences, Yissachar and Zevulun were partners, working together toward one common goal. Perhaps this was Yitzchak's dream, that his two sons work together to mend the world. The dream was not realized by Yitzchak's children, for Esav did not accept the responsibility of serving God. Only in future generations, Yaakov's children bring their grandfather's dream to its fruition.

Perhaps this insight offers a new perspective on an earlier passage in the *parashah*:

בראשית פרק כה, כט-לג

(כט) וַיָּזֶד יַעֲקֹב נָזִיד וַיָּבֹא עֵשָׂו מִן־הַשָּׂדֶה וְהוּא עָיֵף: (ל) וַיֹּאמֶר עֵשָׂו אֶל־יַעֲקֹב הַלְעִיטֵנִי נָא מִן־הָאָדֹם הָאָדֹם הַזֶּה כִּי עָיֵף אָנֹכִי עַל־כֵּן קָרָא־שְׁמוֹ אֱדוֹם: (לא) וַיֹּאמֶר יַעֲקֹב מִכְרָה כַיּוֹם אֶת־בְּכֹרָתְךָ לִי: (לב) וַיֹּאמֶר עֵשָׂו הִנֵּה אָנֹכִי הוֹלֵךְ לָמוּת וְלָמָּה־זֶּה לִי בְּכֹרָה: (לג) וַיֹּאמֶר יַעֲקֹב הִשָּׁבְעָה לִּי כַּיּוֹם וַיִּשָּׁבַע לוֹ וַיִּמְכֹּר אֶת־בְּכֹרָתוֹ לְיַעֲקֹב:

Yaakov cooked pottage, and Esav came from the field, exhausted. Esav said to Yaakov, "Give me, I beg you, some of that red pottage; for I am exhausted." Therefore his name was called "Edom." Yaakov said, "Sell me this day your birthright." Esav said, "Behold, I am on the verge of death. Why do I need this birthright?" Yaakov said, "Swear to me this day." He swore to him, and sold his birthright to Yaakov. (*Bereishit* 25:29–33)

This negotiation seems strange; how can Yaakov be so petty as to use his brother's hunger as leverage to force him to sell his birthright? The text, however, says nothing about hunger: Esav is described—and describes himself—as *exhausted*, and it is this exhaustion that indicated to Yaakov that Yitzchak's vision would not be realized. Yitzchak envisioned a partnership between his two sons, and he invested his parenting in teaching them to join forces—Esav in the field and Yaakov in the tents—as Yissachar and Zevulun would later do. Yaakov and Esav were groomed to be team players. Esav, the fearless hunter, would be in charge of the physical world, while Yaakov's domain would be the spiritual world. Rivkah, however, encouraged Yaakov to abandon his father's fantasy. She had always known that this was not the way things would unfold. God had spoken to her, and she knew that only her younger son would achieve greatness:

בראשית פרק כה:כג
וַיֹּאמֶר ה' לָהּ שְׁנֵי גוֹיִם בְּבִטְנֵךְ וּשְׁנֵי לְאֻמִּים מִמֵּעַיִךְ יִפָּרֵדוּ וּלְאֹם מִלְאֹם יֶאֱמָץ וְרַב יַעֲבֹד צָעִיר:

God said to her, "Two nations are in your womb, and two peoples shall be separated from your bowels. One people shall be stronger than the other, and the elder shall serve the younger." (*Bereishit* 25:23)

Yaakov was caught in the middle of two narratives, two dreams or visions: his father's dream of partnership, and his mother's vision of his superiority over his older brother. When Esav came in from the field exhausted and in search of food, Yaakov realized that his mother's vision, and not his father's dream, would be realized: Esav was exhausted; the weight of his responsibilites weighed upon him, and he became either unable or unwilling to fulfill his role in the partnership. The moment Esav asked Yaakov to tend to his physical needs, he became undeserving of the birthright. He abdicated his rights when he abdicated his responsibilities; Yaakov understood that he would have to adopt both roles, that he would have to take responsibility for both the physical and the spiritual aspects of the partnership. For his part, Esav was relieved; he despised the responsibility, he despised the "birthright," and he was glad to be rid of it:

בראשית פרק כה:לד

(לד) וְיַעֲקֹב נָתַן לְעֵשָׂו לֶחֶם וּנְזִיד עֲדָשִׁים וַיֹּאכַל וַיֵּשְׁתְּ וַיָּקָם וַיֵּלַךְ וַיִּבֶז עֵשָׂו אֶת־הַבְּכֹרָה:

Then Yaakov gave Esav bread and pottage of lentils. He ate and drank, and rose and went on his way. Esav despised the birthright. (*Bereishit* 25:34)

From that moment forward, Yaakov took on both roles. He remained Yaakov, but took on the role of Esav, as well. Perhaps this explains why he said to his father, "I am Esav your firstborn;"[13] contractually, this was the truth. Yaakov had become Esav, and this new facet of Yaakov's personality—the part that grapples with the physical world, the element of strength that his mother wanted him to obtain by whatever means necessary, would be fully developed, to the point where a new name is warranted: Yisrael (Israel).[14]

---

13. *Bereishit* 27:19:

בראשית פרק כז:יט

וַיֹּאמֶר יַעֲקֹב אֶל־אָבִיו אָנֹכִי עֵשָׂו בְּכֹרֶךָ עָשִׂיתִי כַּאֲשֶׁר דִּבַּרְתָּ אֵלָי קוּם־נָא שְׁבָה וְאָכְלָה מִצֵּידִי בַּעֲבוּר תְּבָרֲכַנִּי נַפְשֶׁךָ:

Yaakov said to his father, "I am Esav, your first-born; I have done as you told me. Pray sit up and eat of my game, that you may give me your innermost blessing."

14. *Bereishit* 32:29; also see *Bereishit* 35:10:

בראשית פרק לב:כט

וַיֹּאמֶר לֹא יַעֲקֹב יֵאָמֵר עוֹד שִׁמְךָ כִּי אִם־יִשְׂרָאֵל כִּי־שָׂרִיתָ עִם־אֱלֹהִים וְעִם־אֲנָשִׁים וַתּוּכָל:

"He said, 'Your name shall no longer be Yaakov, but Yisrael, for you have striven with beings divine and human, and have prevailed.'"

Were Yitzchak's expectations for his two sons an error of judgment? Was his dream of a joining of the two different personalities and realms a mistake? Surely, in theory, this type of an arrangement could work. In practice, though, it was impossible—at least, at that point in time. Yitzchak's vision was quite different than Rivkah's; while she had a clear, realistic view, Yitzchak saw things from an idealistic vantage point. He saw the world through eyes of purity and service of God, from the point of view of complete dedication to Jewish destiny. Yitzchak's particular vantage point was, at all times, from atop the altar, high up on a holy mountain; his vision was forever affected by his awesome experience at the *Akeidah*:

בראשית רבה (וילנא) פרשת תולדות פרשה סה:י
דָּבָר אַחֵר, מֵרְאֹת, מִכֹּחַ אוֹתָהּ רְאִיָּה, שֶׁבְּשָׁעָה שֶׁעָקַד אַבְרָהָם אָבִינוּ אֶת בְּנוֹ עַל גַּבֵּי הַמִּזְבֵּחַ בָּכוּ מַלְאֲכֵי הַשָּׁרֵת, הֲדָא הוּא דִכְתִיב (ישעיה לג, ז): הֵן אֶרְאֶלָּם צָעֲקוּ חֻצָה וגו', וְנָשְׁרוּ דְּמָעוֹת מֵעֵינֵיהֶם לְתוֹךְ עֵינָיו, וְהָיוּ רְשׁוּמוֹת בְּתוֹךְ עֵינָיו, וְכֵיוָן שֶׁהִזְקִין כָּהוּ עֵינָיו, הֲדָא הוּא דִכְתִיב: וַיְהִי כִּי זָקֵן יִצְחָק, וגו' דָּבָר אַחֵר, מֵרְאֹת, מִכֹּחַ אוֹתָהּ הָרְאִיָּה, שֶׁבְּשָׁעָה שֶׁעָקַד אַבְרָהָם אָבִינוּ אֶת יִצְחָק בְּנוֹ עַל גַּבֵּי הַמִּזְבֵּחַ, תָּלָה עֵינָיו בַּמָּרוֹם וְהִבִּיט בַּשְּׁכִינָה.

[Why did Yitzchak become blind?] As a result of that event [the *Akeidah*]; for when our father Avraham bound his son Yitzchak, the ministering angels wept, as it says, "Behold, the valiant ones cry outside; the angels of peace weep bitterly" (*Yeshayahu* 33:7). Tears dropped from their eyes into his and left their mark upon them, and so when he became old his eyes dimmed.... Another interpretation of "[Yitzchak's eyes became dull] from seeing" is: [He became blind] through [seeing] that event [the *Akeidah*]; for when our father Avraham bound Yitzchak on the altar, he lifted up his eyes Heavenward and gazed at the *Shechinah*. (*Bereishit Rabbah* 65:10)

Yitzchak's experience as a potential offering caused him to see the world from a lofty, holy perspective, from a point halfway to heaven. He saw the world through holy lenses, as it were, which allowed him to see the holiness in Esav and to disregard or dismiss everything else. He saw the world in an idealized state; he saw "reality" as the way things could be, as they should be—as they will be, some day—which is why Esav's shortcomings apparently escaped him,[15] as did the vicissitudes of fortune Yaakov would have to endure in order to fulfill both roles.

In a very real sense, Yitzchak lived in the future; this had always been his essence, even before he was born; his name, *Yitzchak,* denotes this orientation. It means, literally, "he will laugh"—in future tense. Yitzchak's vision was neither false nor misguided; it was a true vision, but it was a vision that was ahead of its time. Yitzchak's vision will be realized at the end of history, when Esav will, indeed, assume the role his father had envisioned for him—the role Yaakov was forced to play for millennia.

---

15. Lest the reader think we are being "too harsh" on Esav, who was merely the victim of a plot "cooked up" by his mother and executed by his brother, we should note that Esav displays a total lack of sensitivity to the Abrahamic vision when he takes a wife (or two). On a very superficial level Esav behaves like his father and marries at the age of forty (*Bereishit* 26:34). Unlike his father, and in defiance of Avraham's wishes (for Yitzchak) Esav marries not one but two local girls (*Bereishit* 26:35). Both of his parents find Esav's choice disturbing. It should also be noted that later Esav is only bothered that his father is disappointed; his mother's feelings do not seem to concern him. Instead of separating himself from these problematic wives, he takes an additional wife in a misguided attempt to placate his father. (*Bereishit* 28:8-9)

בראשית פרק כו, לד-לה
(לד) וַיְהִי עֵשָׂו בֶּן אַרְבָּעִים שָׁנָה וַיִּקַּח אִשָּׁה אֶת יְהוּדִית בַּת בְּאֵרִי הַחִתִּי וְאֶת בָּשְׂמַת בַּת אֵילֹן הַחִתִּי: (לה) וַתִּהְיֶיןָ מֹרַת רוּחַ לְיִצְחָק וּלְרִבְקָה: ס

And Esav was forty years old when he married Judith the daughter of Beeri the Hittite, and Basemat the daughter of Elon the Hittite. And they made life bitter for Yitzchak and for Rivkah.

בראשית פרק כח:ח-ט
(ח) וַיַּרְא עֵשָׂו כִּי רָעוֹת בְּנוֹת כְּנָעַן בְּעֵינֵי יִצְחָק אָבִיו: (ט) וַיֵּלֶךְ עֵשָׂו אֶל יִשְׁמָעֵאל וַיִּקַּח אֶת מָחֲלַת בַּת יִשְׁמָעֵאל בֶּן אַבְרָהָם אֲחוֹת נְבָיוֹת עַל נָשָׁיו לוֹ לְאִשָּׁה:

And Esav saw that the daughters of Canaan displeased Yitzchak his father. Then Esav went to Yishmael, and took, besides the wives he had, Mahalat the daughter of Yishmael, Avraham's son, the sister of Nevayot, to be his wife.

בראשית רבה [וילנא] פרשה עח ד"ה יד יעבר נא

אָמַר רַבִּי אַבָּהוּ חָזַרְנוּ עַל כָּל הַמִּקְרָא וְלֹא מָצָאנוּ שֶׁהָלַךְ יַעֲקֹב אָצֶל עֵשָׂו לְהַר שֵׂעִיר מִיָּמָיו, אֶפְשָׁר יַעֲקֹב אֱמִתִּי הָיָה וּמְרַמֶּה בּוֹ, אֶלָּא אֵימָתַי הָיָה הוּא בָא אֶצְלוֹ, לֶעָתִיד לָבוֹא, הֲדָא הוּא דִכְתִיב (עובדיה א, כא): וְעָלוּ מוֹשִׁיעִים בְּהַר צִיּוֹן לִשְׁפֹּט אֶת הַר עֵשָׂו.

R. Abbahu said: "We have searched the whole of Scriptures and do not find that Yaakov ever went to Esav to the mountain of Seir (as he said he would). Is it then possible that Yaakov, who was a man of truth, deceived him? When would he come to him? In the Messianic era, as it is written: 'And liberators will ascend Mount Zion to judge the Mountain of Esav (and the kingdom shall be the Lords).' [*Ovadiah* 1:.[12"] (*Bereishit Rabbah* 78:14)

At the End of Days, the descendants of Esav will join forces with the children of Yaakov in order to complete their joint mission—either of their own volition, or through a process of terrifying judgment; either a partnership will finally be forged, or judgment will be pronounced against those who have shirked their responsibility for human destiny and *tikkun olam*.

תהלים פרק קכו

שִׁיר הַמַּעֲלוֹת בְּשׁוּב ה' אֶת-שִׁיבַת צִיּוֹן הָיִינוּ כְּחֹלְמִים: אָז יִמָּלֵא שְׂחוֹק פִּינוּ וּלְשׁוֹנֵנוּ רִנָּה אָז יֹאמְרוּ בַגּוֹיִם הִגְדִּיל ה' לַעֲשׂוֹת עִם-אֵלֶּה: הִגְדִּיל ה' לַעֲשׂוֹת עִמָּנוּ הָיִינוּ שְׂמֵחִים:

A song of ascents. When the Lord restores the fortunes of Zion—we see it as in a dream—then our mouths will be filled with laughter, our tongues, with songs of joy. Then shall they say among the nations, "The Lord has done great things for them!" The Lord will do great things for us and we shall rejoice. (*Tehillim* 126:1-3)

In the end of days, when the vision of Yitzchak comes to fruition, the children of Esav will come home. They will lend a supportive hand to Yaakov, and the joy of the completion of Yitzchak's vision for the perfection of human history will fill the world. Then, but not now, we, too, will experience Yitchak's sublime, spiritual laughter.

Parashat Vayeitzei

Antecedents of a Nation

Yaakov leaves Be'er Sheva and heads toward Charan. Ironically, he leaves laden with blessings, but he has no place to sleep. All the blessings which he possesses do not provide him with any shelter from the elements, and he sleeps under the stars with a stone for a pillow. There, on the ground, he dreams of a ladder[1] that reaches into the Heavens, with angels of God ascending and descending. God appears to Him and promises to give him the Land of Israel and to protect him wherever he goes.[2]

When he awakens, Yaakov is afraid:

> בראשית פרק כח:יז-כב
> וַיִּירָא וַיֹּאמַר מַה־נּוֹרָא הַמָּקוֹם הַזֶּה אֵין זֶה כִּי אִם־בֵּית אֱלֹהִים וְזֶה שַׁעַר הַשָּׁמָיִם: וַיַּשְׁכֵּם יַעֲקֹב בַּבֹּקֶר וַיִּקַּח אֶת־הָאֶבֶן אֲשֶׁר־שָׂם מְרַאֲשֹׁתָיו וַיָּשֶׂם אֹתָהּ מַצֵּבָה וַיִּצֹק שֶׁמֶן עַל־רֹאשָׁהּ: וַיִּקְרָא אֶת־שֵׁם־הַמָּקוֹם הַהוּא בֵּית־אֵל וְאוּלָם לוּז שֵׁם־הָעִיר לָרִאשֹׁנָה: וַיִּדַּר יַעֲקֹב נֶדֶר לֵאמֹר ... וְהָאֶבֶן הַזֹּאת אֲשֶׁר־שַׂמְתִּי מַצֵּבָה יִהְיֶה בֵּית אֱלֹהִים וְכֹל אֲשֶׁר תִּתֶּן־לִי עַשֵּׂר אֲעַשְּׂרֶנּוּ לָךְ:

He said, "How awesome is this place! This is none other than the House of God, and this is the gate to Heaven." When Yaakov awoke in the morning, he took the stone that was under his head, set it up as a monument, and poured oil over it. And he called the name of the place "Beit El" [House of God]; however, Luz was its original name. Yaakov vowed, "...This stone which I have put up as a pillar will become a House of God." (*Bereishit* 28:17–22)

---

1. Though *sulam* is translated as "ladder," we should note that the word is a *hapax legomenon*; this is its only appearance in the biblical text.
2. The blessings Yitzchak gave Yaakov at the end of *Parashat Toldot*, when he was fully aware that his younger son Yaakov stood before him, are repeated and confirmed by God in this encounter; the blessings which Yaakov took surreptitiously are not.

Yaakov encounters God, perhaps for the first time. His immediate response is to erect a monument, a *matzeivah*, which he vows to transform into a House of God upon his return to the Land of Israel. His behavior is understandable: Despite the blessings of fertility that were bestowed upon him, he is but one individual, and his vow is an expression of his aspirations. He hopes that upon his return he will realize the potential, and the blessings he received him will come to fruition.

The monument with which he marks the spot is a symbol of this hope: Although it is now only one rock, it will become an entire House of God. On another level, though, this *matzeivah* is an illustration or a physical manifestation of a greater underlying theme of this *parashah* as well as the *parashah* that follows: The underlying issue of *Vayeitzei* and *Vayishlach* is the transformation of Yaakov from a solitary, lonely "man on the run" to the leader of a clan which will in turn become a great nation. The pillar Yaakov anoints as he leaves his home symbolizes the individual's spiritual quest, while the "House of God" that will one day be built above it symbolizes a nation's place of worship.

However, this monument presents a problem—a technical legal problem—but a problem nonetheless. The Torah states:

דברים פרק טז:כב

וְלֹא־תָקִים לְךָ מַצֵּבָה אֲשֶׁר שָׂנֵא ה' אֱלֹהֶיךָ:

You shall not set up any monument [*matzeivah*] which the Almighty, your God, despises. (*Devarim* 16:22)

Rashi notes that a *matzeivah* is made of but one stone, while an altar is made of many.[3] While the altar will eventually become one of the most important elements of the Temple, the creation of monoliths is forbidden

---

3. Rashi, *Devarim* 16:22:

רש"י, דברים פרק טז:כב

וְלֹא־תָקִים לְךָ מַצֵּבָה - מַצֶּבֶת אֶבֶן אַחַת לְהַקְרִיב עָלֶיהָ אֲפִלּוּ לַשָּׁמָיִם.

"And you shall not build a monument [*matzeivah*]" — i.e., a monument of one stone, not even in order to sacrifice on it to Heaven (to God).

because of their identification with Canaanite idolatry. If a *matzeivah* is "despised by God," why does Yaakov erect one? While it would certainly be unfair to judge the forefathers through the prism of contemporary religious practice, it is still disturbing to find Yaakov doing something that the Torah later explicitly forbids. This raises halachic issues that are intriguing, but beyond our present scope. However the conceptual issue we will address here, starting with Rashi:

רש"י דברים פרק טז:כב
... וְאַעַ"פּ שֶׁהָיְתָה אֲהוּבָה לוֹ בִּימֵי הָאָבוֹת, עַכְשָׁיו שְׂנֵאָהּ מֵאַחַר שֶׁעֲשָׂאוּהָ אֵלּוּ חֹק לַעֲבוֹדָה זָרָה:

…Even though [the making of *matzeivot*] was a beloved practice during the time of the patriarchs, it is now despised. (Rashi, *Devarim* 16:22)

A *matzeivah* made of one stone was an acceptable form of practice before the emergence of the Jewish nation. In their lifetimes, the patriarchs were essentially individuals who embodied national aspirations and potential—represented by the image of the solitary stone, standing alone above the landscape. However, once the Israelite nation comes into existence, the visual representation through which we relate to God evolves as well. When the individual becomes a family which becomes a nation, the means through which we reach out to God must be an altar comprised of many stones gathered together, reflecting the unity of a nation formed by the coming together of many individuals; the solitary stance of a *matzeivah* is no longer appropriate. This is precisely why, after Yaakov's eleven children are born and he heads back to the Land of Israel, God appears to him with the following command:

בראשית פרק לה:א
וַיֹּאמֶר אֱלֹהִים אֶל־יַעֲקֹב קוּם עֲלֵה בֵית־אֵל וְשֶׁב־שָׁם וַעֲשֵׂה־שָׁם מִזְבֵּחַ לָאֵל הַנִּרְאֶה אֵלֶיךָ בְּבָרְחֲךָ מִפְּנֵי עֵשָׂו אָחִיךָ:

And God said to Yaakov, "Go up to Beit El and dwell there and build an altar to God, who appeared to you when you fled from your brother Esav." (*Bereishit* 35:1)

God commands Yaakov to build an altar; evidently, the change in status from individual to nation has occurred. The construction is no longer with a single stone, but with many small ones. Upon analysis of the section preceding God's command, we find that Yaakov was not completely aware of the impending change, or of the fact that it perhaps should already have taken place.

Yaakov had traveled to Charan to marry and start a family. He returns to Israel with his wives and eleven children after extricating himself, with great difficulty, from Lavan's house. In and of itself, this separation is permeated with great theological significance, as we learn from the celebrated passage in the Passover Haggadah in which Lavan is compared unfavorably to Pharaoh:

הגדה של פסח - נוסח ההגדה:
מַה בִּקֵּשׁ לָבָן הָאֲרַמִּי לַעֲשׂוֹת לְיַעֲקֹב אָבִינוּ. שֶׁפַּרְעֹה לֹא גָזַר אֶלָּא עַל הַזְּכָרִים וְלָבָן בִּקֵּשׁ לַעֲקוֹר אֶת הַכֹּל.

What did Lavan the Aramite try to do to our patriarch Yaakov? Pharaoh sought to annihilate only the males, while Lavan sought to uproot everything. (Passover Haggadah)

What did the Sages see in the text that elicited this shocking contrast? The Biblical text does not recount any attempt by Lavan to kill his own children or grandchildren, Yaakov's wives and their sons. Quite the opposite: Lavan seems truly wounded when Yaakov takes his leave. And yet, Yaakov recognizes that he must leave Lavan's house, make a clean break, and return to the Land of Israel. The sinister behavior of Lavan, then, was not attempted murder; rather, it was the seduction of Yaakov to assimilate. Yaakov recognized that he must flee Lavan's house and return to the Land of Israel if there was to be any hope of fulfilling his destiny and bringing the blessings he had received from his father to fruition.

בראשית פרק לא:כ

וַיִּגְנֹב יַעֲקֹב אֶת־לֵב לָבָן הָאֲרַמִּי עַל־בְּלִי הִגִּיד לוֹ כִּי בֹרֵחַ הוּא:

Yaakov outwitted Lavan the Aramite, by leaving without a word. (*Bereishit* 31:20)

When Lavan catches up with him and confronts him, Yaakov explains himself:

בראשית פרק לא:לא

וַיַּעַן יַעֲקֹב וַיֹּאמֶר לְלָבָן כִּי יָרֵאתִי כִּי אָמַרְתִּי פֶּן־תִּגְזֹל אֶת־בְּנוֹתֶיךָ מֵעִמִּי:

Because I was afraid; for I said perhaps you would take by force your daughters from me. (*Bereishit* 31:31)

בראשית פרק לא:מג

וַיַּעַן לָבָן וַיֹּאמֶר אֶל־יַעֲקֹב הַבָּנוֹת בְּנֹתַי וְהַבָּנִים בָּנַי...

Lavan answered Yaakov, "These daughters are my daughters, and these children are my children..." (*Bereishit* 31:43)

From Lavan's perspective, Yaakov, his wives, and his children are all part of his own extended family; they are, to his mind, one people. Therefore, to Lavan, Yaakov's desire to leave seems strange and elitist. By leaving Lavan's house, Yaakov expresses separatist religious and nationalistic aspirations. Removing his family from Lavan's house is a declaration of independence: Yaakov's family is his alone, not Lavan's, and the destinies that await these two families are vastly different. And while Lavan felt he was within his rights to charge Yaakov with creating differences between them—a charge that has been leveled at the Jews throughout the generations—the time had come for Yaakov to demarcate his family as a separate, independent nation. The time had come to return to Beit El and build the House of God. But before he is able to do so, the episode of Dinah unfolds:

בראשית פרק לד:א-ב

וַתֵּצֵא דִינָה בַּת־לֵאָה אֲשֶׁר יָלְדָה לְיַעֲקֹב לִרְאוֹת בִּבְנוֹת הָאָרֶץ: וַיַּרְא אֹתָהּ שְׁכֶם בֶּן־חֲמוֹר הַחִוִּי נְשִׂיא הָאָרֶץ וַיִּקַּח אֹתָהּ וַיִּשְׁכַּב אֹתָהּ וַיְעַנֶּהָ:

> Dinah, the daughter of Leah, whom she bore to Yaakov, went out to see the daughters of the land. Shechem the son of Chamor the Chivi, prince of the land, saw her. He took her and lay with her and abused her. (*Bereishit* 34:1–2)

Dinah goes out to befriend the neighbors, which seems perfectly natural; upon moving to a new land, she seeks companionship. Her behavior is understood as that of an individual girl going to visit her neighbors, and we would not have given it a second thought—had it not been for the unfortunate results. The question is how to view this outrage. Is it merely a local "problem" between neighbors, or is it more?

If the Children of Israel are now a nation, Shechem's violation is not only a violation of Dinah as an individual; it constitutes a breaking of barriers, and casts the entire incident in a different light altogether. Dinah is described as a daughter of Yaakov; Shechem is described as the son of Chamor, "prince of the land"—a very significant description in this context. The daughter of Yaakov, leader of the Jewish nation, is abused by the son of Chamor, the Chivite leader. This is not merely an unfortunate, interpersonal incident, nor is it a family squabble; it is, at the very least, an international incident, and, at worst, a *causus belli*.[4]

---

4. It is worthwhile comparing and contrasting the assault and abuse of Dinah with that of Tamar, who was assaulted by her half-brother Amnon (2 *Shmuel* 13:1-17). In both instances, the more common word *oness* is not used to describe the act of rape; instead, in both instances, the word *va-yaneha* is used, which can be translated as "abuse" or "violation" See *Devarim* 22:24, where the word *innah* (which we have translated here as "abuse") is apparently a synonym for *oness*, "rape." See *Metzudat Zion* (Rabbi Yechiel Hillel Altschuler), *Shoftim* 20:5, who explains that the two are synonymous: *innai* is *oness*, both mean "rape."

דברים פרק כב:כד

(כד) וְהוֹצֵאתֶם אֶת־שְׁנֵיהֶם אֶל־שַׁעַר׀ הָעִיר הַהִוא וּסְקַלְתֶּם אֹתָם בָּאֲבָנִים וָמֵתוּ אֶת־הַנַּעֲרָ עַל־דְּבַר אֲשֶׁר לֹא־צָעֲקָה בָעִיר וְאֶת־הָאִישׁ עַל־דְּבַר אֲשֶׁר־עִנָּה אֶת־אֵשֶׁת רֵעֵהוּ וּבִעַרְתָּ הָרָע מִקִּרְבֶּךָ: ס

You shall take the two of them out to the gate of that town and stone them to death: the girl because she did not cry for help in the town, and the man because he violated another man's wife. Thus you will purge the evil from your midst.

מצודת ציון שופטים פרק כ פסוק ה

עִנּוּ - הוּא הָאֹנֶס כְּמוֹ עַל־דְּבַר אֲשֶׁר־עִנָּה [דברים כב]:

Tamar's words to Amnon offer her understanding of the Dinah-Shechem incident: Dinah, like Tamar, was a victim of a sexual assault. Tamar makes a conscious, carefully-worded reference to the earlier attack on Dinah when she says, "Do not, brother. Do not abuse me [*te'anneini*, from the word *innah*]. Such things are not done in Israel! Don't do such a vile thing! Where will I carry my shame? And you, you will be like any of the scoundrels in Israel!"

(יב) וַתֹּאמֶר לוֹ אַל־אָחִי אַל־תְּעַנֵּנִי כִּי לֹא־יֵעָשֶׂה כֵן בְּיִשְׂרָאֵל אַל־תַּעֲשֵׂה אֶת־הַנְּבָלָה הַזֹּאת: (יג) וַאֲנִי אָנָה אוֹלִיךְ אֶת־חֶרְפָּתִי וְאַתָּה תִּהְיֶה כְּאַחַד הַנְּבָלִים בְּיִשְׂרָאֵל...

Her words echo the narrative of the brother's response to Shechem's attack on Dinah:

And they were extrememly upset for [they felt] a disgrace was brought upon Israel by lying with the daughter of Yaakov, a deed which should not be done. (*Bereishit* 34:5-7).

בראשית פרק לד, ה-ז

וַיִּחַר לָהֶם מְאֹד כִּי־נְבָלָה עָשָׂה בְיִשְׂרָאֵל לִשְׁכַּב אֶת־בַּת־יַעֲקֹב וְכֵן לֹא יֵעָשֶׂה:

Linguistically and thematically, the episodes involving Dinah and Tamar are certainly related (especially verses 12 and14); both involve the rape of a "princess." What is strange about the Dinah episode is the fact that Shechem subsequently falls in love with Dinah, courts her, and vigourously seeks her had in marriage (*Bereishit* 34:3,4). In contrast, after he rapes Tamar, Amnon's lust turns into loathing for his victim.

בראשית פרק לד:ג-ד

וַתִּדְבַּק נַפְשׁוֹ בְּדִינָה בַּת־יַעֲקֹב וַיֶּאֱהַב אֶת־הַנַּעֲרָ וַיְדַבֵּר עַל־לֵב הַנַּעֲרָ: וַיֹּאמֶר שְׁכֶם אֶל־חֲמוֹר אָבִיו לֵאמֹר קַח־לִי אֶת־הַיַּלְדָּה הַזֹּאת לְאִשָּׁה:

Shechem became emotionally attached to Dinah daughter of Yaakov, and he fell in love with the maiden, and spoke to her tenderly (to win her over). And Shechem spoke to his father Chamor, saying "Get me this girl for a wife.

שמואל ב פרק יג:א-יז

(א) וַיְהִי אַחֲרֵי־כֵן וּלְאַבְשָׁלוֹם בֶּן־דָּוִד אָחוֹת יָפָה וּשְׁמָהּ תָּמָר וַיֶּאֱהָבֶהָ אַמְנוֹן בֶּן־דָּוִד: (ב) וַיֵּצֶר לְאַמְנוֹן לְהִתְחַלּוֹת בַּעֲבוּר תָּמָר אֲחֹתוֹ כִּי בְתוּלָה הִיא וַיִּפָּלֵא בְּעֵינֵי אַמְנוֹן לַעֲשׂוֹת לָהּ מְאוּמָה: (ג) וּלְאַמְנוֹן רֵעַ וּשְׁמוֹ יוֹנָדָב בֶּן־שִׁמְעָה אֲחִי דָוִד וְיוֹנָדָב אִישׁ חָכָם מְאֹד: (ד) וַיֹּאמֶר לוֹ מַדּוּעַ אַתָּה כָּכָה דַּל בֶּן־הַמֶּלֶךְ בַּבֹּקֶר בַּבֹּקֶר הֲלוֹא תַּגִּיד לִי וַיֹּאמֶר לוֹ אַמְנוֹן אֶת־תָּמָר אֲחוֹת אַבְשָׁלֹם אָחִי אֲנִי אֹהֵב: (ה) וַיֹּאמֶר לוֹ יְהוֹנָדָב שְׁכַב עַל־מִשְׁכָּבְךָ וְהִתְחָל וּבָא אָבִיךָ לִרְאוֹתֶךָ וְאָמַרְתָּ אֵלָיו תָּבֹא נָא תָמָר אֲחוֹתִי וְתַבְרֵנִי לֶחֶם וְעָשְׂתָה לְעֵינַי אֶת־הַבִּרְיָה לְמַעַן אֲשֶׁר אֶרְאֶה וְאָכַלְתִּי מִיָּדָהּ: (ו) וַיִּשְׁכַּב אַמְנוֹן וַיִּתְחָל וַיָּבֹא הַמֶּלֶךְ לִרְאֹתוֹ וַיֹּאמֶר אַמְנוֹן אֶל־הַמֶּלֶךְ תָּבוֹא־נָא תָּמָר אֲחֹתִי וּתְלַבֵּב לְעֵינַי שְׁתֵּי לְבִבוֹת וְאֶבְרֶה מִיָּדָהּ: (ז) וַיִּשְׁלַח דָּוִד אֶל־תָּמָר הַבַּיְתָה לֵאמֹר לְכִי נָא בֵּית אַמְנוֹן אָחִיךְ וַעֲשִׂי־לוֹ הַבִּרְיָה: (ח) וַתֵּלֶךְ תָּמָר בֵּית אַמְנוֹן אָחִיהָ וְהוּא שֹׁכֵב וַתִּקַּח אֶת־הַבָּצֵק וַתָּלָשׁ וַתְּלַבֵּב לְעֵינָיו וַתְּבַשֵּׁל אֶת־הַלְּבִבוֹת: (ט) וַתִּקַּח אֶת־הַמַּשְׂרֵת וַתִּצֹק לְפָנָיו וַיְמָאֵן לֶאֱכוֹל וַיֹּאמֶר אַמְנוֹן הוֹצִיאוּ כָל־אִישׁ מֵעָלַי וַיֵּצְאוּ כָל־אִישׁ מֵעָלָיו: (י) וַיֹּאמֶר אַמְנוֹן אֶל־תָּמָר הָבִיאִי הַבִּרְיָה הַחֶדֶר וְאֶבְרֶה מִיָּדֵךְ וַתִּקַּח תָּמָר אֶת־הַלְּבִבוֹת אֲשֶׁר עָשָׂתָה וַתָּבֵא לְאַמְנוֹן אָחִיהָ הֶחָדְרָה: (יא) וַתַּגֵּשׁ אֵלָיו לֶאֱכֹל וַיַּחֲזֶק־בָּהּ וַיֹּאמֶר לָהּ בּוֹאִי שִׁכְבִי עִמִּי אֲחוֹתִי: (יב) וַתֹּאמֶר לוֹ אַל־אָחִי אַל־תְּעַנֵּנִי כִּי לֹא־יֵעָשֶׂה כֵן בְּיִשְׂרָאֵל אַל־תַּעֲשֵׂה אֶת־הַנְּבָלָה הַזֹּאת: (יג) וַאֲנִי אָנָה אוֹלִיךְ אֶת־חֶרְפָּתִי וְאַתָּה תִּהְיֶה כְּאַחַד הַנְּבָלִים בְּיִשְׂרָאֵל וְעַתָּה דַּבֶּר־נָא אֶל־הַמֶּלֶךְ כִּי לֹא יִמְנָעֵנִי מִמֶּךָּ: (יד) וְלֹא אָבָה לִשְׁמֹעַ בְּקוֹלָהּ וַיֶּחֱזַק מִמֶּנָּה וַיְעַנֶּהָ וַיִּשְׁכַּב אֹתָהּ: (טו) וַיִּשְׂנָאֶהָ אַמְנוֹן שִׂנְאָה גְּדוֹלָה מְאֹד כִּי גְדוֹלָה הַשִּׂנְאָה אֲשֶׁר שְׂנֵאָהּ מֵאַהֲבָה אֲשֶׁר אֲהֵבָהּ וַיֹּאמֶר־לָהּ אַמְנוֹן קוּמִי לֵכִי: (טז) וַתֹּאמֶר לוֹ אַל־אוֹדֹת הָרָעָה הַגְּדוֹלָה הַזֹּאת מֵאַחֶרֶת אֲשֶׁר־עָשִׂיתָ עִמִּי לְשַׁלְּחֵנִי וְלֹא אָבָה לִשְׁמֹעַ לָהּ:

This happened sometime afterward: Avshalom son of David had a beautiful sister named Tamar, and Amnon son of David became infatuated with her. Amnon was so distraught because of his [half-]sister Tamar that he became sick; for she was a virgin, and it seemed impossible to Amnon to do anything to her. Amnon had a friend named Yonadav, the son of David's brother Shimah; Yonadav was a very clever man. He asked him, "Why are you so dejected, O prince, morning after morning? Tell me!" Amnon replied, "I am in love with Tamar, the sister of my brother Avshalom!" Yonadav said to him, "Lie down in your bed and pretend you are sick. When your father comes to see you, say to him, 'Let my sister Tamar come and give me something to eat. Let her prepare the food in front of me, so that I may look on, and let her serve it to me.'" Amnon lay down and pretended to be sick. The king came to see him, and Amnon said to the king, "Let my sister Tamar come and prepare a couple of cakes in front of me, and let her bring them to me." David sent a message to Tamar in the palace, "Please go to the house of your brother Amnon and prepare some food for him." Tamar went to the house of her brother Amnon, who was in bed. She took dough and kneaded it into cakes in front of him, and cooked the cakes. She took the pan and set out [the cakes], but Amnon refused to eat and ordered everyone to withdraw. After everyone had withdrawn, Amnon said to Tamar, "Bring the food inside and feed me." Tamar took the cakes she had made and brought them to her brother inside. But when she served them to him, he caught hold of her and said to her, "Come lie with me, sister." But she said to him, "Don't, brother. Don't abuse me. Such things are not done in Israel! Don't do such a vile thing! Where will I carry my shame? And you, you will be like any of the scoundrels in Israel! Please, speak to the king; he will not refuse me to

Apparently, Yaakov sees the episode on a personal or familial level. His children, on the other hand, see Shechem's actions as a declaration of war on a national level. They seem to sense something that eludes Yaakov.

בראשית פרק לד:ה-ז

וְיַעֲקֹב שָׁמַע כִּי טִמֵּא אֶת־דִּינָה בִתּוֹ וּבָנָיו הָיוּ אֶת־מִקְנֵהוּ בַּשָּׂדֶה וְהֶחֱרִשׁ יַעֲקֹב עַד־בֹּאָם: ... וּבְנֵי יַעֲקֹב בָּאוּ מִן־הַשָּׂדֶה כְּשָׁמְעָם וַיִּתְעַצְּבוּ הָאֲנָשִׁים וַיִּחַר לָהֶם מְאֹד כִּי־נְבָלָה עָשָׂה בְיִשְׂרָאֵל לִשְׁכַּב אֶת־בַּת־יַעֲקֹב וְכֵן לֹא יֵעָשֶׂה:

> Yaakov heard that his daughter Dinah, had been defiled, and his sons were tending the flocks in the fields; Yaakov was silent until they arrived... The sons of Yaakov came from the field when they heard, and they were saddened and greatly incensed, for [they felt] a disgrace was brought upon **Israel** by lying with the daughter of Yaakov, a deed which should not be done. (*Bereishit* 34:5-7)

Yaakov hears that his **daughter** has been defiled; his sons hear that **Israel** has been disgraced. The sons see the act in a national context. For the first time, the term *Israel* is used to describe what had heretofore been referred to as Yaakov's family. The shift from private, individual life to national existence has already been made in the minds of the sons: Hadn't their father led them out of the house of their grandfather in order to set them apart, to form a separate entity? To them, their unique national destiny, which was clear and unequivocal, was already playing itself out.

Ironically, Yaakov seems unaware that the time had come to be a nation. His response to the sons' call for action is instructive: Yaakov explains that as individuals, as a family, we are outmatched. Perhaps

---

you." But he would not listen to her; he overpowered her and lay with her by force. Then Amnon felt a very great loathing for her; indeed, his loathing for her was greater than the passion he had felt for her. And Amnon said to her, "Get out!" She pleaded with him, "Please don't commit this wrong; to send me away would be even worse than the first wrong you committed against me." But he would not listen to her. He summoned his young attendant and said, "Get that woman out of my presence, and bar the door behind her."

in the future, when we become something more, we will have the wherewithal to respond differently, but now is not the time. How different is the viewpoint of the sons, who see themselves as part of the future, and express a sense of responsibility to the coming generations of the Jewish People who will look to their actions for spiritual guidance. The text records their impassioned response:

בראשית פרק לד:לא
וַיֹּאמְרוּ הַכְזוֹנָה יַעֲשֶׂה אֶת־אֲחוֹתֵנוּ:

Can we let our sister be taken for a whore? (*Bereishit* 34: 31)

Targum (Pseudo)-Yonatan reads between the lines of their response: "What will future generations of the Jewish people understand when they read about these events? What sort of role models are we to be?" the brothers ask. "Shechem has committed an act of war, and we have a responsibility to answer that challenge and to set national standards."[5]

---

5. See Targum (Pseudo)-Yonatan, *Bereishit* 37:31, translated from the Aramaic to Hebrew in the *Keter Yonatan*, as well as the Targum Yerushalmi:

תרגום המיוחס ליונתן - תורה בראשית פרק לד:לא
עֲנִינָן שִׁמְעוֹן וְלֵוִי לָא יָאֵי לְמֵהֱוֵי מִתְאַמַּר בִּכְנִשְׁתְּהוֹן דְיִשְׂרָאֵל עַרְלָאִין סָאִיבוּ לִבְתוּלְתָּא וּפָלְחֵי צַלְמִין טָנִיפוּ לִבְרַתֵּיהּ דְיַעֲקֹב אֱלָהֵין כְּדֵין יָאֵי לְמֵהֱוֵי מִתְאַמַּר עַרְלָאִין אִתְקְטִילוּ בְּגִין בְּתוּלְתָּא וּפָלְחֵי צַלְמִין בְּגִין בְּרַתֵּיהּ דְיַעֲקֹב וְלָא יֶהֱוֵי שְׁכֶם בַּר חֲמוֹר מְלַגְלֵג עֲלָנָא וּכְאִיתָּא מְטַעְיָיא נָפְקַת בְּרָה דְלֵית לַהּ תְּבוֹעַ יַעֲבֵיד יַת אַחֲתָן אִין לָא עֲבַדְנָא יַת פִּתְגָּמָא הָדֵין:

כתר יונתן בראשית פרשת וישלח פרק לד:לא
ענו שמעון ולוי לא יאה להיות נאמר באסיפותיהם [בכנסיותיהם] של ישראל ערלים טמאו לבתולה ועובדי צלמים טנפו לבתו של יעקב אלא כך יאה להיות נאמר ערלים נהרגו בעבור בתולה ועובדי צלמים בעבור ביתו של יעקב ולא יהיה שכם בן חמור מלגלג במילותיו עלינו, וכאשה זונה יצאה בת שאין לה תובע יעשה את אחותנו, אם לא עשינו את הדבר הזה.

Targum Yonatan, *Bereishit* 34:31
And Shimon and Levi answered, "It would not have been fit to be said in the congregations of Israel that the uncircumcised polluted the virgin, and the worshippers of idols debased the daughter of Yaakov: but it is fit that it should be said, The uncircumcised were slain on account of the virgin, and the worshippers of idols on account of the daughter of Yaakov. Shechem son of Chamor will not (now) deride us with his words; for he would have made our sister as a whorish woman and an outcast who has no avenger, if we had not done this thing.

Immediately after the Dinah episode, God calls upon Yaakov to go to Beit El and build the altar, thus fulfilling the vow he made when he fled from Esav. God Himself sees Yaakov's family as the People of Israel; at this point, worship must be formalized. Perhaps the entire incident with Dinah might have been avoided had Yaakov understood this new status earlier, when the term *nation* was used for the first time— immediately prior to the incident with Dinah, after leaving the house of Lavan, when Yaakov prepared for his meeting with Esav:

בראשית פרק לב: ח

וַיִּירָא יַעֲקֹב מְאֹד וַיֵּצֶר לוֹ וַיַּחַץ אֶת־הָעָם אֲשֶׁר־אִתּוֹ ...

Yaakov was greatly afraid and distressed, and he divided the **nation** that was with him. (*Bereishit* 32:8)

In addition to the change of identity that runs through this *parashah*— from Yaakov as an individual to Yisrael the nation, an additional change of identity runs through *Parashat Veyeitzei*. The *parashah* begins with a seemingly clear statement:

תרגום ירושלמי, בראשית ל״ד:ל״א

עַנְיָין תְּרֵין בְּנוֹי דְיַעֲקֹב כַּחֲדָא וְאָמְרִין לְיִשְׂרָאֵל אֲבוּהוֹן לָא יָאֵי הוּא דְיֵיהֱוֵי מִתְאַמַּר בִּכְנִשָׁתְּהוֹן דְיִשְׂרָאֵל וּבְבֵית מֶדְרָשֵׁיהוֹן עָרְלִין סָאִיבוּ בְתוּלָה וּפָלְחֵי צַלְמִין בְּרַתֵּיהּ דְיַעֲקֹב בְּרַם יָאֵי הוּא דְיֵיהֱוֵי מִתְאַמַּר בִּכְנִשָׁתֵיהוֹן דְיִשְׂרָאֵל וּבְבֵית מֶדְרָשֵׁיהוֹן עָרְלִין אִיתְקְטִילוּ עַל עִיסַק בְּתוּלָה פָּלְחֵי צַלְמִין עַל דְסָאִיבוּ לְדִינָה בַּת יַעֲקֹב דְלָא יְהֵי שְׁכֶם בַּר חֲמוֹר מִתְגָּאֵי בְלִבֵּיהּ וַאֲמַר כְּאִיתְּתָא דְלֵית לַהּ אֱנָשׁ תָּבַע עוּלְבָּנָהּ כֵּן יִתְעֲבֵיד לְדִינָה בַּת יַעֲקֹב וְאָמְרִין כְּאִיתְּתָא זַנְיָי וְנָפְקַת בָּרָא מַחְשַׁב יָת אֲחָתָן:

Targum Yerushalmi, Bereishit **34:31**
The two sons of Yaakov answered together, and said to Israel their father, "It would not be fit to be said in the congregations of Israel, in their house of instruction, that the uncircumcised polluted the virgin, and the worshippers of idols the daughter of Yaakov; but it is fit that it be said in the congregations of Israel and in their house of instruction, that the uncircumcised were put to death for the sake of the virgin, and the worshippers of idols because they had defiled Dinah the daughter of Yaakov. And Shechem son of Chamor will not boast in his heart and say, "As a woman who hath no man to avenge her injury, so hath Dinah the daughter of Yaakov been made." And they said, "As an impure woman and an outcast would he have accounted our sister."

בראשית פרק כח:יט

וַיִּקְרָא אֶת־שֵׁם־הַמָּקוֹם הַהוּא בֵּית־אֵל וְאוּלָם לוּז שֵׁם־הָעִיר לָרִאשֹׁנָה:

> And he called the name of the place Beit El; however, Luz was its original name. (*Bereishit* 28:19)

Upon Yaakov's return, the text goes to great lengths to describe his destination.

בראשית פרק לה:ו-ח

וַיָּבֹא יַעֲקֹב לוּזָה אֲשֶׁר בְּאֶרֶץ כְּנַעַן הִוא בֵּית־אֵל הוּא וְכָל־הָעָם אֲשֶׁר־עִמּוֹ: וַיִּבֶן שָׁם מִזְבֵּחַ וַיִּקְרָא לַמָּקוֹם אֵל בֵּית־אֵל כִּי שָׁם נִגְלוּ אֵלָיו הָאֱלֹהִים בְּבָרְחוֹ מִפְּנֵי אָחִיו:

> So Yaakov came to Luz, which is in the land of Canaan, that is, Beit El—he and all the nation which was with him. He built an altar there, and called the place "El Beit El," because there God appeared to him when he fled from his brother. (*Bereishit* 35:6–7)

The altar is built in Luz, which Yaakov himself had earlier renamed Beit El. However, even many years later, Yaakov continues to refer to this place as Luz:

בראשית פרק מח:ג

וַיֹּאמֶר יַעֲקֹב אֶל־יוֹסֵף אֵל שַׁדַּי נִרְאָה־אֵלַי בְּלוּז בְּאֶרֶץ כְּנַעַן וַיְבָרֶךְ אֹתִי:

> Yaakov said to Yosef, "God Almighty appeared to me in Luz and blessed me." (*Bereishit* 48:3)

Why does Yaakov revert to the city's original name? Perhaps the change from Luz to Beit El was not definitive, paralleling the Yaakov-Yisrael duality, the individual-national duality.

What was Luz? Our Sages teach:

Vayeitzei: Antecedents of a Nation | 181

בראשית רבה (וילנא) פרשת ויצא פרשה סט:ח
וְאוּלָם לוּז, הִיא לוּז שֶׁצּוֹבְעִין בָּהּ אֶת הַתְּכֵלֶת, הִיא לוּז שֶׁעָלָה סַנְחֵרִיב וְלֹא בִּלְבְּלָהּ, נְבוּכַדְנֶצַּר וְלֹא הֶחֱרִיבָהּ. הִיא לוּז שֶׁלֹּא שָׁלַט בָּהּ מַלְאַךְ הַמָּוֶת מֵעוֹלָם...

Luz is the place where they dyed the *techeilet* (blue dye). Luz is the place which Sanherev invaded but did not conquer, and which Nevuhadnezar did not destroy. Luz is the place where the Angel of Death had no power. (*Bereishit Rabbah* 69:8)

Luz was a city with quite a formidable spiritual personality: Demonic forces had no control within its boundaries; death was unknown there. In another context, the Sages tell us that a particular part of the spine, called the *luz*, will be the key for the Resurrection of the Dead in the Messianic Age:

ויקרא רבה (וילנא) פרשת מצורע פרשה יח סימן א
אַדְרִיָּנוּס שְׁחִיק עֲצָמוֹת שָׁאַל אֶת רַבִּי יְהוֹשֻׁעַ בַּר חֲנַנְיָא אָמַר לוֹ מֵהֵיכָן הַקָּדוֹשׁ בָּרוּךְ הוּא מֵצִיץ אֶת הָאָדָם לֶעָתִיד לָבוֹא, אָמַר לוֹ מִלּוּז שֶׁל שִׁדְרָה.

Hadrian, may his bones rot, asked Rabbi Yehoshua ben Chananyah, "From which part of the body will the Holy One, blessed be He, cause man to sprout forth in the time of resurrection?" [Rabbi Yehoshua] answered, "From the *luz* of the spinal column." (*Vayikra Rabbah* 18:1)

Luz refers to things that are indestructible, whether it be the *luz* of the spine or the city named Luz. Similarly, Yaakov is indestructible:

תלמוד בבלי מסכת תענית דף ה עמוד ב
אָמַר רַבִּי יוֹחָנָן, יַעֲקֹב אָבִינוּ לֹא מֵת. אָמַר לֵיהּ, וְכִי בִּכְדִי סָפְדוּ סַפְדָּנַיָּא? וְחָנְטוּ חָנְטַיָּא? וְקָבְרוּ קַבְרַיָּא? אָמַר לֵיהּ...מַקִּישׁ הוּא לְזַרְעוֹ, מַה זַּרְעוֹ בַּחַיִּים, אַף הוּא בַּחַיִּים.

Rabbi Yochanan said, "Yaakov our Patriarch never died." They said to him, "Was he not eulogized, embalmed, and buried?" Rabbi Yochanan answered, "…He is connected to his descendants. Just as his descendants live, so he lives." (*Ta'anit* 5b)

Yaakov lives on—though such a statement is not made concerning Avraham or Yitzchak. Why is Yaakov immortal, indestructible? The answer offered by Rabbi Yochanan in this Talmudic discussion refers to the nation of Israel: It is through his descendants that Yaakov lives; more precisely, it is the aspect of Yaakov expressed by the name *Yisrael* that is eternal. The eternal nature of the Jewish people emanates from Yaakov's first encounter with the Almighty under the stars in the city of Luz.

The unique spiritual personality of Luz is also closely identified with the *techeilet*, the dye used to make tzitzit, which was manufactured there. Tzitzit are made up of two colors: white and *techeilet*. In another context, the Gemara reports:

תלמוד בבלי מסכת מנחות דף מג עמוד ב

תַּנְיָא, הָיָה רַבִּי מֵאִיר אוֹמֵר, מַה נִּשְׁתַּנָּה תְּכֵלֶת מִכָּל מִינֵי צִבְעוֹנִין? מִפְּנֵי שֶׁהַתְּכֵלֶת דּוֹמֶה לַיָּם, וְיָם דּוֹמֶה לָרָקִיעַ, וְרָקִיעַ דּוֹמֶה לְסַפִּיר, וְסַפִּיר דּוֹמֶה לְכִסֵּא הַכָּבוֹד. ...

Why was *techeilet* chosen from among all the other colors? *Techeilet* resembles the sea, and the sea resembles the sky. The sky, in turn, resembles the Divine Throne. (*Menachot* 43b)

Techeilet is intended to remind us of the blue of the ocean and the sky, which, like God Himself, are beyond man's grasp, ephemeral and impossible to confine or define.

Rabbi Yosef Dov Soloveitchik, *zt"l*, explained that white represents logic, clarity, while blue represents "meta-logic"—the divine breath that animates and energizes human spirituality.[6] With the mitzvah of *tzitzit*,

---

6. See Rabbi Avraham Besdin, *Man of Faith in the Modern World — Reflections of the Rav*, vol. 2, p. 25ff.

Jews are commanded to clothe themselves in a garment that combines white and blue, the logical and the heavenly, and to conduct their everyday lives wrapped in this seeming contradiction. As we contend with the mundane aspects of our existence, it is so easy to lose sight of the purpose—the *tachlit*—of our existence. The *techeilet* reminds us of our unique *tachlit*—the lofty destiny of the eternal nation of Yisrael. For this reason, we recite the morning *Shema*, in which we accept God's kingship upon ourselves, only when it is possible to distinguish between white and blue, when we are able to discern the *techeilet* from the *lavan* (white): Only when we are cognizant of the combination of logical and meta-logical considerations that guide our lives as Jews, can we fully accept God's dominion.

The *techeilet*, then, is a means of connecting to Heaven. This was, in a sense, the same message conveyed in the vision Yaakov saw at Luz, the "ladder set on the ground with its head reaching the heavens." (*Bereishit* 28:12)

In this light, Yaakov's confrontation with his father-in-law Lavan gains greater significance. The threat of assimilation presented by Lavan seems curious when regarded in purely logical terms: Logically speaking, is there really a difference between one man and the next? From a purely logical perspective, Lavan's argument makes perfect sense. Perhaps that is why he was called "Lavan" (white): his considerations and the arguments he presented were exclusively logical. Yaakov's considerations went beyond the realm of logic, and were bound by the meta-logical elements that distinguish the destiny of his children and their children, for all time. It is these considerations, represented by the *techeilet*, that made it imperative that Yaakov separate from the house of Lavan. Clearly, Yaakov was capable of discerning between *techeilet* and *Lavan*.

The only way a Jew can withstand the threat of assimilation is if he is connected to Heaven. Only the Jew who can see beyond the logical can be free of Lavan. Only a descendant of Yisrael who sees himself as part of a nation with a great and unique mission and destiny will be liberated from Lavan's arguments. For this reason, Yaakov stopped in Luz after leaving the house of Lavan: The vision of the ladder, a singular experience, would be permanently represented by the *techeilet*, which serves as a "ladder" for every Jew who wishes to connect with Heaven. The secret of the eternity of the Jewish people has its origins in the city of Luz, for that is where Yaakov, and through him, all of his descendants, learned how to live with the dialectic represented in the *tzitzit*: *techeilet* and *lavan*: At one and the same moment, we live on the ground but still climb up to the Heavens.

Parashat Vayishlach

The Struggle

Many years have passed since Yaakov left his home. He was on the run, terrified that his brother Esav's murderous plans would fell him. Now, as he prepares to face Esav after so many years and so many changes, Yaakov does not know his brother's state of mind, so he sends a reconnaissance mission ("armed" with gifts), to evaluate the situation. When they return, they come with word that Esav is on the way with four hundred men. The situation looks dire, and Yaakov prepares to meet his brother and face his fate, although he hopes that some kind of reconciliation can be forged, and to that end he prepares (more) gifts. On a practical level, Yaakov's main tactic is to divide the camp in two, in hope that one or the other will escape. On a spiritual plane, Yaakov prays.

Perhaps overwhelmed by the reality of having to choose which camp he will join—or by the knowledge that he is a liability for either camp—Yaakov spends the night alone. And then, as he prepares for the epic showdown with his estranged brother, Yaakov faces another confrontation—one that is altogether different, in every sense of the word:

בראשית פרק לב:כה-לב
(כה) וַיִּוָּתֵר יַעֲקֹב לְבַדּוֹ וַיֵּאָבֵק אִישׁ עִמּוֹ עַד עֲלוֹת הַשָּׁחַר: (כו) וַיַּרְא כִּי לֹא יָכֹל לוֹ וַיִּגַּע בְּכַף־יְרֵכוֹ וַתֵּקַע כַּף־יֶרֶךְ יַעֲקֹב בְּהֵאָבְקוֹ עִמּוֹ: (כז) וַיֹּאמֶר שַׁלְּחֵנִי כִּי עָלָה הַשָּׁחַר וַיֹּאמֶר לֹא אֲשַׁלֵּחֲךָ כִּי אִם־בֵּרַכְתָּנִי: (כח) וַיֹּאמֶר אֵלָיו מַה־שְּׁמֶךָ וַיֹּאמֶר יַעֲקֹב: (כט) וַיֹּאמֶר לֹא יַעֲקֹב יֵאָמֵר עוֹד שִׁמְךָ כִּי אִם־יִשְׂרָאֵל כִּי־שָׂרִיתָ עִם־אֱלֹהִים וְעִם־אֲנָשִׁים וַתּוּכָל: (ל) וַיִּשְׁאַל יַעֲקֹב וַיֹּאמֶר הַגִּידָה־נָּא שְׁמֶךָ וַיֹּאמֶר לָמָּה זֶּה תִּשְׁאַל לִשְׁמִי וַיְבָרֶךְ אֹתוֹ שָׁם: (לא) וַיִּקְרָא יַעֲקֹב שֵׁם הַמָּקוֹם פְּנִיאֵל כִּי־רָאִיתִי אֱלֹהִים פָּנִים אֶל־פָּנִים וַתִּנָּצֵל נַפְשִׁי: (לב) וַיִּזְרַח־לוֹ הַשֶּׁמֶשׁ כַּאֲשֶׁר עָבַר אֶת־פְּנוּאֵל וְהוּא צֹלֵעַ עַל־יְרֵכוֹ:

Yaakov remained alone, and a man wrestled with him until daybreak. When he saw that he could not [defeat] him, he touched the joint of his thigh. Yaakov's hip became dislocated from wrestling with him.

[The man] said, "Release me, for dawn is breaking."

He [Yaakov] said, "I will not release you unless you bless me." He [the man] said, "What is your name?" He said, "Yaakov."

He [the man] said, "Your name shall no longer be called Yaakov, but rather Yisrael, for you have struggled with God and with man and [you] have been victorious."

Yaakov asked, "Please tell me your name."

He said, "Why are you asking for my name?" And he blessed him there.

Yaakov called the place "Peniel" [face of God], "For I have seen God face to face, and my soul was saved."

The sun rose as he left Penuel, and he was limping because of his thigh.

Therefore, the Children of Israel do not eat the *gid hanasheh* which is on the thigh [of an animal] until this very day, for Yaakov's thigh was afflicted on the gid hanasheh. (*Bereishit* 32:25–32)

The text seems deliberately enigmatic and contradictory. If Yaakov is alone, how can someone wrestle with him? With each verse, the difficulties and ambiguities seem compounded:

(כו) וַיַּרְא כִּי לֹא יָכֹל לוֹ וַיִּגַּע בְּכַף־יְרֵכוֹ וַתֵּקַע כַּף־יֶרֶךְ יַעֲקֹב בְּהֵאָבְקוֹ עִמּוֹ:

When **he** saw that **he** could not [defeat] **him**, **he** touched the joint of **his** thigh.

Who is "he" and who is "him"? This verse cannot be understood on its own; only by reading the next verse can we understand the meaning. Why is there so much confusion? And who Yaakov's mysterious adversary?

He said, "What is your name?"
He said, "Yaakov."

Does the adversary not even know with whom he is struggling?

> He said, "Your name shall no longer be called Yaakov, but rather Yisrael, for you have struggled with God and with man and [you] have been victorious.

The adversary, who does not even know the identity of his foe, declares that the one with whom he has been wrestling has been victorious in his struggle with God and man!

> Yaakov asked, "Please tell me your name."
> He said, "Why are you asking for my name?"

Why does Yaakov wish to know the identity of this person?

Despite the complexity of the verses, the Midrash and commentaries are relatively unanimous as to the identity of the assailant: Yaakov wrestled with an angel. In fact, most[1] traditional sources identify the angel as none other than the angel of Esav.[2] As Yaakov prepares to meet his brother after years of estrangement, Esav's angel comes down

---

1. Various sources identify different angels in this passage; most sources identify Yaakov's adversary as the angel of Esav, though some identify the assailant as Michael (an angel generally sympathetic to Jews):

תנחומא בובר וישלח ז
שלח לו מיכאל לעשות עמו מריבה, מה עשה לו המלאך, נדמה לו בדמות רועה, שנאמר ויאבק איש עמו וגו', וירא כי לא יכול לו וגו', ויאמר שלחני וגו' (שם לב כה כו כז).

אלשיך בראשית פרק לב
והנה חלקו רבותינו ז"ל אם מיכאל היה (תנחומא בובר ז), או סמאל שרו של עשו (בראשית רבה עז ב, ועוד).

2. For example, see *Bereishit Rabbah* 77:3, Rashi, *Bereishit* 32:25,

בראשית רבה (וילנא) פרשת וישלח פרשה עז:ג
רַבִּי חָמָא בְּרַבִּי חֲנִינָא אָמַר שָׂרוֹ שֶׁל עֵשָׂו הָיָה, הוּא דַּהֲוָה אָמַר לֵיהּ (בראשית לג, י): כִּי עַל כֵּן רָאִיתִי פָנֶיךָ כִּרְאֹת פְּנֵי אֱלֹהִים וַתִּרְצֵנִי,

רש"י על בראשית ל"ב:כ"ה
(כה) ויאבק איש וּפֵרְשׁוּ רַזַ"ל, שֶׁהוּא שָׂרוֹ שֶׁל עֵשָׂו:

from Heaven in order to "have a go" at Yaakov first. Interestingly, while Yaakov manages to reach a reconciliation with Esav in the morning, he is unable to avoid battle with Esav's heavenly representative the night before. This nocturnal confrontation seems unavoidable; at the very least, it is foreshadowed in the textual account of the twin brothers' earliest struggle.

בראשית פרק כה:כב
וַיִּתְרֹצֲצוּ הַבָּנִים בְּקִרְבָּהּ וַתֹּאמֶר אִם־כֵּן לָמָּה זֶּה אָנֹכִי וַתֵּלֶךְ לִדְרֹשׁ אֶת ה':

But the children struggled in her womb, and she said, "If so, why do I exist?" She went to seek out God. (*Bereishit* 25:22)

The night before the brothers are to re-enact—or perhaps continue—the struggle that began before they were born, Yaakov stands alone despite all that he has accomplished and everything he has acquired over the years.

בראשית פרק לב: כה
וַיִּוָּתֵר יַעֲקֹב לְבַדּוֹ וַיֵּאָבֵק אִישׁ עִמּוֹ עַד עֲלוֹת הַשָּׁחַר:

Yaakov remained **alone**, and a man wrestled with him until daybreak. (*Bereishit* 32: 25)

If Yaakov is truly alone, who can he be wrestling with? The most straightforward answer is that he was, in fact, alone; no one else was there to wrestle with him. Yaakov was wrestling with himself. He was "the man" when no other man was present, the man who is both there and not there. In fact, Yaakov is described with precisely this term *ha-ish*, "the man," at another very critical juncture in his personal history:

בראשית פרק ל, מג
וַיִּפְרֹץ הָאִישׁ מְאֹד מְאֹד וַיְהִי־לוֹ צֹאן רַבּוֹת וּשְׁפָחוֹת וַעֲבָדִים וּגְמַלִּים וַחֲמֹרִים:

The man [*ha-ish*] was exceedingly successful, and he possessed many flocks and maids and servants and camels and donkeys. (*Bereishit* 30:43)

Yaakov has "made it;" he has acheieved tremendous financial success. The blessings which he took surreptitiously from Esav have come to fruition, and it is in this very particular context that the text refers to him as *ha-ish*, "the man." Yaakov's metamorphosis, from a man of the tents[3]—a "yeshiva student", if you will—to successful entrepreneur, is complete.

Yet Yaakov struggles with his success. It was one thing to take the blessings destined for Esav; it is quite another to live with the results of those blessings. As Yaakov prepares to meet his brother, he takes stock of his life; he surveys his household and all the wealth he has accumulated, and he is worried. He separates everything he has, even his beloved family, into different camps—but he is alone,[4] and not for the first time: Yaakov was described as alone when he fled from Esav, spent an awesome night under the stars, and saw the vision of the ladder ascending to heaven. Then, he was destitute; without so much

---

3. See *Bereishit* 25:27 and Rashi's comments *ad loc*:

בראשית פרק כה:כז

(כז) וַיִּגְדְּלוּ הַנְּעָרִים וַיְהִי עֵשָׂו אִישׁ יֹדֵעַ צַיִד אִישׁ שָׂדֶה וְיַעֲקֹב אִישׁ תָּם יֹשֵׁב אֹהָלִים:

When the boys grew up, Esav became a skillful hunter, a man of the outdoors; and Yaakov was a mild man of the tents.

רש"י בראשית פרק כה:כז

"ישב אהלים": אָהֳלוֹ שֶׁל שֵׁם וְאָהֳלוֹ שֶׁל עֵבֶר.

"A man of the tents:" — the tent of Shem and the tent of Ever (*Bereishit Rabbah* 63:10).

4. Perhaps sensitive to this theme, the Talmud (*Chullin* 91a, quoted by Rashi, *Bereishit* 32:25) explains that Yaakov was alone because he had gone back for small (inexpensive) flasks that had been left behind, which is surprising behavior for a person of great wealth. The Talmud may be suggesting that Yaakov is identifying with his earlier (poorer) self.

רש"י בראשית פרק לב:כה

ויותר יעקב. שכח פכים קטנים וחזר עליהם:

"And Yaakov was left alone" — He had forgotten some small jars and he returned for them.

as the clothes on his back, he was forced to use a rock for a pillow. Now, despite the trememdous wealth he has accrued and the impressive household he has built, Yaakov is alone once again as he prepares to meet his brother.

We can easily imagine that in the quiet of that night of waiting, Yaakov looked back on everything that had led up to his impending showdown with his brother, and he wrestled with himself, as it were; he wrestled with his internal contradictions, as the man he had become fought with his truest, innermost self. Had the man of great wealth eclipsed the man of the tents? Had his struggle for survival turned him into something he was not? As he faced his own internal contradictions, he must surely have reminded himself of the Divine blessing and the promise God made on that night of revelation beneath the stars so many years earlier:

בראשית פרק כח:יב-טו

(יב) וַיַּחֲלֹם וְהִנֵּה סֻלָּם מֻצָּב אַרְצָה וְרֹאשׁוֹ מַגִּיעַ הַשָּׁמָיְמָה וְהִנֵּה מַלְאֲכֵי אֱלֹהִים עֹלִים וְיֹרְדִים בּוֹ: (יג) וְהִנֵּה ה' נִצָּב עָלָיו וַיֹּאמַר אֲנִי ה' אֱלֹהֵי אַבְרָהָם אָבִיךָ וֵאלֹהֵי יִצְחָק הָאָרֶץ אֲשֶׁר אַתָּה שֹׁכֵב עָלֶיהָ לְךָ אֶתְּנֶנָּה וּלְזַרְעֶךָ: (יד) וְהָיָה זַרְעֲךָ כַּעֲפַר הָאָרֶץ וּפָרַצְתָּ יָמָּה וָקֵדְמָה וְצָפֹנָה וָנֶגְבָּה וְנִבְרְכוּ בְךָ כָּל־מִשְׁפְּחֹת הָאֲדָמָה וּבְזַרְעֶךָ: (טו) וְהִנֵּה אָנֹכִי עִמָּךְ וּשְׁמַרְתִּיךָ בְּכֹל אֲשֶׁר־תֵּלֵךְ וַהֲשִׁבֹתִיךָ אֶל־הָאֲדָמָה הַזֹּאת כִּי לֹא אֶעֱזָבְךָ עַד אֲשֶׁר אִם־עָשִׂיתִי אֵת אֲשֶׁר־דִּבַּרְתִּי לָךְ:

He had a dream; a stairway was set on the ground and its top reached to the sky, and angels of God were going up and down on it. And the Almighty was standing above him and He said, "I am the Almighty, the God of your father Avraham and the God of Yitzchak. The ground on which you are lying I will assign to you and to your offspring. Your descendants shall be as the dust of the earth; you shall spread out to the west and to the east, to the north and to the south. All the families of the earth shall bless themselves by you and your descendants. Remember, I am with you: I will protect you wherever you go and will bring you back to this land. I will not leave you until I have done what I have promised you." (*Bereishit* 28:12-15)

The blessings God bestowed upon Yaakov that night echoed the blessing he had received from his father Yitzchak—blessings that were intentionally, purposefully given to Yaakov and not to Esav:

בראשית פרק כח:א-ה

(א) וַיִּקְרָא יִצְחָק אֶל־יַעֲקֹב וַיְבָרֶךְ אֹתוֹ וַיְצַוֵּהוּ וַיֹּאמֶר לוֹ לֹא־תִקַּח אִשָּׁה מִבְּנוֹת כְּנָעַן: (ב) קוּם לֵךְ פַּדֶּנָה אֲרָם בֵּיתָה בְתוּאֵל אֲבִי אִמֶּךָ וְקַח־לְךָ מִשָּׁם אִשָּׁה מִבְּנוֹת לָבָן אֲחִי אִמֶּךָ: (ג) וְאֵל שַׁדַּי יְבָרֵךְ אֹתְךָ וְיַפְרְךָ וְיַרְבֶּךָ וְהָיִיתָ לִקְהַל עַמִּים: (ד) וְיִתֶּן־לְךָ אֶת־בִּרְכַּת אַבְרָהָם לְךָ וּלְזַרְעֲךָ אִתָּךְ לְרִשְׁתְּךָ אֶת־אֶרֶץ מְגֻרֶיךָ אֲשֶׁר־נָתַן אֱלֹהִים לְאַבְרָהָם: (ה) וַיִּשְׁלַח יִצְחָק אֶת־יַעֲקֹב וַיֵּלֶךְ פַּדֶּנָה אֲרָם אֶל־לָבָן בֶּן־בְּתוּאֵל הָאֲרַמִּי אֲחִי רִבְקָה אֵם יַעֲקֹב וְעֵשָׂו:

So Yitzchak sent for Yaakov and blessed him. He instructed him, saying, "You shall not take a wife from among the Canaanite women. Arise, go to Paddan-Aram, to the house of Betuel your mother's father, and take a wife there from among the daughters of Lavan, your mother's brother. May God (El Shaddai) bless you, and make you fertile and numerous, so that you become an assembly of peoples. May He grant the blessing of Avraham to you and your offspring, that you may possess the land where you are sojourning, which God assigned to Avraham." Then Yitzchak sent Yaakov off, and he went to Paddan-Aram, to Lavan the son of Betuel the Aramean, the brother of Rivkah, mother of Yaakov and Esav. (*Bereishit* 28:1-5)

The content of Yitzchak's blessing was repeated and reinforced in the blessing Yaakov received directly from God. On the other hand, the blessings intended for Esav, which Yaakov had "taken by guile," were not repeated. The "ill-gotten" blessing invoked material success, for wealth and power and earthly blessings. When God Himself blessed him at Beit El but made no mention of this blessing, Yaakov "heard God's silence" as clearly as he heard God's words. He understood immediately that the blessings for physical plenty were not forthcoming, and beseeched God to provide him with the bare minimum he would need to survive—bread to eat and the most basic clothing.

בראשית פרק כח:יח-כב

(יח) וַיַּשְׁכֵּם יַעֲקֹב בַּבֹּקֶר וַיִּקַּח אֶת־הָאֶבֶן אֲשֶׁר־שָׂם מְרַאֲשֹׁתָיו וַיָּשֶׂם אֹתָהּ מַצֵּבָה וַיִּצֹק שֶׁמֶן עַל־רֹאשָׁהּ: (יט) וַיִּקְרָא אֶת־שֵׁם־הַמָּקוֹם הַהוּא בֵּית־אֵל וְאוּלָם לוּז שֵׁם־הָעִיר לָרִאשֹׁנָה: (כ) וַיִּדַּר יַעֲקֹב נֶדֶר לֵאמֹר אִם־יִהְיֶה אֱלֹהִים עִמָּדִי וּשְׁמָרַנִי בַּדֶּרֶךְ הַזֶּה אֲשֶׁר אָנֹכִי הוֹלֵךְ וְנָתַן־לִי לֶחֶם לֶאֱכֹל וּבֶגֶד לִלְבֹּשׁ: (כא) וְשַׁבְתִּי בְשָׁלוֹם אֶל־בֵּית אָבִי וְהָיָה ה' לִי לֵאלֹהִים: (כב) וְהָאֶבֶן הַזֹּאת אֲשֶׁר־שַׂמְתִּי מַצֵּבָה יִהְיֶה בֵּית אֱלֹהִים וְכֹל אֲשֶׁר תִּתֶּן־לִי עַשֵּׂר אֲעַשְּׂרֶנּוּ לָךְ:

Early in the morning, Yaakov took the stone that he had put under his head and set it up as a pillar and poured oil on the top of it. He named that site Bethel; but previously the name of the city had been Luz. Yaakov then made a vow, saying, "If the Almighty is with me, if He protects me on this journey that I am making, and gives me bread to eat and clothing to wear, and if I return safely to my father's house—the Almighty shall be my God. And this stone, which I have set up as a pillar, shall be God's abode; and of all that You give me, I will set aside a tithe for You." (*Bereishit* 28:18-22)

Now, Yaakov returns with riches—wealth he had not sought, wealth his former self did not need, wealth he may well have thought he did not deserve. As he crosses the Yabok River and sees his reflection, he struggles with questions of identity:[5] *Who am I? Have I he begun to look like Esav? Has the fulfillment of the stolen blessings actually turned me into Esav?*

---

5. Rashi, *Bereishit* 25:27 (based on *Bereishit Rabbbah* 63:10) notes that as young people the twins were far more similar than we usually think.

רש"י בראשית פרק כה:כז

ויגדלו ... ויהי עשו כָּל זְמַן שֶׁהָיוּ קְטַנִּים, לֹא הָיוּ נִכָּרִים בְּמַעֲשֵׂיהֶם, וְאֵין אָדָם מְדַקְדֵּק בָּהֶם, מַה טִּיבָם; כֵּיוָן שֶׁנַּעֲשׂוּ בְנֵי שְׁלֹשׁ עֶשְׂרֵה שָׁנָה, זֶה פֵּרֵשׁ לְבָתֵּי מִדְרָשׁוֹת וְזֶה פֵּרֵשׁ לַעֲ"זְ:

"And they grew ... and Esav was..." — So long as they were young they could not be distinguished by what their behavior and no one paid much attention to their characters, but when they reached the age of thirteen, one went his way to the houses of learning and the other went his way to the idolatrous temples.

It would seem that Esav thought so.

When last we heard from Esav, he swore to kill Yaakov. Now, although decades had passed, Yaakov's emissaries returned with information that confirmed Esav's murderous intentions: He was on his way with an army of four hundred men.[6]

And yet, when they finally stand face to face, a dramatic shift takes place in Esav's temperament. Esav embraces Yaakov, physically and figuratively, and asks Yaakov to travel together with him, to join him in Seir and live together as brothers—quite an unexpected response from someone who has sworn to kill.

We might naturally have expected Esav's anger to have been exacerbated by the sight of Yaakov's great wealth; after all, this blessing of wealth was rightfully his own. What brought about Esav's sudden change of heart? The gifts Yaakov offered can hardly explain this sudden outpouring of fraternal affection; why would Esav have been placated by gifts when he could easily have killed Yaakov, taken his revenge, and walked off with everything?

The only explanation is that Esav now saw something in Yaakov that he had never seen before. Esav saw the "new" Yaakov, the man who had seemingly abandoned his spiritual pursuits in favor of material wealth, and as far as Esav was concerned, there was no longer a reason to hate his brother. In Esav's mind, Yaakov had become Esav. The barriers which had divided them had disappeared; they could now join forces. Esav thought he had achieved an ideological victory, which was far sweeter than any revenge he could have exacted.

This was precisely the cause of Yaakov's inner struggle.

All through the night before his confrontation with his brother, Yaakov struggles with his own success. He struggles with the blessings meant for Esav, and with the Esav that he fears may have become a part of himself. His spiritual self and his physical self collide as he tries to determine his true identity—but is unable to resolve the conflict.

---

6. *Bereishit* 33:1.

בראשית פרק לב:כו-לג

(כו) וַיַּרְא כִּי לֹא יָכֹל לוֹ וַיִּגַּע בְּכַף־יְרֵכוֹ וַתֵּקַע כַּף־יֶרֶךְ יַעֲקֹב בְּהֵאָבְקוֹ עִמּוֹ:.... וְהוּא צֹלֵעַ עַל־יְרֵכוֹ: (לג) עַל־כֵּן לֹא־יֹאכְלוּ בְנֵי־יִשְׂרָאֵל אֶת־גִּיד הַנָּשֶׁה אֲשֶׁר עַל־כַּף הַיָּרֵךְ עַד הַיּוֹם הַזֶּה כִּי נָגַע בְּכַף־יֶרֶךְ יַעֲקֹב בְּגִיד הַנָּשֶׁה:

When he saw that he could not [defeat] him, he touched the joint of his thigh. Yaakov's hip became dislocated from wrestling with him.... And he was limping because of his thigh... Therefore, the Children of Israel do not eat the *gid ha-nasheh* which is on the thigh [of an animal] until this very day, for Yaakov's thigh was afflicted on the *gid ha-nasheh*. (Bereshit 32:26, 33)

In the resolution that is finally achieved, the physical realm is forced to yield, to move at a slower pace. Laws, like that of the *gid ha-nasheh*, will from this time onward create spiritual boundaries within physical experience, making it possible to elevate the physical world to a spiritual plane. This is the first law of *kashrut* revealed to the Children of Israel, and it is a symbolic representation of the limits placed on the physical plane in service of our higher, spiritual identity: A slow, precise process of removal of this sinew from the animal's leg must be performed in order for the meat to be permissible for our consumption. This law reflects the resolution of Yaakov's inner struggle: Although he may have resembled Esav physically, Yaakov was a changed man in spiritual terms. The name he was given by his father at birth, Yaakov, connotes a relationship with Esav;[7] now, this name would be superseded by the name *Yisrael*, which speaks of his relationship with the physical and spiritual realms.

---

7. See *Bereishit* 25:26:

בראשית פרק כה:כו
(כו) וְאַחֲרֵי־כֵן יָצָא אָחִיו וְיָדוֹ אֹחֶזֶת בַּעֲקֵב עֵשָׂו וַיִּקְרָא שְׁמוֹ יַעֲקֹב וְיִצְחָק בֶּן־שִׁשִּׁים שָׁנָה בְּלֶדֶת אֹתָם:

Then his brother emerged, holding on to the heel ['akev] of Esav; so he was named Yaakov. Yitzchak was sixty years old when they were born.

When the Sages identified Yaakov's adversary as "the angel of Esav," they referred to the power of Esav within himself with which Yaakov was struggling, the power which Yaakov feared had taken over his life.[8]

There is an enlightening commentary on this section in the Book of Hoshea, which leaves little doubt that the prophet understood that Yaakov's assailant was not a human adversary, and connects this struggle with the the *in utero* struggle:

הושע פרק יב:ד-ז

(ד) בַּבֶּטֶן עָקַב אֶת־אָחִיו וּבְאוֹנוֹ שָׂרָה אֶת־אֱלֹהִים: (ה) וַיָּשַׂר אֶל־מַלְאָךְ וַיֻּכָל בָּכָה וַיִּתְחַנֶּן־לוֹ בֵּית־אֵל יִמְצָאֶנּוּ וְשָׁם יְדַבֵּר עִמָּנוּ: (ו) וַה' אֱלֹהֵי הַצְּבָאוֹת ה' זִכְרוֹ: (ז) וְאַתָּה בֵּאלֹהֶיךָ תָשׁוּב חֶסֶד וּמִשְׁפָּט שְׁמֹר וְקַוֵּה אֶל־אֱלֹהֶיךָ תָּמִיד:

In the womb he tried to supplant his brother; grown to manhood, he strove with the Almighty.[9] He strove with an angel and prevailed; the other had to weep and implore him. At Beit El [Yaakov] would meet him, there to commune with him. (*Hoshea* 12:4-7)[10]

When the struggle ends, with the break of dawn, Esav appears. Yaakov has spent a dread-filled night, tormented by the thought that he has become Esav, and when they meet at last, Esav seems to concur. Esav reaches out to Yaakov in an unexpected, long awaited act of brotherly love:

---

8. More on the similarity between Yaakov and Esav and their struggle can be found in *Parashat Acharei Mot*.
9. The word *Elo-him* has the meaning of "all-powerful." It may be used to refer to God or angels, or even false idols that people mistakenly believe have power. may refer either to God's identity as all-powerful, thus "Almighty," or to false gods to which mankind attributes certain powers – or even to people of great power.
10. See Rashi, *Hoshea* 12:5:

רש"י הושע פרק יב:ה

ויתחנן לו - כשנאמר לו לא אשלחך כי אם ברכתני (בראשית לב) המלאך היה מבקש ממנו הנח לי עכשיו סופו של הקדוש ברוך הוא ליגלות עליך בבית אל ושם ימצאנו ושם ידב' עמנו והוא ואני נסכים לך על הברכות שבירכך יצחק ואותו מלאך שָׂרוֹ של עֵשָׂו היה והיה מערער על הברכות:

בראשית פרק לג:יב-יג

(יב) וַיֹּאמֶר נִסְעָה וְנֵלֵכָה וְאֵלְכָה לְנֶגְדֶּךָ: (יג) וַיֹּאמֶר אֵלָיו אֲדֹנִי יֹדֵעַ כִּי־הַיְלָדִים רַכִּים וְהַצֹּאן וְהַבָּקָר עָלוֹת עָלָי וּדְפָקוּם יוֹם אֶחָד וָמֵתוּ כָּל־הַצֹּאן:

[Esav] said, "Let us travel and walk together, and I will walk alongside you." [Yaakov] said to him, "My master knows that the children are young and the sheep and cattle weigh heavily on me. If I should overdrive them one day, all the sheep would die." (*Bereishit* 33:12-13)

When Esav sees his brother, sees the man he has become and the wealth he has accrued, he mistakenly believes that Yaakov has abandoned his earlier pursuits in favor of building this empire. Esav suggests that they join forces and travel together, certain that there are no longer irreconcilable differences between them—but Yaakov begs off, explaining that for him, his possessions are a burden. For Esav, physical plenty is the goal, the sought-after prize, but Yaakov considers the physical bounty with which he has been blessed a cumbersome responsibility that holds him back from reaching his true stride, from realizing his spiritual potential—much like his damaged leg, the physical reminder of his nocturnal struggle, which slows him down and inhibits his progress.

בראשית פרק לג:טז-יז

(טז) וַיָּשָׁב בַּיּוֹם הַהוּא עֵשָׂו לְדַרְכּוֹ שֵׂעִירָה: (יז) וְיַעֲקֹב נָסַע סֻכֹּתָה וַיִּבֶן לוֹ בָּיִת וּלְמִקְנֵהוּ עָשָׂה סֻכֹּת עַל־כֵּן קָרָא שֵׁם־הַמָּקוֹם סֻכּוֹת: ס

On that day Esav returned to his way to Sei'ir. Yaakov went to Sukkot and built for himself a house and made booths [*sukkot*] for the cattle. Therefore, the name of the place was called Sukkot. (*Bereishit* 33: 16–17)

As the curtain is lowered on the confrontation scene, Yaakov and Esav part ways: Esav returns to Sei'ir, while Yaakov travels to Sukkot, named for the shelter Yaakov builds for his livestock. Presumably, Yaakov also built a home in this place, where he lived with his family. Why would he prefer to name the place for the insubstantial shelter he constructed to protect his animals?

The association that immediately springs to mind when we read these verses is with Sukkot, the festival in which we reside in booths or huts. While at first this association seems like an anachronism, there may be more to it than meets the eye: During the Festival of Sukkot, we leave the comforts of home and live in a temporary abode, reminding ourselves that the physical world is a temporary one.[11] However, during this same holiday we take four species in hand and pray for rain—*geshem*. A beautiful dialectic is created, at the same time we pray for physical bounty, *gashmiut*, we leave our homes, and enter a transitory, vulnerable hut, an abode under the *Shechinah*.[12] We live in a physical world but must find a way of elevating the physical.

---

11. By definition, a *sukkah* is a temporary abode. See *Sukkah* 23a and 2a:

תלמוד בבלי מסכת סוכה דף כג עמוד א
רבי עקיבא סבר: סוכה דירת עראי בעינן....

Rabbi Akiva holds: a *sukkah* needs to be a temporary residence.

תלמוד בבלי מסכת סוכה דף ב עמוד א
ורבא אמר: מהכא בסכת תשבו שבעת ימים. אמרה תורה: כל שבעת הימים צא מדירת קבע ושב בדירת עראי. עד עשרים אמה - אדם עושה דירתו דירת עראי, למעלה מעשרים אמה - אין אדם עושה דירתו דירת עראי,

Rava said from here: "In sukkot shall you reside seven days" (Leviticus 23:42). The Torah said: the entire seven days, emerge from the permanent residence and reside in a temporary residence, up to twenty cubits, a person can render his residence a temporary residence, above twenty cubits high, one cannot render his residence a temporary residence; rather, permanent residence.

12. See *Zohar, Vayikra* 103a:

זוהר מנוקד חלק ג דף קג/א
תָּא חֲזֵי, עַל כָּל חֶסֶד דְּעָבַד קוּדְשָׁא בְּרִיךְ הוּא בְּיִשְׂרָאֵל. קָשִׁיר עִמְּהוֹן ז' עֲנָנֵי יַקִּירָן, וְקָשִׁיר לְהוּ בִּכְנֶסֶת יִשְׂרָאֵל, דְּהָא עֲנָנָא דִּילָהּ אִתְקְשַׁר בְּשִׁיתָא אָחֳרָנִין. וּבְכֻלְּהוּ שִׁבְעָה, אַזְלוּ יִשְׂרָאֵל בְּמַדְבְּרָא. מַאי קָא טַעֲמָא, בְּגִין דְּכַלְּהוּ קִשְׁרָא דִמְהֵימְנוּתָא נִינְהוּ וְעַל דָּא בַּסֻּכּוֹת תֵּשְׁבוּ שִׁבְעַת יָמִים. מַאי קָא מַיְירֵי. בְּגִין דִּכְתִיב, (שיר השירים ב) בְּצִלּוֹ חִמַּדְתִּי וְיָשַׁבְתִּי וּפִרְיוֹ מָתוֹק לְחִכִּי. וּבָעֵי בַר נָשׁ לְאַחֲזָאָה גַּרְמֵיהּ, דְּיָתִיב תְּחוֹת צִלָּא דִּמְהֵימְנוּתָא:

For this very reason, the verse describing Yaakov's behavior in the aftermath of his dual confrontations is a fitting conclusion to this section as a whole: Yaakov recognizes that the physical wealth which which he has been blessed is transitory. Moreover, Yaakov comes to understand his wealth as a means to an end: His destiny is not defined by the physical but rather by the quest to elevate the physical. In order to stress this message, he names the first place he settles after meeting Esav and coming to terms with his material existence, "Sukkot."

Perhaps this message, of elevating the mundane was already discerned at the start if Yaakov's sojourn. Underneath the stars, Yaakov saw a ladder which reached to the heavens, and the angels went up and then came down. Man too, should take the bounty of this world and find a way to connect it to heaven, and then return to his or her mission in this world.

And just as Yaakov headed toward Sukkot after his confrontation with Esav, each year Jews head to Sukkot immediately after Yom Kippur, the day of personal and national reckoning.

One of the most confounding aspects of Yom Kippur is the scapegoat:

ויקרא פרק טז:ז-י

(ז) וְלָקַח אֶת־שְׁנֵי הַשְּׂעִירִם וְהֶעֱמִיד אֹתָם לִפְנֵי ה' פֶּתַח אֹהֶל מוֹעֵד: (ח) וְנָתַן אַהֲרֹן עַל־שְׁנֵי הַשְּׂעִירִם גֹּרָלוֹת גּוֹרָל אֶחָד לַה' וְגוֹרָל אֶחָד לַעֲזָאזֵל: (ט) וְהִקְרִיב אַהֲרֹן אֶת־הַשָּׂעִיר אֲשֶׁר עָלָה עָלָיו הַגּוֹרָל לַה' וְעָשָׂהוּ חַטָּאת: (י) וְהַשָּׂעִיר אֲשֶׁר עָלָה עָלָיו הַגּוֹרָל לַעֲזָאזֵל יָעֳמַד־חַי לִפְנֵי ה' לְכַפֵּר עָלָיו לְשַׁלַּח אֹתוֹ לַעֲזָאזֵל הַמִּדְבָּרָה:

Aharon shall take the two he-goats and let them stand before God at the entrance of the Tent of Meeting; and Aharon shall place lots upon the two goats, one marked "For God" and the other marked "For Azazel." Aharon shall bring forward the goat designated by lot for God, which he is to offer as a sin offering; while the goat designated by lot for Azazel shall be left standing alive before God, to make expiation with it and to send it off to the wilderness for Azazel. (*Vayikra* 16:7-10)

In attempting to explain the concept of the Yom Kippur scapegoat, the *se'ir la'azazel*, Ramban[13] explains that this peculiar "sacrifice" is

---

13. Ramban's comments on *Vayikra* 16:8 are based on a teaching found in *Pirkei de-Rabbi Eliezer*, depending on the edition chapter 45 or 46.

רמב"ן ויקרא פרק טז:ח

...ור"א כתב אמר רב שמואל אף על פי שכתוב בשעיר החטאת שהוא לשם, גם השעיר המשתלח הוא לשם. ואין צורך, כי המשתלח איננו קרבן, שלא ישחט. ואם יכולת להבין הסוד שהוא אחר מלת עזאזל תדע סודו וסוד שמו, כי יש לו חברים במקרא, ואני אגלה לך קצת הסוד ברמז בהיותך בן שלשים ושלש תדענו. והנה ר"א נאמן רוח מכסה דבר, ואני הרכיל מגלה סודו שכבר גלו אותו רבותינו ז"ל במקומות רבים:

אמרו בבראשית רבה (סה י) ונשא השעיר עליו (להלן פסוק כב), זה עשו שנאמר (בראשית כז יא) הן עשו אחי איש שעיר, את כל עונותם, עונות תם שנאמר ויעקב איש תם (שם כה כז):

ומפורש מזה בפרקי רבי אליעזר הגדול (פרק מו), לפיכך היו נותנין לו לסמאל שוחד ביום הכפורים שלא לבטל את קרבנם, שנאמר גורל אחד לה' וגורל אחד לעזאזל, גורלו של הקדוש ברוך הוא לקרבן עולה, וגורלו של עזאזל שעיר החטאת וכל עונותיהם של ישראל עליו, שנאמר ונשא השעיר עליו. ראה סמאל שלא נמצא בהם חטא ביום הכפורים, אמר לפני הקדוש ברוך הוא, רבון כל העולמים יש לך עם אחד בארץ כמלאכי השרת שבשמים, מה מלאכי השרת יחפי רגל כך הן ישראל יחפי רגל ביום הכפורים. מה מלאכי השרת אין בהם אכילה ושתיה כך ישראל אין בהם אכילה ושתיה ביום הכפורים. מה מלאכי השרת אין להם קפיצה כך ישראל עומדין על רגליהם ביום הכפורים. מה מלאכי השרת שלום מתוך ביניהם כך הן ישראל שלום מתוך ביניהם ביום הכפורים. מה מלאכי השרת נקיים מכל חטא כך הן ישראל נקיים מכל חטא ביום הכפורים. והקדוש ברוך הוא שומע עדותן של ישראל מן הקטיגור שלהם ומכפר על המזבח ועל המקדש ועל הכהנים ועל כל עם הקהל שנאמר וכפר את מקדש הקדש וגו', ע"כ אגדה זו. והנה הודיענו שמו ומעשהו:

וזה סוד הענין, כי היו עובדים לאלהים אחרים, הם המלאכים, עושים להם קרבנות והם להם לריח ניחוח כענין שנאמר (יחזקאל טז יט) ושמני וקטרתי נתת לפניהם, ולחמי אשר נתתי לך סולת ושמן ודבש האכלתיך ונתתיהו לפניהם לריח ניחוח ויהי נאם ה' אלהים. ואתה צריך להתבונן בכתוב במקרא ובמסורות:

והנה התורה אסרה לגמרי קבלת אלהותם וכל עבודה להם, אבל צוה הקדוש ברוך הוא ביום הכפורים שנשלח שעיר במדבר לשר המושל במקומות החרבן, והוא הראוי לו מפני שהוא בעליו ומאצילות כחו יבא חורב ושממון כי הוא העילה לכוכבי החרב והדמים והמלחמות והמריבות והפצעים והמכות והפירוד והחרבן, והכלל נפש לגלגל מאדים, וחלקו מן האומות הוא עשו שהוא עם היורש החרב והמלחמות, ומן הבהמות השעירים והעזים, ובחלקו עוד השדים הנקראים מזיקין בלשון רבותינו, ובלשון הכתוב (להלן יז ז) שעירים, כי כן יקרא הוא ואומתו שעיר. ואין הכונה בשעיר המשתלח שיהיה קרבן מאתנו אליו חלילה, אבל שתהיה כונתנו לעשות רצון בוראנו שצונו כך:

והמשל בזה, כמי שעשה סעודה לאדון וצוה האדון את האיש העושה הסעודה תן מנה אחת לעבדי פלוני, שאין העושה הסעודה נותן כלום לעבד ההוא ולא לכבודו יעשה עמו, רק הכל נתן לאדון והאדון נותן פרס לעבדו, ושמר זה מצותו ועשה לכבוד האדון כל אשר צוהו, ואמנם האדון לחמלתו על בעל הסעודה רצה שיהיו כל עבדיו נהנין ממנו שיספר בשבחו ולא בגנותו:

וזה טעם הגורלות, כי אילו היה הכהן מקדיש אותם בפה לה' ולעזאזל, היה כעובד אליו ונודר לשמו, אבל היה מעמיד אותם לפני ה' פתח אהל מועד, כי שניהם מתנה לה' והוא נתן מהם לעבדו החלק אשר יבא לו מאת השם, הוא הפיל להם גורל וידו חלק להם, כענין שנאמר

actually a bribe for an angel named Samaʹel, who is called to testify in the Heavenly Court as a character witness for the Jewish people[14]—in

(משלי טז לג) בחיק יוטל את הגורל ומה' כל משפטו וגם אחרי הגורל היה מעמידו לפני ה' לומר שהוא שלו ואין אנחנו מכוונים בשילוחו אלא לרצונו לשם, כמו שאמר (פסוק י) יעמד חי לפני ה' לכפר עליו לשלח אותו וגו', ולכך לא נשחוט אותו אנחנו כלל:

ותרגם אונקלוס לשמא דהשם ולעזאזל, כי האחד לשם ה' ולא לו, והשני לעזאזל ולא לשמו של עזאזל.

ומפני זה אמרו רבותינו (ת"כ פרק יג ט) ואת חקותי (להלן יח ד), דברים שיצר הרע מק־טרג בהם ואומות העולם משיבין עליהם, לבישת שעטנז ופרה אדומה ושעיר המשתלח. ולא מצאו בקרבנות תשובה לאומות העולם עלינו, כי הם על אישי ה', אבל בשעיר המשתלח ישיבו עלינו, כי יחשבו שאנו עושים כמעשיהם. וכן בפרה אדומה, מפני שהיא נעשית מחוץ למחנה, ועניינה דומה לענין שעיר המשתלח להעביר רוח הטומאה, כענין שנאמר בעתיד (זכריה יג ב) את הנביאים ואת רוח הטומאה אעביר מן הארץ. ומזה תבין טעם כבוס בגדי המשלח את השעיר לעזאזל והשורף את הפרה, ומה שהזכירו רבותינו (זבחים קד א) בכבוס הבגדים של פרים הנשרפים ושעירים הנשרפים:

והנה רמז לך ר"א שתדע סודו כשתגיע לפסוק ולא יזבחו עוד את זבחיהם לשעירים. והמלה מורכבת, וחבריה רבים. והנה הענין מבואר, זולתי אם תחקור מה ענין לשכלים הנבד־לים ולרוחות בקרבן. וזה יודע ברוחות, בחכמת נגרומנסי"א, ויודע גם בשכלים, ברמזי התורה למבין סודם, ולא אוכל לפרש. כי היינו צריכים לחסום פי המתחכמים בטבע הנמשכים אחרי היוני אשר הכחיש כל דבר זולתי המורגש לו, והגיס דעתו לחשוב הוא ותלמידיו הרשעים, כי כל ענין שלא השיג אליו הוא בסברתו איננו אמת:

פרקי דרבי אליעזר פרק מו
שֶׁיּוֹם הַכִּפֻּרִים מְכַפֵּר עַל הַקַּלּוֹת וְעַל הַחֲמוּרוֹת, שֶׁנֶּאֱמַר [שם טז, ל] כִּי בַיּוֹם הַזֶּה יְכַפֵּר עֲלֵיכֶם וְגוֹ', מִכֹּל חַטֹּאתֵיכֶם, מֵחַטֹּאתֵיכֶם אֵין כְּתִיב, אֶלָּא מִכֹּל חַטֹּאתֵיכֶם: יוֹם שֶׁנִּתְּנָה תוֹרָה אָמַר סַמָּאֵל [נ"א: שטן] לִפְנֵי הַקָּדוֹשׁ בָּרוּךְ הוּא, רִבּוֹנוֹ שֶׁל עוֹלָם, עַל כָּל הָרְשָׁעִים נָתַתָּ לִי רְשׁוּת, וְעַל הַצַּדִּיקִים אֵין אַתָּה נוֹתֵן לִי רְשׁוּת. אָמַר לוֹ הֲרֵי יֵשׁ לְךָ רְשׁוּת עֲלֵיהֶן בְּיוֹם הַכִּפֻּרִים אִם יֵשׁ לָהֶם חֵטְא, וְאִם לָאו אֵין לְךָ עֲלֵיהֶן רְשׁוּת, לְפִיכָךְ נוֹתְנִים לוֹ שֹׁחַד בְּיוֹם הַכִּפֻּרִים, שֶׁלֹּא לְבַטֵּל קָרְבָּן שֶׁל יִשְׂרָאֵל, שֶׁנֶּאֱמַר [שם ח] גּוֹרָל אֶחָד לַה' וְגוֹרָל אֶחָד לַעֲזָאזֵל, גּוֹרָלוֹ שֶׁל הַקָּדוֹשׁ בָּרוּךְ הוּא קָרְבַּן עוֹלָה, וְגוֹרָלוֹ שֶׁל עֲזָאזֵל שְׂעִיר חַטָּאת. וְכָל עֲוֹנוֹתֵיהֶם שֶׁל יִשְׂרָאֵל הָיָה עָלָיו, שֶׁנֶּאֱמַר [שם כב] וְנָשָׂא הַשָּׂעִיר עָלָיו אֶת כָּל עֲוֹנֹתָם. רָאָה סַמָּאֵל [נ"א: השטן] שֶׁלֹּא נִמְצָא בָהֶם חֵטְא בְּיוֹם הַכִּפֻּרִים, אָמַר לְפָנָיו רִבּוֹנוֹ שֶׁל עוֹלָם, יֵשׁ לְךָ עַם אֶחָד בָּאָרֶץ כְּמַלְאֲכֵי הַשָּׁרֵת בַּשָּׁמַיִם. מַה מַּלְאֲכֵי הַשָּׁרֵת אֵין לָהֶם קְפִיצִין, כָּךְ הֵם יִשְׂרָאֵל עוֹמְדִים עַל רַגְלֵיהֶם בְּיוֹם הַכִּפֻּרִים. מַה מַּלְאֲכֵי הַשָּׁרֵת אֵין לָהֶם אֲכִילָה וּשְׁתִיָּה, כָּךְ יִשְׂרָאֵל אֵין לָהֶם אֲכִילָה וּשְׁתִיָּה בְּיוֹם הַכִּפֻּרִים. מַה מַּלְאֲכֵי הַשָּׁרֵת נְקִיִּים מִכָּל חֵטְא, כָּךְ יִשְׂרָאֵל נְקִיִּים מִכָּל חֵטְא בְּיוֹם הַכִּפֻּרִים. מַה מַּלְאֲכֵי הַשָּׁרֵת שָׁלוֹם מְתַוֵּךְ בֵּינֵיהֶם, כָּךְ הֵם יִשְׂרָאֵל שָׁלוֹם מְתַוֵּךְ בֵּינֵיהֶם בְּיוֹם הַכִּפֻּרִים. וְהַקָּדוֹשׁ בָּרוּךְ הוּא שׁוֹמֵעַ עֲתִירָתָן שֶׁל יִשְׂרָאֵל מִן הַקַּטֵּגוֹר שֶׁלָּהֶם, וּמְכַפֵּר עַל הַמִּזְבֵּחַ וְעַל הַכֹּהֲנִים וְעַל כָּל עַם הַקָּהָל לְמִגָּדוֹל וְעַד קָטָן, שֶׁנֶּאֱמַר [ויקרא טז, לג] וְכִפֶּר אֶת מִקְדַּשׁ הַקֹּדֶשׁ:

---

14. See Rav Soloveitchik's commentary on this Ramban in *On Repentance* (edited by P. Peli), 317ff. Without the Rav's explanation, this Ramban is all but impenetrable.

much the same way that Yaakov attempted to appease Esav with gifts. Who is Samael? The Midrash, commenting on our *parashah*, explains:[15]

מדרש תנחומא (ורשא) פרשת וישלח

וַיִּוָּתֵר יַעֲקֹב לְבַדּוֹ וַיֵּאָבֵק אִישׁ עִמּוֹ, זֶה סַמָּאֵל שָׂרוֹ שֶׁל עֵשָׂו שֶׁבִּקֵּשׁ לְהָרְגוֹ, שֶׁנֶּאֱמַר: וַיַּרְא כִּי לֹא יָכֹל לוֹ, וַנַּעֲשָׂה צוֹלֵעַ.

---

15. The larger context of the Midrash is Yaakov's failure to fulfill the vow he made when he woke after seeing the vision of angels ascending and descending the heavenly ladder; see note 115, below.

מדרש תנחומא (ורשא) פרשת וישלח

וְאָמַר רַבִּי יַנַּאי, הַנּוֹדֵר וְאֵינוֹ מְשַׁלֵּם, פִּנְקָסוֹ מִתְבַּקֶּרֶת לִפְנֵי הַקָּדוֹשׁ בָּרוּךְ הוּא וְאוֹמֵר: הֵיכָן פְּלוֹנִי בֶּן פְּלוֹנִי שֶׁנָּדַר נֶדֶר בְּיוֹם פְּלוֹנִי. בֹּא וּרְאֵה, כְּשֶׁהָלַךְ יַעֲקֹב לַאֲרַם נַהֲרַיִם מַה כְּתִיב שָׁם, וַיִּדַּר יַעֲקֹב נֶדֶר לֵאמֹר וְגוֹ' (בראשית כח, כ). הֵשִׁיבוּ עַל כָּל דָּבָר וְדָבָר. הָלַךְ וְנִתְעַשֵּׁר וּבָא וְיָשַׁב לוֹ וְלֹא שָׁלֵם אֶת נִדְרוֹ, הֵבִיא עָלָיו עֵשָׂו וּבִקֵּשׁ לְהָרְגוֹ. נָטַל מִמֶּנּוּ כָּל אוֹתוֹ דּוֹרוֹן, עִזִּים מָאתַיִם, וְלֹא הִרְגִּישׁ. הֵבִיא עָלָיו הַמַּלְאָךְ וְרָפַשׁ עִמּוֹ וְלֹא הִרְגִּישׁ, שֶׁנֶּאֱמַר: וַיִּוָּתֵר יַעֲקֹב לְבַדּוֹ וַיֵּאָבֵק אִישׁ עִמּוֹ, זֶה סַמָּאֵל שָׂרוֹ שֶׁל עֵשָׂו שֶׁבִּקֵּשׁ לְהָרְגוֹ, שֶׁנֶּאֱמַר: וַיַּרְא כִּי לֹא יָכֹל לוֹ, וַנַּעֲשָׂה צוֹלֵעַ. כֵּיוָן שֶׁלֹּא הִרְגִּישׁ, בָּאת עָלָיו צָרַת דִּינָה, שֶׁנֶּאֱמַר: וַתֵּצֵא דִינָה. כֵּיוָן שֶׁלֹּא הִרְגִּישׁ, בָּאת עָלָיו צָרַת רָחֵל, שֶׁנֶּאֱמַר: וַתָּמָת רָחֵל וַתִּקָּבֵר. מְסַיֵּעַ לֵהּ לְרַב שְׁמוּאֵל בַּר נַחְמָן דְּאָמַר, כָּל הַנּוֹדֵר וְאֵינוֹ מְשַׁלֵּם גּוֹרֵם לְאִשְׁתּוֹ שֶׁתָּמוּת, שֶׁנֶּאֱמַר: אִם אֵין לְךָ לְשַׁלֵּם וְגוֹ'.

R. Yannai asserted: The ledger of the man who makes a vow which he fails to fulfill is examined in the presence of the Holy One, blessed be He. He asks: Where is that person who made a vow on a certain day? Observe that it is written concerning the time that Yaakov went to Aram-Naharaim: And Yaakov vowed a vow, saying: "If God be with me" (*Bereishit* 28:20). At first He granted his every request. He went there and became wealthy, but when he returned without fulfilling his vow, He turned Esav against him, and Esav sought to kill him. And though Esav took the two hundred she-goats from him, Yaakov did not trouble to perform his vow. Whereupon He turned the angel against him and they wrestled together, but still he did not take note, as it is said: Yaakov remained alone and a man wrestled with him" — this is Samael, the guardian angel of Esav, who wished to kill him, as is said: When he saw that he prevailed not against him, he touched the hollow of his thigh (v. 27). When he still was not persuaded to fulfill his vow, the anguish occasioned by Dinah's experience befell him, as is said: And Dinah went out. When he continued to refrain from carrying out his vow, the tragedy of Rachel's death occurred, as it is said, "And Rachel died and was "buried (*Bereishit* 35:19). This confirms the opinion of R. Shmuel the son of Nahman that one who vows and fails to fulfill his vow brings about the death of his wife, as it is said: "If do not have the means to pay, why should he take away your bed from under you?" (Prov. 22:27).

> "Yaakov remained alone and a man wrestled with him" — this is Sama'el, the guardian angel of Esav, who wished to kill him.
> (*Midrash Tanchuma, Vayishlach* 8)

Just as the connection between Yaakov's *sukkot* and the Festival of Sukkot reveals the inner meaning of the holiday, so, too, regarding the connection with Yom Kippur: This is a day of introspection and self-appraisal, of spiritual stock-taking and soul-searching. On Yom Kippur, every Jew takes a long, hard look at the person he or she has become, and measures his or her present self against the person he or she should be. On this day, we are commanded to offer a scapegoat, to "give the devil his due," as it were, in a ritual of atonement that enables us to readjust our perspective on our physical existence. This is what Yaakov did on the eve of his personal day of reckoning, and precisely the strategy he employed in order to win Esav over and avoid catastrophe.

The *Zohar*[16] makes this connection clear: Yaakov received the blessings from his father on Rosh Hashanah, and fled in the days between Rosh Hashanah and Yom Kippur. Years later, according to the *Zohar*, the confrontation between Yaakov and the spiritual representative of Esav takes place on Yom Kippur Eve, at the hour of *Kol Nidrei*,[17] but this struggle is resolved by daybreak—the hour the *kohen gadol* begins the Yom Kippur ritual, the hour when Yaakov/Yisrael confronts Esav.[18]

When the nocturnal struggle is over, Yaakov is a changed man. He is given a new name, and he, in turn, gives the place of this confrontation a name: *Peniel*, "the face of God." Yaakov's profound self-analysis and inner struggle bring him "face to face" with God—just as the process of *teshuvah* (repentance) that results from profound introspection leads every penitent to a rendezvous with God.

---

16. *Zohar, Vayikra* 100b.
17. It is interesting to note that the first *neder* (vow) Yaakov made, in Beit El, was that upon his return to Israel he would build a house of God—the sanctuary in which the *kohen gadol* would perform the Yom Kippur ritual. See *Midrash Tanchuma Vayishlach* 8 cited above.
18. See *Zohar, Bamidbar* 203a. The question, "Who are these?" (i.e., are we behaving like Yaakov or Esav?) is asked every Yom Kippur, by Satan.

Vayishlach: The Struggle

תלמוד בבלי מסכת יומא דף פו עמוד א
אָמַר רַבִּי לֵוִי, גְּדוֹלָה תְשׁוּבָה - שֶׁמַּגַּעַת עַד כִּסֵּא הַכָּבוֹד, שֶׁנֶּאֱמַר, (הושע יד) "שׁוּבָה יִשְׂרָאֵל עַד ה' אֱלֹהֶיךָ"

> Great is repentance, for it reaches up to the Throne of Glory, as it says, "Return, O Israel, to the Almighty, your God." [*Hoshea* 14:2]. (*Yoma* 86a)

The confrontation with Esav that ensued is the prototype for Yom Kippur: The gifts with which Yaakov attempts to appease his would-be accuser parallel the scapegoat offering; the introspection and prayer through the night; the face-off between the spiritual and physical aspects of his personality; the reconciliation Yaakov achieves between the warring sides of his psyche as he rededicates himself to using his physical blessings to better serve his spiritual mission. Yaakov's struggle and eventual victory encapsulate the story of the Days of Awe, and of the spiritual destiny of the Jewish People.

If the confrontation between Yaakov and Esav takes place on Yom Kippur, then, by extension, the confrontation with his anonymous opponent takes place the previous night—*Kol Nidrei* night, Yom Kippur Eve. All that night, Yaakov struggled with the Esav within him: Was he still Yaakov or had he become Esav? Had his possessions and his preoccupation with acquiring those possessions changed him? By taking Esav's blessing, had he in fact taken on Esav's persona?

The verses tell us that Yaakov wrestled with the angel; the Gemara comments on these verses:

תלמוד בבלי מסכת חולין צא.
דְּאָמַר רַבִּי יְהוֹשֻׁעַ בֶּן לֵוִי, מְלַמֵּד שֶׁהֶעֱלוּ אָבָק בְּרַגְלֵיהֶם עַד כִּסֵּא הַכָּבוֹד....

> For Rabbi Yehoshua ben Levi taught: This teaches us that the combatants raised dust from their feet that rose up to the Divine Throne. (*Chullin* 91a)

The *Zohar* elaborates:

זוהר חלק א דף קע/א

וַיֵּאָבֵק אִישׁ עִמּוֹ, מַאי וַיֵּאָבֵק. (גליון דאמר רבי יהושע בן לוי, מלמד דסליקו אבק ברגליהון עד כורסי יקרא. כתיב הכא בהאבקו עמו, וכתיב (נחום א) אבק רגליו, וההוא מלאך שרו של עשו היה, ואיהו סמאל. בגין כך, דינו הוא שיעלה אבק דרגליו עד כסא הכבוד, שהוא מקום המשפט.)

Rabbi Yehoshua ben Levi said: This teaches that the dust arose from their feet up to the Throne of Glory. It is written here, "When he wrestled with him," and it also is written, "the dust of his feet" (*Nachum* 1). And this angel was the Guardian of Esav. And who is he? Samael. It is appropriate that the dust of their feet went up to the Throne of Glory, for that is the place of judgment. (*Zohar, Bereishit* 170a in a marginal note)

The *Zohar* understands that judgment filled the air that night. Would the angel of Esav be able to attest to Yaakov's innocence as he would for generations of Jews in the future?

בראשית לב:כז

... וַיֹּאמֶר לֹא אֲשַׁלֵּחֲךָ כִּי אִם־בֵּרַכְתָּנִי:

He [Yaakov] said, "I will not release you unless you bless me." (*Bereishit* 32:27)

Yaakov wants the angel's blessing, and eventually he receives it, as the verses attest:

בראשית פרק לב:ל-לב

(ל) ... וַיְבָרֶךְ אֹתוֹ שָׁם: (לא) וַיִּקְרָא יַעֲקֹב שֵׁם הַמָּקוֹם פְּנִיאֵל כִּי־רָאִיתִי אֱלֹהִים פָּנִים אֶל־פָּנִים וַתִּנָּצֵל נַפְשִׁי: (לב) וַיִּזְרַח־לוֹ הַשֶּׁמֶשׁ כַּאֲשֶׁר עָבַר אֶת־פְּנוּאֵל....

...And he blessed him there. Yaakov called the place "Peniel" [face of God], "For I have seen God face to face, and my soul was saved." The sun rose as he left Penuel .... (*Bereishit* 32:30-32)

This is what Yaakov feels as morning breaks: He has seen God's face, as it were, by looking deeply into himself, by fighting his own internal battle.

בראשית פרק לב:לב
(לב) וַיִּזְרַח־לוֹ הַשֶּׁמֶשׁ כַּאֲשֶׁר עָבַר אֶת־פְּנוּאֵל וְהוּא צֹלֵעַ עַל־יְרֵכוֹ:

The sun rose as he left Penuel, and he was limping because of his thigh. (*Bereishit* 32:32)

Yaakov limped away from that confrontation, physically weaker but spiritually transformed and empowered. Armed with his new insight, invigorated by his spiritual mission, Yaakov now knew how to respond to the challenges that awaited him. His identity would no longer be defined by his relationship with his brother Esav; he had now become Yisrael. The physical and spiritual were no longer at odds, and he was ready, as never before, to confront Esav. Together, the divergent aspects of his personality accompany Yaakov/Yisrael with every step he takes as he moves toward his destiny—at a slower pace physically, but spiritually invigorated.

Parashat Vayeshev

The Light of Mashiach

Parashat Vayeishev begins with a cryptic statement:

בראשית לז:א
וַיֵּשֶׁב יַעֲקֹב בְּאֶרֶץ מְגוּרֵי אָבִיו בְּאֶרֶץ כְּנָעַן:

Yaakov settled in the land in which his fathers dwelled, in the land of Canaan. (*Bereishit* 37:1)

Yaakov had come to the point in his life when he could finally settle down. The Hebrew term for "settled" is *va-yeishev*, while the term for "dwelled" is *megurei*, from the word *gur*, rooted in the word *ger*, "stranger."[1] In this short verse, then, we are told that Yaakov succeeded in settling where his father and grandfather before him only managed to dwell. Interestingly, in his later years, when Yaakov stands before Pharaoh and the latter asks him his age, Yaakov responds:

בראשית מז:ט
וַיֹּאמֶר יַעֲקֹב אֶל־פַּרְעֹה יְמֵי שְׁנֵי מְגוּרַי שְׁלֹשִׁים וּמְאַת שָׁנָה מְעַט וְרָעִים הָיוּ יְמֵי שְׁנֵי חַיַּי וְלֹא הִשִּׂיגוּ אֶת־יְמֵי שְׁנֵי חַיֵּי אֲבֹתַי בִּימֵי מְגוּרֵיהֶם:

---

1. Yaakov describes the time he spent in Lavan's house with the word *"garti"* (Bereishit 32:5), implying that the time spent outside of the Land of Israel was a time of "strangeness" for him.

בראשית לב:ה
וַיְצַו אֹתָם לֵאמֹר כֹּה תֹאמְרוּן לַאדֹנִי לְעֵשָׂו כֹּה אָמַר עַבְדְּךָ יַעֲקֹב עִם־לָבָן גַּרְתִּי וָאֵחַר עַד־עָתָּה:

The days of my dwellings are one hundred and thirty years, few and bad have been the days of my life, and they do not match the days of my fathers' dwellings. (*Bereishit* 47:9)

Yaakov describes his life and times with the word *megurei*, "dwellings," as opposed to the term with which the present *parashah* begins: *Vayeishev*, "he settled." Did Yaakov in fact settle, or did he merely dwell?[2]

Rashi cites a Midrash to explain the meaning of Yaakov's "settling."

רש״י, בראשית לז:ב

וַיֵּשֶׁב: בִּקֵּשׁ יַעֲקֹב לֵישֵׁב בְּשַׁלְוָה, קָפַץ עָלָיו רָגְזוֹ שֶׁל יוֹסֵף – צַדִּיקִים מְבַקְשִׁים לֵישֵׁב בְּשַׁלְוָה, אָמַר הַקָּבָּ"ה לֹא דַיָּן לַצַדִּיקִים מַה שֶּׁמְּתֻקָּן לָהֶם לָעוֹלָם הַבָּא, אֶלָּא שֶׁמְּבַקְשִׁים לֵישֵׁב בְּשַׁלְוָה בָּעוֹלָם הַזֶּה:

"And he settled" —Yaakov wished to settle in tranquility, but the episode of [literally, the anger of] Yosef confronted him. The righteous wish to live in tranquility; God says, "Is it not sufficient for the righteous what is awaiting them in the next world that they [also] wish to live in tranquility in this world!?" (Rashi, *Bereishit* 37:2, based on *Bereishit Rabbah* 84:3)

This concept is quite puzzling. What does it mean that Yaakov wished to live in tranquility? Did Yaakov wish to "retire" from active patriarchal service and enjoy his "golden years"? Certainly, Yaakov's life was difficult, but was this a reason to abandon his mission for the sake of "the good life"? There must be a deeper meaning to the "tranquility" Yaakov was seeking. Rav Yosef Dov Soloveitchik, *zt"l*, suggested Yaakov was seeking spiritual tranquility. When he returned to the Land of Israel, after overcoming the challenges presented by Lavan and Esav, Yaakov anticipated nothing less than the onset of Messianic Age. This would

---

2. Apparently, Yaakov here refers to all his days, including his sojourn in the house of Lavan, and his present stay in Egypt.

explain the Midrashic reference to the World to Come: Yaakov sought spiritual utopia here on earth. This is reflected in God's comment: Tzaddikim strive for spiritual perfection. They are not satisfied with what God has waiting for them in the World to Come; they desire perfection here and now as well.[3]

But how could Yaakov possibly think that a state of perfection or tranquility could be attained at that juncture in history? Had God not promised Avraham that his descendants would be enslaved for four hundred years?

בראשית פרק טו, יג-טז
(יג) וַיֹּאמֶר לְאַבְרָם יָדֹעַ תֵּדַע כִּי־גֵר| יִהְיֶה זַרְעֲךָ בְּאֶרֶץ לֹא לָהֶם וַעֲבָדוּם וְעִנּוּ אֹתָם אַרְבַּע מֵאוֹת שָׁנָה: (יד) וְגַם אֶת־הַגּוֹי אֲשֶׁר יַעֲבֹדוּ דָּן אָנֹכִי וְאַחֲרֵי־

---

3. I heard this idea in a lecture I attended in 1983. Also, see *Chumash Mesoras Harav Bereishis* page 273, which cites a lecture delivered in Boston in 1974.

The same idea can be found in the writings of Rav Pinchas Horowitz, *Panim Yafot* to *Bereishit* 37:1.

Also see Rabbi Kasher's *Torah Sheleimah, Parashat Vayeshev* page 1385 note one (citing a midrash from manuscript) found in *Midrash Yelamdenu* (Mann) *Yalkut Talmud Torah Bereishit* 553:

פנים יפות בראשית פרק לז
(א) וישב יעקב וגו׳. פירש"י ביקש יעקב לישב בשלוה קפץ עליו רוגזו של יוסף [ב"ר פד, א]. ...איתא במדרש [ב"ר פד, ה] מגורי אביו בגימטריא רנ"ט, מיום שאמר הקדוש ברוך הוא לא־ברהם ידוע תדע עד שעה שנתיישב יעקב אבינו בארץ מגורי אביו, <u>יש לפרש מה שאמר [שם] ביקש לישב בשלוה, דהיינו שחשב שכבר נשלמו הת' שנה שנגזרה בין הבתרים,</u> דהיינו שחשב שנותיו ושנות אביו שהוא היה כשבא אצל אביו צ"ח שנה כדאיתא בפ"ק דמגילה [יז א] ממילא היה שנות אביו קנ"ח, ולפי שלא היו השנים שווים שהרי יצחק נולד בפסח ויעקב בתשרי והוי בצירוף רנ"ט כמספר מגורי, וחשב יעקב שנות הבנים המובלעים בשנות האבות עולים ג"כ בחשבון, וחשב מאה של אברהם שהרי בברית בין הבתרים היה בן ע"ה וכשעקם היה קע"ה, וחשב ג"כ שנות ראובן שהיה בן ט"ו שנה כשבא אצל אביו, שהרי בן י"ג היה במעשה שכם דמניה ילפינן [ב"ר פ, ט] דמקרי איש לי"ג שנה, וחשב הט' שנים שהיה אצל אביו עד שהיה יוסף בן שבע עשרה שנה, ג"פ לו וליצחק ולראובן היה הכל ת' שנה, לכך ביקש לישב בשלוה כיון דלדעתו נשלם הגלות:

מדרש ילמדנו (מאן) ילקוט תלמוד תורה - בראשית אות קנג
א"ר אלעזר מהו וישב יעקב, מלמד שחשב יעקב בדעתו ואמר: כבר אמר הב"ה לאברהם להיות בניו גרים, הרי אני הייתי גר עשרים שנה בבית לבן משועבד בצאנו, וכיון שראה שעשו הלך לעיר אחרת אמר: בזה יתקיים השעבוד ארבע מאות שנה, ונתישבה דעתו. אמר הב"ה: מחשבתי עמוקה ממחשבתך, שנ׳ כי לא מחשבותי מחשבותיכם (יש׳ נ"ה, ח'), מיד הביא עליו עלילה על ידי יוסף.

כֵּן יֵצְאוּ בִּרְכֻשׁ גָּדוֹל: (טו) וְאַתָּה תָּבוֹא אֶל־אֲבֹתֶיךָ בְּשָׁלוֹם תִּקָּבֵר בְּשֵׂיבָה טוֹבָה: (טז) וְדוֹר רְבִיעִי יָשׁוּבוּ הֵנָּה כִּי לֹא־שָׁלֵם עֲוֹן הָאֱמֹרִי עַד־הֵנָּה:

> [God] said to Avraham, "Know that your descendants will be strangers in a land which is not theirs. They will be slaves and abused for four hundred years. The nation which enslaves them will be judged by Me. They will subsequently leave with great fortune. The fourth generation will return here, for the sin of the Emori will not be complete until then." (*Bereishit* 15:13–16)

How could Yaakov ignore the four hundred years of slavery stipulated in the Divine decree?

In fact, there are conflicting sources regarding the period of the Israelites' enslavement in Egypt: From the text of the Haggadah (which, in turn, is taken from earlier rabbinic sources), we learn that God was lenient in the calculation, and after a mere 210 years the Israelites were liberated.[4] And yet, the Torah explicitly states that the Jews left Egypt "at the end of four hundred and thirty years."[5] The contradiction

---

4. In the words of the Haggadah, God did a "calculation."

הגדה של פסח - נוסח ההגדה:

בָּרוּךְ שׁוֹמֵר הַבְטָחָתוֹ לְיִשְׂרָאֵל, בָּרוּךְ הוּא, שֶׁהַקָּדוֹשׁ בָּרוּךְ הוּא חִשַּׁב אֶת הַקֵּץ לַעֲשׂוֹת כְּמָה שֶׁאָמַר לְאַבְרָהָם אָבִינוּ בִּבְרִית בֵּין הַבְּתָרִים. שֶׁנֶּאֱמַר, וַיֹּאמֶר לְאַבְרָם יָדֹעַ תֵּדַע כִּי גֵר יִהְיֶה זַרְעֲךָ בְּאֶרֶץ לֹא לָהֶם וַעֲבָדוּם וְעִנּוּ אֹתָם אַרְבַּע מֵאוֹת שָׁנָה. וְגַם אֶת הַגּוֹי אֲשֶׁר יַעֲבֹדוּ דָּן אָנֹכִי וְאַחֲרֵי כֵן יֵצְאוּ בִּרְכֻשׁ גָּדוֹל:

Blessed is He who keeps His promise to Israel, blessed be He! For the Holy One, blessed be He, calculated the end [of the bondage], in order to do as He had said to our father Avraham at the "Covenant between the Portions," as it is said: "And He said to Avraham, 'You shall know that your seed will be strangers in a land that is not theirs, and they will enslave them and make them suffer, for four hundred years. But I shall also judge the nation whom they shall serve, and after that they will come out with great wealth.'"

5. *Shemot* 12:41:

שמות פרק יב פסוק מא

וַיְהִי מִקֵּץ שְׁלֹשִׁים שָׁנָה וְאַרְבַּע מֵאוֹת שָׁנָה וַיְהִי בְּעֶצֶם הַיּוֹם הַזֶּה יָצְאוּ כָּל־צִבְאוֹת ה' מֵאֶרֶץ מִצְרָיִם:

among the sources was quite apparent to our sages, and they addressed this question in the Midrash: Which was it: four hundred years, four hundred and thirty years, four generations? The Midrash reconciles the apparent contradiction by pointing out that God's revelation to Avraham, in which both four hundred years and four generations were mentioned, took place thirty years prior to the birth of Yitzchak. God stipulated that Avraham's descendants would be enslaved by a foreign power for four hundred years, and the clock was set in motion the moment Avraham's son was born; the calculation of the four hundred years of oppression begins with Yitzchak's birth. Thus, the Exodus came "at the end of four hundred and thirty years" from the moment God made this covenant with Avraham, which was four hundred years from the moment Yitchak was born.[6] Yitzchak and Yaakov, as well as Yaakov's twelve sons, were subject to foreign rule for one hundred and ninety years, followed by the period of actual slavery in Egypt which was 210 years in duration.

What, however, is the significance of the four generations mentioned in God's covenant with Avraham?

At the end of the four hundred and thirtieth year, to the very day, all the ranks of God departed from the land of Egypt.

6. See *Rosh Hashanah* 10b-11a:

תלמוד בבלי מסכת ראש השנה דף י עמוד ב

תַּנְיָא, רַבִּי אֱלִיעֶזֶר אוֹמֵר, בְּתִשְׁרֵי נִבְרָא הָעוֹלָם. בְּתִשְׁרֵי נוֹלְדוּ אָבוֹת. בְּתִשְׁרֵי מֵתוּ אָבוֹת. בְּפֶסַח נוֹלַד יִצְחָק. בְּרֹאשׁ הַשָּׁנָה נִפְקְדוּ שָׂרָה, וְרָחֵל, וְחַנָּה. בְּרֹאשׁ הַשָּׁנָה יָצָא יוֹסֵף מִבֵּית הָאֲסוּרִין: [דף יא ע"א] בְּרֹאשׁ הַשָּׁנָה בָּטְלָה עֲבוֹדָה מֵאֲבוֹתֵינוּ בְּמִצְרָיִם. בְּנִיסָן נִגְאֲלוּ (יִשְׂרָאֵל), וּבְתִשְׁרֵי עֲתִידִין לִיגָּאֵל. רַבִּי יְהוֹשֻׁעַ אוֹמֵר, בְּנִיסָן נִבְרָא הָעוֹלָם. בְּנִיסָן נוֹלְדוּ אָבוֹת. בְּנִיסָן מֵתוּ אָבוֹת. בְּפֶסַח נוֹלַד יִצְחָק. בְּרֹאשׁ הַשָּׁנָה נִפְקְדוּ שָׂרָה, רָחֵל, וְחַנָּה. בְּרֹאשׁ הַשָּׁנָה יָצָא יוֹסֵף מִבֵּית הָאֲסוּרִין. בְּרֹאשׁ הַשָּׁנָה בָּטְלָה עֲבוֹדָה מֵאֲבוֹתֵינוּ בְּמִצְרָיִם. בְּנִיסָן נִגְאֲלוּ וּבְנִיסָן עֲתִידִין לִיגָּאֵל.

It is taught Rabbi Eliezer says: In Tishrei the world was created; in Tishrei the Patriarchs were born; in Tishrei the Patriarchs died; on Passover Isaac was born; on Rosh Hashanah Sarah, Rachel, and Hannah were remembered; on Rosh Hashanah Joseph came out from prison; on Rosh Hashanah our forefathers' slavery in Egypt ceased; in Nisan they were redeemed; in Tishrei in the future they will be redeemed. Rabbi Yehoshua says: In Nisan the world was created; in Nisan the Patriarchs were born; in Nisan the Patriarchs died; on Passover Isaac was born; on Rosh Hashanah Sarah, Rachel, and Hannah were remembered; on Rosh Hashanah Joseph came out from prison; on Rosh Hashanah our forefathers' slavery in Egypt ceased; in Nisan they were redeemed; and in Nisan in the future they will be redeemed.

מכילתא דרבי ישמעאל בא - מסכתא דפסחא פרשה יד

... אָמַר הַקָּדוֹשׁ בָּרוּךְ הוּא אִם עוֹשִׂין תְּשׁוּבָה אֲנִי גוֹאֲלָם לְדוֹרוֹת וְאִם לָאו אֲנִי גוֹאֲלָם לְשָׁנִים.

The Holy One, blessed be He, said, "If they do *teshuvah* I [calculate] their redemption in generations; if not, I will [calculate] their redemption in years." *(Mechilta de-Rabbi Yishmael, Bo* 14)[7]

---

7. Also see *Midrash Tanchuma, Bo* 9:2:

מדרש תנחומא, בא ט':ב'

וּמוֹשַׁב בְּנֵי יִשְׂרָאֵל אֲשֶׁר יָשְׁבוּ בְּמִצְרָיִם שְׁלֹשִׁים שָׁנָה וְאַרְבַּע מֵאוֹת שָׁנָה. וּכְתִיב: וַעֲבָדוּם וְעִנּוּ אֹתָם אַרְבַּע מֵאוֹת שָׁנָה (בראשית טו, יג). הֲרֵי שְׁנֵי פְּסוּקִים מַכְחִישִׁין זֶה אֶת זֶה. כֵּיצַד? עַד שֶׁלֹּא נוֹלַד יִצְחָק, נִגְזְרָה גְּזֵרָה. וּמִשֶּׁנּוֹלַד יִצְחָק, חִשֵּׁב הַקָּדוֹשׁ בָּרוּךְ הוּא, שֶׁנֶּאֱמַר: כִּי גֵר יִהְיֶה זַרְעֲךָ (בראשית טו, יג). וְאַבְרָהָם חִשֵּׁב מִשְּׁעַת הַגְּזֵרָה. כְּתִיב אַרְבַּע מֵאוֹת שָׁנָה. וּכְתִיב וְדוֹר רְבִיעִי יָשׁוּבוּ הֵנָּה (בראשית טו, טז). הָא כֵּיצַד? עָשׂוּ תְּשׁוּבָה, אֶגְאָלֵם לְדוֹרוֹת. וְאִם לָאו, לְשָׁנִים. וַיְהִי מִקֵּץ שְׁלֹשִׁים שָׁנָה וְגוֹ'. כְּשֶׁהִגִּיעַ הַקֵּץ, לֹא עִכְּבָם כְּהֶרֶף עַיִן. בַּחֲמִשָּׁה עָשָׂר בְּנִיסָן נִגְזְרָה גְּזֵרָה וְנִדְבַּר עִם אַבְרָהָם אָבִינוּ בֵּין הַבְּתָרִים. בַּחֲמִשָּׁה עָשָׂר בְּנִיסָן בָּאוּ מַלְאֲכֵי הַשָּׁרֵת לְבַשְּׂרוֹ עַל יִצְחָק. בַּחֲמִשָּׁה עָשָׂר בְּנִיסָן נוֹלַד יִצְחָק. בַּחֲמִשָּׁה עָשָׂר בְּנִיסָן נִגְאֲלוּ מִמִּצְרָיִם. בַּחֲמִשָּׁה עָשָׂר בְּנִיסָן עֲתִידִין לְהִגָּאֵל מִשִּׁעְבּוּד גָּלֻיּוֹת. וַיְהִי מִקֵּץ שְׁלֹשִׁים שָׁנָה. קֵץ אֶחָד לְכֻלָּם.

Now the time that the children of Israel dwelt in Egypt was four hundred and thirty years (*Shemot* 12:40). Yet it is written, "And shall serve them, and they shall afflict them four hundred years" (*Bereishit* 15:13). Since these two verses are obviously contradictory, how can they be reconciled? The first decree was issued prior to the birth of Yitzchak, but after Yitzchak's birth, the Holy One, blessed be He, reconsidered the matter, as it is said: 'Your descendents will be strangers, and they shall afflict them four hundred years.' Avraham reflected on this subject at the time of the decree. It is written: And they shall afflict them four hundred years, but it is also written: In the fourth generation, they shall return here (*Bereishit* 15:16). How can these verses be reconciled? These verses suggest that, if they repent, I will redeem them after four generations, but if not, after four hundred years. "And it came to pass at the end of four hundred and thirty years" (*Shemot* 12:41). At the end of that time he did not delay them as long as the blink of an eye. It was on the fifteenth day of Nisan that he issued the decree and spoke to Avraham our father, at the time of making the covenant-between-the-parts. It was on the fifteenth day of Nisan that ministering angels came to inform him about the birth of Yitzchak; it was on the fifteenth day of Nisan that Yitzchak was born; it was on the fifteenth day of Nisan that they were redeemed from Egypt; and it is on the fifteenth day of Nisan that they will be redeemed from servitude to the nations. The same day was designated for all these events.

The details of the promise to Avraham were not etched in stone; they were flexible. The central idea was that Avraham's descendants would be enslaved and abused, and would eventually leave the place of their oppression with great wealth. Apparently, Yaakov believed that this sequence had already occurred, that all these elements of God's promise had been fulfilled in his own life story. He must have thought that his oppression at the hands of Lavan and the years of labor which ended in his return to Israel with tremendous material wealth had fulfilled God's words to Avraham, and redemption could now take place. His children, after all, were the fourth generation of Avraham's family.

And then, all of a sudden, Yaakov's worldview was derailed by the saga of Yosef and his brothers. "The anger of Yosef" shattered his illusions of tranquility and fulfillment.

When the enemy was Nimrod, Yishmael, Lavan, or Esav, confrontation was understandable, inevitable—even anticipated. But an internal struggle such as this did not seem to be part of the Divine Plan. Yaakov was certain that all the adversaries had been neutralized, and that the era of spiritual tranquility was dawning. With his sons at his side, Yaakov was confident that the Messianic Age had arrived. This new struggle was unanticipated, but the Messianic Age could not begin (nor can *Sefer Bereishit* come to an end) before this final intrigue within the family of Israel was played out. Thus, toward the end of the book of *Bereishit* when Yaakov meets up with Pharaoh, in his succinct retrospective of his life, he tells the Egyptian monarch that he had, in fact "dwelled," but had not succeed in "settling." He never achieved this sought-after tranquility.

The narratives that comprise the bulk of *Sefer Bereishit* are more than stories; the vicissitudes of the lives of our forefathers are far more than ancient tales. They are spiritual realities pregnant with meaning, which shape the contours of Jewish history. If we are to understand the significance of the teachings in *Bereishit* in general, and this *parashah* in particular, we must read them through the prism of "*ma'aseh avot siman labanim*,[8] the actions of the forefathers serve as a portent for their

---

8. See *Midrash Tanchuma, Lech Lecha* section 9, and Ramban, *Bereishit* 12:6:

מדרש תנחומא (ורשא) פרשת לך לך סימן ט:ג,ד

אָמַר רַבִּי יְהוֹשֻׁעַ דְּסִכְנִין, סִימָן נָתַן לוֹ הַקָּדוֹשׁ בָּרוּךְ הוּא לְאַבְרָהָם, שֶׁכָּל מַה שֶּׁאֵרַע לוֹ אֵרַע לְבָנָיו. כֵּיצַד? בָּחַר בְּאַבְרָהָם מִכָּל בֵּית אָבִיו, שֶׁנֶּאֱמַר: אַתָּה הוּא ה' הָאֱלֹהִים אֲשֶׁר בָּחַרְתָּ בְּאַבְרָם וְהוֹצֵאתוֹ מֵאוּר כַּשְׂדִּים וְשַׂמְתָּ שְּׁמוֹ אַבְרָהָם (נחמיה ט, ז). וּבָחַר בְּבָנָיו מִשִּׁבְעִים אֻמּוֹת, שֶׁנֶּאֱמַר: כִּי עַם קָדוֹשׁ אַתָּה לַה' אֱלֹהֶיךָ וּבְךָ בָּחַר ה' לִהְיוֹת לוֹ לְעַם סְגֻלָּה מִכֹּל הָעַמִּים אֲשֶׁר עַל פְּנֵי הָאֲדָמָה (דברים יד, ב). לְאַבְרָהָם נֶאֱמַר לֶךְ לְךָ, וּלְבָנָיו נֶאֱמַר אַעֲלֶה אֶתְכֶם מֵעֳנִי מִצְרַיִם אֶל אֶרֶץ הַכְּנַעֲנִי וְהַחִתִּי וְהָאֱמֹרִי וְהַפְּרִזִּי וְהַחִוִּי וְהַיְבוּסִי אֶל אֶרֶץ זָבַת חָלָב וּדְבָשׁ (שמות ג, יז). לְאַבְרָהָם נֶאֱמַר: וַאֲבָרֶכְךָ וַאֲגַדְּלָה שְׁמֶךָ וֶהְיֵה בְּרָכָה וַאֲבָרֲכָה מְבָרְכֶיךָ. וּלְבָנָיו נֶאֱמַר: יְבָרֶכְךָ ה'. לְאַבְרָהָם נֶאֱמַר: וְאֶעֶשְׂךָ לְגוֹי גָּדוֹל, וּלְבָנָיו נֶאֱמַר: וּמִי גּוֹי גָּדוֹל (דברים ד, ח). אַבְרָהָם כְּתִיב בּוֹ: אֶחָד הָיָה אַבְרָהָם (יחזקאל לג, כד). וְיִשְׂרָאֵל: וּמִי כְעַמְּךָ יִשְׂרָאֵל וְגוֹ' (דה"א יז, כא). לְאַבְרָהָם נֶאֱמַר: וַיְהִי רָעָב בָּאָרֶץ וַיֵּרֶד אַבְרָם מִצְרַיְמָה לָגוּר שָׁם כִּי כָבֵד הָרָעָב בָּאָרֶץ. וּלְבָנָיו כֵּיוָן שֶׁשָּׁבוּ לְמִצְרַיִם, וְהָרָעָב כָּבֵד בָּאָרֶץ (בראשית מג, א). אַבְרָהָם עַל יְדֵי הָרָעָב יָרַד לְמִצְרַיִם, וְאַף בָּנָיו עַל יְדֵי הָרָעָב יָרְדוּ לְמִצְרַיִם, שֶׁנֶּאֱמַר: וַיֵּרְדוּ אֲחֵי יוֹסֵף עֲשָׂרָה לִשְׁבֹּר בָּר מִמִּצְרָיִם (בראשית מב, ג). אַבְרָהָם כְּשֶׁיָּרַד נִזְדַּוְּגוּ לוֹ הַמִּצְרִים, וַיִּרְאוּ הַמִּצְרִים אֶת הָאִשָּׁה כִּי יָפָה הִיא מְאֹד (בראשית יב, יד). אַף לְבָנָיו, הָבָה נִתְחַכְּמָה לוֹ פֶּן יִרְבֶּה וְהָיָה כִּי תִקְרֶאנָה מִלְחָמָה וְנוֹסַף גַּם הוּא עַל שֹׂנְאֵינוּ וְנִלְחַם בָּנוּ וְעָלָה מִן הָאָרֶץ (שמות א, י).

אַבְרָהָם נִזְדַּוְּגוּ לוֹ אַרְבָּעָה מְלָכִים, אַף לְיִשְׂרָאֵל עֲתִידִין כָּל הַמְּלָכִים לְהִתְרַגֵּשׁ עֲלֵיהֶם, שֶׁנֶּאֱמַר: לָמָּה רָגְשׁוּ גוֹיִם וּלְאֻמִּים יֶהְגּוּ רִיק (תהלים ב, א). וְאוֹמֵר: יִתְיַצְּבוּ מַלְכֵי אֶרֶץ וְרוֹזְנִים נוֹסְדוּ יַחַד עַל ה' וְעַל מְשִׁיחוֹ (תהלים ב, ב). מָה אַבְרָהָם יָצָא הַקָּדוֹשׁ בָּרוּךְ הוּא וְנִלְחַם בְּשׂוֹנְאָיו, שֶׁנֶּאֱמַר: מִי הֵעִיר מִמִּזְרָח צֶדֶק יִקְרָאֵהוּ לְרַגְלוֹ יִתֵּן לְפָנָיו גּוֹיִם וּמְלָכִים יַרְדְּ יִתֵּן כֶּעָפָר חַרְבּוֹ כְּקַשׁ נִדָּף קַשְׁתּוֹ (ישעיה מא, ב), אַף כָּךְ עָתִיד הַקָּדוֹשׁ בָּרוּךְ הוּא לַעֲשׂוֹת לְבָנָיו, שֶׁנֶּאֱמַר: וְיָצָא ה' וְנִלְחַם בַּגּוֹיִם הָהֵם כְּיוֹם הִלָּחֲמוֹ בְּיוֹם קְרָב (זכריה יד, ג).

R. Yehoshua of Sikhnin was of the opinion that the Holy One, blessed be He, gave Avraham a sign that whatever happened to him would likewise happen to his descendants. He chose Avraham from among all those in his father's house, as it is said, "You are the Almighty God who chose Avram, and brought him forth out of Ur Kasdim, and gave him the name of Avraham' (Nechemiah 9:7). And He selected Avraham's sons to be His chosen ones among the seventy nations, as is said, "For you are a Holy people to the Almighty your God, and God has chosen you to be His own treasured nation out of all the peoples that are upon the face of the earth" (*Devarim* 14:2). He said to Avraham, "Go, for your sake… to the land that I will show you," and to Avraham's sons, He said, "I will bring you up out of the affliction of Egypt to the land of the Canaanite, and the Hittite, and the Emorite… to a land flowing with milk and honey" (*Shemot* 3:17). He promised Avraham: 'And I will bless you, and make your name great; and you will be a blessing' (*Bereishit* 12:2), and he told his sons, "God will bless you and keep you" (*Bamidbar* 6:24). To Avraham He said, "I will make you a great nation" (*Bereishit* 12:2), and to his descendants He said, "And what greater nation is there…" (*Devarim* 4:8). Concerning Avraham it is written, "Avraham was unique," (*Yechezkel* 33:24), and of Israel it is said: 'And who is like our people Israel, a unique nation on the earth' (1 *Divrei HaYamim* 17:21). In reference to Avraham it is said, "And the was a famine in the land" (*Bereishit* 12:10), and about his descendants it is said, "When they returned to Egypt, there was already famine in the land" (*Bereishit* 43:1). Avraham

descendants." Put another way, 'History repeats itself,' or, in theological terms, 'Jewish history is Jewish destiny.'

When Yosef and his brothers clash, the spiritual power for future internal disputes is unleashed. It is no accident that the festival of Chanukah, which, at its core, marks the end of a tragic period of

descended to Egypt because of famine, and his sons also, descended because of famine, as is said, "And Yosef's ten brothers went down to buy grain from Egypt" (*Bereishit* 42:3). When Avraham descended the Egyptians approached him, "and the Egyptians saw the woman that she was very beautiful" (*Bereishit* 12:14), and concerning his descendants, the Egyptians declared, "Come, let us deal wisely with them lest they multiply, and it comes to pass that a war breaks out, they will join our enemies, and fight against us, and emigrate out of the land" (*Shemot* 1:10).

The four kings attacked Avraham, and in the future all the kings will war against Israel, as it is said, "Why are the nations in an uproar, and why do the peoples mutter in vain?" (*Tehillim* 2:1), and it says elsewhere, "The kings of the earth stand up, and the rulers take counsel together against God and against His anointed one: (*Tehillim* 2:2). Just as in the case of Avraham, the Holy One, blessed be He, waged war against those who hated him, as it is said, "Who has raised up one from the east, at whose steps victory attends? He gives nations before him, and makes him rule over kings; his sword makes them as the dust, his bow as the driven stubble" (*Yeshayahu* 41:2), so too the Holy One, blessed be He, will wage war in the future in behalf of his descendants, as is said, "Then shall God go forth and fight against those nations, as when he fights in the day of battle" (*Zechariah* 14:3).

רמב״ן, בראשית יב:ו
ויעבר אברם בארץ עד מקום שכם - אומר לך כלל תבין אותו בכל הפרשיות הבאות בענין אברהם יצחק ויעקב, והוא ענין גדול, הזכירוהו רבותינו בדרך קצרה, ואמרו (תנחומא ט) כל מה שאירע לאבות סימן לבנים, ולכן יאריכו הכתובים בספור המסעות וחפירת הבארות ושאר המקרים, ויחשוב החושב בהם כאלו הם דברים מיותרים אין בהם תועלת, וכולם באים ללמד על העתיד, כי כאשר יבוא המקרה לנביא משלשת האבות יתבונן ממנו הדבר הנגזר לבא לזרעו:...

"'And Avram passed through the land to the place of Shechem" — I will tell you a general principle—understand it in all of the coming sections about Avraham, Yitzchak and Yaakov, and it is a great matter. Our rabbis mentioned it in a brief way, and said, "Everything that occurred to our forefathers is a sign for the children" (*Midrash Tanchuma* 9). And therefore the verses will write at length in recounting the journeys and the digging of the wells and the other events. And one who thinks about them can think as if they were superfluous things with no purpose. But all of the events come to teach about the future, for when an event occurs to a prophet, [meaning] one of the three forefathers, he will contemplate from it the matter that is decreed to come to his descendents...

fratricidal conflict, is celebrated each year during the weeks when the Torah portions regarding Yosef and his brothers are read. The destruction of the Second Temple is attributed to *sinat chinam*, unwarranted hatred between brothers—the very same hatred that underlies the plot of these Torah portions. The civil war fought by the Maccabees against the Hellenized Jews is seen as a repercussion—in the most literal sense of re-percussion, the repeated beating of the same drum—of the conflict in *Parashat Vayeshev*. The Midrash that describes the deaths of the Ten Martyrs in the days of the *Tannaim*, a central part of the liturgy of Yom Kippur, is another far-reaching echo of Yosef's story.

Once internal conflict arises, a new type of solution is required; the methods employed against external threats are of no use. This is the lesson of *Vayeishev*: Not only would tranquility not be achieved in Yaakov's lifetime, but the insidious power of internal conflict would haunt future generations. The text of the Torah makes this clear in its unique way:

בראשית לז:לו

וְהַמְּדָנִים מָכְרוּ אֹתוֹ אֶל־מִצְרָיִם לְפוֹטִיפַר סְרִיס פַּרְעֹה שַׂר הַטַּבָּחִים׃

The Midianites sold [Yosef] to Egypt, to Potifar, eunuch of Pharaoh, the Chief Executioner. (*Bereishit* 37:36)

בראשית לט:א

וְיוֹסֵף הוּרַד מִצְרָיְמָה וַיִּקְנֵהוּ פּוֹטִיפַר...

Yosef was brought down to Egypt, where he was purchased by Potifar…. (*Bereishit* 39:1)

Ancient and modern scholars alike have noted a difficulty in the text: The last verse of Chapter 37 and the first verse of Chapter 39 are almost identical. Between these two verses, time seems to stand still in the life of Yosef, while Chapter 38 recounts the life of Yehudah over many years: Yehudah marries and raises a family, and his children, in turn, marry—

Vayeshev: The Light of Mashiach | 223

and die. The Torah finds it necessary to take us into the life and character of Yehudah before it can proceed to tell us about Yosef's fate. Why?

To understand this peculiar ordering of the text, we must first recall the larger context: Yosef was sent by his father to look for his ten older brothers. When the brothers see Yosef approaching from afar, they plot to kill him. Reuven, who, as the eldest, would be held most responsible, suggests that they throw him into a pit, and the "narrator" shares Reuven's thoughts with us.

בראשית לז:כא-כב

וַיִּשְׁמַע רְאוּבֵן וַיַּצִּלֵהוּ מִיָּדָם וַיֹּאמֶר לֹא נַכֶּנּוּ נָפֶשׁ: וַיֹּאמֶר אֲלֵהֶם| רְאוּבֵן אַל־תִּשְׁפְּכוּ־דָם הַשְׁלִיכוּ אֹתוֹ אֶל־הַבּוֹר הַזֶּה אֲשֶׁר בַּמִּדְבָּר וְיָד אַל־תִּשְׁלְחוּ־בוֹ לְמַעַן הַצִּיל אֹתוֹ מִיָּדָם לַהֲשִׁיבוֹ אֶל־אָבִיו:

Reuven heard this and rescued [Yosef]. "We will not take his life!" he said. Reuven said to them, "Do not commit bloodshed. Throw him into this pit in the desert, and do not lay a hand on him." [His plan was] to rescue [Yosef] from [his brothers] and bring him back to his father. (*Bereishit* 37: 21-22)

In the hope of rescuing Yosef later, Reuven convinces his brothers to "let nature take its course." What follows is one of the harshest scenes in the Bible: The brothers sit down to break bread as Yosef languishes in the pit.[9] At this point, Yehudah speaks (for the first time in the entire Torah):

בראשית לז:כו-כז

וַיֹּאמֶר יְהוּדָה אֶל־אֶחָיו מַה־בֶּצַע כִּי נַהֲרֹג אֶת־אָחִינוּ וְכִסִּינוּ אֶת־דָּמוֹ: לְכוּ וְנִמְכְּרֶנּוּ לַיִּשְׁמְעֵאלִים וְיָדֵנוּ אַל־תְּהִי־בוֹ כִּי־אָחִינוּ בְשָׂרֵנוּ הוּא וַיִּשְׁמְעוּ אֶחָיו:

---

9. While the brothers contemplate first the murder and then the sale of Yosef as they break bread, little do they realize that by selling Yosef as a slave, they have taken the first step toward the enslavement of their own children. How appropriate that when the Jews leave Egypt, they are commanded first to sit as a family and have a Passover seder—a family meal that includes the *entire* family.

And Yehudah said to his brothers, "What will we gain if we kill our brother and cover his blood? Let us sell him to the Yishmaelites and let not our hands be upon him, for he is our brother and our flesh." His brothers acquiesced. (*Bereishit* 37: 26-27)

Yehudah takes responsibility, displays leadership; on the other hand, he also displays callousness and an almost Machiavellian cynicism. His conclusion, "Let us not kill him, for he is our brother and our flesh," yet in the same breath suggesting that they sell him as a slave, is shocking.

With Yosef gone, the brothers are presented with a new problem: How are they to inform their father, Yaakov, of Yosef's disappearance? They dip his coat of many colors in the blood of a slaughtered goat and present it to their father:

בראשית לז:לב

...וַיֹּאמְרוּ זֹאת מָצָאנוּ הַכֶּר־נָא הַכְּתֹנֶת בִּנְךָ הִוא אִם־לֹא:

...We have found this. Do you recognize it? Is it your son's coat? (*Bereishit* 37: 32)

The brothers didn't actually lie to Yaakov; they merely deceived him. According to the midrash,[10] Yehudah was still the leader, and it was he who spoke. Yaakov, who immediately recognized the coat and assumed the worst, began to mourn for his son in a way that only a bereaved father can.

It is at this point that the narrative shifts its focus to Yehudah's personal life story:

בראשית לח:א

וַיְהִי בָּעֵת הַהִוא וַיֵּרֶד יְהוּדָה מֵאֵת אֶחָיו ...

---

10. *Bereishit Rabbah* 84:19:

בראשית רבה (וילנא) פרשת וישב פרשה פד סימן יט

(בראשית לז, לב): וַיְשַׁלְּחוּ אֶת כְּתֹנֶת הַפַּסִּים וגו'. אָמַר רַבִּי יוֹחָנָן אָמַר הַקָּדוֹשׁ בָּרוּךְ הוּא לִיהוּדָה אַתָּה אָמַרְתָּ (בראשית לז, לב): הַכֶּר נָא, חַיֶּיךָ שֶׁתָּמָר אוֹמֶרֶת לְךָ (בראשית לח, כה): הַכֶּר נָא. (בראשית לז, לג): וַיַּכִּירָהּ וַיֹּאמֶר כְּתֹנֶת בְּנִי, אָמַר לֵית אֲנָא יָדַע מָה אֲנָא חָמֵי, כְּתֹנֶת בְּנִי חַיָּה רָעָה אֲכָלָתְהוּ וגו', אָמַר רַב הוּנָא נִצְנְצָה בּוֹ רוּחַ הַקֹּדֶשׁ, חַיָּה רָעָה אֲכָלָתְהוּ, זוֹ אִשְׁתּוֹ שֶׁל פּוֹטִיפַר.

It came to pass, at that time, that Yehudah parted ways with [literally, went down from] his brothers….(*Bereishit* 38:1)

Rashi explains that Yehudah's "descent" was the result of his lowered esteem in his brothers' eyes. The brothers blamed Yehudah for their father's bereavement, and therefore for Yosef's disappearance.

רש"י, בראשית פרק לח:א
וַיְהִי בָּעֵת הַהִוא - לָמָּה נִסְמְכָה פָּרָשָׁה זוֹ לְכָאן, וְהִפְסִיק בְּפָרָשָׁתוֹ שֶׁל יוֹסֵף? לְלַמֵּד שֶׁהוֹרִידוּהוּ אֶחָיו מִגְּדֻלָּתוֹ כְּשֶׁרָאוּ בְּצָרַת אֲבִיהֶם, אָמְרוּ: אַתָּה אָמַרְתָּ לְמָכְרוֹ, אִלּוּ אָמַרְתָּ לַהֲשִׁיבוֹ הָיִינוּ שׁוֹמְעִים לָךְ:

"And it came to pass" — Why is this section placed here, interrupting the story of Yosef's life? To teach that his brothers lowered him from his high position. When they saw their father's grief they said, "You are the one who told us to sell him! Had you said, 'Return him to his father,' we would have listened to you." (Rashi, *Bereishit* 38:1)

Yehudah takes leave of his father's house; he has lost his brothers' respect, and he sets out to build a new family for himself. The midrash attempts to explain this seeming tangent in the narrative:

בראשית רבה (וילנא) פרשת וישב פרשה פה:א
ויהי בעת ההיא: רַבִּי שְׁמוּאֵל בַּר נַחְמָן פָּתַח (ירמיה כט, יא): כִּי אָנֹכִי יָדַעְתִּי אֶת הַמַּחֲשָׁבֹת, שְׁבָטִים הָיוּ עֲסוּקִין בִּמְכִירָתוֹ שֶׁל יוֹסֵף, וְיוֹסֵף הָיָה עָסוּק בְּשַׂקּוֹ וּבְתַעֲנִיתוֹ, רְאוּבֵן הָיָה עָסוּק בְּשַׂקּוֹ וְתַעֲנִיתוֹ, וְיַעֲקֹב הָיָה עָסוּק בְּשַׂקּוֹ וּבְתַעֲנִיתוֹ, וִיהוּדָה הָיָה עָסוּק לִקַּח לוֹ אִשָּׁה, וְהַקָּדוֹשׁ בָּרוּךְ הוּא הָיָה עוֹסֵק בּוֹרֵא אוֹרוֹ שֶׁל מֶלֶךְ הַמָּשִׁיחַ, וַיְהִי בָּעֵת הַהִיא וַיֵּרֶד יְהוּדָה. (ישעיה סו, ז): בְּטֶרֶם תָּחִיל יָלָדָה, קֹדֶם שֶׁלֹּא נוֹלַד מְשַׁעְבֵּד הָרִאשׁוֹן נוֹלַד גּוֹאֵל הָאַחֲרוֹן

"It came to pass at that time" Rabbi Shmuel bar Nachman expounded: "Because I know the thoughts…" (*Yirmiyahu*

29:11). The brothers were occupied with the selling of Yosef, Yosef was occupied with his sackcloth and fasting, Reuven was occupied with his sackcloth and fasting, Yaakov was occupied with his sackcloth and fasting, Yehudah was occupied with taking a wife for himself, and God was busy creating the light of the King Mashiach. "And it came to pass at that time that Yehudah parted" (*Yeshayahu* 66:7): …Before the first pangs of labor,' Before the first enslaver is born, the final Redeemer is born. (*Bereishit Rabbah* 85:1)

In its own way, the Midrash, asks a question that is all too familiar to the modern reader: Where was God? How did He allow the sale of Yosef to proceed? The answer is nothing short of amazing: While this unspeakable travesty was unfolding, as the innocent and righteous Yosef was being abused, tortured, and sold by his own brothers—which eventually brings the entire Jewish People to Egypt, into the clutches of slavery and unspeakable suffering—God was busy creating the light of Mashiach. What are we to make of this bizarre response?

Yaakov sought tranquility, but God had a different plan. The slavery and redemption foretold to Avraham had not yet been fulfilled, but God was already busy setting the final redemption in motion, weaving the threads of a plan that began with the sale of Yosef and crystallized with the "descent of Yehudah." Yosef, who was always uniquely capable of seeing the larger picture and visualizing long-term strategy, came to recognize the Divine Hand involved in the events of his life. It began, he eventually understood, when he wandered the countryside in search of his brothers.

בראשית לז:טו-יז

וַיִּמְצָאֵהוּ אִישׁ וְהִנֵּה תֹעֶה בַּשָּׂדֶה וַיִּשְׁאָלֵהוּ הָאִישׁ לֵאמֹר מַה־תְּבַקֵּשׁ: וַיֹּאמֶר אֶת־אַחַי אָנֹכִי מְבַקֵּשׁ הַגִּידָה־נָּא לִי אֵיפֹה הֵם רֹעִים: וַיֹּאמֶר הָאִישׁ נָסְעוּ מִזֶּה כִּי שָׁמַעְתִּי אֹמְרִים נֵלְכָה דֹּתָיְנָה וַיֵּלֶךְ יוֹסֵף אַחַר אֶחָיו וַיִּמְצָאֵם בְּדֹתָן:

A man found [Yosef] wandering, lost in a field. The man asked him, "What are you seeking?" [Yosef] said, "I am seeking my brothers. Tell me, please, where they are grazing [their flocks]?" The man said, "They left here, for I heard them say, 'Let us go to Dotan.'" Yosef went after his brothers and found them in Dotan. (*Bereishit* 37:15–17)

Had this unnamed man not found him wandering in the fields and directed him, Yosef would never have found his brothers, and would have returned home to his father. God made sure that, one way or another, Yosef would find his brothers, that he would be sold, that he would end up in Egypt, and that his brothers would follow. Yaakov's tranquility would have to wait.

Yosef eventually came to understand this encounter with the mysterious man in the field—as well as the entire chain of events that followed it—as an act of Divine Will. When he was reunited with his brothers years later, he attempted to explain to them the mysterious ways in which God takes an active role in human history:

בראשית מה:ה-ח

וְעַתָּה׀ אַל־תֵּעָצְבוּ וְאַל־יִחַר בְּעֵינֵיכֶם כִּי־מְכַרְתֶּם אֹתִי הֵנָּה כִּי לְמִחְיָה שְׁלָחַנִי אֱלֹהִים לִפְנֵיכֶם: כִּי־זֶה שְׁנָתַיִם הָרָעָב בְּקֶרֶב הָאָרֶץ וְעוֹד חָמֵשׁ שָׁנִים אֲשֶׁר אֵין־חָרִישׁ וְקָצִיר: וַיִּשְׁלָחֵנִי אֱלֹהִים לִפְנֵיכֶם לָשׂוּם לָכֶם שְׁאֵרִית בָּאָרֶץ וּלְהַחֲיוֹת לָכֶם לִפְלֵיטָה גְּדֹלָה: וְעַתָּה לֹא־אַתֶּם שְׁלַחְתֶּם אֹתִי הֵנָּה כִּי הָאֱלֹהִים וַיְשִׂימֵנִי לְאָב לְפַרְעֹה וּלְאָדוֹן לְכָל־בֵּיתוֹ וּמֹשֵׁל בְּכָל־אֶרֶץ מִצְרָיִם:

Now do not be saddened and do not be angered that you have sold me here, for **God** has sent me ahead to be a source of sustenance. For these two years there is famine in the land, and for another five years there will be no sowing and harvesting. **God** sent me ahead of you to set aside for you a remnant of the land and to save your lives by great deliverance. And now, it is not you who has sent me here but **God**.... (*Bereishit* 45:5–8)

God's plan took the form of a mysterious man in the field. This seemingly insignificant event shaped the course of Yosef's life; it was the Will wof God, guiding him to his destiny in Egypt. While this does not exonerate the brothers for their nefarious behavior, the will of God is ultimately apparent in the world. Rashi tells us that the anonymous person in the field was the angel Gavriel, whose very name denotes *gevurah* (strength), God's attribute of d(justice).

It is this "Hand of God" that the midrash describes: At the moment Yosef was being sold into slavery, God was occupied with weaving the mantle of Mashiach, while Yehudah was involved in his personal life. What does this mean?

When Yehudah's oldest son, Eir, dies, one would expect Yehudah to gain some insight into his father's pain. He now knows intimately, firsthand, what Yaakov feels and what it means to mourn one's own child. When Yehudah's second son, Onan, dies, we would expect Yehudah to be tormented with guilt; it would be a natural response for him to blame his own actions for the tragic deaths of his sons. We would expect Yehudah to approach his father, admit his guilt, and tell him, "Yosef is alive!" But Yehudah seems cold and indifferent.

When Tamar, Yehudah's daughter-in-law, approaches him, he callously tells her to wait for his third son, despite having no intention of giving him to her for a husband. Some time later, Yehudah's own wife dies, and he seeks illicit comfort in the company of the type of woman who plies her trade on the side of the road. Unbeknownst to him, his daughter-in-law Tamar, who has come to realize that Yehudah has not been honest with her, has disguised herself as a prostitute.

When she becomes pregnant, Yehudah, unaware that he is the father, orders that she be killed. She then presents Yehudah's signet ring, staff, and coat, which she held as collateral, in lieu of the goat she was to receive as her wages. The Midrash points out that Tamar's "wages," a goat, also conveyed a powerful message:

בראשית רבה (וילנא) פרשת וישב פרשה פה:ט
אָמַר הַקָּדוֹשׁ בָּרוּךְ הוּא לִיהוּדָה אַתָּה רִמִּיתָ בְּאָבִיךָ בִּגְדִי עִזִּים, חַיֶּיךָ שֶׁתָּמָר מְרַמָּה בָּךְ בִּגְדִי עִזִּים.

God said to Yehudah, "You deceived your father with a goat. By your life, Tamar will deceive you with a goat." (*Bereishit Rabbah* 85:9)

Tamar confronts Yehudah, presenting the personal effects of the man by whom she became pregnant:

בראשית לח: כה-כו
הִוא מוּצֵאת וְהִיא שָׁלְחָה אֶל־חָמִיהָ לֵאמֹר לְאִישׁ אֲשֶׁר־אֵלֶּה לּוֹ אָנֹכִי הָרָה וַתֹּאמֶר הַכֶּר־נָא לְמִי הַחֹתֶמֶת וְהַפְּתִילִים וְהַמַּטֶּה הָאֵלֶּה:

When she was being taken out [to be executed], she sent [the items] to her father-in-law with the message, "I am pregnant by the man who is the owner of these articles." She said [to Yehudah], "Do you recognize [these objects]? Who is the owner of this seal, this wrap, and this staff?" (*Bereishit* 38:25)

The Midrash explains:

בראשית רבה (וילנא) פרשת וישב פרשה פה:יא
אָמַר רַבִּי יוֹחָנָן אָמַר לוֹ הַקָּדוֹשׁ בָּרוּךְ הוּא לִיהוּדָה אַתָּה אָמַרְתָּ לְאָבִיךָ (בראשית לז, לב): הַכֶּר נָא, חַיֶּיךָ שֶׁתָּמָר אוֹמֶרֶת לְךָ הַכֶּר נָא.

Rabbi Yochanan said: God said to Yehudah, "You said to your father, 'We have found this. Do you recognize it? Is it your son's coat?' (*Bereishit* 37:32). By your life, Tamar will say to you, 'Do you recognize...?'" (*Bereishit Rabbah* 85:11)

The Midrash draws a straight line from the relationship between Yehudah and Tamar to the relationship between Yehudah and his father; Yehudah is rehabilitated from his earlier sin by Tamar. When Tamar says the words, "Do you recognize," Yehudah hears the echo of his own words all those years before, when he looked his father in the eye and shattered his father's world by saying, "Do you recognize it? Is it your son's coat?"[11] At last, Yehudah breaks through the walls of his own selfishness; he sees Tamar—and so much more. He sees himself, and he sees what he has done, the wrongs he has committed—against his daughter-in-law, and against his father. The next verse encapsulates his transformation:

בראשית לח:כו

וַיַּכֵּר יְהוּדָה וַיֹּאמֶר צָדְקָה מִמֶּנִּי...

Yehudah recognized, and said, "She is more righteous than I…" (*Bereishit* 38:26)

With these words, the idea of Mashiach is born: The capacity to recognize when we have sinned and to take responsibility is the starting point for both personal and national redemption. From this point on, Yehudah is a changed person, perhaps the first true *baal teshuvah*. From the relationship between Yehudah and Tamar, our kings emerge—David,[12] and his descendant, the Mashiach. The midrash refers to this concept in its unique symbolic language: Tamar challenges Yehudah with his own staff:

---

11. In 1975 Robert Alter published a brilliant analysis of this section in which he pointed out these connections, and lamented: "At this late date there exists no serious literary analysis of the Bible." See "A Literary Approach to the Bible," *Commentary* December 1975. When this article was later expanded into a larger book, *The Art of Biblical Narrative* (Basic Books, 1981), Alter noted (p. 10) that the Midrash had anticipated his analysis. "It is instructive that the two verbal cues indicating the connection between the story of the selling of Joseph and the story of Tamar and Judah were duly noted more than 1500 years ago in the Midrash."

12. David, too sinned, and had the courage to admit his mistake. See 2 *Shmuel* 12:13:

שמואל ב' יב:יג

וַיֹּאמֶר דָּוִד אֶל נָתָן חָטָאתִי לַה'...

בראשית רבה (וילנא) פרשת וישב פרשה פה:ט

וּמַטְּךָ, זֶה מֶלֶךְ הַמָּשִׁיחַ.

The staff [is the scepter] of the King Mashiach. (*Bereishit Rabbah* 85:9)

When Tamar asks Yehudah to identify his staff, she challenges him to find the courage to admit his guilt and take responsibility, to manifest the greatness which she sees within him. She challenges him to change. This is the lesson that Mashiach will one day teach the world: Every person controls his or her own destiny. No matter what mistakes have been made, they can be fixed, redeemed, turned into tools for greater understanding and empathy, insight and courage.

Neither Yehudah nor David, the progenitors of the Messiah, were like Yosef, who heroically withstood temptation. Rather, they were both guilty of sin. This flawed personality, and not the perfect, superhuman ideal, is the Jewish prototype for the Messiah. Moreover, the lineage of the Messiah traces back to the incestuous relationship between Lot and his daughter, which resulted in the birth of Moav, the founder of the tribe to which Ruth, the great-grandmother of David, was born.

The seemingly unrelated, apparently tangential, and unmistakably sordid relationships recorded in *Sefer Bereishit* lead inexorably to the birth of David, and, eventually, the Messiah.[13] Yosef is perhaps the more obvious candidate for proto-Messiah; Yosef certainly plays a key role—some might argue that his is the leading role—in the remainder of the book of *Bereishit*. Indeed, Yosef is the prototype for a second type of Messiah—known, appropriately enough, as "Mashiach ben

---

13. In the darkest days of the Holocaust, a formally anti-Zionist rabbi, Yisachar Shlomo Teichtal, came to the realization that God uses "broken vessels," and that the rebuilding of Israel could well be accomplished by "sinful" non-religious Jews. Rabbi Teichtal came to understand that from sin, redemption may yet arise. See *Eim Habanim Semeichah* (translated by Rabbi Moshe Lichtman in Kol Mevaser: Jerusalem 2000).

Yosef."[14] However, Yosef, who withstands temptation, is not the same as Yehudah, who sins, acknowledges his own failure, and is transformed.

As a result of the episode of Yosef, the Jews were enslaved in Egypt; because of the *teshuvah* of Yehudah, the Jews will be redeemed at the End of Days, when a spirit of change will permeate the world, spearheaded by a descendant of Yehudah. History will reach its apex and the light of Mashiach, created all those years ago during the sale of Yosef, will shine bright. At that time, all the children of Yaakov, and with them all the people of the world, will finally achieve the tranquility Yaakov so eagerly hoped to find.

---

14. See *Sukkah* 52a. According to the Vilna Gaon's understanding, this second Messiah (ben Yosef) is the central figure in the messianic process. See *Kol Hator*; the ideas contained in this work are ascribed by followers of the Vilna Gaon to their master.

Worse Than You Thought

One of the most horrific episodes in the book of *Bereishit*, and perhaps in the entire Torah, is the sale of Yosef. Jealousy morphs into hatred, which leads to the brink of murder: Brothers who seem devoid of any fraternal love, at first plot to murder, and then "settle for" selling Yosef into slavery—or worse.

Perhaps our progress through the book of *Bereishit* has numbed us to this unimaginable state of affairs; otherwise, how could we possibly read about thoughts of fratricide and the callous sale of one brother by the other and not be shocked? Apparently, this sort of behavior is the norm, the leading motif or theme, of *Bereishit*: Brothers are unable to live together in peace, beginning with Kayin and Hevel, leading up to Avraham and Lot (who, though not brothers, were close relatives), Yitzchak and Yishmael, Yaakov and Esav—harmonious family life is a rare commodity in the first chapters of the book. Why would we expect anything else as we approach the final chapters?

The end of last week's *parashah* hardly gave us any reasons to be optimistic: Yaakov's sons are loose cannons, and there do not seem to have been any consequences for their inexcusable behavior. A straightforward reading of the text indicates that one son was intimate with his father's concubine (35:22), two others took murderous vengeance on an entire city (34:25-29), and the remaining sons apparently ransacked and plundered that city, and took the idols worshipped by their victims for their own use (35:2).

These three sins (murder, sexual impropriety, and idolatry) are the most severe offenses in Jewish thought, yet not only do the sons who perpetrated these crimes remain members in good standing of

Yaakov's family, there is barely a word of moral outrage recorded in the text; Yaakov's censure of his children is nothing if not restrained. His objections and remonstrations are purely pragmatic. To be sure, before he dies, Yaakov will have a word with his wayward sons, yet they are not banished or shunned, disowned or distanced. Traditional Jewish commentaries on these chapters of *Bereishit* tend to downplay or reinterpret the textual description of their crimes, but the straightforward reading of the text is morally jarring.

Another instance of distinctly unbrotherly behavior between relatives involves Yaakov and his wives. When Yaakov, who has invested seven years of hard labor for the right to marry Rachel, finds that his father-in-law Lavan has tricked him into marrying her sister Leah, why does Yaakov accept the situation so blandly? The marriage to Leah was the product of deception, and should not have been legally or morally binding; why does Yaakov agree to continue, and even expand, his association with these crazy, deceitful people? It isn't hard to conclude that his "wife," Leah, and his wife-to-be, Rachel, were in collusion—not to mention his father-in-law Lavan. Yaakov should have run as fast as he could to escape this family.

Perhaps there is one answer to all these questions.

When Yaakov was young, his father Yitzchak had a dream that was never realized. What Yitzchak wanted more than anything was for his sons to work together. He wanted his family to be united. Perhaps the lessons of his own youth had taught Yitzchak about the tragedy of a broken family: Soon after his own birth, Hagar and Yishmael were banished from his father's house, and midrashic sources tell us that Yitzchak never stopped trying to make the family whole again. For example:

בראשית רבה (וילנא) פרשת חיי שרה פרשה ס

בְּאֵר לַחַי רֹאִי, הָלַךְ לְהָבִיא אֶת הָגָר, אוֹתָהּ שֶׁיָּשְׁבָה עַל הַבְּאֵר וְאָמְרָה לְחַי הָעוֹלָמִים רְאֵה בְּעֶלְבּוֹנִי. (בראשית כד, סג):

רש"י בראשית פרשת חיי שרה פרק כד
מִבּוֹא בְּאֵר לַחַי רֹאִי. שֶׁהָלַךְ לְהָבִיא הָגָר לְאַבְרָהָם אָבִיו שֶׁיִּשָּׂאֶנָּה (בראשית רבה):

"He had just come from the well of Lachai-Roi" —For he had gone there to bring Hagar back to Avraham that he might take her again as his wife. (Rashi, *Bereishit* 24:62)

Yitzchak was a man of conciliation, and he dreamed of *his* sons growing up together, and remaining united—as he and his half-brother Yishmael had not.

Rivkah, on the other hand, knew that it was not to be. She had been told by God Himself that her sons would never form a unified family. They were destined to part ways from the outset, and their differences would grow as time went on. She knew there would be conflict; the rift was not to be bridged. Yaakov and Esav had separate identities and separate destinies that would preclude the sort of cooperation Yitzchak dreamed of.

Yaakov received his education from both of his parents. Even though he obeyed his mother and took the blessing Yitzchak had designated for Esav, Yaakov also internalized and cherished the values he learned from his father: Family should stick together.

This explains Yaakov's strange passivity when he is tricked into marrying Leah. When Yaakov sees Rachel's dedication to her sister, when he understands the lengths to which Rachel will go to protect Leah from shame and rejection, Yaakov is overwhelmed. He understands without a doubt that he has found the perfect woman: Rachel embodies the values his father Yitzchak had taught him. Sisters who will go to any lengths to protect one another's honor, sisters who "have one another's back," are the antithesis of his own experience. They are a living example of the sort of family cohesion Yitzchak had dreamed of but that had eluded both him and his sons. When Yaakov understood that Rachel had helped Leah at her own expense, not only didn't Yaakov run away, he fell even more deeply in love with Rachel.

בראשית פרק כט

(יח) וַיֶּאֱהַב יַעֲקֹב אֶת־רָחֵל וַיֹּאמֶר אֶעֱבָדְךָ שֶׁבַע שָׁנִים בְּרָחֵל בִּתְּךָ הַקְּטַנָּה:
(ל) וַיָּבֹא גַּם אֶל־רָחֵל וַיֶּאֱהַב גַּם־אֶת־רָחֵל מִלֵּאָה וַיַּעֲבֹד עִמּוֹ עוֹד שֶׁבַע־שָׁנִים אֲחֵרוֹת:

(18) Jacob loved Rachel. He said, "I will serve you seven years for Rachel, your younger daughter." … 30) He went in also to Rachel, and he loved also Rachel more than Leah, and served with him yet seven other years. (*Bereishit* 29:18, 30)

This also explains why Yaakov, while displeased with his sons, did not disown or banish them. He did not want to create another Yishmael or Lot; that would have been the easy way out. Yaakov was determined to keep his family intact. Even the outrageous behavior of Shimon and Levi was an outgrowth of this same world view: They "had their sister's back," and would not allow her to be victimized; their response was visceral, vengeful—and an expression of family cohesion that took the words out of Yaakov's mouth. Even Reuven's outrageous behavior may be seen as an attempt to re-engineer the dynamics between Rachel and Leah; Reuven sensed his mother Leahs' pain when, even after Rachel's death, Yaakov remained distant.[1]

Perhaps Yaakov's love for Yosef was an outgrowth of his love for Rachel: Yaakov favored Yosef, the son of Rachel, whom Yaakov loved more than anyone or anything else in the world. Yaakov never

---

1. As per Rashi, *Bereishit* 35:22:

רש״י בראשית פרשת וישלח פרק לה:כב

וישכב. מתוך שֶׁבִּלְבֵּל מִשְׁכָּבוֹ, מַעֲלֶה עָלָיו הַכָּתוּב כְּאִלּוּ שְׁכָבָהּ; וְלָמָּה בִּלְבֵּל וְחִלֵּל יְצוּעָיו? שֶׁכְּשֶׁמֵּתָה רָחֵל נָטַל יַעֲקֹב מִטָּתוֹ, שֶׁהָיְתָה נְתוּנָה תָּדִיר בְּאֹהֶל רָחֵל וְלֹא בִּשְׁאָר אֹהָלִים, וּנְתָנָהּ בְּאֹהֶל בִּלְהָה; בָּא רְאוּבֵן וְתָבַע עֶלְבּוֹן אִמּוֹ, אָמַר אִם אֲחוֹת אִמִּי הָיְתָה צָרָה לְאִמִּי, שִׁפְחַת אֲחוֹת אִמִּי תְּהֵא צָרָה לְאִמִּי? לְכָךְ בִּלְבֵּל:

"And he lay" — Because he had disturbed his couch Scripture accounts it to him as though he had actually sinned in this manner. But why did he disturb his couch? When Rachel died Yaakov removed to Bilhah's tent and Reuven came and protested against the slight thus inflicted on his mother (Leah). He said: "If my mother's sister was her rival, is that any reason why the handmaid of my mother's sister should become a rival to her!" On this account he disturbed the couch.

considered that there might be toxic fallout from this love; after all, Leah had entered into the marriage with her eyes wide open. She knew from the outset that Yaakov had always loved Rachel more, and that he always would. Surely her children understood that as well. But just as Rachel fiercely defended her sister, Yaakov was convinced that all of the children, raised in a loving family by mothers who protected and cared for one another, would create a strong bond, and would evolve into a new kind of nation.

With this in mind, the sale of Yosef seems even worse than we initially thought: The brothers failed to internalize the teachings of their father and grandfather, failed to value family unity, and failed to learn from their mothers about the lengths to which siblings should go to protect one another. When they plotted to kill Yosef, and when they eventually sold him into bondage, the brothers not only rejected Yosef, they rejected the values which their father and mothers held so dear.

It is unclear whether Yaakov ever learned of the circumstances that led Yosef to Egypt; perhaps he imagined that Yosef had been kidnapped by strangers. We can only hope that Yaakov never found out that not only did his sons not "have Yosef's back," they were ready to put a knife in it.

Parashat Miketz

Yosef HaTzaddik

The story of Yosef is well known: As the favorite son, Yosef becomes the object of the jealousy and derision of his brothers. He is sold into slavery, and, after many trials and tribulations, rises to the second most powerful position in Egypt. Many years later he confronts his brothers, and the visions for which his brothers mocked him in his youth come to fruition.

Biblical stories are often quite compelling, and this saga is truly great literature. For Jews, however, these stories are much more than a "good read." Many levels or layers of meaning and insight are encapsulated in the verses of these stories, and the account of Yosef's life is no exception. Each verse, each word used to tell Yosef's story, is loaded with theological and mystical implications.

בראשית לז:ב
אֵלֶּה ׀ תֹּלְדוֹת יַעֲקֹב יוֹסֵף בֶּן־שְׁבַע־עֶשְׂרֵה שָׁנָה...

These are the generations of Yaakov: Yosef was seventeen years old... (*Bereishit* 37:2)

The story of Yaakov is inextricably linked with Yosef; of all the sons, Yosef holds the key to Yaakov's legacy. The fulfillment or completeness of Yaakov, the "generations of Yaakov," will be realized through Yosef.

בראשית לז:ג
וְיִשְׂרָאֵל אָהַב אֶת־יוֹסֵף מִכָּל־בָּנָיו...

And **Yisrael** loved Yosef more than all his sons... (*Bereishit* 37:3)

Yisrael—and not Yaakov—loved Yosef more than the other sons. The use of this name reflects national identity and national destiny, and not the sentimental, personal relationship between Yaakov and his children. Yaakov's mission was a spiritual one; if he favored Yosef, it was because he believed that Yosef was best suited to fulfill that mission.

בראשית לז:ה
וַיַּחֲלֹם יוֹסֵף חֲלוֹם...

And Yosef dreamed a dream… (*Bereishit* 37:5)

Yosef was a visionary; perhaps this was one of the reasons why Yisrael favored him. Yosef had a unique ability to dream and to understand the meaning of dreams. Yisrael—the name used to describe the third of our founding fathers, as opposed to the name Yaakov that refers to his personal life and times—identified Yosef as the son most capable of carrying the nation's spiritual mission forward. Like his father and grandfather, Yaakov looked to the future: Avraham, Yitzchak, and Yaakov were not merely three highly accomplished spiritual individuals. They formed a dynasty; Yisrael identified Yosef as the link in the *shalshelet* (which means "chain" or "dynasty," from the root *shalosh*, "three") that would hold the entire chain together.

The dynasty began when God forged a covenant with Avraham:

בראשית יז:א-יב
וַיְהִי אַבְרָם בֶּן־תִּשְׁעִים שָׁנָה וְתֵשַׁע שָׁנִים וַיֵּרָא ה' אֶל־אַבְרָם וַיֹּאמֶר אֵלָיו אֲנִי־אֵל שַׁדַּי הִתְהַלֵּךְ לְפָנַי וֶהְיֵה תָמִים: וְאֶתְּנָה בְרִיתִי בֵּינִי וּבֵינֶךָ וְאַרְבֶּה אוֹתְךָ בִּמְאֹד מְאֹד: וַיִּפֹּל אַבְרָם עַל־פָּנָיו וַיְדַבֵּר אִתּוֹ אֱלֹהִים לֵאמֹר: אֲנִי הִנֵּה בְרִיתִי אִתָּךְ וְהָיִיתָ לְאַב הֲמוֹן גּוֹיִם: וְלֹא־יִקָּרֵא עוֹד אֶת־שִׁמְךָ אַבְרָם וְהָיָה שִׁמְךָ אַבְרָהָם כִּי אַב־הֲמוֹן גּוֹיִם נְתַתִּיךָ: וְהִפְרֵתִי אֹתְךָ בִּמְאֹד מְאֹד וּנְתַתִּיךָ לְגוֹיִם וּמְלָכִים מִמְּךָ יֵצֵאוּ: וַהֲקִמֹתִי אֶת־בְּרִיתִי בֵּינִי וּבֵינֶךָ וּבֵין זַרְעֲךָ אַחֲרֶיךָ לְדֹרֹתָם לִבְרִית עוֹלָם לִהְיוֹת לְךָ לֵאלֹהִים וּלְזַרְעֲךָ אַחֲרֶיךָ: וְנָתַתִּי לְךָ וּלְזַרְעֲךָ אַחֲרֶיךָ אֵת | אֶרֶץ מְגֻרֶיךָ אֵת כָּל־אֶרֶץ כְּנַעַן לַאֲחֻזַּת עוֹלָם וְהָיִיתִי

Miketz: Yosef HaTzaddik | 243

לָהֶם לֵאלֹהִים: וַיֹּאמֶר אֱלֹהִים אֶל־אַבְרָהָם וְאַתָּה אֶת־בְּרִיתִי תִשְׁמֹר אַתָּה וְזַרְעֲךָ אַחֲרֶיךָ לְדֹרֹתָם: זֹאת בְּרִיתִי אֲשֶׁר תִּשְׁמְרוּ בֵּינִי וּבֵינֵיכֶם וּבֵין זַרְעֲךָ אַחֲרֶיךָ הִמּוֹל לָכֶם כָּל־זָכָר: וּנְמַלְתֶּם אֵת בְּשַׂר עָרְלַתְכֶם וְהָיָה לְאוֹת בְּרִית בֵּינִי וּבֵינֵיכֶם: וּבֶן־שְׁמֹנַת יָמִים יִמּוֹל לָכֶם כָּל־זָכָר לְדֹרֹתֵיכֶם...

Avraham was ninety-nine years old. God appeared to Avraham, and said to him, "I am El Shaddai;[1] walk with Me and be complete. I will make a covenant between Me and you and multiply you exceedingly." Avraham prostrated himself, and God said to him: "This is My covenant with you; you will father many nations. You will no longer be called Avram; your name shall be Avraham because I have made you the father of a many nations. I will cause you to multiply exceedingly and make nations from you; kings will descend from you. And I will uphold the covenant between us, and with your offspring and their descendants through the generations, in an everlasting covenant, to be their God and the God of their children after them. And I will give to you and your descendants the land in which you dwell, the entire Land of Canaan, as an eternal inheritance, and I will be their God." God said to Avraham: "And you shall safeguard the covenant with Me; you, and your descendants throughout the generations. This is My covenant which you shall keep between Me and you, and your descendants after you: Every male child among you shall be circumcised. You shall circumcise the flesh of your foreskin, and it shall be a sign of the covenant between Me and you. Every eight-day-old male among you, throughout the generations, shall be circumcised...." (*Bereishit* 17:1–12)

This epiphany takes place prior to the birth of Yitzchak. Avram becomes Avraham, the new name signifying his new identity and

---

1. As with all names of God, the word itself is considered too holy to be used commonly. Thus, with the exclusion of the recitation of blessings or in mandated Torah reading in the synagogue, none of the names of God are pronounced by the devout as they appear in the text: *Elohim* is pronounced *Elokim*, *El* is pronounced *Kel*, *Shaddai* is pronounced *Shakkai*, and the Tetragrammaton (*yud-hei-vav-hei*) is replaced with *Hashem* (meaning, quite simply, "The Name").

spiritual mission as a father of nations and progenitor of a covenantal community. Avraham is commanded to circumcise all his descendants. As a result of these changes, Yitzchak will come into the world and the chain will continue: The covenant creates a new relationship between Avraham and God that will be carried on by Avraham's children. With the commandment of circumcision, the dynasty begins.

This passage, almost-literally pregnant with religious, national, and historic importance, contains another significant element: This is the first time *El Shaddai* appears in the Torah. The significance of this fact becomes apparent when we note its subsequent appearances in the text: When Yitzchak orders Yaakov not to take a wife from among the local women, he sends him away with a blessing:

בראשית כח:ג-ד

וַיִּקְרָא יִצְחָק אֶל־יַעֲקֹב וַיְבָרֶךְ אֹתוֹ וַיְצַוֵּהוּ וַיֹּאמֶר לוֹ לֹא־תִקַּח אִשָּׁה מִבְּנוֹת כְּנָעַן: קוּם לֵךְ פַּדֶּנָה אֲרָם בֵּיתָה בְתוּאֵל אֲבִי אִמֶּךָ וְקַח־לְךָ מִשָּׁם אִשָּׁה מִבְּנוֹת לָבָן אֲחִי אִמֶּךָ: וְאֵל שַׁדַּי יְבָרֵךְ אֹתְךָ וְיַפְרְךָ וְיַרְבֶּךָ וְהָיִיתָ לִקְהַל עַמִּים: וְיִתֶּן־לְךָ אֶת־בִּרְכַּת אַבְרָהָם לְךָ וּלְזַרְעֲךָ אִתָּךְ לְרִשְׁתְּךָ אֶת־אֶרֶץ מְגֻרֶיךָ אֲשֶׁר־נָתַן אֱלֹהִים לְאַבְרָהָם:

Yitzchak called Yaakov and blessed him, and commanded him, saying: "Do not take a wife from among the Canaanites. Go, travel to Padan Aram, to the house of Betuel, your maternal grandfather, and take a wife there, from the daughters of Lavan, your uncle. *El Shaddai* shall bless you and make you fruitful and multiply you, and you will become a large nation. He will give the blessing of Avraham to you and to your descendants along with you, to inherit the land in which you live, which the Almighty promised to Avraham. (*Bereishit* 28:1–4)

When the blessing of nationhood, given to Avraham by *El Shaddai*, is passed on to Yaakov, the Name of God invoked is, once again, *El Shaddai*. God Himself uses this term in his communication of this blessing to Yaakov:

Miketz: Yosef HaTzaddik

בראשית לה:י-יא

וַיֹּאמֶר־לוֹ אֱלֹהִים שִׁמְךָ יַעֲקֹב לֹא־יִקָּרֵא שִׁמְךָ עוֹד יַעֲקֹב כִּי אִם־יִשְׂרָאֵל יִהְיֶה שְׁמֶךָ וַיִּקְרָא אֶת־שְׁמוֹ יִשְׂרָאֵל: וַיֹּאמֶר לוֹ אֱלֹהִים אֲנִי אֵל שַׁדַּי פְּרֵה וּרְבֵה גּוֹי וּקְהַל גּוֹיִם יִהְיֶה מִמֶּךָּ וּמְלָכִים מֵחֲלָצֶיךָ יֵצֵאוּ:

The Almighty said to him, "Your name is Yaakov, [but] you shall no longer be called Yaakov, but rather Yisrael shall be your name," and He named him Yisrael. The Almighty said to him, "I am *El Shaddai*. Be fruitful and multiply; a nation and a congregation of nations shall descend from you, and kings will emerge from your loins." (*Bereishit* 35:10–11)

Each time God bestows the blessing of progeny upon the patriarchs, He refers to Himself with the Divine Name *El Shaddai*. In fact, these are the <u>only</u> instances in which this Divine Name is used until this point in the Torah; it is not used in any other context. Instead, the more familiar Tetragrammaton (translated as "Eternal") or *Elokim* (which we translate as "Almighty") are used.[2]

---

2. There are sources that note the unmistakable similarity of the name Shaddai to the Hebrew *shadayim*, meaning "breasts,", which would explain why this name always seems related to blessings of fertility. See *Zohar, Shemot* 253a, and *Ben Yehoyada* on *Shabbat* 97a:

זוהר כרך ב (שמות) פרשת פקודי [המתחיל בדף רכ עמוד א]

... וּמִיּוֹמָא דְּאִתְחָרַב בֵּי מַקְדְּשָׁא, לָא עָאלוּ הָכָא נִשְׁמָתֵין אַחֲרָנִין. וְכַד יִסְתַּיְּימוּן אִלֵּין, הֵיכָלָא קַיְּימָא בְּרֵיקַנְיָא, וְיִתְפַּקַּד מִלְּעֵילָּא, וּכְדֵין יֵיתֵי מַלְכָּא מְשִׁיחָא. וְאִתְּעַר הֵיכָלָא דָּא לְעֵילָּא, וְיִתְּעַר הֵיכָלָא לְתַתָּא.
וּבְרָזָא דְּהֵיכָלָא דָּא כְּתִיב, (שיר השירים ד) שְׁנֵי שָׁדַיִךְ כִּשְׁנֵי עֳפָרִים וְגו'. בְּגִין דְּבַהֵיכָלָא דָּא הַהוּא רוּחָא דְּקָאָמְרָן, וְהַהוּא חֵיוָתָא, אַפִּיק תְּרֵין נְהוֹרִין כְּלִילָן דָּא בְּדָא, מִתְקַשְׁרָן דָּא בְּדָא, וְאִקְרוּן אֵ"ל שַׁדָּ"י. אִלֵּין אִקְרוּן שַׁדָּ"י, וְאֵ"ל דִּלְתַתָּא, מִתְחַבְּרָן דָּא בְּדָא, וְאָעִיל דָּא בְּדָא, וְאִקְרֵי אֵ"ל שַׁדָּ"י. בְּגִין דְּיָנִיק מִכְּלָלָא דְּאִלֵּין שָׁדַיִם.
וְהַאי אֵ"ל דְּאִיהוּ מִסִּטְרָא דִּימִינָא, נָטִיל מֵאֲתָר דָּא, כָּל אִינוּן רַחֲמִין, דְּקַיְּימֵי לְאַתְזָנָא הַהוּא הֵיכָלָא דִּלְתַתָּא, דְּאִקְרֵי זְכוּתָ"א, עַל שְׁמָא דְּהַאי רוּחָא דְּבֵיהּ דְּקָאָמְרָן. הַאי שַׁדַּי, יָנִיק לְכָל אִינוּן תַּתָּאִין, וּלְכָל אִינוּן הֵיכָלִין, וּלְכָל אִינוּן דִּלְבַר, דְּקַיְּימֵי מִסִּטְרָא דָּא, דְּאִקְרוּן יִתְדוֹת הַמִּשְׁכָּן, כְּמָה דְּאוֹקִימְנָא. וְעַל דָּא אִקְרֵי שַׁדַּי, בְּגִין דִּמְסַפְּקָא מְזוֹנָא לְכֻלְּהוּ תַּתָּאֵי, כְּמָה דְּאִיהוּ מְקַבְּלָא, מִסִּטְרָא דִּימִינָא ...

ספר בניהו בן יהוידע על שבת דף צז/א

שם. מחיקו הוא דשבה כבשרו. נראה לי בס"ד תחלה א"ל הבא נא ידך בחיקך, והיינו חקך אות ש' שהיא עומדת בחק שמך, ותתן עליה אותיות יד אז יהיה צירוף יד"ש המורה על הלקאה

The next appearance of *El Shaddai* is in this week's Torah portion, *Parashat Miketz*. Yaakov is finally persuaded—with great difficulty—to allow the brothers to take Binyamin to Egypt. His parting words to his sons are as much a prayer as a blessing:

בראשית מג:יד-טו

וְאֵל שַׁדַּי יִתֵּן לָכֶם רַחֲמִים לִפְנֵי הָאִישׁ וְשִׁלַּח לָכֶם אֶת־אֲחִיכֶם אַחֵר וְאֶת־בִּנְיָמִין וַאֲנִי כַּאֲשֶׁר שָׁכֹלְתִּי שָׁכָלְתִּי:

May *El Shaddai* grant you mercy before the man [the leader of Egypt]. May He send your other brother [Shimon], as well as Binyamin, back; as for me, just as I mourned [for Yosef] I will mourn [for Binyamin]. (*Bereishit* 43:14)

Yaakov is tormented by the prospect of losing Binyamin. He has mourned Binyamin's brother Yosef for decades, and is consumed with dread that he will lose the only son that remains from his beloved Rachel. However, if we view this dialogue as Yaakov speaking not only as a father but as the leader of a nation, the statement takes on a different meaning. He fears for the future of his nation—the nation promised to him and his father and grandfather by *El Shaddai*.

In the last days of Yaakov's life, he invokes *El Shaddai* twice, both in discussions with Yosef: First, Yaakov recounts the crucial moments of his life story. Once again, the topic is children or descendants, as Yaakov prepares to bless Yosef's sons—the only grandchildren to receive his blessing directly.

בראשית פרק מח:ג-ד

(ג) וַיֹּאמֶר יַעֲקֹב אֶל־יוֹסֵף אֵל שַׁדַּי נִרְאָה־אֵלַי בְּלוּז בְּאֶרֶץ כְּנָעַן וַיְבָרֶךְ אֹתִי:

(ד) וַיֹּאמֶר אֵלַי הִנְנִי מַפְרְךָ וְהִרְבִּיתִךָ וּנְתַתִּיךָ לִקְהַל עַמִּים ...

לשון דישה, והוא אחר שעשה צירופים על שם שדי, אך אחר כך בטובה א"ל השב נא ידך בחקך, תיבת השב מורה על חזרה לאחור, כלומר צירוף יד עם חקך שהוא ש' שנעשה יד"ש השב אותו לאחור שנעשה שם שדי ביושר, כי ידש למפרע שד"י, ושם זה יורה על הטובה והוא לשון שדים של יניקה, וגם עוד ראיתי בספר קה"י שהביא מן ספר דן ידין שכינה החכמה באותיות שדי, ובגילוי אור החכמה מסתלק הצרעת כנודע מדברי רבינו האר"י ז"ל בשה"מ.

Yaakov said to Yosef, "*El Shaddai* appeared to me in Luz and blessed me. He said to me, 'I will make you fruitful and numerous and a host of nations will spring forth from you…" (*Bereishit* 48:3-4)

The last time *Shaddai* is used in *Sefer Bereishit* is in Yaakov's deathbed blessing to Yosef.

בראשית מט: כה-כו
מֵאֵל אָבִיךָ וְיַעְזְרֶךָּ וְאֵת שַׁדַּי וִיבָרְכֶךָּ בִּרְכֹת שָׁמַיִם מֵעָל בִּרְכֹת תְּהוֹם רֹבֶצֶת תָּחַת בִּרְכֹת שָׁדַיִם וָרָחַם: בִּרְכֹת אָבִיךָ גָּבְרוּ עַל-בִּרְכֹת הוֹרַי עַד-תַּאֲוַת גִּבְעֹת עוֹלָם תִּהְיֶיןָ לְרֹאשׁ יוֹסֵף וּלְקָדְקֹד נְזִיר אֶחָיו:

May the God [*El*] of your father help you, and *El Shaddai* shall bless you, blessings of the Heavens above, blessings of the depths which crouch below, blessings of the breast and womb. The blessings of your father are potent beyond those of my ancestors, to the utmost boundary of the everlasting hills. They shall be on the head of Yosef, and on the crown of the head of he who was separated from his brothers. (*Bereishit* 49:25–26)

Yaakov passes on to Yosef the powerful blessings he himself received from God directly, as well as from his own father and grandfather. Once again, the Name associated with this blessing of progeny is *El Shaddai*.

These are the only passages in *Sefer Bereishit* where the name *El Shaddai* appears, which leads us to two conclusions: First, that *Shaddai* is intrinsically connected with the blessing of progeny, and second, that of all of Yaakov's children this blessing is bestowed specifically upon Yosef.

What is the meaning of *El Shaddai*?

תלמוד בבלי מסכת חגיגה דף יב עמוד א
וְהַיְינוּ דְּאָמַר רֵישׁ לָקִישׁ, מַאי דִּכְתִיב, (בראשית יז) "אֲנִי אֵ-ל שַׁדַּי", אֲנִי אֵ-ל שֶׁאָמַרְתִּי לְעוֹלָמִי "דַּי"! אָמַר רֵישׁ לָקִישׁ, בְּשָׁעָה שֶׁבָּרָא הַקָּדוֹשׁ בָּרוּךְ הוּא אֶת הַיָּם, הָיָה מַרְחִיב וְהוֹלֵךְ, עַד שֶׁגָּעַר בּוֹ הַקָּדוֹשׁ בָּרוּךְ הוּא, וְיִבְּשׁוֹ...

And this is the teaching of Resh Lakish: "What is the meaning of 'I am Kel Shakkai'? I am He who told the world, 'Enough!'" Reish Lakish taught: "When the Holy One, blessed be He, created the sea, it kept on expanding until the Holy One, blessed be He, chastised it, and it stopped...." (*Chagigah* 12a)

Resh Lakish explained that the Hebrew word *dai*, which means "enough," "stop," "cease and desist," forms the core of the Divine Name *Shaddai*: The forces of Creation, when unleashed, threatened to overwhelm what had been created. Nature had to be restrained from overexpanding, so God set boundaries, creating a tension between the various forces of nature that enabled our world to exist.

The Name of God used in the description of Creation is *Elokim*, the Almighty or Omnipotent. According to Kabbalistic tradition, *Elokim* does not describe the essence of God; it expresses one aspect of God, one facet that is revealed to us. Kabbalistic texts more commonly refer to God as *Ein Sof*, the One "without limits," or "The Infinite." At first glance, we might think that *Elokim*, "Almighty," best describes God's role in the cosmic drama. Why, then, do the Kabbalists prefer *Ein Sof*?

The Kabbalists grapple with a fundamental problem: The essence of God is transcendental, completely beyond man's grasp or ability to categorize, and therefore beyond articulation. Consequently, even the term "Almighty" is, in effect, an anthropomorphism; it describes God as the possessor of all the powers we can conceive of, all the powers known to us or imagined by our limited minds—which is, in God's terms, a very limited purview indeed. The *Zohar* attempts to point out our inability to grasp or express that which lies beyond us, suggesting that the first verse of the Torah should be translated as "In the beginning, *Elokim* was created [by the transcendental *Ein Sof*]..." (*Tikkunei Zohar, Tikkunim Chadashim, Ha-Iidra Kaddisha*).[3]

---

3. See *Tikkunei Zohar* 4b, 98a, 111b:

תיקוני זהר דף ד/ב

וְשֵׁם יהו"ה אִיהוּ עַמּוּדָא דְאֶמְצָעִיתָא, אֱמֶת, וּשְׁכִינְתֵּיהּ תּוֹרַת אֱמֶת, בָּהּ אִתְבְּרִיאַת כָּרְסַיָּא דְאִיהִי אֱלֹהִ"ם, וְהַיְינוּ בְּרֵאשִׁית בָּרָא אֱלֹהִ"ם, בְּאוֹרַיְיתָא דְאִיהִי רֵאשִׁית בָּרָא כָּרְסַיָּא דְאִיהִי אֱלֹהִ"ם, דְּהָכִי סָלִיק הַכִּסֵּ"א לְחוּשְׁבַּן אֱלֹהִ"ם.

Miketz: Yosef HaTzaddik | 249

The name *Elokim* is identified with the unbridled forces of nature[4]; it

תיקוני זהר דף צח/א

בְּרֵאשִׁית בָּרָא אלהי"ם דָּא מטטרו"ן, דְּבָרָא לֵיהּ קוּדְשָׁא בְּרִיךְ הוּא קַדְמוֹן וְרֵאשִׁית לְכָל צְבָא הַשָּׁמַיִם דִּלְתַתָּא, וְדָא אִיהוּ אָדָם הַקָּטֹן, דְּקוּדְשָׁא בְּרִיךְ הוּא עָבַד לֵיהּ בְּדִיוּקְנָא וְצִיּוּרָא דִּלְעֵילָא בְּלָא עִרְבּוּבְיָא, וַעֲלֵיהּ אִתְּמָר (בראשית א כד) תּוֹצֵא הָאָרֶץ נֶפֶשׁ חַיָּה לְמִינָהּ, וְאִיהוּ עֵץ פְּרִי עוֹשֶׂה פְּרִי לְמִינוֹ (שם יא ז), כְּגַוְונָא דִלְעֵילָא וַי מָאן דְּעָבִיד עִרְבּוּבְיָא לְעֵילָא וּלְתַתָּא, דְּהַאי אִילָנָא דְעָר בּוּבְיָא, עִרְבּוּבְיָא מֵאִילָנָא דְמוֹתָא, בְּגִין דָּא אִתְקְרֵי מַטֶּה, דְּאִתְהַפֵּךְ לְנָחָשׁ לְאַלְקָאָה בֵּיהּ לְחַיָּיבַיָּא, וּמָאן אִיהוּ דְאָפִיךְ לֵיהּ קוּדְשָׁא בְּרִיךְ הוּא דְשַׁלִּיט עָלֵיהּ וְהָא אוּקְמוּהָ.

תיקוני זהר דף קיא/ב

אָמְרוּ לֵיהּ רַבִּי רַבִּי, הָא אִילָנָא שְׁלִים בְּיהו"ה, אַמַּאי נָחִית א' מִן בְּרֵאשִׁית, אֶלָּא בְּגִין דְּאִיהוּ נְבִיעוּ לְאַשְׁקָאָה אִילָנָא, דְּמִתַּמָּן אלהי"ם מָלְיָא"ה מִכָּל תֵּשַׁע סְפִירָאן, דְּאִינוּן בְּבְרֵאשִׁית, שִׁית אִינוּן שִׁית סְפִירָאן, בָּרָא תְּלַת סְפִירָאן עִלָּאִין, אלהי"ם אִיהוּ עֲשִׂירָאָה מַלְיָאה מְכֻּלְּהוּ תֵּשַׁע, שְׁלִימוּ דְכֻלְהוּ, וּבְגִין דָּא בְּרֵאשִׁית בָּרָא אלהי"ם, אֶת הַשָּׁמַיִם וְאֶת הָאָרֶץ, אָתוּ לְנַשְּׁקָא לֵיהּ פָּרַח לְעֵילָא.

4. This Divine Name has the same numeric value as *ha-teva* (nature). This teaching is hinted at in the writings of Rabbenu Bachya (*Bereishit* 2:4); it appears in the writings of Rabbi Moshe of Cordovero's *Pardes Rimonim* (*Shaar* 12, chapter 2), and is cited by the *Shla Ha-Kadosh* from the *Pardes Rimonim*, and by numerous later writers:

רבנו בחיי על בראשית פרק ב פסוק ד

לא הזכיר השם המיוחד עד עתה בכל ששת ימי בראשית. ועל דרך הפשט שם אלהים נופל על מעשה הטבע ומעיד השם המיוחד על החידוש ושם המיוחד מעיד על קדמותו ומציאותו יתברך, ועל כן לא הזכיר השם המיוחד בכל מעשה הטבע רק שם אלהים כי התורה רצתה להתחיל בסיפור החידוש, ועל כן הוצרך להזכיר השם המורה על המחדש והוא הכינוי שנתחדש לו בבריאת עולמו, ואילו היתה כוונת התורה להתחיל בסיפור קדמותו ומציאותו יתברך היה ראוי להזכיר השם המיוחד המעיד על זה, ועל כן הזכיר הנגלה והסתיר הנסתר:

ספר השל"ה הקדוש - מסכת פסחים מצה עשירה {תע}

וּכְבָר כָּתְבוּ הַרְבֵּה מְפָרְשִׁים עִנְיָן זֶה, שֶׁשֵּׁם אֱלֹהִים מוֹרֶה עַל הַטֶּבַע (וְכֵן מִנְיַן 'הַטֶּבַע', כְּמִנְיַן 'אֱלֹהִים', (הפרדס שער י"ב פ"ב). וְשֵׁם ידו"ד מוֹרֶה עַל שֶׁהוּא הָיָה הֹוֶה יִהְיֶה, מְהַוֶּה הַכֹּל בִּרְצוֹנוֹ וּבְחֶפְצוֹ לְשַׁנּוֹת וּלְשַׁדֵּד:

שפתי כהן על בראשית פרק א פסוק כז

שכן אלהים בגימטריא הטבע

ספר פרדס רמונים - שער יב פרק ב

אבל נכתב בשם אלקים באותיות אלקים לרמוז אל תוקף דין הגבורה כי היא עולם הטבע. וכן עולה שם אלקים במנין הטב"ע שהוא בו. והטעם כי השמיטה היתה בגבורה כפי המוסכם בין רוב המפרשים. והשמיטה הטביעה בעולמה כפי טבעה ורצונה כי הטבע רצון אלקי הוא. ולכן בריאת העולם היה בדין גמור עד שראה שלא יכול לעמוד ושתף עמה מדת הרחמים כדפי' רז"ל:

ספר מגלה עמוקות על התורה - פרשת חקת

ע"ד השכל חטאו בשני ההנהגות שהקב"ה מנהיג עולמו באלקים הנהגת הטבע ובמשה הנהגת השגחה לכן נאמר וידבר באלקים אלקים בגימט' הטבע

is this aspect of God that creates heaven and earth in six days. However, in the Kabbalistic description of Creation, the world's emergence is made possible by the transcendental God "holding back" His transcendence and allowing a finite world to exist. This process is known as *tzimtzum* ("contraction" or "self-limitation"); the result is the creation of "nature." The aspect of God expressed in the Divine Name *Shakkai* denotes this limitation of nature.

Avraham came to recognize God through nature[5]; God's response was to give Avraham the mitzvah of circumcision, which implies that man must perfect nature, rise above it, control his natural instincts—in imitation of God's own self-limitation. For the Jewish People to emerge, Avraham must connect with the Infinite by developing the ability to rise above "nature." This is the symbol of the eighth day: There are seven days of the week in the process of creation; the eighth day lies beyond the natural, beyond the physical. The Jewish People could not emerge as a nation until they accepted the mitzvah of circumcision; the self-limitation that is the essence of the Covenant of Avraham is the prerequisite for the birth of a holy nation, a "kingdom of priests."

More than any other biblical figure, Yosef epitomizes the ability to control base human instinct: He resists sexual temptation, he overcomes the human tendency toward vengefulness, spite, and hatred—even when these might have been perfectly well-deserved. Yosef, and no other, is known as "Yosef the Tzaddik," and Kabbalistic sources refer to him as *Yesod*—the foundation. He completes the process of self-limitation that brings about the transition from family to nationhood: Yosef internalizes the concept of *tzimtzum* expressed in the Divine attribute of *Shaddai*.

ספר קהלת יעקב - ערך בם

במוכן הוא חילוף שם אלהים באותיות שלאחריו והוא יותר דין מבחינת אלהים הרב ז"ל (פרי עץ חיים שער חג המצות פרק א'), והרב החסיד מוהר"ר ישראל דק"ק קאזניץ אמר טעם על מה שנקרא במוכן כי בחינת אלהים הוא בטבע כי אלהים בגימטריא הטבע, והטבע אינו שופע אלא במוכן לה שנולד במזל זה, וגם אותיות במוכן שאחר אלהים ודברי פי חכם חן:

ספר מבוא לחכמת הקבלה - חלק א שער ז פרק ה

אלקים הוא המכסה אור הוי"ה ב"ה הנקרא שם העצם. לכן אלקים בגימ' הטבע הנהגת הטבע. וע"ז נאמר כבוד אלקים הסתר דבר, כבוד לשון לבוש, כטעם רבי יוחנן דקרי למאניה מכבדותי:

5. See above on *Parashat Lech Lecha* for a summary of the midrashim on this topic.

As the long and oppressive exile in Egypt comes to an end, the Israelites set about collecting their unpaid wages from their Egyptian taskmasters, in fulfillment of the promise God made to Avraham centuries earlier:

בראשית פרק טו, יג-יד
...וַעֲבָדוּם וְעִנּוּ אֹתָם ... וְאַחֲרֵי־כֵן יֵצְאוּ בִּרְכֻשׁ גָּדוֹל:

"…They will enslave them and abuse them…and then [Your descendents] will leave with great possessions." (*Bereishit* 15:14)

Moshe, their leader, heads instead to the Nile River to collect Yosef's remains. Why did Moshe occupy himself personally with the task of fulfilling the promise made by the brothers to Yosef to redeem his remains from Egypt? Could this responsibility not have been delegated, perhaps to one of Yosef's direct descendants?

While still an infant, Moshe was hidden in an ark and set afloat on the Nile. Pharaoh's daughter found him and took him in, saving him from the death sentence her own father had issued for all Jewish males. Moshe's sister Miriam offered to find a nurse for the baby, and Pharaoh's daughter agreed. Thus, Moshe was returned to his parents' home for two years, until he was weaned; he then went back to Pharaoh's place, where he was raised as the son of Pharaoh's daughter (*Shemot* 2). Moshe's parents had a brief opportunity to educate their son prior to his return to the daughter of Pharaoh and to life in the palace. What sort of things did they teach him? Clearly, they succeeded in inculcating in him an awareness of his Jewish identity:

שמות ב:יא
וַיְהִי | בַּיָּמִים הָהֵם וַיִּגְדַּל מֹשֶׁה וַיֵּצֵא אֶל־אֶחָיו וַיַּרְא בְּסִבְלֹתָם וַיַּרְא אִישׁ מִצְרִי מַכֶּה אִישׁ־עִבְרִי מֵאֶחָיו:

It was in those days, when Moshe was grown, that he went out to his **brothers** and looked on their burdens, and he saw an Egyptian beating a Hebrew, one of his **brothers**. (*Shemot* 2:11)

Despite his life of privilege and comfort in the palace, Moshe knew and acknowledged the Israelite slaves as his **brothers**. His parents had obviously taught him well, had equipped him with the tools to retain his Jewish identity in the palace. Surely, there could have been no better role model than their great-great uncle Yosef. Who but Yosef had spent long years in the palace, living among the uppermost echelon of Egyptian society, and, despite all its depravity and seductiveness, retained his identity? The example of Yosef the Tzaddik almost certainly inspired Moshe, fortified him in the years of separation from his family, and gave him hope for a reconciliation—as well as a deep understanding that God's plan for the salvation of the Jewish People sometimes requires that individuals be placed in this situation for the good of the nation. Yosef, once again, is the *Yesod*—the foundation upon which the Exodus from Egypt was built.

And so, in a gesture of gratitude for the uplifting example and inspiration Yosef provided, Moshe himself lifted Yosef's remains from the Nile and out of Egypt. Had Yosef been merely one more distant relative, Moshe could have delegated the chore of locating his remains to someone else. Rather, it was Yosef the Tzaddik, the foundation of Moshe's faith in Jewish unity and Jewish destiny, the symbol of man's ability to control his own nature, the human manifestation of *Shaddai*, whom Moshe liberated.[6] Kabbalisitic thought stresses the spiritual connection between Moshe and Yosef:

זוהר חלק ג דף רלו/א (רעיא מהימנא ספר במדבר פרשת פנחס)
וַיִּקַּח מֹשֶׁה אֶת עַצְמוֹת יוֹסֵף עִמּוֹ. עַצְמוֹת צַדִּיק יְסוֹד עָלְמִין, דַּרְגָּא דְּיוֹסֵף הַצַּדִּיק.

"Moshe took the remains of Yosef with him" (*Shemot* 11:19) — the remains of the Tzaddik who is the foundation of the world, the level of Yosef the Tzaddik. (*Zohar, Bamidbar* 236a)

---

6. On a more basic level, we may posit that Moshe, as a descendant of Levi, felt an historic responsibility to "right the wrong" and to return Yosef home. According to tradition, it was Levi who first suggested to kill Yosef; perhaps Moshe felt particular responsibility for the schism created by the sale of Yosef, and this was his way of making amends and healing the nation's wounds of discord.

It should come as no surprise, then, that when God speaks to Moshe for the first time, He addresses this spiritual connection, and uses it to explain the task He is about to bestow upon Moshe:

שמות ו:ב-ג

וַיְדַבֵּר אֱלֹהִים אֶל־מֹשֶׁה וַיֹּאמֶר אֵלָיו אֲנִי ה': וָאֵרָא אֶל־אַבְרָהָם אֶל־יִצְחָק וְאֶל־יַעֲקֹב בְּאֵל שַׁדָּי וּשְׁמִי ה' לֹא נוֹדַעְתִּי לָהֶם:

The Almighty spoke to Moshe, and said to him, "I am the Eternal God [Hashem]. I appeared to Avraham, Yitzchak, and Yaakov as *El Shaddai*, and My Eternal Name [*Hashem Elokim*] I did not make known to them." (*Shemot* 6:2–3)

To fulfill his mission, Moshe will need a different type of relationship with God than the one enjoyed by the patriarchs. These relationships are expressed in the different names through which God reveals Himself: The aspect of God expressed by *Shaddai* is a powerful one, and surely no holy nation of Jews could have come into existence without it. God, however, has many more plans for the Jews—plans that Moshe is now tasked with setting in motion: Standing at Mount Sinai, receiving the Torah, taking possession of the Land of Israel, and, eventually, mending and perfecting the world. For these missions to be accomplished, more Divine Light must be revealed, other aspects of God must become known and manifest in this world. The blessings bestowed upon the Patriarchs by *El Shaddai* were brought to full expression in Yosef, the *Yesod* or foundation of the Jewish People, but the building which will stand on this foundation had yet to be built. That would require a new relationship with God, a new covenant that would be forged at Mount Sinai, built upon the foundation laid by our Forefathers.

A Cherished Chalice

As a young man, Yosef was a dreamer of dreams. There were those who considered these dreams nothing more than delusions of grandeur, but Yosef knew the dreams would come true.

As a dreamer, Yosef knew how to read symbols; he understood things others often missed, enabling him to see into the future with clarity. From the moment Yosef takes his place on the stage of history, everyone who comes into contact with him—other than his brothers—sees that he is gifted; Yosef is revered, but feared. In at least one instance, this unusual combination saved his life: Yosef's first "home" in Egypt was in the household of the chief executioner, Potifar. Surely a man with such a vocation was neither friendly nor forgiving. Yet when Yosef is (falsely) accused of cuckolding the executioner, somehow he emerges unscathed. Potifar, who killed people for a living, could quite easily have dispatched Yosef with one quick chop of the guillotine; strangely enough, Potifar doesn't lay a finger on Yosef. The executioner was no fool; simply put, he was terrified of Yosef.[1] Potifar saw how his personal fortunes had soared from the moment Yosef arrived. He understood that God was with Yosef, and he was afraid that if he harmed Yosef, not only would he lose his new-found wealth, but he might also be subjected to the wrath of Yosef's God. Perhaps Potifar knew his own

---

1. Alshich, *Bereshit* 39:20:

אלשיך על בראשית פרשת וישב פרק לט פסוק כ

...אמנם, הנה אין ספק כי אם היה אדוני יוסף מאמין לדברי אשתו לא היה נותנו בבית הסוהר רק רודפו עד המיתו. אך מאשר ראה כי ה' אתו כמו שכתבנו למעלה וירא אדוניו כי ה' אתו, ומה גם לרבותינו ז"ל (בראשית רבה פו ה) שאמרו שראה שכינה על ראשו, על כן היה נכוה בשתי אשות, אומר בלבו אוי לי אם אומר כי האמת עם אשתי וחטאתי לה' אשר עם יוסף, ואוי לי אם לא אומר כי תהיה לי לחרפה שתצא שם רע על אשתי. ועל כן הפשיר הדבר ויתנהו בית הסוהר. וגם זה ביראת אלהים - פן יענש - לקחו בדברים טובים אל ייחר בעיני יוסף ויענש אדוניו עליו.

wife well enough not to believe her accusation; perhaps he knew Yosef well enough to know that he was an upstanding, trustworthy man and not some sort of Rasputin. Either way, Potifar arrives at a rather elegant resolution of the problem: He incarcerates Yosef in his prison, knowing that even from the dungeon Yosef may still be an asset.[2]

Yosef, for his part, displayed nothing but loyalty—both to his earthyl master and to the Master of the Universe, to Potifar and to God—when he withstood the advances of Potifar's wife:

בראשית פרק לט, ח-ט

(ח) וַיְמָאֵן | וַיֹּאמֶר אֶל־אֵשֶׁת אֲדֹנָיו הֵן אֲדֹנִי לֹא־יָדַע אִתִּי מַה־בַּבָּיִת וְכֹל אֲשֶׁר־יֶשׁ־לוֹ נָתַן בְּיָדִי: (ט) אֵינֶנּוּ גָדוֹל בַּבַּיִת הַזֶּה מִמֶּנִּי וְלֹא־חָשַׂךְ מִמֶּנִּי מְאוּמָה כִּי אִם־אוֹתָךְ בַּאֲשֶׁר אַתְּ־אִשְׁתּוֹ וְאֵיךְ אֶעֱשֶׂה הָרָעָה הַגְּדֹלָה הַזֹּאת וְחָטָאתִי לֵאלֹהִים:

Now that I am here, my master gives no thought to anything in this house, and all that he owns he has placed in my hands. There is no one in this house who holds more authority than I, and he has withheld nothing from me except yourself, since you are his wife. How then could I do this most wicked thing, and sin before God?" (*Bereishit* 39:8-9)

---

2. R. S.R. Hirsch and Malbim, *Bereishit* 39:20:

רש"ר הירש בראשית פרשת וישב פרק לט פסוק כ

בבית הסהר. אחרי שכבר שמענו שניתנו לבית הסוהר, הרי מיותר להוסיף כי היה שם בבית הסוהר. פוטיפר היה ממונה גם על בית הסוהר הממלכתי (ראה להלן מ, ג). הוא העביר את יוסף "אל בית הסהר", למען יביא שם תועלת, כדרך שעד כה הביא בביתו; ובדרך זו היה שם אסיר בבית הסוהר. אם כך, הרי בעומק נפשו היה משוכנע מצדקתו של יוסף והיה אנוס להגיב רק למען כבודו:

מלבי"ם בראשית פרשת וישב פרק לט פסוק כ

ויקח. לקחו בעצמו לא ע"י שוטרי בית הסוהר רק לקחו באהבה מצד שהוא מצד אדוני יוסף, ויכול להפקיד אותו שיעשה עבודתו בבית הסוהר, ויתנהו אל בית הסוהר שיעבוד עבודתו שם, ויען היה מקום בבית הסוהר ששם ישבו הפחותים אומר שנתנו אל צד הזה ששם אסורים אסירי המלך השרים והפרתמים. ומבואר שהוא לא היה אסור רק היה שם חפשי עובד עבודתו, ועז"א ויהי שם בבית הסוהר, כי בית הסוהר היה שייך לבית פוטיפר והיה צריך עבדים גם שם, והיה יכול לתתו שם גם בלי פשע:

Yosef's description of his own position of authority and the trust his master has placed in him differs subtly from the "narrator's" description, several verses earlier, of the relationship between Potifar and Yosef:

בראשית פרק לט, ה-ו

(ה) וַיְהִי מֵאָז הִפְקִיד אֹתוֹ בְּבֵיתוֹ וְעַל כָּל־אֲשֶׁר יֶשׁ־לוֹ וַיְבָרֶךְ ה' אֶת־בֵּית הַמִּצְרִי בִּגְלַל יוֹסֵף וַיְהִי בִּרְכַּת ה' בְּכָל־אֲשֶׁר יֶשׁ־לוֹ בַּבַּיִת וּבַשָּׂדֶה: (ו) וַיַּעֲזֹב כָּל־אֲשֶׁר־לוֹ בְּיַד־יוֹסֵף וְלֹא־יָדַע אִתּוֹ מְאוּמָה כִּי אִם־הַלֶּחֶם אֲשֶׁר־הוּא אוֹכֵל וַיְהִי יוֹסֵף יְפֵה־תֹאַר וִיפֵה מַרְאֶה:

> And from the time that [Potifar] put Yosef in charge of his household and of all that he owned, God blessed the Egyptian's house for Yosef's sake, so that the blessing of God was upon everything that he owned, in the house and outside. [Potifar] left all that he had in Yosef's hands and he did not withhold anything save the bread that he ate. And Yosef was good looking and handsome. (*Bereishit* 39:5-6)

The text tells us that only one aspect of Potifar's household was beyond Yosef's authority: the "bread." When Yosef describes the limits of his own authority, he replaces this expression with a reference to his master's wife. The switch is deliberate, and is one more indication of Yosef's talent at utilizing and understanding symbolism. The symbol of bread is what lands Yosef in prison, and it continues to be an ominous symbol in the dream of the king's baker; to Yosef, the recurring symbol is as clear as day.

On the other hand, the sommelier's dream contained no such ominous symbols; he would live and would be returned to his former position. He would once again bear the king's chalice, and through him Yosef's abilities would be made known. Apparently, the sommelier, like Potifar, both revered and feared Yosef's powers. He seems to have been unsure whether Yosef only read the future, or if he was responsible for creating it.³ Either way, the sommelier does his best to steer clear of Yosef. He tries to forget the entire incident, and to put a safe distance between himself and the man with the frightening abilities.

When Pharaoh is tormented by his own dreams, the sommelier steps forward, racked with guilt⁴; he knows that Yosef had predicted his personal future, and is convinced that Yosef can see the future of Pharaoh and all of Egypt.

Pharaoh's dreams had particular significance for Yosef, not only because of their importance for the Egyptian economy, or even because they catapulted him from prison to prestige. Pharaoh's dreams held the key to the fulfillment of Yosef's dreams: When he heard Pharaoh recount his recurring visions, Yosef was able to see, for the first time, how and under what circumstances he would be reunited with his brothers. He knew, without a doubt, that his brothers would soon be on their way to Egypt, seeking food. The dreams he had seen as a young man would be fulfilled:

בראשית פרק לז, ה-ח

(ה) וַיַּחֲלֹם יוֹסֵף חֲלוֹם וַיַּגֵּד לְאֶחָיו וַיּוֹסִפוּ עוֹד שְׂנֹא אֹתוֹ: (ו) וַיֹּאמֶר אֲלֵיהֶם שִׁמְעוּ נָא הַחֲלוֹם הַזֶּה אֲשֶׁר חָלָמְתִּי: (ז) וְהִנֵּה אֲנַחְנוּ מְאַלְּמִים אֲלֻמִּים בְּתוֹךְ הַשָּׂדֶה וְהִנֵּה קָמָה אֲלֻמָּתִי וְגַם נִצָּבָה וְהִנֵּה תְסֻבֶּינָה אֲלֻמֹּתֵיכֶם וַתִּשְׁתַּחֲוֶיןָ לַאֲלֻמָּתִי: (ח) וַיֹּאמְרוּ לוֹ אֶחָיו הֲמָלֹךְ תִּמְלֹךְ עָלֵינוּ אִם מָשׁוֹל תִּמְשֹׁל בָּנוּ וַיּוֹסִפוּ עוֹד שְׂנֹא אֹתוֹ עַל חֲלֹמֹתָיו וְעַל דְּבָרָיו:

---

3. See Malbim and *Ha'amek Davar*, *Bereishit* 41:13:

מלבי״ם בראשית פרשת מקץ פרק מא פסוק יג

(יג) ויהי. ובכ״ז כאשר פתר לנו כן היה באופן שאותי השיב על כני, <u>הוא השיב אותי על כני לא אתה</u>, ואתו תלה, <u>הוא תלה את שר האופים</u>, כי כ״ז נעשה ע״י דבורו:

העמק דבר בראשית פרשת מקץ פרק מא פסוק יג
<u>אתי השיב. הפותר. שכך היא סגולת נפשו שההחלום הולך אחר פתרונו</u> כדאיתא ברכות דנ״ה:

4. When he speaks to Pharaoh, the sommelier speaks of his *sins* in the plural, how he had sinned against Pharaoh and Yosef. See Bereishit 41:9, and comments of Hizkuni:

חזקוני בראשית פרשת מקץ פרק מא פסוק ט

(ט) את חטאי <u>מה שסרחתי על פרעה ומה ששכחתי את יוסף</u>.

Miketz: A Cherished Chalice | 259

Once Yosef had a dream which he told to his brothers; and they hated him even more. He said to them, "Hear this dream which I have dreamed: We were binding sheaves in the field, when suddenly my sheaf stood up and remained upright; your sheaves gathered around and bowed low to my sheaf." His brothers answered, "Do you mean to reign over us? Do you mean to rule over us?" (*Bereishit* 37:5-8)

As the story unfolds, Yosef's dreams come true; his brothers bow low, humbling themselves before the man who holds their fate and the fate of their hungry children in his hands. But Yosef's "victory" is hollow; the fulfillment of his dreams is marred by the brothers' lack of recognition.

בראשית פרק מב, ו-ח
(ו) וְיוֹסֵף הוּא הַשַּׁלִּיט עַל־הָאָרֶץ הוּא הַמַּשְׁבִּיר לְכָל־עַם הָאָרֶץ וַיָּבֹאוּ אֲחֵי יוֹסֵף וַיִּשְׁתַּחֲווּ־לוֹ אַפַּיִם אָרְצָה: (ז) וַיַּרְא יוֹסֵף אֶת־אֶחָיו וַיַּכִּרֵם וַיִּתְנַכֵּר אֲלֵיהֶם וַיְדַבֵּר אִתָּם קָשׁוֹת וַיֹּאמֶר אֲלֵהֶם מֵאַיִן בָּאתֶם וַיֹּאמְרוּ מֵאֶרֶץ כְּנַעַן לִשְׁבָּר־אֹכֶל: (ח) וַיַּכֵּר יוֹסֵף אֶת־אֶחָיו וְהֵם לֹא הִכִּרֻהוּ:

Now Yosef was the vizier of the land; it was he who dispensed rations to all the people of the land. And Yosef's brothers came and bowed low to him, with their faces to the ground. When Yosef saw his brothers, he recognized them; but he acted like a stranger toward them and spoke harshly to them. He asked them, "Where do you come from?" And they said, "From the land of Canaan, to procure food." For though Yosef recognized his brothers, they did not recognize him. (*Bereishit* 42:6-8)

While Potifar, the prison warden, the sommelier, and Pharaoh were all aware of Yosef's greatness and powers, those who were closest to him could not see past their own hatred and jealousy. They could not imagine that their tormentor, the viceroy of the world's greatest superpower, was in fact an old adversary, the brother whom they had mocked for his delusions of grandeur.

Yosef has a plan; he is determined to open their eyes as the first step toward healing the rift. And so, Yosef—the dreamer and interpreter of dreams—speaks to them in symbols. They are sent on their way back to their father's house in Canaan with food in their bags and an incarcerated brother (Shimon) left behind. Yosef alone sees the symbolism of their situation, the inner meaning: When Yosef languished in the pit, screaming for mercy, these same brothers sat and broke bread, filling their bellies at their brother's expense. When they sold Yosef, they chose money over their brother—and so, in an act of symbolism colored with poetic justice, Yosef sees to it that they leave for home not only with food in their bags, but with their money as well. After all, don't these people prefer food and money to a brother?

Throughout the ordeal, the brothers do not begin to guess the true identity of the man who has latched on to them; in fact, they don't ever seem to entertain the obvious questions: Who is he? What does he want from us? What have we ever done to him to deserve such treatment? Their manner and demeanor is of innocent victims, yet they are far from innocent, and it is their erstwhile victim who is now in control.

The brothers return to Egypt, this time with their youngest brother, Binyamin. Yosef greets them; the "mistake" through which the money ended up in their bags is excused. Yosef (via his emissary) explains that it his understanding that God has been looking out for them. (*Bereishit* 43:23)

Once again, Yosef orchestrates a scene that is ripe with symbolic meaning—but only he understands it. He gathers all of his brothers, and they sit down to a meal together. Once again, the brothers fail to recognize the significance of the moment; they do not recognize Yosef, and therefore they do not know that they are whole.

The brothers seem relived; Yosef's hospitality indicates that they will not be charged with theft or espionage. They let their guard down, and they raise their glasses and drink with their host, who has now taken on the role of sommelier. Yosef alone understands the symbolism of wine in the story of his life; the brothers are unaware of the circumstances of Yosef's ascension to power. They have avoided asking about their inquisitor's identity or history.

Once again, Yosef sends them away; once again, their money is returned—but this time, another item is added to their bags: Yosef's chalice.

When they are tracked down and detained, they are accused of repaying Yosef's benevolence with malevolence, of stealing the magical chalice he uses for divination. Why did Yosef choose this, of all things, to ensnare them?

The brothers are completely at a loss. They are no longer able to act, to speak in their own defense. They become deflated, and believe that their predicament is God's way of punishing them for a crime committed long ago. They analyze the strange accusation with which they have been charged. Perplexed, they posit that the inscrutable man who has been tormenting them is immersed in the occult, which is the source of his uncanny knowledge about them and their family. For the brothers to accept this explanation, they must embrace a world of black magic and supernatural powers.

The true explanation, a far less far-fetched explanation, eluded them: Yosef, the interpreter of dreams, was communicating through the use of symbols. He hoped to speak to his brothers on a much deeper level than the superficiality of words, to make them face their past, and the symbol of the chalice was part of Yosef's message.

Yosef's rise to power was made possible by his interpretation of the sommelier's dream. By placing the cup back in the hand of the sommelier, Yosef would one day leave his prison. The chalice, Yosef understood, was a symbol for his own life. The chalice told Yosef's future, just as Yosef told the future through the chalice.

The brothers were not guilty of stealing the chalice, However they were guilty of "stealing" Yosef, the person whom the chalice represented.

Yosef understood the symbolic representation of the future in each of the dreams he interpreted. Yosef was a vessel for communicating the future, and the magical chalice, a vessel of divination, was a symbolic representation of Yosef's unique vision. In his confrontation with his brothers, Yosef used the symbol of his own dreams to awaken his brothers to the sins of their past. As the visions of his youth came to fruition, Yosef hoped he could heal his family by helping his brothers see, through the use of symbols, what they had so steadfastly avoided seeing for so many years.

Parashat Vayigash

The Beauty of Yosef

Parashat Vayigash begins as Yosef and Yehudah approach a showdown: Soon Yosef will reveal himself and send for his father. Throughout the generations, scholars have been perturbed by Yosef's seeming callousness: Why did it take Yosef so long to orchestrate this reunion? One could argue that the primary victim of this delay was Yaakov, who spent twenty-two years in needless mourning. We might excuse Yosef's desire for vengeance against his brothers for their perfidy, but this seems inconsistent with Yosef's reputation as a *tzaddik*. Certainly, when vengeance impinges on Yosef's filial responsibilities, any delay which causes his father Yaakov to remain bereft and hungry even one day longer than necessary—when Yosef had it within his power to solve both problems with ease—seems inexcusable.

In his commentary on the Torah, Ramban poses this question,[1] which, in a sense, hovers over the last three *parshiyot*: Why

---

1. To be more precise, in the Ramban's formulation, this is not so much a question as it is evidence of Yosef's larger plan: Yosef was motivated by the need to bring the dreams of his youth to fruition; were this not the case, we would be forced to question Yosef's willful delay of the reunion with his father. Also see the comments of the Riva and the Rosh, who base their interpretation on a rabbinic tradition that all the participants in the sale of Yosef took an oath of silence regarding the entire episode. This explains why God, who joins the group, as it were, does not reveal anything to Yaakov, and why Yosef does not reach out to his father: At the very moment he is cut off from the group by the actions of his brothers, Yosef takes this oath of silence upon himself and refrains from contacting Yaakov—in effect proving that he is, despite it all, still "one of the gang," still a member of the family—and of the Jewish People. On the other hand, Yosef dreams that he has eleven brothers who will bow down to him, implicitly declaring that Reuven, despite his sin, is still part of the family. Perhaps this is what motivated Reuven's attempt to save Yosef. See footnote 9 below and *Bereishit* 37:21-22:

didn't Yosef try to contact his father? After all, the distance between Israel and Egypt is no more than a six-day journey (Ramban, *Bereishit* 42:9). Why didn't Yosef send a letter to his father, informing him that he was alive and well? When Yosef was placed at the head of Potifar's household, he must have had the ways and means to contact Yaakov. Certainly once he became the second most powerful man in Egypt he should have had all the connections necessary to send a message to his father. Yaakov could have been spared years of anguish, decades of mourning, for his favorite son. Didn't Yosef return his father's love? How could he bear the self-imposed estrangement from his father for all those years?[2]

פירוש הריב"א על התורה בראשית פרשת ויגש פרק מה פסוק א
הוציאו כל איש מעלי. פי' בקו' מפני הבושת שיבייש אחיו. וי"מ שנשבע להם שלא לגלות לאדם מכירתו כי כאשר מכרוהו נשבע להם שלא ישוב עוד לבית אביו ושלא יודיע לאביו שהוא חי ושהוא נמכר. ושלא יאמר לשום אדם שהוא בן יעקב וכן עשה בעל כרחו דאם לא כן כשהיה גדול בבית אדוניו וגם ט' שנים שהיה מלך במצרים מדוע לא שלח לאביו לאמר הנני כאן במצרים כי היה יודע שאביו היה מצטער עליו. אלא על כרחך נשבע להם כן:

פירוש הרא"ש על התורה בראשית פרשת ויגש פרק מה פסוק א
ולא יכול יוסף להתאפק. תימא יש איך המתין כל כך יוסף להודיע לאביו שהיה שרוי בצער גדול כי הוא חי. ויש לומר בשעת החרם שתפו את יוסף עמהם שלא לגלות הדבר ואף כי היה מוכרח כיון שלא מיחה בם היה נכלל עמהם ולפיכך המתין עד שבאו כולם והתירו את החרם בהסכמת כולם דכל דבר שבמנין צריך מנין אחר להתירו. ומכאן ראייה שכל אדם שיושב בבית הכנסת ויש בדעתו להוציא עצמו מתקנת הקהל ומהחרם צריך שיוציא בשפתיו שכל דברים שבלב אינם דברים שא"לכ יהיה נאסר בכללם בחרם:

2. Ramban, *Bereishit* 42:9:

רמב"ן בראשית פרשת מקץ פרק מב פסוק ט
ויזכר יוסף את החלומות אשר חלם להם - עליהם, וידע שנתקיימו שהרי השתחוו לו, לשון רש"י. <u>ולפי דעתי שהדבר בהפך, כי יאמר הכתוב כי בראות יוסף את אחיו משתחוים לו זכר כל החלומות אשר חלם להם וידע שלא נתקיים אחד מהם בפעם הזאת, כי יודע בפתרונם כי כל אחיו ישתחוו לו בתחילה מן החלום הראשון, והנה אנחנו מאלמים אלומים, כי "אנחנו" ירמוז לכל אחיו אחד עשר, ופעם שנית ישתחוו לו השמש והירח ואחד עשר כוכבים מן החלום השני, וכיון שלא ראה בנימין עמהם חשב זאת התחבולה שיעליל עליהם כדי שיביאו גם בנימין אחיו אליו לקיים החלום הראשון תחילה: ועל כן לא רצה להגיד להם אני יוסף אחיכם, ולאמר מהרו ועלו אל אבי וישלח העגלות כאשר עשה עמהם בפעם השניה, כי היה אביו בא מיד בלא ספק. ואחרי שנתקיים החלום הראשון הגיד להם לקיים החלום השני. ולולי כן היה יוסף חוטא חטא גדול לצער את אביו ולהעמידו ימים רבים בשכול ואבל על שמעון ועליו, ואף אם היה רצונו לצער את אחיו קצת איך לא יחמול על שיבת אביו, אבל את הכל עשה יפה בעתו לקיים החלומות כי ידע שיתקיימו באמת:</u> גם העניין השני שעשה להם בגביע לא שתהיה כוונתו לצערם, אבל חשד אולי יש להם שנאה בבנימין שיקנאו אותו באהבת אביהם

Ramban's answer is that Yosef could not contact his father until his dreams had come true. Yaakov and his sons would have to come to Egypt and bow before Yosef, vindicating Yosef's vision and his behavior.

Other commentaries have taken issue with this approach. Dreams are God's domain, they say; let God worry about bringing Yosef's dreams to fruition. It is man's job to behave ethically, and the ethical thing would have been for Yosef to inform Yaakov that he, Yosef, was indeed alive.[3]

כקנאתם בו, או שמא הרגיש בנימין שהיה ידם ביוסף ונולדה ביניהם קטטה ושנאה, ועל כן לא רצה שילך עמהם בנימין אולי ישלחון בו ידם עד בדקו אותם באהבתו: ולזה נתכוונו בו רבותינו בבראשית רבה (צג ט) אמר רבי חייא בר' אבא כל הדברים שאתה קורא שדיבר יהודה בפני אחיו עד שאתה מגיע ולא יכול יוסף להתאפק היה בו פיוס ליוסף פיוס לאחיו, פיוס לבנימין. פיוס ליוסף, ראה היאך נותן נפשו על בניה של רחל וכו': <u>וכן אני אומר שכל הענינים האלה היו ביוסף מחכמתו בפתרון החלומות, כי יש לתמוה אחר שעמד יוסף במצרים ימים רבים והיה פקיד ונגיד בבית שר גדול במצרים, איך לא שלח כתב אחד לאביו להודיעו ולנחמו, כי מצרים קרוב לחברון כששה ימים, ואילו היה מהלך שנה היה ראוי להודיעו לכבוד אביו, ויקר פדיון נפשו ויפדנו ברוב ממון:</u> אבל היה רואה כי השתחוויית אחיו לו וגם אביו וכל זרעו אתו, אי אפשר להיות בארצם, והיה מקוה להיותו שם במצרים בראותו הצלחתו הגדולה שם, וכל שכן אחרי ששמע חלום פרעה שנתברר לו כי יבאו כלם שמה ויתקיימו כל חלומותיו:

3. See Rabbi Yitzchak Arama, *Akeidat Yitzchak*, Bereishit 29:10, and *Kli Yakar*, Bereishit 42:7:

עקידת יצחק בראשית שער כט:י (פרשת מקץ)

והוא מה שראוי לחבר אל זה הספור והוא למה לא הודיע יוסף לאביו את כל כבודו שם כי יש לאל ידו להניחו מרגזו ומעצבו וכל שכן בשנות הרעב להציל ממות נפשו ולחיותו. ותמהני ממה שכתב הרמב"ן ז"ל שעשה כדי שיתקיימו חלומותיו כי מה תועלת לו בשתיקיימו ואף כי יהיה תועלת לא היה לו לחטוא כנגד אביו. אבל היה לחשוך עצמו מחטוא לו והחלומות העושם יגש פתרונם גם שתראה סכלות עצומה שישתדל האדם לקיים חלומותיו שהרי הם הדברי' אשר יעשו שלא מדעת הבעלים:

כלי יקר בראשית פרשת מקץ פרק מב פסוק ז

...והנה בענין דיבור קשות, ישתומם כל משכיל מה ראה יוסף על ככה לצער את אביו ואת אחיו חנם. ומה שפירש הרמב"ן שעשה כל זה כדי שיתקיימו החלומות וכו', אם ירצה ה' בקיומם המה יתקיימו מעצמם ויוסף מה פעל. והנראה לי בזה שמה שלא גילה לאביו עדיין כי הוא חי לפי שחשב אם הקדוש ברוך הוא לא גילה לו כן אם כן רצה הקדוש ברוך הוא בצערו עשרים ושתים שנה כנגד מדה כנגד מדה ואיך יגלה הוא מה שכיסה הקדוש ברוך הוא, כי מצא בשכלו שנגזר על אביו צער עשרים ושתים שנים שלמים מיום ליום כנגד אותן עשרים ושתים שנים שלא קיים מצות כיבוד אביו, ואחר שנשלמו אז נתודע יוסף אל אחיו, ומה שציער את אחיו עשה כל זה למרק עוונם במה שמכרו אחיהם וגדול עוונם מנשוא וצריכין מירוק יסורין מדה כנגד מדה:

Despite this valid rebuttal, we may defend Ramban's approach if we consider the possibility that Yosef understood his youthful dreams as prophecy.[4] This would also explain why he felt compelled to share his visions with his brothers and his father: He knew full well that failure to communicate prophecy can cause incalculable dysfunctionality within a family. He had heard and seen the results of his grandmother Rivkah's failure to share the prophecy regarding her two sons. Perhaps Yosef hoped to avoid the harsh consequences of failure to communicate God's message. Yosef was convinced that he had been granted prophecy, and he went to great lengths to prove it and to see to it that this prophecy would come to true.[5]

---

4. The *Netziv, Bereishit* 42:9, understands the dreams as a prophetic message:

העמק דבר בראשית פרשת מקץ פרק מב פסוק ט
את החלומות: שני החלומות, והודיעו הכתוב שלא מחמת נקימה ח״ו התהלך עמם בעקשות כזה, אלא משום שנזכר החלומות שהוא כעין נבואה, שהרי החלום הראשון כבר נתקיים, וא״כ עליו לראות שיקוים גם השני, ואם לא יעשה כן יהיה כנביא שמוותר על דברי עצמו, על כן ביקש סיבה שיגיע לזה:

5. There is another approach which also assumes that the dreams were the fulfillment of a prophecy—not a new independent prophecy, but rather the prophecy given to Avraham, in which God informed him that his descendants would be enslaved and abused in a foreign land (which may, in turn, be related to Yaakov's dream of the ladder). After enduring his own enslavement and abuse, Yosef understood that his brothers, too, must be enslaved in order for the redemption to ensue. In this light, he interpreted his own dreams: If he would be the one to enslave his brothers, if they would bow down to him, he could treat them humanely, and spare them—and their descendants—the oppression and cruelty they would suffer at the hands of a foreign despot. See *Tzror Hamor, Bereishit* 47:28; The Chida's commentary on *Tehillim, Yosif Tehillot*, 77:15; *Me'oran shel Yisrael, Parashat Miketz* (quoted in *Yismach Yisrael, ad loc.*). For further treatment on Yosef's dreams see *Echoes of Eden: Bereishit* (2011; OU-Gefen Press, Jerusalem), pp. 291-307:

צרור המור על בראשית פרק מז פסוק כח
ואורו וגדולתו של אברהם היה יעקב ע״ה, כדכתיב (ישעי׳ כט, כב) כה אמר ה׳ אל בית יעקב אשר פדה את אברהם, ובברכות יעקב נאמר ויתן לך את ברכת אברהם (לעיל כח, ד), ובמראה הסולם של יעקב נתקיים העולם ונקשר קצתו בקצתו, דכתיב (שם כח, יב) סולם מוצב ארצה וראשו מגיע השמימה. וכאן נתבשר יעקב בגלות מצרים ובגאולתו. וחלומות יוסף נתקשרו בחלומות אביו, להורות על ירידת מצרים, בענין שיתקיים גזירת בין הבתרים. בענין שיעקב ובניו ירדו מצרים, לסבול הגלות הנרמז לאברהם:

A contemporary commentator, Rabbi Yoel Bin-Nun[6], has suggested that perhaps the question should be reversed: Rather than wondering why Yosef did not contact Yaakov, we should consider that Yosef might have spent twenty-two years wondering why Yaakov had not come looking for him, had not contacted him in any way. Yosef may not have had any idea that the brothers had led their father to believe that he was dead; in fact, Yosef may have had every reason to believe that his father had engineered his exile. Yaakov was surely aware of the enmity between Yosef and his brothers; why, then, did Yaakov send Yosef to look in on

---

יוסף תהלות על תהילים פרק עז פסוק טו חיד"א
אפשר במה שביאר הרב עיר וקדיש מהר"י קוב"ו ז"ל בספר גבעות עולם יסודתו בהררי קדש רז"ל והמפרשים דמה שנמכר יוסף לעבד כיפר העדות של גזרת בין הבתרים ומפני זה לקו עשר מכות על העבדות של ישראל שלא היו חייבים וז"ש וגם את הגוי אשר יעבודו דן אנכי:

ספר ישמח ישראל - מאורן של ישראל - פרשת מקץ
ירחמיאל ישראל יצחק דאנציגר (אדמו"ר מאלכסנדר) ספח לספר ומאוחר יותר הודפס בסופו נקרא בשם 'מאורן של ישראל' נכתב על ידי הרב יהודה משה טיברג האדמו"ר החמישי בשרשלת החסידות, והם מאמרים ששמע בעצמו מפי האדמו"ר.

[מכתי"ק מרן הגה"ק הרבי רש"פ מגריצא זמללה"ה] [ב]. ויאסוף אותם אל משמר שלשת ימים (מ"ב ל"ז). כולם תמהו שיוסף לא הודיע ליעקב אביו שהוא במצרים גם אחרי עלותו לגדולה, ועוד על אשר המר בלבבו לקחת את בנימין מעם פני אביו אשר נפשו קשורה בנפשו, ומה גם אשר השביע במרורים את בנימין אחיו אשר לא היה במכירתו, שדיברו בזה כל המפרשים. ונראה לפרש שכאשר נגזרה גזירת בין הבתרים על זרע אברהם והיה מוכרח להתקיים עכ"פ, וראה יוסף הצדיק כי למחיה שלחו אלקים לפניהם, כמ"ש הראשונים ז"ל (ע' שלה"ק תושב"כ פר' מקץ) כי יוסף ירד בראשונה למצרים להיות מרכבה להשראת השכינה שם, ואיתא במדרש (ע' ב"ר פ"ו, א', ובגמ' שבת פ"ט ע"ב) כי ראוי היה יעקב אבינו לירד למצרים בשלשלאות של ברזל, אך אמר הקב"ה בני בכורי הוא וא"א להוליכו שם בבזיון ע"ש, ומבואר בדברי המדרש כי לולא שהיה בנו בכורו היה ראוי לירד בשלשלאות כי כן היתה גזירת הגלות כדרך הגולים, לזאת אלו השבטים הקדושים שהם היו עיקר בנין בית ישראל, ועליהם נגזרה גזירת ברית בין הבתרים, היו מוכרחים לירד למצרים כדרך הגולים, שלא היו עוד נקראים בשם בני בכורי כמו יעקב עצמו, וכשראה יוסף כי בעצמו טרם עלותו לגדולה ברזל באה נפשו, הבין כי כן מוכרחים כל אחיו השבטים לבוא למצרים, וע"כ ויאסף אותם אל משמר כאשר באו, ואילו היה מודיע לאביו כזאת, הרי היה בנימין בא עם יעקב בכבוד גדול, ע"כ הוכרח לצוות להביאו ראשונה מבלי הגד לו, וגם אותו לקח למשמר על אודות הגביע, בכדי לקבל עליהם גזירת הקב"ה.

---

6. Alon Shevut L'Bogrim (Alon Shevut Alumni Journal), vol. 5 (Kislev 5755), pp. 29–39. http://files8.webydo.com/92/9266067/UploadedFiles/6B6C-C6CC-74EE-7183-B951-082E4294506C.pdf
http://etzion.org.il/en/intractable-question-why-did-yosef-not-send-word-his-father

them? Yaakov had heard Yosef's ill reports of the other sons, and knew that the brothers resented Yosef for reporting their misdeeds; why did he ask Yosef to report on them once again? Could Yosef have imagined that this was Yaakov's way of solving the problem in his household, of allowing the other sons to dispose of the source of conflict within the family? To put it plainly, did Yosef suspect that Yaakov was involved in the plot against him?

Let us consider the extended family's history: Whenever brothers did not get along, the solution was to separate. It began with Avraham and Lot; though not actually brothers, when they saw that they could not coexist, they parted ways. The same is true of Yishmael, who was forcibly sent away from Avraham's house so that he would not be a bad influence on Yitzchak. Yaakov was sent abroad when it became clear that his brother Esav wanted to kill him. Despite the fact that his father Yitzchak loved him, Esav left the Land of Canaan when Yaakov returned, even though they had achieved a reconciliation. Perhaps Yosef felt that because of all the dissension he had stirred up in his father's house, Yaakov had decided to send him away. Rabbi Bin-Nun suggests that only upon hearing Yehudah quote his father as saying that Yosef was "ripped apart by beasts" (*Bereishit* 44:28),[7] Yosef realized that his father was under the assumption that he, Yosef, was dead. Only then Yosef revealed himself to his brothers and sent for his father.[8]

While this interpretation is certainly highly original, it is not supported by any of the classic commentaries on the Torah; moreover, it paints Yosef as a maladjusted individual who is highly insecure in his father's love—a portrayal that contradicts everything we know about

---

7. *Bereishit* 44:28:

בראשית מד:כח
וַיֵּצֵא הָאֶחָד מֵאִתִּי וָאֹמַר אַךְ טָרֹף טֹרָף וְלֹא רְאִיתִיו עַד־הֵנָּה:

8. The first time the fate of Yosef was mentioned by the brothers, they simply said "he is no more," which might have implied either a geographical separation or a polite reference to his death.

בראשית מב:יג
וַיֹּאמְרוּ שְׁנֵים עָשָׂר עֲבָדֶיךָ אַחִים ׀ אֲנַחְנוּ בְּנֵי אִישׁ־אֶחָד בְּאֶרֶץ כְּנָעַן וְהִנֵּה הַקָּטֹן אֶת־אָבִינוּ הַיּוֹם וְהָאֶחָד אֵינֶנּוּ:

Yosef from the verses themselves. Yosef is his father's favorite, and he enjoys a special position in the family.[9] His father makes no secret of his affection and his high regard, and gives Yosef a coat of many colors (which may be the garb of royalty[10] and not merely a fashion statement or a token of his favored status). When Yosef confronts his brothers, his behavior does not seem reactive; from the moment his brothers arrive in Egypt, Yosef seems to have a well thought out plan.[11] In fact, he seems to have anticipated their arrival, and personally oversees the sale of food, rather than delegating this task to a lesser functionary, to ensure that the confrontation is inevitable. When Yosef returns the money to his brothers' bags, he sets the stage for the next step: planting the "stolen" chalice in Binyamin's bag. Had Yosef concluded that his family wanted nothing to do with him, he could have easily avoided seeing them, or he could have simply allowed them to purchase food and leave. Alternatively, he could have taken revenge upon them immediately, imprisoning or enslaving them or even putting them to death. Yet Yosef seems to have something else in mind, and he appears to know precisely how to achieve it.

---

9. It should be noted that when the Torah describes this special relationship, we are told that Yisrael—and not Yaakov—loves Yosef, using the name that refers to the patriarch of the nation, and not as a private individual. The implication is that Yosef was given special attention because of his unique capabilities: His father saw that Yosef was most capable in terms of the spiritual mission God had bestowed upon Avraham's descendants. On the other hand, one could posit that Yaakov treated Yosef with extra love, more attention, because Yosef was the child most devastated by the loss of his mother, who died when he was ten years old. Perhaps Yaakov felt that Yosef needed more love than his other sons, who all had doting mothers. This may explain another episode in the family's complicated home life: Reuven is accused of either sleeping with Bilhah, or of moving Yaakov's bed to the tent of his mother Leah. Apparently, Reuven was miffed that even after Rachel's death, Yaakov did not show "favored wife status" to Leah. Reuven considered Yaakov's cohabitation with Bilhah—who was a handmaid of Rachel—as an affront to Leah's status as a full-fledged wife. However, if we consider that Bilhah acted as surrogate mother to Binyamin, whose mother died in childbirth, we may better understand why Yaakov chose her tent over Leah's: He chose the tent of his newborn, orphaned son Binyamin, to assure that he would receive the love he sorely lacked. See *Bereishit* 35:21, and Talmud Bavli 55b.

10. See 2 *Shmuel* 13:18.

11. For a more detailed analysis of Yosef's plan, see *Echoes of Eden: Bereishit* (2011; OU-Gefen Press, Jerusalem), pp. 308-321 and 325-340.

Our Sages teach us that one of the major lessons of *Sefer Bereishit* is *ma'aseh avot siman l'banim*—history repeats itself.[12] The narrative sections of the Torah describe spiritual realities that will be repeated at other junctures in Jewish history. The confrontation between Yosef and his brothers is surely no exception: There must be deeper significance to these episodes, something more than Yosef's personal insecurities or his quest for revenge.

Rabbi Shimshon of Sens, one of the authorities of the school of Tosafot, suggested that Yosef could not simply contact his father:[13]

תוספות השלם [ר"ש משנץ]
ותירץ רבי שמשון ז"ל שאם היה שולח לאביו כל הדברים מיד כל אחיו היו בורחים זה מכאן וזה לכאן מפני הבושה אבל לקחם מעט מעט בדברים והושיבם שלא יתביישו ולטובה נתכון.

Had Yosef sent a message about everything that had happened, his brothers would have scattered in every direction in shame. Therefore, Yosef worked slowly to bring them back, and thus avoid shaming them. His intention was good. (*Tosafot ha-Shalem*)

According to Rabbi Shimshon, the dreams of Yosef's youth had nothing to do with his plan. Rather, he had a problem: How do you inform your father that your brothers sold you as a slave? This idea is further developed in the comments of Rabbi Shimshon Rafael Hirsch.

---

12. See *Midrash Tanchuma*, *Lech Lecha* section 9, and Ramban, *Bereishit* 12:6, quoted in full above: p. 187-189, *Parashat Vayeshev*, note 8.
13. Also cited in *Moshav Zekeinim* 45:1:

מושב זקנים בראשית מה:א
ולא יכול יוסף להתאפק. תימה צדיק כיוסף שהיה יודע שאביו מצער עליו כל היום למה לא שלח לו מיד והודיעו לו שהיה שליט וחי והיה לו לשלוח אל תצטער עלי שאני חי. ותי' רבי' שמשון ז"ל שאם היה שולח לאביו כל הדברים מיד, כל אחיו היו בורחים זה לכאן וזה לכאן מפני הבושת, אבל לקחם מעט מעט בדברים והושיבם שלא יתביישו ולטובה נתכוון, הר"י.
וע"ל בשעת החרם שתפו את יוסף שלא לגלות את הדבר, ואף כי היה מוכרח שלא היה מוחה בם, היה נכלל בכללם עמהם, ולפי' המתין עד שבאו כולם והתירו החרם בהסכמת כולם דכל דבר שבמניין צריך מניין אחר להתירו.

רש"ר הירש בראשית פרשת מקץ פרק מב פסוק ט

יוסף זכר את חלומותיו, זכר איך - על יסוד חלומות אלה - חשדו בו באחיו בתאוות שלטון, עד כי ראו סכנה צפויה לעצמם, וראו את עצמם זכאים גם לבצע פשע, כביכול להגנה עצמית. אם כך היה הדבר כאשר עוד התהלך ביניהם בכתונת פסים, איך ייראו ממנו עתה בחיל ורעדה, כאשר היה "מלך", ועוד היתה לו סיבה לשנוא אותם ולהתנקם בהם כטבע האדם ההמוני... אם אין טעות בידינו, הרי שיקולים אלה הם שהניאו את יוסף מלשלוח הודעה לאביו בשנות אושרו. מה בצע ליעקב לזכות בבן אחד ולשכל תחתיו עשרה, ולראות מתיחות ואיבה שרויות בין בניו?! אך למטרה גדולה זו הוא נזקק לכל התחבולות הללו, והיו אלה - לדעתנו - ראויות בהחלט לחכמתו של יוסף.

> Yosef remembered his dreams, remembered how, on the basis of those dreams, his brothers suspected him of being power-hungry, to the point that they felt threatened by him, and felt they were justified in committing a crime of self-defense, as it were. If this was so while he still lived among them as a brother dressed in a coat of many colors, how much more would they fear him as a "king"—and one with a reason to hate them and, quite naturally, to seek revenge for what they had done to him, as any other person would…. If I am not mistaken, Yosef's consideration in not sending a letter to his father in his years of success was: what would Yaakov gain in getting one son back, if in the process he would lose ten? … Therefore Yosef used all this subterfuge, which, to my mind, was certainly worthy of Yosef's wisdom. (Rav Hirsch, *Bereishit* 42:9)

According to this approach, Yosef's behavior was completely selfless. To have been reunited with his father would clearly have been a source of great personal satisfaction, but it would have had tragic consequences for his brothers. Yosef chose self-imposed isolation in order to preserve the family.

Other commentaries believe that Yosef was motivated by the desire to help his brothers **mend their ways**, to do *teshuvah,* to repent for the sin they had committed. Thus, rather than revealing his identity to his brothers or contacting his father, Yosef orchestrated a series of events which would bring Binyamin to Egypt and provide his brothers with the opportunity to defend and protect the youngest son of Rachel.[14]

---

14. See Seforno, *Bereishit* 43:34, 44:2 and Abarbanel, *Bereishit* 43, section 17, whose approach is expanded by the *Kli Yakar, Bereishit* 42:7. This may also be the understanding of the *Akeidat Yitzchak*, chapter 30. Ramban (*Bereishit* 42:9) also mentions this consideration.

ספורנו בראשית מג:לד
ותרב משאת בנימין. לראות אם יקנאו בו:

ספורנו בראשית מד:ב
תשים בפי אמתחת הקטן. לראות איך ימסרו עצמם עליו כדי להצילו:

אברבנאל על בראשית - פרק מג פסוק טו- מד, יז
כי הנה עם כל הנסיון שעשה יוסף לאחיו בעלילת המרגלים, עוד נשאר ספק בלבו האם היה להם אהבה עם בנימין, או אם היו עדיין שונאים את בני רחל אמו. ולכן רצה להביא את בנימין בפרט בנסיון הגביע, לראות אם ישתדלו להצילו. אבל חשש עם זה, אולי יחשבו אחיו שהיה אמת שבנימין גנב את הגביע, כמו שרחל אמו גנבה את התרפים לאביה (לעיל לא, יט). ואולי מפני זה יאמרו הנפש החוטאת היא תמות, ולא ידרשו בעדו בכל כוחם, לא לשנאתם אותו כי אם לבושתם מרוע המעשה. הנה מפני זה ציווה יוסף לשום עם הגביע כסף שברו, וכן כספיהם של כולם. ובידיעתם, שבזה יכירו הם שלא היה מאשמת בנימין ורשעתו כי אם מעלילת האדון. אם יחמלו עליו וישתדלו להוציאו מעבדות, יוודע שהם אוהבים אותו, ויהיו בעיני יוסף בעלי תשובה גמורים, ויתוודע אליהם וייטיב עמהם כמו שעשה. אבל אם המה יעזבוהו לעבד, יוודע שעדיין המה עומדים במרדם, ויתהפך להם יוסף לאויב והוא ילחם בם. הנה התבאר צורך נסיון ענין הגביע, ולמה היה בפרט בבנימין, ולמה הושם כספם באמתחותם.

עקידת יצחק בראשית שער ל (פרשת מקץ-ויגש)
(ד) נראה שכוונות יוסף היתה גם כן בתחילה לבדוק בהם אם היו עדיין בשנאתם אותו או אם נחמו ממעשיהם והוא לא ראה שתתכן לו זה אם לא בשיבחנם על דבר אחיו בן אמו לראות מה יעשו כשיראו אותו בצער או בסכנה ולזה מיד חשב עלילת הגביע אשר לא היה שם אלא בנימן והוצרך להתעולל עלילות ולגלגל ביאתן לשם.

כלי יקר בראשית פרשת מקץ פרק מב פסוק ז
וקרוב לזה פירש מהר״י אברבנאל, והנני מוסיף על דבריו לפרש כל הפרטים והקורות, כי עלילה ראשונה של מרגלים אתם למרק העוון שחשבו את יוסף למרגל ורכיל לראות ערות אחיהם, כי בבואו אליהם דותינה כתיב ובטרם יקרב אליהם וגו', כי המה חשבו שרצונו להתקרב אליהם ולרגל מה יעשו אחיו כדי לחזור ולהביא איזו דבה רעה עליהם, וכל רכיל גורם לשפיכת דמים כמו שנאמר (יחזקאל כב ט) אנשי רכיל היו בך למען שפוך דם, לפיכך בטרם יקרב אליהם להרוג אותם יתנכלו המה להמיתו, כי חשבו שהבא להורגך השכם להורגו בטרם יקרב אליך הוא. ולכך נאמר ויזכור את החלומות קודם שאמר אליהם מרגלים אתם.

These interpretations are not necessarily mutually exclusive; both Rabbi Shimshon of Sens and Rabbi Hirsch believe that Yosef's behavior was motivated by considerations far beyond his personal interest; both opinions highlight the lofty spiritual level on which Yosef operated.

A close reading of the text on the one hand, and a survey of midrashic and kabbalistic sources on the other, will allow us to gain a deeper understanding of Yosef and shed light on the general question of his motivations.

First, let us return to the text, and pick up the thread of Yosef's rise to power as it began in the house of Potifar. Interestingly, it is at this point—and not in the earlier chapters in which Yosef is first introduced, that the Torah comments on Yosef's physical appearance:

לפי שנזכר שחלם לו והנה תסובנה אלומותיכם ולא פירש מהו הסיבוב, אלא ודאי שסופם להיות בעלילות מרגלים כי כל מרגל הולך ומסבב את כל העיר לראות מהיכן היא נוחה ליכבש, וראיה ממה שנכנסו בעשרה שערי העיר סחור סחור ועל ידי סבוב זה ישתחוו לאלומתו של יוסף, כי יבואו בעלילת מרגלים אתם לראות ערות הארץ באתם. ובזה נתמרק העוון שחשבו את יוסף למרגל הבא לראות ערות מעשיהם: וכנגד מה שהשליכו את יוסף לבור ויאסוף אותם אל משמר, פירש רש"י בית האסורים דהיינו בור כמו שאמר ביוסף ויתנהו אל בית הסוהר, ויוסף אמר כי שמו אותי בבור, והוכרח רש"י לפרש כן שאם היה בית המשמר באיזה חדר לא היה מדה כנגד מדה, לפיכך ויקח מאתם את שמעון כי הוא השליכו לבור. ואמרו דרך וידוי אבל אשמים אנחנו וגו', לפי ששמעו שאמר יוסף את האלהים אני ירא וגו' וראו האמת שכך הוא שהרי גמל חסד עמהם ושלח רעבון ביתם ולא עיכב כי אם את שמעון, אם כן אין לתלות כל הקורות במושל עז ומעליל, שהרי הוא ירא אלהים, אלא ודאי שעוונותם הטו אלה, ועל כן היו מתוודים אחר שאמר את האלהים אני ירא ולא קודם לכך שנתן את כולם במאסר, לפי שאחר כך ראו עין בעין שבמדה שמדדו נמדד להם: ועלילת הגביע היתה, כדי שעל ידו יהיו בחשש עבדות כמו שפסקו על עצמם הננו עבדים לאדוני, כי בזה יתמרק העוון שמכרו את יוסף לעבד. וכשסיפרו כל הקורות ליעקב אמר אם כן איפוא זאת עשו, מהו לשון איפוא, אלא שאמר אם זאת האיפה היוצאת למדוד למדוד לכם, באיפה ומידה, בסאסאה בשלחה תריבנה (ישעיה כז ח) ואינו במקרה כי אם בהשגחה, זאת עשו קחו מזמרת הארץ בכליכם וגו', כדי לכפר על מה שמכרוהו לישמעאלים נושאים נכאת וצרי ולוט, כך יביאו מנחה מן המינים אלו כדי שעל ידי מושל זה יתמרק כל העוון, ואף על פי שיעקב לא ידע מן המכירה מכל מקום רוח ה' דיבר בו להביא מנחה מן מינים אלו, ואל שדי יתן לכם רחמים, כי בזה יתמרק העוון שלא נתנו רחמים לאחיהם בהתחננו אליהם:

רמב"ן בראשית פרשת מקץ פרק מב פסוק ט

...גם העניין השני שעשה להם בגביע לא שתהיה כוונתו לצערם, אבל חשד אולי יש להם שנאה בבנימין שיקנאו אותו באהבת אביהם כקנאתם בו, או שמא הרגיש בנימין שהיה ידם ביוסף ונולדה ביניהם קטטה ושנאה, ועל כן לא רצה שילך עמהם בנימין אולי ישלחו בו ידם עד בדקו אותם באהבתו:

ולזה נתכוונו בו רבותינו בבראשית רבה (צג ט) אמר רבי חייא בר' אבא כל הדברים שאתה קורא שדיבר יהודה בפני אחיו עד שאתה מגיע ולא יכול יוסף להתאפק היה בו פיוס ליוסף פיוס לאחיו, פיוס לבנימין. פיוס ליוסף, ראה היאך נותן נפשו על בניה של רחל וכו':

בראשית לט:ו

...וַיְהִי יוֹסֵף יְפֵה־תֹאַר וִיפֵה מַרְאֶה:

> ... And Yosef was handsome and of fine appearance. (*Bereishit* 39:6)

Editorial comments of this kind are rare enough; in this case, it is all the more curious that the Torah inserts this comment at this particular juncture. By this point, we have been following Yosef's life story for several chapters. Would it not have been more logical to describe Yosef's physical appearance earlier in the narrative—in the chapters describing his birth, his youth, or at the point when the focus of the narrative first shifts in his direction? Instead, this information is provided after Yosef has endured his brothers' ridicule, after they sell him into slavery, after he is bought by an Egyptian minister. A straightforward reading of the text might dismiss this anomaly by reasoning that this verse serves as an introduction to the following episode involving Potifar's wife, in which, for the first time, Yosef's physical appearance becomes relevant. And yet, when we read this verse in the context of our search for Yosef's motivation, a deeper level emerges: The verse which describes Yosef's appearance is the very same verse that describes his rise to a position of power:

בראשית לט:ו

וַיַּעֲזֹב כָּל־אֲשֶׁר־לוֹ בְּיַד־יוֹסֵף ... וַיְהִי יוֹסֵף יְפֵה־תֹאַר וִיפֵה מַרְאֶה:

> [Potifar] placed all that he had in the hands of Yosef...and Yosef was handsome and of fine appearance. (*Bereishit* 39:6)

This verse marks the first time Yosef had the ability to contact his father; he had risen to a position of prominence in a very influential household. And yet, in this same verse, the Torah chooses to describe Yosef's good looks! The strange juxtaposition should alert us to the possibility that something much deeper than Yosef's physical appearance is being described.

An additional clue to deeper strata of meaning is the only parallel of this phrase in the Torah, also found in *Bereishit*:

בראשית כט:יז
וְרָחֵל הָיְתָה יְפַת־תֹּאַר וִיפַת מַרְאֶה:

And Rachel was beautiful and of fine appearance. (*Bereishit* 29:17)

As both the Midrash and the *Zohar* point out, Yosef had inherited his mother's beauty:

בראשית רבה [וילנא] פרשה פו
(בראשית לט, ו): וַיְהִי יוֹסֵף יְפֵה תֹאַר וִיפֵה מַרְאֶה, אָמַר רַבִּי יִצְחָק זְרוֹק חֻטְרָא לְאַוְיָרָא וְעַל עִקָּרֵיהּ נָפִיק, לְפִי שֶׁכָּתוּב (בראשית כט, יז): וְרָחֵל הָיְתָה יְפַת תֹּאַר וגו' לְפִיכָךְ וַיְהִי יוֹסֵף וגו'.

"And Yosef was handsome and of fine appearance" (*Bereishit* 39:6) — Rabbi Yitzchak said, "Throw a stick to the ground, and it will land near the place it came from. For it says, 'Rachel was beautiful and of fine appearance.' Therefore, [the text says] 'Yosef was handsome and of fine appearance.' (*Bereishit Rabbah* 86:6)

As the modern saying goes, an apple doesn't fall far from the tree; the source of Yosef's beauty was the beauty of Rachel. The *Zohar* goes a bit further in its description:

זוהר חלק א דף רטז/ב
כֵּיוָן דְּחָמָא לְיוֹסֵף, וַהֲוָה קָאִים קַמֵּיהּ, כַּד יַעֲקֹב מִסְתַּכֵּל בְּיוֹסֵף, הֲוָה אִשְׁתְּתִיל בְּנַפְשֵׁיהּ, כְּאִלּוּ חָמָא לְאִמֵּיהּ דְּיוֹסֵף. דְּשַׁפִּירוּ דְּיוֹסֵף דָּמֵי לְשַׁפִּירוּ דְּרָחֵל.

Whenever Yosef would walk by Yaakov, he would look at Yosef and his soul would be restored, as if he was looking at Yosef's mother, for the beauty of Yosef resembled the beauty of Rachel. (*Zohar, Bereishit* 216b)

On the other hand, numerous rabbinic sources teach—both implicitly and explicitly—that Yosef bore an uncanny, unmistakable resemblance to his father!

בראשית רבה [וילנא] פרשה פד:ח

וְיִשְׂרָאֵל אָהַב אֶת יוֹסֵף (בראשית לז, ג), ..., רַבִּי יְהוּדָה אוֹמֵר שֶׁהָיָה זִיו אִיקוֹנִין שֶׁלּוֹ דּוֹמֶה לוֹ.

"And Yisrael loved Yosef:" ...Rabbi Yehudah said, [Yosef's] face was like [Yaakov's] own. (*Bereishit Rabbah* 84:8)

The *Zohar* also stresses the resemblance between father and son:

זוהר חלק א דף קפ/א

'אֵלֶּה תּוֹלְדוֹת יַעֲקֹב יוֹסֵף', כָּל מַאן דְּהֲוָה מִסְתַּכֵּל בְּדִיּוּקְנָא דְיוֹסֵף הֲוָה אָמַר דְּדָא הוּא דִיוּקְנָא דְיַעֲקֹב. תָּא חֲזֵי, דִּבְכֻלְהוּ בְּנֵי יַעֲקֹב לָא כְּתִיב אֵלֶּה תּוֹלְדוֹת יַעֲקֹב רְאוּבֵן, בַּר יוֹסֵף, דְּדִיּוּקְנֵיהּ דָּמֵי לְדִיּוּקְנָא דְּאֲבוֹי:

"These are the generations of Yaakov, Yosef..." — Whoever would look at Yosef would see the image of Yaakov. Come and see, the verse does not say 'These are the generations of Yaakov, Reuven...'; only Yosef [is noted in this way] because he was the image of his father. (*Zohar, Bereishit* 180a)

The similarity between father and son gives us new insight into the Talmud's comments regarding Yosef's reaction to the seductive advances of Potifar's wife:

תלמוד בבלי מסכת סוטה דף לו עמוד ב

"וַתִּתְפְּשֵׂהוּ בְּבִגְדוֹ לֵאמֹר שִׁכְבָה עִמִּי", בְּאוֹתָהּ שָׁעָה בָּאתָה דְיוֹקְנוֹ שֶׁל אָבִיו וְנִרְאֵית לוֹ בַּחַלּוֹן.

"[Potifar's wife] grabbed him by the clothing..." — At that moment the image of his father appeared to him in the window. (*Sotah* 36b)

When Yosef looks in the window, he sees his own reflection[15]; the striking resemblance to his father jolts him back to his senses, and saves him from temptation. But if Yosef looked so much like his father, what is meant by the statement that he had inherited his mother's beauty? What, indeed, was the essence of Rachel's beauty? Surely the Torah is not speaking about traits that are only skin deep; Rachel's beauty must also represent some spiritual characteristic.

The answer may be found in a different context altogether: In a lengthy midrashic discussion of the destruction of the First Temple, God summons Avraham, Yitzchak, Yaakov, Moshe, and Yirmiyahu to stand before Him in defense of the Jewish People. Each offers an argument as to why God should rebuild the Temple. God, however, is unmoved by their arguments.

איכה רבה [וילנא] פתיחתתות ד"ה כד רבי יוחנן

בְּאוֹתָהּ שָׁעָה קָפְצָה רָחֵל אִמֵּנוּ לִפְנֵי הַקָּדוֹשׁ בָּרוּךְ הוּא וְאָמְרָה רִבּוֹנוֹ שֶׁל עוֹלָם, גָּלוּי לְפָנֶיךָ שֶׁיַּעֲקֹב עַבְדְּךָ אֲהָבַנִי אַהֲבָה יְתֵרָה וְעָבַד בִּשְׁבִילִי לְאַבָּא שֶׁבַע שָׁנִים, וּכְשֶׁהִשְׁלִימוּ אוֹתָן שֶׁבַע שָׁנִים וְהִגִּיעַ זְמַן נִשּׂוּאַי לְבַעֲלִי, יָעַץ אָבִי לְהַחֲלִיפֵנִי לְבַעֲלִי בִּשְׁבִיל אֲחוֹתִי, וְהֻקְשָׁה עָלַי הַדָּבָר עַד מְאֹד כִּי נוֹדְעָה לִי הָעֵצָה, וְהוֹדַעְתִּי לְבַעֲלִי וּמָסַרְתִּי לוֹ סִימָן שֶׁיַּכִּיר בֵּינִי וּבֵין אֲחוֹתִי כְּדֵי שֶׁלֹּא יוּכַל אָבִי לְהַחֲלִיפֵנִי, וּלְאַחַר כֵּן נִחַמְתִּי בְּעַצְמִי וְסָבַלְתִּי אֶת תַּאֲוָתִי וְרִחַמְתִּי עַל אֲחוֹתִי שֶׁלֹּא תֵצֵא לְחֶרְפָּה, וְלָעֶרֶב חִלְּפוּ אֲחוֹתִי לְבַעֲלִי בִּשְׁבִילִי, וּמָסַרְתִּי לַאֲחוֹתִי כָּל הַסִּימָנִין שֶׁמָּסַרְתִּי לְבַעֲלִי, כְּדֵי שֶׁיְּהֵא סָבוּר שֶׁהִיא רָחֵל. וְלֹא עוֹד אֶלָּא שֶׁנִּכְנַסְתִּי תַּחַת הַמִּטָּה שֶׁהָיָה שׁוֹכֵב עִם אֲחוֹתִי וְהָיָה מְדַבֵּר עִמָּהּ וְהִיא שׁוֹתֶקֶת וַאֲנִי מְשִׁיבַתּוּ עַל כָּל דָּבָר וְדָבָר, כְּדֵי שֶׁלֹּא יַכִּיר לְקוֹל אֲחוֹתִי וְגָמַלְתִּי חֶסֶד עִמָּהּ, וְלֹא קִנֵּאתִי בָהּ וְלֹא הוֹצֵאתִיהָ לְחֶרְפָּה. וּמָה אֲנִי שֶׁאֲנִי בָּשָׂר וָדָם עָפָר וָאֵפֶר לֹא קִנֵּאתִי לְצָרָה שֶׁלִּי וְלֹא הוֹצֵאתִיהָ לְבוּשָׁה וּלְחֶרְפָּה, וְאַתָּה מֶלֶךְ חַי וְקַיָּם, רַחֲמָן, מִפְּנֵי מָה קִנֵּאתָ לַעֲבוֹדַת כּוֹכָבִים שֶׁאֵין בָּהּ מַמָּשׁ, וְהִגְלֵיתָ בָּנַי וְנֶהֶרְגוּ בַחֶרֶב וְעָשׂוּ אוֹיְבִים בָּם כִּרְצוֹנָם. מִיָּד נִתְגַּלְגְּלוּ רַחֲמָיו שֶׁל הַקָּדוֹשׁ בָּרוּךְ הוּא וְאָמַר, בִּשְׁבִילֵךְ רָחֵל אֲנִי מַחֲזִיר אֶת יִשְׂרָאֵל לִמְקוֹמָן, הֲדָא הוּא דִכְתִיב (ירמיה ל״א, י״ד): כֹּה

---

15. There is some poetic license at play here: "Windows" in those days would not have had reflective glass. The Talmud probably intends to say that Yosef had an epiphany of his father that appeared to be looking at him through the window.

אָמַר ה' קוֹל בְּרָמָה נִשְׁמָע נְהִי בְּכִי תַמְרוּרִים רָחֵל מְבַכָּה עַל בָּנֶיהָ מֵאֲנָה לְהִנָּחֵם עַל בָּנֶיהָ כִּי אֵינֶנּוּ. וּכְתִיב (ירמיה לא, יד): כֹּה אָמַר ה' מִנְעִי קוֹלֵךְ מִבֶּכִי וְעֵינַיִךְ מִדִּמְעָה כִּי יֵשׁ שָׂכָר לִפְעֻלָּתֵךְ וגו', וּכְתִיב (ירמיה לא, יד): וְיֵשׁ תִּקְוָה לְאַחֲרִיתֵךְ נְאֻם ה' וְשָׁבוּ בָנִים לִגְבוּלָם.

At that moment, our matriarch Rachel burst in before the Holy One, blessed be He, and said, "Master of the Universe, it is well known to You that Your servant Yaakov loved me exceedingly and toiled for my father on my behalf for seven years. When those seven years were completed and the time arrived for my marriage with my husband, it came to my attention that my father was conspiring to switch my sister for me. It was very hard for me, because the plot was known to me and I disclosed it to my husband; and I gave him a sign whereby he could distinguish between me and my sister, so that my father would not be able to make the substitution.

"Afterwards I relented, suppressed my desire, and had pity upon my sister so that she should not be exposed to shame. In the evening, they substituted my sister for me with my husband, and I gave to my sister all the signs which I had arranged with my husband so that he should think that she was Rachel.... I performed *chesed* for her, was not jealous of her, and did not expose her to shame.

"If I, a creature of flesh and blood, formed of dust and ashes, was not envious of my rival and did not expose her to shame and contempt, why should You, a King who lives eternally and is merciful, be jealous of idolatry in which there is no reality, and exile my children and let them be slain by the sword, and allow their enemies to do with them as they wish?"

Immediately, the mercy of the Holy One, blessed be He, was aroused. "For you, Rachel, I will return Israel to their place." That is [the meaning of the] verse, "Thus says God, 'A voice in Ramah is heard—a bitter cry, Rachel crying for her children.

She refuses to be comforted for her children, for they are gone'" (*Yirmiyahu* 31:14-16), and it says, "Thus says God, 'Refrain your voice from weeping and your eyes from their tears, for your deeds shall be rewarded,'" and it says, "'And there is hope for the future,' says God, 'and your children shall return to their borders.'" (*Eichah Rabbah*, introduction, section 24)

The beauty, the greatness of Rachel, is her ability to sacrifice her personal needs and desires for the sake of her sister. Yosef displays this same trait, but only when he comes of age, in Egypt. For this reason, his beauty is described in the same verse that describes his dominion over the house of Potifar: This was the first time that Yosef had the ability to contact his father; thus, for the first time, the "beauty" of Yosef, the self-sacrifice he took upon himself in order to protect his brothers and his father, shone through. Yosef's beauty, inherited from his mother, became apparent at exactly this point, and so it is described precisely in this verse.

God rewarded Rachel for her self-sacrifice by allowing her children a second chance: The Second Temple was built upon the foundation of Rachel's love, *chesed*, and self-sacrifice—all of which were inherited by Yosef. When the Children of Israel ceased to follow her example, when they treated one another with a lack of respect, with hatred and jealousy—as they did when they sold Yosef into slavery, and as they did, once again, generations later—exile, slavery, and suffering ensued. The spiritual forces unleashed in Yosef's lifetime played out throughout Jewish history. The exile and enslavement of the sons of Yaakov was set in motion when they sold Yosef; this very same spiritual dynamic of *sinat chinam* (groundless hatred) eventually caused the destruction of the Second Temple.

Once the power of *sinat chinam* had been unleashed on the world by the brothers, Yosef endeavored to create a spiritual antidote. This, and not revenge or self-aggrandizement, was what motivated his behavior. With this motivation in mind, we come full circle: Yosef engineers the showdown with very specific—and very unselfish—results in mind.

A closer look at the original source of conflict between Yosef and his brothers brings the climactic confrontation into sharper relief: Yosef dreamed that his brothers would all bow down to him. The brothers, on the other hand, understood that their leader—as a family, and as a nation—was Yehudah.[16] Some have even claimed that the brothers misinterpreted Yosef's dreams as a rejection of Yehudah's leadership; they believed Yosef to be guilty of *meridah be-malchut* (treason)[17]—a capital offense. Yosef, however, understood his dream as the key to the future: The brothers must rally around him, a son of Rachel, as well as around Yehudah, the son of Leah, in their lifetime, in order to establish a spiritual precedent of unity for the future.

When the brothers come to Egypt searching for food, Yosef confronts them. Yosef the visionary, the interpreter of dreams, the man who excels in long-range planning, has surely anticipated their arrival for quite some time. The moment he heard Pharaoh's dream, he knew that the entire region would be struck by famine, and that his brothers would have to come to Egypt if they were to survive. He surely had played this scene out in his mind over and over again through the years.[18]

---

16. It may be argued that Yehudah's ascendency to the leadership role was the direct result of his behavior in this confrontation: He alone stepped up, taking responsibility and protecting his family against the strange demands of this mysterious despot (Yosef).

17. See *Shlah Ha-Kodesh, Torah Ohr Parshiyot Vayeshev, Miketz, Vayigash*, Section 40:

של"ה פרשת וישב מקץ ויגש תורה אור
וזה הוא ראובן היה חושב שלפי עומק הדין יוסף הוא בן מות, כי מורד במלכות בית דוד.

18. See *Pesikta Zutrata Bereishit* 42 *siman* 6; *Bechor Shor, Bereishit* 42:7; *Chizkuni, Bereishit* 42:6:

פסיקתא זוטרתא (לקח טוב) בראשית פרשת מקץ פרק מב סימן ו
ויוסף הוא השליט על הארץ הוא המשביר. לא רצה למנות אחר על המכירה אלא הוא בעצמו, לפי שידע שעתידין היו אחיו לבא מצרימה כדי שיכירם:

ר' יוסף בכור שור בראשית פרשת מקץ פרק מב פסוק ז
ויכירם: כי היה מצפה להם שמא יבואו מפני הרעב, כי דרכם של אבות לבא מצרים מפני הרעב, כמה שנאמר "ויהי רעב בארץ מצרים וירד אברם מצרימה", וכן יצחק עד שהקב"ה אמר לו: "אל תרד מצרימה", והם אינם מצפים שיהיה מלך.

While he must have yearned for news of his father on a personal level, one primary question filled Yosef's mind: Do his brothers regret their actions? Are they haunted by nightmare visions of their brother's frightened face? How have they treated Binyamin? Is Binyamin alive, or did he meet the same horrible fate as Yosef because of their jealousy?

The Torah describes the scene:

בראשית מב:ז-ח
וַיַּרְא יוֹסֵף אֶת־אֶחָיו וַיַּכִּרֵם וַיִּתְנַכֵּר אֲלֵיהֶם וַיְדַבֵּר אִתָּם קָשׁוֹת וַיֹּאמֶר אֲלֵהֶם מֵאַיִן בָּאתֶם וַיֹּאמְרוּ מֵאֶרֶץ כְּנַעַן לִשְׁבָּר־אֹכֶל: וַיַּכֵּר יוֹסֵף אֶת־אֶחָיו וְהֵם לֹא הִכִּרֻהוּ:

> Yosef saw his brothers and recognized them. He acted like a stranger to them and spoke to them harshly, saying, "Where have you come from?" They said, "From the land of Canaan to buy food." Yosef recognized his brothers, but they did not recognize him. (*Bereishit* 42:7–8)

The text is puzzling and redundant, stressing twice in as many verses that Yosef recognized his brothers.[19] The "recognition" makes the confrontation with Yehudah almost palpable; the word *va-yaker* hangs heavily in the air and forces us to compare the development of the two protagonists: Only when Yehudah "recognized" and took responsibility for his own misdeeds (*Bereishit* 38:26)[20] did he become a role model, a true leader, and the progenitor of the Messiah. Here, once again, the

---

חזקוני בראשית פרשת מקץ פרק מב פסוק ו
ויוסף הוא השליט על הארץ ואעפ"כ הוא המשביר לכל עם הארץ שהוא בעצמו מקבל את הכסף מכל הבאים כדי שאם יבואו אחיו יבואו לפניו ואם אחרים יקבלו את הכסף לא ידע כשיבואו אחיו. [המשביר המוכר].

19. The commentaries explain that the first use of *va-yaker* implies a more general sense of recognition: Yosef saw that these were his brothers; the second *va-yaker* indicates that he recognized each one. See Seforno, *Bereishit* 42:7-8;

ספורנו, בראשית מב: ז-ח
ויכירם. שהם אחיו לא שהכיר אחד לאחד: ויכר יוסף את אחיו. אחד לאחד ואחר כך:

20. See discussion on *Vayeishev*, above.

Torah hammers home this same "recognition" on the part of Yosef, indicating that he has undergone a similar process of growth, a similar metamorphosis. Like Yehudah, Yosef becomes a true leader. Yosef's motives are pure; he behaves as he does for the sake of his family and his nation, for the sake of Heaven.

And yet, Yosef continues to interrogate his brothers; he accuses them of espionage.[21] Each time they respond, they unwittingly open the door for more questions. Yosef asks them where they are from, and they respond with too much information, restating the obvious: **"From the land of Canaan, to buy food."**

This strange response is precisely the wrong answer: It allows Yosef to make a positive identification, but at the same time dashes his hopes that they have come to search for their long-lost brother. Yosef's greatest hope is that the brothers regret what they have done; his wish, his fantasy, is that they will make use of this trip to Egypt—the land to which they had sold Yosef as a slave—as an opportunity to look for him, to apologize, to bring him home. We might well imagine what would have happened if they had admitted to being "spies"—not political or military spies

---

21. See Mahari Karo's (Rav Yosef Karo) commentary on *Bereishit* 42:9, where he postulates that accusing them of espionage was a clever preemptive maneuver on Yosef's part: He anticipated that the brothers would start asking questions about the strange minister who was treating them so badly, and would soon discover his identity, foiling Yosef's larger plan. By accusing them of being spies, he prevented them from doing "research" for fear of appearing too inquisitive.

פירוש מהר"י קארו ז"ל על התורה - בראשית פרק מב פסוק ט

וי"ל כי כל מה שעשה יוסף לאחיו היתה כונתו לשם שמים כדי שבזה יתכפר להם העון שעשו וז"ש ויזכור להם יוסף וגו' <u>ולזה אמר מרגלים אתם כדי לסתמום פיהם ושלא יוכלו לשאול מי האיש הלזה כי המרגל לא יוכל לשאול שום דבר מזה וכו' ומה שלא שלח אגרת לאביו לפי שאמר אבי רוח הקדש העלים ממנו</u> ג"כ אני כמו כן ומש"ה וירא יוסף לפי שבב' דברים יכיר <u>האי את חבירו בראות או בקול ותיכף וירא יוסף את אחיו הכירם בראות ולפי שהם ג"כ</u> ראוהו ולא הכירוהו עשה בעצמו התנכרות כמו שתאמר המצנפת על פניו וכנגד הקול <u>שלא יכירוהו בקולו וידבר אתם קשות בכעס כדי שלא ירגישו בקולו</u> וכשהשיבו הם ואמרו כנים אנחנו שנים עשר אחים וגו' אמר הוא וגו' לפי שאינו לפי שאינו רוצה אביו שילמד מעשיכם וז"ש הוא אשר דברתי מרגלים אתם והקטן נשאר את אביו לפי שאינו רוצה אביו שילמד מעשיכם וז"ש הוא אשר דברתי מרגלים אתם וגו' ומה שבחרנו שישאר האחד לפי שלמעלה אמר שלחו מכם אחד ויקח את אחיכם ויבחנו דבריכם ר"ל תביאו הקטן אלי ואייסר אותו בשוטים עד שיודה האמת ואז יבחנו דבריכם האמת אתכם.

hoping to destabilize or overthrow the government, but "spies" searching for a lost brother: Surely, Yosef would have immediately, even joyfully, revealed his identity: "I am Yosef, the brother you seek!" Instead, they declare, immediately and somewhat defensively, that their visit has only one purpose: They have come for food—nothing more, nothing less. In an attempt to lead them in the desired direction, Yosef suggests that they are, in fact, looking for something (or someone) else; he accuses them of being spies, of snooping around Egypt's soft underbelly—where, Yosef assumes, the brothers might logically look for him.[22]

The brothers do not understand what this man is asking them. They strenuously and repeatedly deny seeking anything other than food. The dialogue is confused and cryptic; what is Yosef trying to get out of his brothers? What does he hope their response will be? The answer is remarkably simple.

בראשית פרק מב:יג-יד
וַיֹּאמְרוּ שְׁנֵים עָשָׂר עֲבָדֶיךָ אַחִים| אֲנַחְנוּ בְּנֵי אִישׁ־אֶחָד בְּאֶרֶץ כְּנָעַן וְהִנֵּה הַקָּטֹן אֶת־אָבִינוּ הַיּוֹם וְהָאֶחָד אֵינֶנּוּ: וַיֹּאמֶר אֲלֵהֶם יוֹסֵף הוּא אֲשֶׁר דִּבַּרְתִּי אֲלֵכֶם לֵאמֹר מְרַגְּלִים אַתֶּם:

They reply, "Your servants are twelve. We are brothers, sons of one man from the land of Canaan. The youngest is with our

---

22. Yosef accuses them of scouting the *ervat ha-aretz*, literally, the "nakedness of the land." This strange term can have two meanings: Either it refers to the country's strategic weak points, or it refers to the seedy parts of town, the "red light district" and its infamous flesh-peddlers. Yosef was well aware of the opinion his brothers had formed of him all those years ago; he had been a good-looking teenager, and was most certainly sold into a particular type of slavery; they could not have imagined he would have amounted to much more than that. In fact, the Sages of the Talmud and Midrash state that Potifar purchased Yosef as a sex slave. See *Sotah* 13b, *Bereishit Rabbah* 86:3:

תלמוד בבלי מסכת סוטה דף יג עמוד ב
וַיִּקְנֵהוּ פּוֹטִיפַר סְרִיס פַּרְעֹה", אָמַר רַב, שֶׁקְּנָאוֹ לְעַצְמוֹ; (בָּא גַּבְרִיאֵל וְסֵרְסוֹ) בָּא גַּבְרִיאֵל וּפְרָעוֹ. מֵעִיקָּרָא כְּתִיב, "פּוֹטִיפַר", וּלְבַסּוֹף כְּתִיב, (שם מא) "פּוֹטִי פֶרַע":

בראשית רבה (וילנא) פרשת וישב פרשה פו:ג
סְרִיס פַּרְעֹה, שֶׁנִּסְתָּרֵס בְּגוּפוֹ, מְלַמֵּד שֶׁלֹּא לְקָחוֹ אֶלָּא לְתַשְׁמִישׁ וְסֵרְסוֹ הַקָּדוֹשׁ בָּרוּךְ הוּא בְּגוּפוֹ...

father, and one is no longer with us." Yosef responded, "That is precisely what I meant [literally, 'he is the one I spoke of'] when I said you are spies." (Bereishit 42:13-14)

Yosef shows his hand; he explicitly accuses them of searching for their missing brother.[23] He wants them to admit that they are spies; he hopes they will confess that they have come to Egypt seeking the brother they had mistreated years ago. He seeks a sign that they feel remorse, that they want to right the wrong they had committed. He wants a sign that they have done *teshuvah*.

בראשית פרק מב:יד

וַיֹּאמְרוּ שְׁנֵים עָשָׂר עֲבָדֶיךָ אַחִים׀ אֲנַחְנוּ ... וְהָאֶחָד אֵינֶנּוּ: וַיֹּאמֶר אֲלֵהֶם יוֹסֵף הוּא אֲשֶׁר דִּבַּרְתִּי אֲלֵכֶם לֵאמֹר מְרַגְּלִים אַתֶּם:

They said, "We are twelve brothers…and one is no longer with us." Yosef replied, "**He is the one I spoke of** when I said you are spies." (*Bereishit* 42:14)

The brothers miss the opportunity; they feel no remorse, nor do they have any intention of searching for Yosef while they are in Egypt. They have come for food, and nothing more. Yosef has no choice but to accept this and shift to a contingency plan. He creates a second, albeit lesser, opportunity to heal the Rachel-Leah fault line that has torn the family apart: Ideally the rift should have been healed with the brothers rallying around Yosef, but when they prove unwilling or unable to do so, Yosef

---

23. See comments of the Seforno, *Bereishit* 42:14:

ספורנו בראשית פרשת מקץ פרק מב פסוק יד

הוא אשר דברתי אליכם. אותו האחד שאתם אומרים שאיננו ואינכם מפרשים אנה הלך הוא שהלך בעצתכם להגיד מה שראיתם או שהסכמתם כדי לרגל כמו שאמרתי:

The very one of whom you have said that he is no longer, although you refused to be specific about what happened to him, is the one who went back to report all that you have seen here, or that you have decided to stay a while in order to engage in spying.

creates an opportunity for the brothers to rally around Binyamin. If they are able to treat a son of Rachel like a brother, if they are prepared to protect him and acknowledge his status within the family, perhaps they can still be forgiven.

Binyamin becomes the unifying force—among the brothers, and later, among the tribes: In the Land of Israel, the Temple will stand in Binyamin's territory, a place above the discord and jealousy the brothers felt for Yosef. However, all of this is a result of Yosef's contingency plan, and is not what he had originally envisioned. Because the rectification for the brothers' sale of Yosef took place when they rallied around Binyamin, and not around Yosef, their *teshuvah*—and their unity— was incomplete. The *teshuvah* involving Binyamin was not sufficient to eradicate the sin of the brothers; only *teshuvah* involving Yosef himself could have provided the complete antidote for the power of *sinat chinam* the brothers had unleashed. This is what lies behind Rashi's cryptic comment on the verse describing the reunion of Yosef and Binyamin:

רש"י בראשית פרק מה:יד
ויפול על צוארי בנימין אחיו ויבך - ויבך על שני מקדשות שעתידין להיות בחלקו של בנימין וסופן לחרב:

"He fell on his brother Binyamin's shoulder and cried" — [Yosef cried] for the two Temples which would stand in the portion of Binyamin and be destroyed. (Rashi, *Bereishit* 45:14)

The brothers' *teshuvah* was enough to allow the Temple to be built in the territory of Binyamin, but it was not enough to prevent its eventual destruction. When the unifying factor upon which the Temple is founded crumbles, the Temple falls, destroyed by *sinat chinam*. The love and self-sacrifice of Rachel can build the edifice, but for it to stand, all the descendants of Yaakov would have to learn and internalize these traits.

Perhaps we should consider Ramban's comments from the perspective of spiritual antecedents, of *maasei avot siman la-banim*:

Yosef waited for the fruition of his dreams before contacting his father because he understood that the brothers would have to accept his role—not as a substitute for Yehudah but as a preparation for Yehudah's ultimate leadership, just as Mashiach ben Yosef prepares the way for Mashiach ben David (a descendent of Yehudah).[24]

According to tradition, Mashiach ben Yosef will unite all the Jewish people in preparation for the arrival of Mashiach ben David, but he will die in the process (*Sukkah* 52a); like Rachel, whose self-sacrifice allowed the building of the Second Temple, the self-sacrifice of Mashiach ben Yosef **and his willingness to be subservient to Mashiach ben David** will allow the building of the Third Temple. The spiritual model is Yosef, who chose not to contact his father even though it would have made his own life much more pleasant, because he understood that the ultimate goal could not be achieved without the self-sacrifice he learned from his mother Rachel.

Yosef—the dreamer, the visionary, the interpreter of dreams—saw what his brothers could not. He dedicated his life to his brothers, and he was the great provider for others. He sentenced himself to decades of loneliness so that his brothers would have the chance to be redeemed, and suffered self-imposed isolation so that the family's wounds could be healed.

Like his mother, Yosef was truly beautiful.

---

24. In retrospect, it becomes clear why the story of Yehudah had to be developed (in Chapter 38) before the Yosef story could continue.

Emotional Truth:
Becoming Brothers Once Again

As the story of Yosef and his bothers nears its dramatic conclusion, the brothers are in deep trouble.[1] Accused of theft, and seemingly caught red-handed, their future looks bleak. Technically, they can return home, leaving Binyamin behind; in truth, they cannot return to their father without him. *Parashat Vayigash* begins as Yehudah delivers a dramatic, impassioned speech, in which he recounts recent history. But before we turn to Yehudah's version of the events, let us first recap the preceding chapters from a more dispassionate perspective.

The story of Yosef and his brothers begins with Yaakov's favoritism, which fans the flames of the brothers' jealousy and hatred. They plan to kill him, and eventually sell him into slavery. The ensuing story of Yosef's life in Egypt includes enslavement, a spurned seductress, incarceration in a dungeon, and his meteoric rise to the second highest position in Egypt. Like the mythical phoenix, Yosef rises from being an imprisoned servant to unimaginable power. He tells Pharaoh what the future holds, and formulates a plan to protect the Egyptian economy and to establish the empire's superpower status in the time of regional upheaval that will soon begin. Yosef is placed in charge of this massive, long-range project, and as a result, of the entire population of Egypt during a severe seven-year famine (*Bereishit* 41:37-42).

---

1. This essay is based on a lecture I delivered on December 12, 2013, originally entitled "Honesty and Empathy." http://www.yutorah.org/lectures/lecture.cfm/801844/rabbi-ari-kahn/honesty-and-empathy/. Subsequently, in collaboration with my father Rabbi Dr. Pinchas Kahn, some of the ideas were further developed and references were added.

The brothers and Yosef have become strangers; neither knows what has happened to the other. They suffer not only from geographical distance, but from emotional distance as well. The brothers are unaware of any of the things that happened to Yosef in Egypt; Yosef is equally in the dark as to the experience of the brothers, the residual effect of what they had done to him, or the devastating effect upon their father Yaakov (*Bereishit* 37:31-36, also 42:36 and 43:1-14). And so, when Yosef and his brothers finally meet in Egypt, they carry entirely different sets of "emotional baggage" which, although related, are essentially different. Yosef is the ruler of the land, a man of tremendous power, who nevertheless sees himself as the victim. The brothers know nothing of his feelings or experiences; they don't even know who he is—and Yosef knows equally little about the brother's lives and feelings, whether repressed or conscious, since they parted ways decades earlier.

Yosef proceeds to put the brothers through a number of strange and difficult tasks (*Bereishit* 42:7–44:17). In all likelihood, these tasks are meant to clarify a number of things for Yosef. First, the brothers' reaction to having sold him into slavery: To what degree do they regret what they had done,[2] and where does their father Yaakov fit into the entire episode? Was he part of the plot? Had he died of a broken heart?[3] Yosef's unstated agenda may have been to clarify his brothers' reactions to the outrage they had perpetrated against him, and then to prod them into coming to terms with their responsibility for selling him into slavery.

When the brothers arrive in Egypt, they are immediately on the defensive, for a simple reason: Yosef recognizes them, and he lashes out. They are under attack, but have no idea why. Yosef immediately accuses them of being spies. They wilt under pressure, and respond in a manner that makes them seem guilty: They speak too much, offer

---

2. On two occasions, Yosef imprisons or enslaves one brother and sends the others home, re-enacting his own fate at their hands, as if to test them: Will they repeat their behavior, or learn from their sins?

3. See above, *Parashat Vayigash*.

too much information. They were asked only one question, "Where are you from," and the only response necessary was "From the land of Canaan."⁴ Instead, they offer proclamations: They claim to be innocent, honorable men who are only seeking food. The superfluous claims are important to them; precisely because they carry a burden of guilt, they feel an uncontrollable need to establish their innocence. Of course, as Shakespeare described another such case, they "protest too much." Such declarations serve only to raise, and not allay, doubts about their honesty.

בראשית פרק מב: יא
כֻּלָּנוּ בְּנֵי אִישׁ־אֶחָד נָחְנוּ כֵּנִים אֲנַחְנוּ לֹא־הָיוּ עֲבָדֶיךָ מְרַגְּלִים:

We are all one man's sons; **we are honest men;**⁵ your servants are no spies. (*Bereishit* 42:11)

For the brothers, proving their honesty and being truthful is of the utmost importance. And so, we fully expect Yehudah's address to Yosef, in the climactic scene of their ongoing confrontation, to be completely truthful. A careful reading of his words reveals distortions of fact that are therefore of particular significance.

Setting the stage for the final speech, Yosef's final ploy is to have his chalice secretly placed in Binyamin's sack. Later, when the chalice is "discovered" by Yosef's soldiers, Binyamin is accused of thievery and sentenced to slavery under the Egyptian viceroy (Yosef himself). The brothers' reaction is confused and illogical: Rather than waiting to see if the charge is supported by facts, once again they say too much, and immediately proclaim that the person in whose bag the chalice is found shall be put to death. This is not only a rash and unfortunate pronouncement; it is also extremely shortsighted and disconnected from very recent realities: Had their money not mysteriously been

---

4. See *Bereishit* 42:7.
5. The Hebrew *ki keinim anachnu*, is variously translated as; "we are honest men" (American Standard Version, 1901 & 1995; Darby Bible and our translation, see note 3), "we are true men" (King James Version, 1611) and "we are upright men" (Jewish Publication Society Bible, translation 1999).

returned to their bags on their previous trip? Were they so myopic that they believed they were deserving of that earlier "coincidental windfall," and the possibility that someone had planted money in their bags never occurred to them?

The "negotiations" between the brothers and Yosef's men seem comical. The brothers constantly suggest far more severe punishments than the Egyptian soldiers require: First, the soldiers reject their offer of a death sentence for the guilty party. Yosef's men insist that only the guilty individual will be sentenced to slavery; the brothers counter that all of them should be enslaved. This, too, is rejected by Yosef's emissaries. The angst and the confusion of the brothers is palpable.

Finally, Yehudah steps forward and speaks. He is majestic both in terms of his assumption of leadership, and in the nature of the address itself. Uncowering, he dares to addresses the viceroy directly, and the narrative reaches an emotional crescendo as he delivers an impassioned speech to his inscrutable and powerful adversary. In general terms, Yehudah pleads for the welfare of his elderly father; specifically, he asks that Binyamin be returned to their father, who loves him and cannot live without him. Yehudah volunteers to take Binyamin's place, to serve as a slave in his stead. The words Yehudah uses are of particular interest.

בראשית פרק מד:יח-לד

וַיִּגַּשׁ אֵלָיו יְהוּדָה וַיֹּאמֶר בִּי אֲדֹנִי יְדַבֶּר־נָא עַבְדְּךָ דָבָר בְּאָזְנֵי אֲדֹנִי וְאַל־יִחַר אַפְּךָ בְּעַבְדֶּךָ כִּי כָמוֹךָ כְּפַרְעֹה: אֲדֹנִי שָׁאַל אֶת־עֲבָדָיו לֵאמֹר הֲיֵשׁ־לָכֶם אָב אוֹ־אָח: וַנֹּאמֶר אֶל־אֲדֹנִי יֶשׁ־לָנוּ אָב זָקֵן וְיֶלֶד זְקֻנִים קָטָן וְאָחִיו מֵת וַיִּוָּתֵר הוּא לְבַדּוֹ לְאִמּוֹ וְאָבִיו אֲהֵבוֹ: וַתֹּאמֶר אֶל־עֲבָדֶיךָ הוֹרִדֻהוּ אֵלָי וְאָשִׂימָה עֵינִי עָלָיו: וַנֹּאמֶר אֶל־אֲדֹנִי לֹא־יוּכַל הַנַּעַר לַעֲזֹב אֶת־אָבִיו וְעָזַב אֶת־אָבִיו וָמֵת: וַתֹּאמֶר אֶל־עֲבָדֶיךָ אִם־לֹא יֵרֵד אֲחִיכֶם הַקָּטֹן אִתְּכֶם לֹא תֹסִפוּן לִרְאוֹת פָּנָי: וַיְהִי כִּי עָלִינוּ אֶל־עַבְדְּךָ אָבִי וַנַּגֶּד־לוֹ אֵת דִּבְרֵי אֲדֹנִי: וַיֹּאמֶר אָבִינוּ שֻׁבוּ שִׁבְרוּ־לָנוּ מְעַט־אֹכֶל: וַנֹּאמֶר לֹא נוּכַל לָרֶדֶת אִם־יֵשׁ אָחִינוּ הַקָּטֹן אִתָּנוּ וְיָרַדְנוּ כִּי־לֹא נוּכַל לִרְאוֹת פְּנֵי הָאִישׁ וְאָחִינוּ הַקָּטֹן אֵינֶנּוּ אִתָּנוּ: וַיֹּאמֶר עַבְדְּךָ אָבִי אֵלֵינוּ אַתֶּם יְדַעְתֶּם כִּי שְׁנַיִם יָלְדָה־לִּי אִשְׁתִּי: וַיֵּצֵא הָאֶחָד מֵאִתִּי וָאֹמַר אַךְ טָרֹף טֹרָף וְלֹא רְאִיתִיו עַד־הֵנָּה: וּלְקַחְתֶּם גַּם־אֶת־זֶה מֵעִם פָּנַי

Vayigash: The Emotional Truth | 295

וְקָרְבוּ אָסוֹן וְהוֹרַדְתֶּם אֶת־שֵׂיבָתִי בְּרָעָה שְׁאֹלָה: וְעַתָּה כְּבֹאִי אֶל־עַבְדְּךָ אָבִי וְהַנַּעַר אֵינֶנּוּ אִתָּנוּ וְנַפְשׁוֹ קְשׁוּרָה בְנַפְשׁוֹ: וְהָיָה כִּרְאוֹתוֹ כִּי־אֵין הַנַּעַר וָמֵת וְהוֹרִידוּ עֲבָדֶיךָ אֶת־שֵׂיבַת עַבְדְּךָ אָבִינוּ בְּיָגוֹן שְׁאֹלָה: כִּי עַבְדְּךָ עָרַב אֶת־הַנַּעַר מֵעִם אָבִי לֵאמֹר אִם־לֹא אֲבִיאֶנּוּ אֵלֶיךָ וְחָטָאתִי לְאָבִי כָּל־הַיָּמִים: וְעַתָּה יֵשֶׁב־נָא עַבְדְּךָ תַּחַת הַנַּעַר עֶבֶד לַאדֹנִי וְהַנַּעַר יַעַל עִם־אֶחָיו: כִּי־אֵיךְ אֶעֱלֶה אֶל־אָבִי וְהַנַּעַר אֵינֶנּוּ אִתִּי פֶּן אֶרְאֶה בָרָע אֲשֶׁר יִמְצָא אֶת־אָבִי:

Then Yehudah came near to him, and said, "O my lord, let your servant, I beg you, speak a word in my lord's ears, and let not your anger burn against your servant; for you are as Pharaoh. **My lord asked his servants, saying, Have you a father, or a brother**? And we said to my lord, 'We have a father, an old man, **and a child of his old age, a little one;** and his brother is dead, and he alone is left of his mother, and his father loves him.' And you said to your servants, 'Bring him down to me, that I may set my eyes upon him.' And we said to my lord, The **lad** cannot leave his father; for if he should leave his father, his father would die. And you said to your servants, Unless your youngest brother comes down with you, you shall see my face no more. And it came to pass when we came up to your servant my father, we told him the words of my lord. And our father said, 'Go again, and buy us a little food.' And we said, We can not go down; **if our small brother** be with us, then will we go down; for we may not see the man's face, **unless our: our small brother** be with us. And your servant my father said to us, you know that my wife bore me two sons; And the one went out from me, and I said, Surely **he is torn in pieces**; and I have not seen him since. And if you take this also from me, and harm befall him, you shall bring down my gray hairs with sorrow to Sheol. Now therefore when I come to your servant my father, and the lad is not with us; seeing that his life is bound up in the lad's life; It shall come to pass, when he sees that the lad is not with us, that he will die; and your servants shall bring down the gray hairs of your servant our father with sorrow to Sheol. For your servant guaranteed the lad's safety to my father, saying,' If I do not bring him to you, then I shall bear the blame to my father forever. Now therefore, I beg you, let your servant remain instead of the lad a slave to my lord; and let the lad go up with his brothers. For how shall I go up to my father, and the lad be not with me? lest perhaps I see the evil that shall come on my father. (*Bereishit* 44:18-34)

Yehudah has so much at stake: His brother's fate, and his own, are in his hands; his own reputation and position of leadership among the brothers hangs in the balance; their father's emotional and physical well-being is in jeopardy. Yehudah does his utmost to convince Yosef; he holds nothing back. He tries his hand at emotional manipulation, and places the onus of guilt on Yosef for having created this quagmire. And yet, as we have noted, Yehudah and his brothers display a desperate need to be regarded as innocent and truthful. If nothing else, Yosef has proven to be a formidable foe; Yehudah would be a fool to allow himself to be caught in a lie by a foe such as this. With so much at stake, we would expect Yehudah to take great care to be precise, to speak the truth, to be honest and honorable—yet close scrutiny of the text reveals significant departures from this objective. In a fascinating conflation and confusion of events and episodes, Yehudah creates an intertextual mishmash, which must be unraveled if we are to understand both the historical lies and the emotional truth Yehudah conveys.

Let us return to Yehudah's introductory statements. Yehudah claims that Yosef had asked whether the brothers have a father or brother (verse 19). In fact, Yosef never asked such a question. Rather, it was the brothers, when placed under moderate pressure, who had volunteered this information:

בראשית פרק מב:ט-יג

וַיִּזְכֹּר יוֹסֵף אֵת הַחֲלֹמוֹת אֲשֶׁר חָלַם לָהֶם וַיֹּאמֶר אֲלֵהֶם מְרַגְּלִים אַתֶּם לִרְאוֹת אֶת־עֶרְוַת הָאָרֶץ בָּאתֶם: וַיֹּאמְרוּ אֵלָיו לֹא אֲדֹנִי וַעֲבָדֶיךָ בָּאוּ לִשְׁבָּר

אֹכֶל: (יא) כֻּלָּנוּ בְּנֵי אִישׁ־אֶחָד נָחְנוּ כֵּנִים אֲנַחְנוּ לֹא־הָיוּ עֲבָדֶיךָ מְרַגְּלִים: (יב) וַיֹּאמֶר אֲלֵהֶם לֹא כִּי־עֶרְוַת הָאָרֶץ בָּאתֶם לִרְאוֹת: (יג) וַיֹּאמְרוּ שְׁנֵים עָשָׂר עֲבָדֶיךָ אַחִים ׀ אֲנַחְנוּ בְּנֵי אִישׁ־אֶחָד בְּאֶרֶץ כְּנָעַן וְהִנֵּה הַקָּטֹן אֶת־אָבִינוּ הַיּוֹם וְהָאֶחָד אֵינֶנּוּ:

Recalling the dreams that he had dreamed about them, Yosef said to them, "You are spies, you have come to see the land in its nakedness." But they said to him, "No, my lord! Truly, your servants have come to procure food. **We are all of us sons of the same man; we are honest men**; your servants have never been spies!" And he said to them, "No, you have come to see the land in its nakedness!" And they replied, "**We your servants were twelve brothers, sons of a man in the land of Canaan**; the youngest, however, is now with our father, and one is no more." (*Bereishit* 42: 9-13).

Clearly, Yehudah is preoccupied with the question of their intra-familial relationships. Are they, in fact, all brothers? Even Binyamin? Even "the one who is no more"? It appears that in expressing these feelings during his address to Yosef, Yehudah unconsciously sets the stage for the emotional message that will follow.

Yehudah continues: "You asked if we have a father or brother, and we said we have an elderly father and a *yeled zekunim katan*," "a child of his old age, a little one" (*Bereishit* 44:20). This is not completely accurate. While Binyamin is the youngest, it is Yosef, and not Binyamin, who has been referred to in this manner; Yosef is Yaakov's *ben zekunim*, the "son of his old age" (*Bereishit* 37:3).[6] Moreover, Yosef is referred to by his brothers as a "child" ("*yeled*") (*Bereishit* 42:22),[7] whereas Binyamin is referred to as

---

6. In this context, *zekunim* may refer to Yosef's wisdom rather than Yaakov's advanced age; see Rashi, based on the Targum:

בראשית לז: ג
וְיִשְׂרָאֵל אָהַב אֶת־יוֹסֵף מִכָּל־בָּנָיו כִּי־בֶן־זְקֻנִים הוּא לוֹ וְעָשָׂה לוֹ כְּתֹנֶת פַּסִּים:

7. See *Bereishit* 42:22.

בראשית מב: כב
וַיַּעַן רְאוּבֵן אֹתָם לֵאמֹר הֲלוֹא אָמַרְתִּי אֲלֵיכֶם ׀ לֵאמֹר אַל־תֶּחֶטְאוּ בַיֶּלֶד וְלֹא שְׁמַעְתֶּם וְגַם־דָּמוֹ הִנֵּה נִדְרָשׁ:

a "lad" (*na'ar*) in Yehudah's negotiations with his father (*Bereishit* 43:8).[8] Indeed, in the course of his speech, Yehudah oscillates between the use of "child" (*yeled*) and "lad" (*naar*) so frequently, it is almost dizzying: "Child" appears in verses 20, 23 and twice in 26, while "lad" is used in verses 22, 30, 31, 32, twice in 33, and 34. Furthermore, while Binyamin is the youngest, the "baby" of the family, he is not all that young: Soon after this confrontation between Yosef and Yehudah, the text lists the children and grandchildren of Yaakov who come to Egypt as per Yosef's instructions (*Bereishit* 46:21). Among them, Binyamin is mentioned—as are his ten children! A rough estimation of the chronology of *Bereishit* puts Binyamin's age somewhere between thirty to thirty-two years old at this point. Why call a father of ten a child?[9]

The confusing elements in Yehudah's speech suggest that there is a disconnect between what he says and what he is thinking. Ostensibly, Yehudah is speaking to his Egyptian interlocutor about Binyamin, but he seems to be thinking of someone else—his long-lost brother Yosef; the fates of Yosef and Binyamin have begun to merge in Yehudah's mind. Apparently, Yosef's strategy has succeeded: Yehudah has undergone a metamorphosis. He is no longer speaking about Binyamin, or only about Binyamin. He has been forced to allow the earlier episode of Yosef to float up to a higher level of his subconscious. Yosef is now, finally, on his mind; his responsibility for Yosef's fate begins to seep through in this moment of crisis—and the words he uses allow us to glimpse what is just below the surface of his speech.

Another interesting distortion is seen in verse 28. Yehudah retells his father's reaction as follows:

---

8. See *Bereishit* 43:8:

בראשית מג:ח
וַיֹּאמֶר יְהוּדָה אֶל־יִשְׂרָאֵל אָבִיו שִׁלְחָה הַנַּעַר אִתִּי וְנָקוּמָה וְנֵלֵכָה וְנִחְיֶה וְלֹא נָמוּת גַּם־אֲנַחְנוּ גַם־אַתָּה גַּם־טַפֵּנוּ:

9. Binyamin is referred to as a child by the brothers in their report to Yaakov about the encounter with the "ruler of Egypt" (*Bereishit* 42:32). This may reflect their understanding of Yaakov's feelings toward Binyamin, or their own attitude toward their youngest brother.

Vayigash: The Emotional Truth | 299

בראשית פרק מד:כז-כט
וַיֹּאמֶר עַבְדְּךָ אָבִי אֵלֵינוּ אַתֶּם יְדַעְתֶּם כִּי שְׁנַיִם יָלְדָה־לִּי אִשְׁתִּי: וַיֵּצֵא הָאֶחָד מֵאִתִּי וָאֹמַר אַךְ טָרֹף טֹרָף וְלֹא רְאִיתִיו עַד־הֵנָּה: וּלְקַחְתֶּם גַּם־אֶת־זֶה מֵעִם פָּנַי וְקָרָהוּ אָסוֹן וְהוֹרַדְתֶּם אֶת־שֵׂיבָתִי בְּרָעָה שְׁאֹלָה:

And your servant my father said to us, you know that my wife bore me two sons; And the one went out from me, and I said, Surely **he is torn in pieces**; and I have not seen him since. And if you take this also from me, and harm befall him, you shall bring down my gray hairs with sorrow to Sheol.

But this is not what Yaakov actually said. The text reported his actual response in great detail, as follows:

בראשית פרק מב: לו-לח
וַיֹּאמֶר אֲלֵהֶם יַעֲקֹב אֲבִיהֶם אֹתִי שִׁכַּלְתֶּם יוֹסֵף אֵינֶנּוּ וְשִׁמְעוֹן אֵינֶנּוּ וְאֶת־בִּנְיָמִן תִּקָּחוּ עָלַי הָיוּ כֻלָּנָה: וַיֹּאמֶר רְאוּבֵן אֶל־אָבִיו לֵאמֹר אֶת־שְׁנֵי בָנַי תָּמִית אִם־לֹא אֲבִיאֶנּוּ אֵלֶיךָ תְּנָה אֹתוֹ עַל־יָדִי וַאֲנִי אֲשִׁיבֶנּוּ אֵלֶיךָ: וַיֹּאמֶר לֹא־יֵרֵד בְּנִי עִמָּכֶם כִּי־אָחִיו מֵת וְהוּא לְבַדּוֹ נִשְׁאָר וּקְרָאָהוּ אָסוֹן בַּדֶּרֶךְ אֲשֶׁר תֵּלְכוּ־בָהּ וְהוֹרַדְתֶּם אֶת־שֵׂיבָתִי בְּיָגוֹן שְׁאוֹלָה:

Their father Yaakov said to them, "You have brought me grief: Yosef is no more and Shimon is no more, and now you would take Binyamin. These things always happen to me!" Then Reuven said to his father, "You may kill my two sons if I do not bring him back to you. Put him in my care, and I will return him to you." But he said, "My son must not go down with you, for his brother is dead and he alone is left. If he meets with disaster on the journey you are taking, you will send my white head down to *Sheol* in grief." (*Bereishit* 42:36-38)

The phrase *"he is torn in pieces"* was used many years earlier, when the brothers brought Yosef's bloody clothes to Yaakov and allowed him to draw the inescapable conclusion:

בראשית פרק לז: לג

... וַיַּכִּירָהּ וַיֹּאמֶר כְּתֹנֶת בְּנִי חַיָּה רָעָה אֲכָלָתְהוּ טָרֹף טֹרַף יוֹסֵף:

> [Yaakov] recognized it, and said, "It is my son's coat; an evil beast has devoured him; Yosef is without doubt **torn in pieces**." (*Bereishit* 37:33)

As Yehudah stands unknowingly before Yosef, the memory of that horrible cry comes flooding back to him; his father's pain and his own guilt ring in his ears. He hears, once again, Yaakov's haunting cry, and the words slip seamlessly into his re-telling of a more recent conversation with his father.

As Yehudah presents his case to the Egyptian despot, he warns that his elderly father will die without his beloved youngest son; his description of Yaakov's anguish is telling:

בראשית פרק מד: כט-לא

וּלְקַחְתֶּם גַּם־אֶת־זֶה מֵעִם פָּנַי וְקָרָהוּ אָסוֹן וְהוֹרַדְתֶּם אֶת־שֵׂיבָתִי בְּרָעָה שְׁאֹלָה: ... וְהָיָה כִּרְאוֹתוֹ כִּי־אֵין הַנַּעַר וָמֵת וְהוֹרִידוּ עֲבָדֶיךָ אֶת־שֵׂיבַת עַבְדְּךָ אָבִינוּ בְּיָגוֹן שְׁאֹלָה:

> And if you take this also from me, and harm befall him, **you shall bring down my gray hairs with sorrow to Sheol.**... It shall come to pass, when he sees that the lad is not with us, that he will die; and your servants shall **bring down the gray hairs of your servant our father with sorrow to Sheol.** (*Bereishit* 44: 29-31).

Once again, Yehudah misreports Yaakov's parting statement. When he negotiated with Yehudah about sending Binyamin, Yaakov never mentioned going to his own grave in sorrow; Yaakov used this expression twice before—once when Yosef was assumed dead (*Bereishit* 37:35)[10] and once in Yaakov's negotiations with Reuven (*Bereishit* 42:38)[11]—but never in his conversation with Yehudah. Nonetheless, Yehudah utilizes this dramatic turn of phrase in his speech, either because his own emotional state causes him to conflate all these traumatic scenes, or as a means of shifting his own deep-seated guilt onto his adversary's shoulders. Yehudah knows Yaakov's pain; his ears are still ringing with Yaakov's anguished cry decades earlier, and with Yaakov's words to Reuven. All of these emotions and memories become entangled, and Yehudah finally voices his own unbearable guilt:

בראשית מד: לב-לד

כִּי עַבְדְּךָ עָרַב אֶת־הַנַּעַר מֵעִם אָבִי לֵאמֹר אִם־לֹא אֲבִיאֶנּוּ אֵלֶיךָ וְחָטָאתִי לְאָבִי כָּל־הַיָּמִים: ... כִּי־אֵיךְ אֶעֱלֶה אֶל־אָבִי וְהַנַּעַר אֵינֶנּוּ אִתִּי פֶּן אֶרְאֶה בָרָע אֲשֶׁר יִמְצָא אֶת־אָבִי:

For I have guaranteed the safety of the lad to my father, saying, 'If I do not bring him back to you, **then I shall bear the blame to my father forever...** For how shall I go up to my father, and the lad be not with me? **How will I bear to see the evil that shall befall my father?** (*Bereishit* 44:32-34).

---

10. *Bereishit* 37:35:

בראשית לז:לה

וַיָּקֻמוּ כָל־בָּנָיו וְכָל־בְּנֹתָיו לְנַחֲמוֹ וַיְמָאֵן לְהִתְנַחֵם וַיֹּאמֶר כִּי־אֵרֵד אֶל־בְּנִי אָבֵל שְׁאֹלָה וַיֵּבְךְּ אֹתוֹ אָבִיו:

And all his sons and all his daughters rose up to comfort him; but he refused to be comforted; and he said, **For I will go down to Sheol to my son, mourning.** Thus his father wept for him.

11. *Bereishit* 42: 38:

בראשית מב:לח

וַיֹּאמֶר לֹא־יֵרֵד בְּנִי עִמָּכֶם כִּי־אָחִיו מֵת וְהוּא לְבַדּוֹ נִשְׁאָר וּקְרָאָהוּ אָסוֹן בַּדֶּרֶךְ אֲשֶׁר תֵּלְכוּ־בָהּ וְהוֹרַדְתֶּם אֶת־שֵׂיבָתִי בְּיָגוֹן שְׁאוֹלָה:

... my son will not go down with you, for his brother is dead, and he alone remains, and if disaster strikes on the way he goes, you will cause me to go to my grave in deep mourning—with hair white [from mourning] (*Bereishit* 42:38).

Distortions of speech and recall are understood in psychological analysis as the breaking through of repressed emotions. When a number of such 'breakthroughs' form a common theme, the distortions may be attributed to a common source, a single, disturbing issue with which the speaker is preoccupied. The psychoanalyst Ernest Jones, quoting Freud, noted that, "... a word said in mistake is a manifestation of a second, suppressed thought, and thus arises outside the train of thought that the speaker intended to express. It may be a word or phrase entirely foreign to the train of thought, being taken in its entirety from the outlying thought, or it may be a compromise formation, in which both come to expression."[12]

Yosef responds to Yehudah's speech on many levels, parallel to the levels of Yehudah's own speech. When Yehudah focuses on his father's pain, Yosef abandons his disguise. Yosef never wanted to cause his father pain; quite the opposite. His father's misery tormented him.

Despite his demons, which seem to be dancing just below the surface of his impassioned plea, Yehudah is heroic. Binyamin has been caught stealing, jeopardizing the entire family; Yehudah could quite easily have taken his remaining brothers, cut their losses, and denounced the "problematic" branch of the family. Yehudah could easily have reasoned that Rachel and her sons were all tainted by the same evil: Rachel had stolen her father Lavan's *terafim* years earlier, placing the entire family in peril; her son Yosef was a bad apple—self-centered and vain. And now her younger son Binyamin had been caught in an act of selfishness and thievery. Simply turning and walking away could have been Yehudah's most logical solution to his own dilemma. Instead, Yehudah takes charge, and takes responsibility. He mobilizes the brothers and is willing to be enslaved so Binyamin can go free.[13]

Another subconscious dilemma shows through the language Yehudah employs in his speech to Yosef; his emotions bubble to the

---

12. E. Jones, *Papers on Psychoanalysis* (Boston: Beacon Press, 1961 [first published as *Papers on Psycho-Analysis*. London: Balliere Tindall & Cox. 1912]), p. 44. See examples brought in his book from *The Egoist* by George Meredith on pp. 48-49.
13. Rabbi Ari Kahn, *Echoes of Eden: Bereishit* (Jerusalem and New York: Gefen Publishing and OU Press, 2011), p.320.

surface and he expresses his own inner world without necessarily being aware of it: Yehudah is wracked with guilt for the pain he has caused his father, and so he deflects his guilt by accusing the cruel Egyptian ruler (Yosef) of the very same crime of which he is guilty: "If you take away the son that my father loves, he will die! How can you do this to him?" In fact, this is precisely what Yehudah had done years earlier, and his feelings of guilt and pain break through into his speech.

Perhaps Yehudah's new voice, as representative of the brothers, was more than just a means of communicating with their Egyptian tormentor. Yehudah's speech reveals that he is traumatized, and the moment he steps up to take the lead, he assumes the collective guilt for what they all had done to Yosef, and for the pain they had caused their father Yaakov.

Yosef, the interpreter of dreams *par excellence*, understands Yehudah's emotional communication perfectly. He hears Yehudah's subconscious struggle breaking through; he hears Yehudah's regret and remorse. He senses that the brothers have changed, and that they feel guilty about what they had done. But Yosef is not their therapist, nor can he be. He is the aggrieved brother, the victim. Yosef, understanding exactly what Yehudah is saying and feeling, responds succinctly—but with immense emotional power: "I am Yosef; is my father still alive?" (*Bereishit* 45:3), as if to say, "Are you really so concerned about Yaakov's well-being that you claim he will die if his beloved son is taken from him?" He challenges and chastises: "I am Yosef. Could my father be alive? Can he have survived what you have already done, what you did to me?"[14]

With that, Yehudah is rendered speechless; there can be no answer. All of the brothers' neat explanations vanish. No justifications will work. The stark truth of Yosef's existence stares them down, shocks them into silence. They have no words, only guilt. The Sages compare this experience to the Day of Judgment, when the All-Knowing God conducts a final

---

14. See the commentary of Seforno, *Bereishit* 45:3, for an in-depth discussion. Also see *Echoes of Eden: Bereishit*, pp. 320-321.

reckoning of man's deeds. No finesse, no legalese, no justifications: On that day, only the humiliation of facing the truth remains.[15]

Apparently, what Yosef seeks is not revenge; given his position of power, that could have been easily achieved. The erstwhile protege of the chief executioner of Egypt was surely well-versed in the ways of punishment and pain, but this is not the path Yosef chooses. Nor

---

15. See *Midrash Sechel Tov* (Buber), *Vayigash* 45:3; *Chagigah* 4b, *Midrash Tanchuma* (Buber) *Vayigash, siman 7, Midrash Tanchuma, Vayigash siman 5:*

שכל טוב (בובר) בראשית פרשת ויגש פרק מה סימן ג

ג) ויאמר יוסף אל אחיו אני יוסף העוד אבי חי. בתחלה שאל שלום אביו: ולא יכלו לענות אותו. אפילו על שלום אביו, למה: כי נבהלו מפניו. א"ר אליעזר בן עזריה אוי לנו מיום הדין, אוי לנו מיום התוכחה, ומה יוסף שהוא בשר ודם כשהוכיח את אחיו לא יכלו לעמוד בתוכחתו, בתוכחותיו של הקדוש ברוך הוא מלך מלכי המלכים שהוא עד ודיין ובעל דין, ויושב על כסא רם ונשא בדין, ודן את כל אדם לפי מעשיו על אחת כמה וכמה שאין בריה יכולה לעמוד לפניו, שנא' אם תוכיח ה' מי יעמוד, וכתיב כי לא יצדק לפניך כל חי (תהלים קמג ב):

תלמוד בבלי מסכת חגיגה דף ד עמוד ב

רַבִּי אֶלְעָזָר, כִּי הֲוָה מַטֵּי לְהַאי קְרָא, בָּכֵי: (בראשית מה) "וְלֹא יָכְלוּ אֶחָיו לַעֲנוֹת אֹתוֹ כִּי נִבְהֲלוּ מִפָּנָיו", וּמַה תּוֹכֵחָה שֶׁל בָּשָׂר וָדָם כָּךְ, שֶׁל הַקָּדוֹשׁ בָּרוּךְ הוּא לֹא כָּל שֶׁכֵּן?

מדרש תנחומא (בובר) פרשת ויגש סימן ז

כיון שאמר להם אני יוסף (אחיכם) לא יכלו אחיו לענות אותו כי נבהלו מפניו (שם /בראשית מ"ה/), ר' אלעזר ב"ר שמעון בשם ר' אלעזר בן עזריה אמר ומה אם יוסף שאמר לאחיו אני יוסף, וידעו מה שעשו בו, לא יכלו לענות אותו, כשיבא הקדוש ברוך הוא להתוכח עם כל אחד ואחד מן הבריות ולומר לו מעשיו כמו שכתוב כי הנה יוצר הרים ובורא רוח ומגיד לאדם מה שיחו (עמוס ד יג) על אחת כמה וכמה שאין בריה יכולה לעמוד.

מדרש תנחומא פרשת ויגש סימן ה

אָמַר רַבִּי יוֹחָנָן, וַי לָנוּ מִיּוֹם הַדִּין, וַי לָנוּ מִיּוֹם תּוֹכֵחָה. וּמַה, יוֹסֵף כְּשֶׁאָמַר לְאֶחָיו אֲנִי יוֹסֵף, פָּרְחָה נִשְׁמָתָן. כְּשֶׁיַּעֲמֹד הַקָּדוֹשׁ בָּרוּךְ הוּא לָדִין דִּכְתִיב בֵּיהּ (מלאכי ג, ב) וּמִי מְכַלְכֵּל אֶת יוֹם בּוֹאוֹ וּמִי הָעוֹמֵד בְּהֵרָאוֹתוֹ שֶׁכָּתוּב בּוֹ כִּי לֹא יִרְאַנִי הָאָדָם וָחָי (שמות לג, כ) עַל אַחַת כַּמָּה וְכַמָּה, וּמַה זֶה נִבְהֲלוּ אֶחָיו מִפָּנָיו כְּשֶׁיָּבוֹא הַקָּדוֹשׁ בָּרוּךְ הוּא לִתְבֹּעַ עֶלְבּוֹן הַמִּצְוֹת וּפִשְׁעָהּ שֶׁל תּוֹרָה, עַל אַחַת כַּמָּה וְכַמָּה.

Rabbi Yochanan declared: Woe unto us on judgment day, woe unto us on the day of rebuke, for if Yosef could cause them to faint by saying "I am your brother Yosef," what will happen when the Holy One, blessed be He, arises to judge us, since it is written about Him: "Who may abide the day of His coming? And who shall stand when He appears?" (Malachi 3:2), and "For no man shall see Me and live" (*Shemot* 3:20)? If a mere human could confound his brothers, how much more so will we be confounded when the Holy One, blessed be He, examines us concerning our arrogance toward the commandments and our transgressions of the Torah.

does he seek to humiliate his brothers; that was never his objective. He wants to remind them of the past, to remind them that there is someone they have forgotten—himself.[16] He wants them to understand that even if they have managed to forget, their father Yaakov never ceased mourning for his "dead" son—and for that ongoing pain, they must take responsibility. Yehudah, who himself had lost not one but two of his own sons, should have been more sensitive to the pain Yaakov was forced to endure—for a son who was quite alive.

When Yehudah takes upon himself the role of protector and spokesperson for his brothers, when he places himself in peril and speaks to the humanity and empathy of his enemy, the first glimpses of Jewish royalty shine through—glimpses that will be more fully manifest in his descendants, the Davidic dynasty.[17] Perhaps, though, these regal qualities are not what made Yehudah and his descendants worthy; perhaps, instead, it was the deep scars, the sense of responsibility, and the trauma of finally realizing what pain and suffering he had caused, that made Yehudah the ultimate Jewish leader. This very human aspect of Yehudah—his readiness to accept his guilt and to chart a path toward rehabilitation, is his true source of strength and majesty.

Yehudah's words were fraught with imprecision, misrepresentation, and even outright distortion, but behind those words lay very truthful emotions. The man who poured out his heart in Egypt was not the same callous Yehuda who had engineered the sale of his brother and broke his father's heart. This transformed Yehuda desperately hoped to protect his brother, and to minimize his father's pain experienced. This emotionally raw, vulnerable Yehudah gained Yosef's respect; **this** Yehudah was the forerunner of kings.

---

16. *Echoes of Eden: Bereishit*, p.321.
17. Arguably, the first step toward Yehudah's rehabilitation took place in his interaction with Tamar, when he declared, "She is more righteous than I" (*Bereishit* 38:26). See *Explorations*: Parashat Vayeshev, "The Light of the Messiah."

Parashat Vayechi

Who Is First?

In the penultimate scene of Yaakov's life, Yosef is summoned to his ailing father's sick bed, and he brings his two sons with him. Previously, Yaakov had made Yosef promise to bury him in the Land of Israel. As his final days slip away, Yaakov stands poised to bless Yosef's sons and grant them equal status among the tribes; Yaakov assigns Efraim and Menashe a place among his own sons, rather than among his grandsons. Their status as tribes effectively gives their father Yosef a "double portion," the birthright of the first-born son.

Were Yaakov's parting interactions with Yosef merely additional expressions of the favoritism Yaakov had displayed toward Yosef in his youth? Why did Yaakov make his deathbed request for burial in the ancestral tomb specifically of Yosef, and not all of his sons? While we may say that it was Yosef, among all the sons, who had the power to fulfill this request, surely there would have been no harm in addressing all the sons as a group. And why were Yosef's sons alone raised to a status far above all of Yaakov's other grandchildren? Why were they, and by extension their father Yosef, favored with a double inheritance? Was this blessing a continuation of the preferential treatment that had sparked the brothers' jealousy and led them to sell Yosef into slavery?

After announcing this double inheritance, Yaakov asks that Efraim and Menashe approach him and receive his blessing, but when they stand at their grandfather's bedside, Yaakov appears to become confused:

בראשית פרק מח:ח
וַיַּרְא יִשְׂרָאֵל אֶת־בְּנֵי יוֹסֵף וַיֹּאמֶר מִי־אֵלֶּה:

And Yisrael saw Yosef's sons, and (Yisrael) said, "Who are these?" (*Bereishit* 48:8)

There are several possible explanations for this confusion: In a subsequent verse, we are told that Yaakov (Yisrael) had limited eyesight (*Bereishit* 48:10). Perhaps he simply could not see, or was no longer able to see well enough to distinguish between them.[1] A second possibility is that Yosef's Egyptian-born sons looked strange and unfamiliar to Yaakov, due to their regal dress and foreign upbringing.[2] A third possibility, raised by Rashi, is that Yaakov's lack of clarity was not a problem of eyesight but of clairvoyance: At that moment, Yaakov lost his prophetic vision. He became frightened, not confused, and his question was not aimed at clarifying the names or identities of his grandsons, but of their worthiness, their spiritual identity:

רש"י, בראשית פרשת ויחי פרק מח פסוק ח
וירא ישראל את בני יוסף -בִּקֵּשׁ לְבָרְכֵם, וְנִסְתַּלְּקָה שְׁכִינָה מִמֶּנּוּ, לְפִי שֶׁעָתִיד יָרָבְעָם וְאַחְאָב לָצֵאת מֵאֶפְרַיִם וְיֵהוּא וּבָנָיו מִמְּנַשֶּׁה:

ויאמר מי אלה- מֵהֵיכָן יָצְאוּ אֵלּוּ, שֶׁאֵינָן רְאוּיִן לִבְרָכָה:

"And Yisrael saw Yosef's sons..." — he wished to bless them but the Divine Presence departed from him because he saw that from Efraim would be born the wicked kings Yerovam and Ahav, and from Menasheh Yehu and his sons (*Midrash Tanchuma, Vayechi* 6).

---

1. Rashbam, *Bereishit* 48:8:

רשב"ם בראשית פרשת ויחי פרק מח פסוק ח
וירא ישראל - אעפ"י שכת' לפנינו (ו)לא יוכל לראות, יש רואה דמות אדם ואינו מכיר דמות פניו. ...

2. Malbim, *Bereishit* 48:8:

מלבי"ם בראשית פרשת ויחי פרק מח פסוק ח
וירא ישראל. מלבושי העברים היו משונים ממלבושי המצרים, ויוסף שהיה קרוב למלכות, וכן בניו היו לובשים כמלבושי שרי מצרים, וכמ"ש של בית ר"ג היו משנים מהלכתן משום כבוד מלכות, וע"כ תמה יעקב ואמר מי אלה, ויאמר יוסף בני הם, והם צדיקים ויראי ה', ומה שאתה רואה אותם משונים במלבושיהם מפני אשר נתן לי אלהים בזה, שנולדו בזה המקום והמקום והמצב מחייב זאת:

"(Yisrael) asked, 'Who are these?'" — from where did these come, who are unfit for blessing?

According to Rashi, there was evil lurking in the future, something that Yaakov had never seen before, and this caused him to lose his *ruach ha-kodesh* and to question whether these sons of Yosef were in fact deserving of the blessing he was about to bestow on them. Yaakov saw evil in the future: Yerovam, Achav, and Yehu, three wicked kings of Israel, were descendants of Yosef.

Yaakov could not imagine that Yosef would spawn such offspring. He had never seen any negative sides to his favorite son's personality. Yosef was the golden child, Yaakov's favorite.[3] From a very young age, Yaakov knew that Yosef was destined for greatness. He dressed Yosef in the special, regal clothes, making it plain to anyone who saw him that Yosef was the anointed one.

For the most part, Yosef's dreams were consonant with Yaakov's expectations and aspirations: Yosef, the son of his beloved wife Rachel, was not like his other children, and his dreams of economic and political dominance simply echoed what Yaakov had already intuited: Yosef was born to lead. Yaakov's other children, however, did not take kindly to the predictions of their own subservience. Their jealousy led to hatred, which nearly led to murder, ultimately resulted in the sale of Yosef.

From the moment, he retells his dreams to his father and brothers, Yosef's dreams remain just below the surface of the narrative for the remainder of Bereishit. Thus, the brothers refer to what they believe to be Yosef's delusions of grandeur as they plot to dispose of him:

בראשית פרק לז: יט-כ

וַיֹּאמְרוּ אִישׁ אֶל־אָחִיו הִנֵּה בַּעַל הַחֲלֹמוֹת הַלָּזֶה בָּא: וְעַתָּה לְכוּ וְנַהַרְגֵהוּ וְנַשְׁלִכֵהוּ בְּאַחַד הַבֹּרוֹת וְאָמַרְנוּ חַיָּה רָעָה אֲכָלָתְהוּ וְנִרְאֶה מַה־יִּהְיוּ חֲלֹמֹתָיו:

---

3. The text (*Bereishit* 37:3) stresses that Yisrael loved Yosef because he was a "*ben zekunim*" which is understood by Rashi as a clever son. The name Yisrael tends to be used on a more national as opposed to personal level, indicating that Yisrael favored Yosef for his leadership skills, in the context of nationhood—favoritism that would prove to be well-founded later in Yosef's life.

Then one said to the other, "Here comes that **dreamer**. Come now, let us kill him and throw him into one of the pits; and we can say, "A savage beast devoured him"; then we shall see what becomes of his **dreams**! (*Bereishit* 37:19-20)

Many years later, when the brothers come searching for food, they do not imagine that Yosef's dreams of power and economic superiority were not delusions but prophecies. They bow to Yosef, as his dream predicted they would; they beg him for food, as his dreams predicted they would. For Yosef, the dreams are a real and powerful element of his consciousness; he remembers the dreams from the moment his brothers re-enter his life:

בראשית פרק מב:ו-ט
וְיוֹסֵף הוּא הַשַּׁלִּיט עַל־הָאָרֶץ הוּא הַמַּשְׁבִּיר לְכָל־עַם הָאָרֶץ וַיָּבֹאוּ אֲחֵי יוֹסֵף וַיִּשְׁתַּחֲווּ־לוֹ אַפַּיִם אָרְצָה: וַיַּרְא יוֹסֵף אֶת־אֶחָיו וַיַּכִּרֵם וַיִּתְנַכֵּר אֲלֵיהֶם וַיְדַבֵּר אִתָּם קָשׁוֹת וַיֹּאמֶר אֲלֵהֶם מֵאַיִן בָּאתֶם וַיֹּאמְרוּ מֵאֶרֶץ כְּנַעַן לִשְׁבָּר־אֹכֶל: וַיַּכֵּר יוֹסֵף אֶת־אֶחָיו וְהֵם לֹא הִכִּרֻהוּ: וַיִּזְכֹּר יוֹסֵף אֵת הַחֲלֹמוֹת אֲשֶׁר חָלַם לָהֶם וַיֹּאמֶר אֲלֵהֶם מְרַגְּלִים אַתֶּם לִרְאוֹת אֶת־עֶרְוַת הָאָרֶץ בָּאתֶם:

Now Yosef was the vizier of the land; it was he who dispensed rations to all the people of the land. And Yosef's brothers came and bowed low to him, with their faces to the ground. When Yosef saw his brothers, he recognized them; but he acted like a stranger toward them and spoke harshly to them. He asked them, "Where do you come from?" And they said, "From the land of Canaan, to procure food." For though Yosef recognized his brothers, they did not recognize him. Recalling the **dreams** that he had **dreamed** about them, Yosef said to them, "You are spies, you have come to see the land in its nakedness." (*Bereishit* 42:6-9)

In an exchange dripping with delicious irony, the brothers bow to the powerful supplier of food, yet they do not know that is their long-lost, nearly-murdered brother, whom they had kidnapped and sold. Yosef alone remembers the dreams, and the dreams have come true.[4] Yet we can ask if it is truly a fulfillment of Yosef's dream. Afterall, when the brothers bowed they did know they were bowing to Yosef. Can we say that the brothers have truly bowed to Yosef if they do not know who he is? Must they actually experience and internalize their subservience to their brother, or acknowledge Yosef's greatness, for the dreams to be fulfilled? It seems almost like the famous philosophical conundrum: If a tree falls in the forest and no one hears...

Setting this question aside for the moment, we might remind ourselves that the dreams are a subtext, as we have noted, and not the central theme of the tension that builds in the course of their encounter. The larger issue seems to be that Yosef is gauging his brothers' morality: Have they remained the same jealous, devious bunch? Is his younger brother Binyamin safe? Is his father still alive? Have they been transformed by the years of separation? Do they regret how they treated him? Is there still a chance for reconciliation?

From the moment Yosef heard Pharaoh's dreams, he knew that his brothers would arrive—sooner rather than later. He also knew that as soon as they arrived, they would bow—but there was much more that he did not know. And so, when they do arrive, and when they bow to him, oblivious to his true identity, Yosef watches and listens carefully. He puts them through a series of rigorous tests in order to answer his own questions, and in the end the brothers—particularly Yehudah— pass the test: Yehudah is prepared to sacrifice himself and become a slave so that Binyamin can be free. Yosef, who has first-hand insight as to the physical and emotional price this entails, is moved; Yehudah's extraordinary gesture allows Yosef to bring the charade to an end, and to reveal his identity.

---

4. Many debate the extent to which Yosef's dreams were fulfilled: Only ten of his brothers, and not eleven, bowed before him; their father (and Yosef's mother) did not bow, either. Nonetheless, the substance of the dreams did, indeed, come to fruition: Yosef provided food and sustenance to the entire family, and had a position of great power—symbolized by the brothers' sheaves bowing to Yosef's sheaf, and the stars bowing to him, respectively.

The real question is, what's next? Essentially, only Yosef can answer this question; after all, he holds all the cards. Yosef is in charge—not only of Egypt, and of the fate of his brothers, but also of the type of reconciliation, if any, they can expect, and the new rules of engagement.

There are three obvious possibilities:

First: Yosef punishes his brothers. He recalls everything he went through because of them—the humiliation, slavery, mortal danger, and estrangement from his beloved father. As we have already noted,[5] the former apprentice to the chief executioner of Egypt surely had the knowledge, power and means to subject his brothers to unimaginable pain. Alternatively, sentencing them to live out their lives as slaves might have been the just and equitable punishment for their perfidy. Nonetheless, Yosef has no thoughts of revenge.

Second: Yosef wipes the slate clean, expunges the past, and starts from scratch, building a new relationship with his now-transformed brothers, on equal footing with them at last. This approach would arguably go a long way toward excising the cancerous feelings of jealousy and hatred which are in danger of growing even stronger than they had been, festering and metastasizing on the fertile ground of Yosef's success.

Yosef chooses a third path: While he does not take revenge, he does not seek equality. An analysis of the language of the verses that describe their relationship reveals his plan, his thoughts—and his dreams for the future.

בראשית פרק מה:ג

וַיֹּאמֶר יוֹסֵף אֶל־אֶחָיו אֲנִי יוֹסֵף הַעוֹד אָבִי חָי וְלֹא־יָכְלוּ אֶחָיו לַעֲנוֹת אֹתוֹ כִּי נִבְהֲלוּ מִפָּנָיו:

Yosef said to his brothers, "I am Yosef. Is **my** father still alive?" But his brothers could not answer him, so shaken were they on account of him. (*Bereishit* 45:3)

---

5. See above, *Parashat Vayigash*.

Yosef speaks, and the text stresses that it is to his brothers that he addresses himself. This very loaded term gives us hope for fraternity and brotherhood, but that hope quickly disappears: Yosef asks, "Is **my father** still alive?" Had he wished for reconciliation, he would surely have included them: "Is **our** father still alive?"

The bothers are in shock; they are speechless. Yosef tries, once again, to engage them. There are many things he can say to assure them of his identity, and he urges them to come close—but then he chooses to remind them of the most painful parts of their relationship, using words that must have cut like the jagged edge of a knife:

בראשית פרק מה:ד
וַיֹּאמֶר יוֹסֵף אֶל־אֶחָיו גְּשׁוּ־נָא אֵלַי וַיִּגָּשׁוּ וַיֹּאמֶר אֲנִי יוֹסֵף אֲחִיכֶם אֲשֶׁר־מְכַרְתֶּם אֹתִי מִצְרָיְמָה:

Then Yosef said to his brothers, "Please, come forward to me." And when they came forward, he said, "I am your brother Yosef, whom you sold into Egypt. (*Bereishit* 45:4)

Yosef assures them he is, in fact, their brother, that he has returned from the grave they dug for him in their minds; he is the same Yosef they had sold all those years ago. Once again, Yosef creates a moment of closeness—"I am Yosef your **brother**"—but quickly follows with a crushing dose of blunt truth: "whom you sold into [slavery in] Egypt." Had he sought reconciliation, there were so many other words he could have used to convince them of his identity. But Yosef continues, and a deviousness emerges:

בראשית פרק מה:ה-ז
וְעַתָּה| אַל־תֵּעָצְבוּ וְאַל־יִחַר בְּעֵינֵיכֶם כִּי־מְכַרְתֶּם אֹתִי הֵנָּה כִּי לְמִחְיָה שְׁלָחַנִי אֱלֹהִים לִפְנֵיכֶם: כִּי־זֶה שְׁנָתַיִם הָרָעָב בְּקֶרֶב הָאָרֶץ וְעוֹד חָמֵשׁ שָׁנִים אֲשֶׁר אֵין־חָרִישׁ וְקָצִיר: וַיִּשְׁלָחֵנִי אֱלֹהִים לִפְנֵיכֶם לָשׂוּם לָכֶם שְׁאֵרִית בָּאָרֶץ וּלְהַחֲיוֹת לָכֶם לִפְלֵיטָה גְּדֹלָה: וְעַתָּה לֹא־אַתֶּם שְׁלַחְתֶּם אֹתִי הֵנָּה כִּי הָאֱלֹהִים וַיְשִׂימֵנִי לְאָב לְפַרְעֹה וּלְאָדוֹן לְכָל־בֵּיתוֹ וּמֹשֵׁל בְּכָל־אֶרֶץ מִצְרָיִם:

> Now, do not be distressed or reproach yourselves because you sold me to this place; it was to save life that God sent me ahead of you. It is now two years that there has been famine in the land, and there are still five years to come in which there shall be no yield from tilling. God has sent me ahead of you to ensure your survival on earth, and to save your lives in an extraordinary deliverance. So, it was not you who sent me here, but God; and He has made me a father to Pharaoh, lord of all his household, and ruler over the whole land of Egypt. (*Bereishit* 45:5-8)

With an artfully crafted explanation that displays his brilliance, Yosef praises God for bringing him to Egypt and to his lofty position, and at the same time exonerates his brothers, removing them completely from the narrative. On the one hand, he explains that God's master-plan brought him to Egypt and secured him in a position of unimaginable power. Many lives, including their own, will be saved. But lest they receive any credit, even incidental credit, for anything good that results from Yosef rise to power, he stresses that this was all the work of God. The sub-text is extraordinary: Yosef knew, from the start, that he would achieve greatness. He tried to tell them, to share his worldview, but they scorned him and scoffed at his predictions. They were so far off the mark, he tells them, that they cannot take any credit for the fortuitous outcome, because they were oblivious to the truth all along. They were nothing more than pawns, marionettes whose strings were pulled by the master of the Divine drama that catapulted Yosef to the top. He alone, he tells them in his just-subtle enough speech, has always been the star of the show. He has always been the main character; they are merely "extras" in a cast of thousands. Yosef gives God all the credit; he wants them to understand that God is on his side.

Yosef's speech is stunning. These are not the words of a man seeking peace, love, fraternity, or reconciliation. The speech is self-serving from start to finish, bordering on narcissistic, and these same tropes are echoed in his instructions for breaking the news to his father that he is alive:

Vayechi: Who Is First?

בראשית פרק מה:ט-יג

מַהֲרוּ֮ וַעֲל֣וּ אֶל־אָבִי֒ וַאֲמַרְתֶּ֣ם אֵלָ֗יו כֹּ֤ה אָמַר֙ בִּנְךָ֣ יוֹסֵ֔ף שָׂמַ֧נִי אֱלֹהִ֛ים לְאָד֖וֹן לְכָל־מִצְרָ֑יִם רְדָ֥ה אֵלַ֖י אַֽל־תַּעֲמֹֽד: וְיָשַׁבְתָּ֣ בְאֶֽרֶץ־גֹּ֗שֶׁן וְהָיִ֤יתָ קָרוֹב֙ אֵלַ֔י אַתָּ֕ה וּבָנֶ֖יךָ וּבְנֵ֣י בָנֶ֑יךָ וְצֹאנְךָ֥ וּבְקָרְךָ֖ וְכָל־אֲשֶׁר־לָֽךְ: וְכִלְכַּלְתִּ֤י אֹֽתְךָ֙ שָׁ֔ם כִּי־ע֛וֹד חָמֵ֥שׁ שָׁנִ֖ים רָעָ֑ב פֶּן־תִּוָּרֵ֛שׁ אַתָּ֥ה וּבֵֽיתְךָ֖ וְכָל־אֲשֶׁר־לָֽךְ: וְהִנֵּ֤ה עֵֽינֵיכֶם֙ רֹא֔וֹת וְעֵינֵ֖י אָחִ֣י בִנְיָמִ֑ין כִּי־פִ֖י הַֽמְדַבֵּ֥ר אֲלֵיכֶֽם: וְהִגַּדְתֶּ֣ם לְאָבִ֗י אֶת־כָּל־כְּבוֹדִי֙ בְּמִצְרַ֔יִם וְאֵ֖ת כָּל־אֲשֶׁ֣ר רְאִיתֶ֑ם וּמִֽהַרְתֶּ֛ם וְהוֹרַדְתֶּ֥ם אֶת־אָבִ֖י הֵֽנָּה:

Now, hurry back to my father and say to him: "Thus says your son Yosef, 'God has made me lord of all Egypt; come down to me without delay. You will dwell in the region of Goshen, where you will be near me—you and your children and your grandchildren, your flocks and herds, and all that is yours. There I will provide for you;—for there are yet five years of famine to come—that you and your household and all that is yours may not suffer want." You can see for yourselves, and my brother Binyamin for himself, that it is indeed I who am speaking to you. And you must tell my father everything about my high station in Egypt and all that you have seen; and bring my father here with all speed." (Bereishit 45:9-13)

Yosef wants his father to know that God has placed him as leader and lord over Egypt; again, he refers to his father, not their (collective) father, and his own personal glory, power, and honor. The benevolent Yosef lets it be known that he will care for them all, provide them with food, homes, and all their other needs—yet his benevolence comes at a price. He infantilizes his brothers by caring for them, creating total dependence on his good graces rather than employing them in meaningful, productive positions.[6] His benevolence feeds and strengthens his dreams; the reality he creates surpasses even his dreams.

---

6. See comments of Radak to *Bereishit* 46:34. Yosef did not want his brothers to receive government positions. Presumably Paroh would adduce if having one "Yosef" work for him changed the economy of Egypt—imagine what a team of twelves "Yosefs" could do.

רד"ק בראשית פרשת ויגש פרק מו:לד

(לד) בעבור תשבו בארץ גשן - לפי שהיתה ארץ מקנה, ועוד כדי שלא יקח אתכם לעבודת המלך:

What do the brothers hear? How do they interpret his kindness? Apparently, they see what they had always seen: Yosef's narcissism. Even when Yosef embraces them and cries on the shoulders of each of his brothers, only Binyamin reciprocates; the other brothers stand stone cold, either in shock or in disgust. They are convinced that they had been right about Yosef from the start.

בראשית פרק מה:יד-טו
וַיִּפֹּל עַל־צַוְּארֵי בִנְיָמִן־אָחִיו וַיֵּבְךְּ וּבִנְיָמִן בָּכָה עַל־צַוָּארָיו: וַיְנַשֵּׁק לְכָל־אֶחָיו וַיֵּבְךְּ עֲלֵהֶם וְאַחֲרֵי כֵן דִּבְּרוּ אֶחָיו אִתּוֹ:

With that he embraced his brother Binyamin around the neck and wept, and Binyamin wept on his neck. He kissed all his brothers and wept upon them; only then were his brothers able to talk to him. (*Bereishit* 45:14-15)

Yosef shares with his brothers a state secret, there would be five more years of drought and hunger. Yosef prides himself into seeing into the future, and shares with his brothers, they should tell Yaakov who should hurry down.

As the brothers leave, Yosef shows favoritism to his full brother Binyamin, mistakes from the past will not be corrected, they will be institutionalized, for Yosef the story has a happy ending. He has been vindicated, and now all his brothers know it. The tree which fell in the forest could now be heard loud and clear.

בראשית פרק מה: כב-כד
לְכֻלָּם נָתַן לָאִישׁ חֲלִפוֹת שְׂמָלֹת וּלְבִנְיָמִן נָתַן שְׁלֹשׁ מֵאוֹת כֶּסֶף וְחָמֵשׁ חֲלִפֹת שְׂמָלֹת: וּלְאָבִיו שָׁלַח כְּזֹאת עֲשָׂרָה חֲמֹרִים נֹשְׂאִים מִטּוּב מִצְרָיִם וְעֶשֶׂר אֲתֹנֹת נֹשְׂאֹת בָּר וָלֶחֶם וּמָזוֹן לְאָבִיו לַדָּרֶךְ: וַיְשַׁלַּח אֶת־אֶחָיו וַיֵּלֵכוּ וַיֹּאמֶר אֲלֵהֶם אַל־תִּרְגְּזוּ בַּדָּרֶךְ:

To each of them, moreover, he gave a change of clothing; but to Binyamin he gave three hundred pieces of silver and five changes of clothing. And to his father he sent the following: ten donkeys laden with the best things of Egypt, and ten she-asses laden with grain, bread, and provisions for his father on the journey. As he sent his brothers off on their way, he told them, "Do not be quarrelsome on the way." (*Bereishit* 45:22-24)

Upon returning to Yaakov, the brothers share the news in more subdued tones: Yosef is alive, and he rules over Egypt. After overcoming his initial disbelief, Yaakov comes back to life, and his spirit of prophecy returns.

בראשית פרק מה: כה-כח
וַיַּעֲלוּ מִמִּצְרָיִם וַיָּבֹאוּ אֶרֶץ כְּנַעַן אֶל־יַעֲקֹב אֲבִיהֶם: וַיַּגִּדוּ לוֹ לֵאמֹר עוֹד יוֹסֵף חַי וְכִי־הוּא מֹשֵׁל בְּכָל־אֶרֶץ מִצְרָיִם וַיָּפָג לִבּוֹ כִּי לֹא־הֶאֱמִין לָהֶם: וַיְדַבְּרוּ אֵלָיו אֵת כָּל־דִּבְרֵי יוֹסֵף אֲשֶׁר דִּבֶּר אֲלֵהֶם וַיַּרְא אֶת־הָעֲגָלוֹת אֲשֶׁר־שָׁלַח יוֹסֵף לָשֵׂאת אֹתוֹ וַתְּחִי רוּחַ יַעֲקֹב אֲבִיהֶם: וַיֹּאמֶר יִשְׂרָאֵל רַב עוֹד־יוֹסֵף בְּנִי חָי אֵלְכָה וְאֶרְאֶנּוּ בְּטֶרֶם אָמוּת:

They went up from Egypt and came to their father Yaakov in the land of Canaan. And they told him, "Yosef is still alive, and he is ruler over the whole land of Egypt." His heart went numb, for he did not believe them. But when they recounted all that Yosef had said to them, and when he saw the wagons that Yosef had sent to transport him, the spirit of their father Yaakov was revived. "Enough!" said Yisrael. "My son Yosef is still alive! I must go and see him before I die." (*Bereishit* 45:25-28)

Yosef's dreams had come true, but Yaakov's vision surpassed the vision of Yosef. God spoke to Yaakov directly, and enabled him to see much farther into the future than Yosef could see:

בראשית פרק מו, א-ד
וַיִּסַּע יִשְׂרָאֵל וְכָל־אֲשֶׁר־לוֹ וַיָּבֹא בְּאֵרָה שָּׁבַע וַיִּזְבַּח זְבָחִים לֵאלֹהֵי אָבִיו יִצְחָק: וַיֹּאמֶר אֱלֹהִים׀ לְיִשְׂרָאֵל בְּמַרְאֹת הַלַּיְלָה וַיֹּאמֶר יַעֲקֹב׀ יַעֲקֹב וַיֹּאמֶר הִנֵּנִי: וַיֹּאמֶר אָנֹכִי הָאֵל אֱלֹהֵי אָבִיךָ אַל־תִּירָא מֵרְדָה מִצְרַיְמָה כִּי־לְגוֹי גָּדוֹל אֲשִׂימְךָ שָׁם: אָנֹכִי אֵרֵד עִמְּךָ מִצְרַיְמָה וְאָנֹכִי אַעַלְךָ גַם־עָלֹה וְיוֹסֵף יָשִׁית יָדוֹ עַל־עֵינֶיךָ:

> So Yisrael set out with all that was his, and he came to Beer Sheva, where he offered sacrifices to the God of his father Yitzchak. God called to Yisrael in a vision by night: "Yaakov! Yaakov!" He answered, "I am here." And He said, "I am God, the God of your father. Fear not to go down to Egypt, for *I will make you there into a great nation*. I Myself will go down with you to Egypt, and I Myself will also bring you back; and Yosef's hand shall close your eyes." (*Bereishit* 46:1-4)

Yaakov is told that his children will become a great and numerous nation during their sojourn in Egypt; clearly, this vision extends well beyond five years into the future that Yosef is able to see. Yaakov understands that this exile will continue for hundreds of years. He knows that the fruition of the covenant God made with Avraham has begun; slavery and affliction will soon follow. Yosef can amuse himself with his power, but Yaakov knows it is temporary. Although Yaakov lives out his years in Egypt, reunited with the son he always loved, but he is nonetheless preoccupied with the future.

Now, we return to the deathbed scene. Yaakov is taken aback; he sees something coming, something evil that emerges from Yosef, something he had never seen before: Yosef's descendants will be self-centered, narcissistic leaders who will lead the nation astray. In shock, Yaakov asks, "Who are these people?"[7] — even though the people standing at

---

7. See my essay "Who Are These": https://www.aish.com/tp/i/moha/48937092.html, specifically note the *Zohar* cited which links the question of Yaakov: "Who are these" *mi eleh*, with the declaration made when the Golden Calf in the desert and the pair of golden calves by Yerovam were constructed and worshiped. ("these are your gods Israel – *eleh alohecha Yisrael*).

זוהר חלק א דף רכז/א

וַיַּרְא יִשְׂרָאֵל אֶת בְּנֵי יוֹסֵף וַיֹּאמֶר מִי אֵלֶּה, אָמַר רַבִּי יִצְחָק, הַאי קְרָא קַשְׁיָא, דִּכְתִיב וַיַּרְא יִשְׂרָאֵל, וּכְתִיב וְעֵינֵי יִשְׂרָאֵל כָּבְדוּ מִזֹּקֶן לֹא יוּכַל לִרְאוֹת, אִי לֹא יוּכַל לִרְאוֹת, מַהוּ וַיַּרְא יִשְׂרָאֵל. אֶלָּא דְּחָמָא בְּרוּחַ קוּדְשָׁא, אֵינוּן בְּנֵי יוֹסֵף, דְּאִינּוּן יָרָבְעָם וַחֲבֵירָיו. דְּיָרָבְעָם עָבַד תְּרֵין עֶגְלֵי זָהָב, וְאָמַר (מלכים א יב) אֵלֶּה אֱלֹהֶיךָ יִשְׂרָאֵל. וּבְגִין כָּךְ, מִי אֵלֶּה, מַאן הוּא דִּזַמִּין לְמֵימַר אֵלֶּה אֱלֹהֶיךָ לְטַעֲוָון אָחֳרָן, וּבְגִין כָּךְ וַיַּרְא יִשְׂרָאֵל אֶת בְּנֵי יוֹסֵף: מִכַּאן, דְּצַדִּיקַיָּיא חָמָאן עוֹבָדָא לְמֵרָחוֹק, וְקוּדְשָׁא בְּרִיךְ הוּא מְעַטֵּר לוֹן בְּעִטְרָא דִּילֵיהּ, מַה קוּדְשָׁא בְּרִיךְ הוּא חָמֵי לְמֵרָחוֹק, כְּמָה דִּכְתִיב, (בראשית א) וַיַּרְא אֱלֹהִים אֶת כָּל אֲשֶׁר עָשָׂה וְהִנֵּה טוֹב מְאֹד, דְּקוּדְשָׁא בְּרִיךְ הוּא חָמָא כָּל עוֹבָדִין, עַד לָא יַעֲבֵד לוֹן, וְכֻלְּהוּ אַעֲבָרוּ קַמֵּיהּ:

his bedside are Yosef's sons Efraim and Menashe, whom we have every reason to believe were fine, upstanding young men. Yaakov feels his prophetic vision slipping away in the face of something sinister, and he is shocked and alarmed: This is a side of Yosef he had never seen—but perhaps should have seen. Our Sages point out Yosef's immaturity and narcissism from a very early stage in his life story:

בראשית פרק לז:ב

אֵלֶּה ׀ תֹּלְדוֹת יַעֲקֹב יוֹסֵף בֶּן־שְׁבַע־עֶשְׂרֵה שָׁנָה הָיָה רֹעֶה אֶת־אֶחָיו בַּצֹּאן וְהוּא נַעַר אֶת־בְּנֵי בִלְהָה וְאֶת־בְּנֵי זִלְפָּה נְשֵׁי אָבִיו וַיָּבֵא יוֹסֵף אֶת־דִּבָּתָם רָעָה אֶל־אֲבִיהֶם:

This is the line of Yaakov: At seventeen years of age, Yosef tended the flocks with his brothers, and he was a lad (*naar*) to the sons of his father's wives Bilhah and Zilpah. And Yosef brought bad reports of them to their father. (*Bereishit* 37:2)

רש"י בראשית פרק לז:ב

וְהוּא נַעַר - שֶׁהָיָה עוֹשֶׂה מַעֲשֵׂה נַעֲרוּת, מְתַקֵּן בִּשְׂעָרוֹ, מְמַשְׁמֵשׁ בְּעֵינָיו, כְּדֵי שֶׁיִּהְיֶה נִרְאֶה יָפֶה:

"…and he was a lad (*naar*)" — His actions were childish: he dressed his hair, he touched up his eyes so that he should appear good-looking. (Rashi, *Bereishit* 37:2, based on *Bereishit Rabbah* 84:7)

"And Yisrael saw the sons of Yosef, and he said: "Who are these?" — This verse seems to contradict the statement a few verses later that "the eyes of Yisrael were dim from age, so that he could not see." What this verse really means, however, is that he saw through the Holy Spirit those later descendants of Yosef, Yeravam, and his fraternity. Yeravam made two golden calves and said, "These are your gods, O Israel" (1 *Melachim* 12:28). Hence Yisrael now said, "Who are these?" That is, "Who is he that will one day say *these* to idols?" From this passage, we learn that the righteous see into the distant future and God crowns them with His own crown." (*Zohar, Bereishit*, 227b)

בראשית פרק לט:ו

וַיַּעֲזֹב כָּל־אֲשֶׁר־לוֹ בְּיַד־יוֹסֵף וְלֹא־יָדַע אִתּוֹ מְאוּמָה כִּי אִם־הַלֶּחֶם אֲשֶׁר־הוּא אוֹכֵל וַיְהִי יוֹסֵף יְפֵה־תֹאַר וִיפֵה מַרְאֶה:

He left all that he had in Yosef's hands and, with him there, he paid attention to nothing save the food that he ate. Now Yosef was well built and handsome. (*Bereishit* 39:6)

רש"י בראשית פרק לט:ו

וַיְהִי יוֹסֵף יְפֵה תֹאַר וִיפֵה מַרְאֶה - כֵּיוָן שֶׁרָאָה עַצְמוֹ מוֹשֵׁל, הִתְחִיל אוֹכֵל וְשׁוֹתֶה וּמְסַלְסֵל בִּשְׂעָרוֹ אָמַר הַקָּבָּ"ה אָבִיךָ מִתְאַבֵּל, וְאַתָּה מְסַלְסֵל בִּשְׂעָרֶךָ, אֲנִי מְגָרֶה בְךָ אֶת הַדּוֹב! מִיָּד...:

"And Yosef was well built and handsome" — As soon as he saw that he was ruler (in the house) he began to eat and drink and curl his hair. The Holy One, blessed be He, said to him, "Your father is mourning and you curl your hair! I will let a bear loose against you" (*Midrash Tanchuma, Vayeshev* 8). Immediately… (Rashi, *Bereishit* 39:6)

The Rabbis see something that evades Yaakov's detection, something self-absorbed in Yosef's personality. Yosef is certain that he is destined to lead, and he is attracted to the trappings of leadership.

In Yosef's descendants, specifically the kings cited above, this dysfunction morphs into a pathological spiritual sickness. Yerovam thinks it wise to repeat the greatest offense committed by his ancestors, and builds not one but two golden calves. He stations guards at the border crossings to prevent Jews from making pilgrimages to Jerusalem. Yerovam is willing to lead an entire generation astray just to assure his exalted position.

In one of the most extreme expressions of this illness, the Rabbis tell of a conversation between God and Yerovam:

תלמוד בבלי מסכת סנהדרין דף קב עמוד א
אַחַר הַדָּבָר הַזֶּה לֹא שָׁב יָרָבְעָם מִדַּרְכּוֹ הָרָעָה [מלכים א:יג] מַאי ,אַחַר'?
אָמַר רַבִּי אַבָּא, אַחַר שֶׁתְּפָשׂוֹ הַקָּדוֹשׁ בָּרוּךְ הוּא לְיָרָבְעָם בְּבִגְדוֹ, וְאָמַר לוֹ,
חֲזֹר בָּךְ, וַאֲנִי וְאַתָּה וּבֶן יִשַׁי נְטַיֵּל בְּגַן עֵדֶן. אָמַר לוֹ, מִי בָרֹאשׁ? אָמַר לוֹ, בֶּן
יִשַׁי בָּרֹאשׁ. אִי הָכִי - לָא בָּעֵינָא:

"And after this matter, Yerovam did not repent from his evil ways" (I Kings 13:33). What does "after" refer to? Rabbi Abba says: After the Holy One, Blessed be He, grabbed Yerovam by his garment, and said to him: Repent, and you and I and the son of Yishai will stroll together in the Garden of Eden. (Yerovam) said to Him: Who will be in the lead? (God) said to (Yerovam): The son of Yishai will be in the lead. (Yerovam) said: If so, I am not interested. (*Sanhedrin* 102a)

This passage expresses the almost unimaginable, unmitigated gall of Yerovam: God "grabbed Yerovam by his garment," a phrase that directly links Yerovam with his forefather Yosef. He is offered a stroll with God and the Messiah in the Garden of Eden, the most exclusive journey (pilgrimage?) in the most exclusive, exalted company—but his first question is, "Who is first?" Who will take the lead? Can Yerovam have imagined that God Himself would take a back seat to a mortal king? God seems to go along, hoping to teach Yerovam a lesson in humility, and does not put Himself in the lead, but when Yerovam hears that he himself will not be the star of the show—he rejects God!

This is the side of Yosef the brothers always saw. They sensed that his first, perhaps his only, concern was self-aggrandizement. And yet, Yosef's clothes were left behind when he escaped from the clutches of Mrs. Potifar, while Yerovam's garments are torn from him as he escapes the grasp of God—and there, in a nutshell, lies the complexity of Yosef. Yosef managed to suppress the negative aspects of his personality; Yerovam did not. But the brothers could not see this. When they looked at Yosef, they saw only the vainglorious, self-righteous, pretentious side of his personality. While Yaakov was blind to Yosef's darker side, the brothers were blind to the positive side. They knew nothing about Yosef's spiritual struggles and victories. They knew nothing of the temptations he faced and overcame. They did not hear him speak about God to all those around him, even at his own peril. They did not know that he took no personal credit for interpreting Pharaoh's dreams and saving Egypt. They did not know how truly great he was. And so, even when he delivers a speech and makes a commitment to set aside the past and care for them and their families, they hear the "B side" of the record: Yosef "forgives" them "for nothing;" he intimates that they were unimportant details in the story. Once again, they see and the parts of his personality they had always hated. Even worse, they were afraid of him:

בראשית פרק נ: יד-כא

וַיָּשָׁב יוֹסֵף מִצְרַיְמָה הוּא וְאֶחָיו וְכָל הָעֹלִים אִתּוֹ לִקְבֹּר אֶת אָבִיו אַחֲרֵי קָבְרוֹ אֶת אָבִיו: וַיִּרְאוּ אֲחֵי יוֹסֵף כִּי מֵת אֲבִיהֶם וַיֹּאמְרוּ לוּ יִשְׂטְמֵנוּ יוֹסֵף וְהָשֵׁב יָשִׁיב לָנוּ אֵת כָּל הָרָעָה אֲשֶׁר גָּמַלְנוּ אֹתוֹ: (טז) וַיְצַוּוּ אֶל יוֹסֵף לֵאמֹר אָבִיךָ צִוָּה לִפְנֵי מוֹתוֹ לֵאמֹר: (יז) כֹּה תֹאמְרוּ לְיוֹסֵף אָנָּא שָׂא נָא פֶּשַׁע אַחֶיךָ וְחַטָּאתָם כִּי רָעָה גְמָלוּךָ וְעַתָּה שָׂא נָא לְפֶשַׁע עַבְדֵי אֱלֹהֵי אָבִיךָ וַיֵּבְךְּ יוֹסֵף בְּדַבְּרָם אֵלָיו: (יח) וַיֵּלְכוּ גַּם אֶחָיו וַיִּפְּלוּ לְפָנָיו וַיֹּאמְרוּ הִנֶּנּוּ לְךָ לַעֲבָדִים: (יט) וַיֹּאמֶר אֲלֵהֶם יוֹסֵף אַל תִּירָאוּ כִּי הֲתַחַת אֱלֹהִים אָנִי: (כ) וְאַתֶּם חֲשַׁבְתֶּם עָלַי רָעָה אֱלֹהִים חֲשָׁבָהּ לְטֹבָה לְמַעַן עֲשֹׂה כַּיּוֹם הַזֶּה לְהַחֲיֹת עַם רָב: (כא) וְעַתָּה אַל תִּירָאוּ אָנֹכִי אֲכַלְכֵּל אֶתְכֶם וְאֶת טַפְּכֶם וַיְנַחֵם אוֹתָם וַיְדַבֵּר עַל לִבָּם:

Yosef returned to Egypt, he and his brothers and all who had gone up with him to bury his father. When Yosef's brothers saw that their father had died, they said, "What if Yosef still bears a grudge against us and pays us back for all the wrong that we did him!" So they sent this message to Yosef, "Before his death your father left this instruction: So shall you say to Yosef, 'Forgive, I urge you, the offense and guilt of your brothers who treated you so harshly.' Therefore, please forgive the offense of the servants of the God of your father." And Yosef was in tears as they spoke to him. His brothers went to him themselves, flung themselves before him, and said, "We are prepared to be your slaves." But Yosef said to them, "Have no fear! Am I a substitute for God? Besides, although you intended me harm, God intended it for good, so as to bring about the present result—the survival of many people. And so, fear not. I will sustain you and your children." Thus, he reassured them, speaking kindly to them. (*Bereishit* 50:14-21)

Despite living as a reunited family for seventeen years, the brothers were far from convinced that this was the true Yosef. They were convinced that the detente achieved was only due to their father's presence. Now, with Yaakov dead and buried, Yosef would take his revenge. Yosef for his part is shocked by their mistrust, hurt by the knowledge that they could even suspect him of such thoughts. He repeats the speech he had given when he first revealed his identity, and again exonerates them, explaining that this was God's will.

If Yosef's goal was rapprochement, he failed; if, however, his goal was to demonstrate his superiority, he was successful.

Yosef remains a complex character. He achieved dizzying power, unimaginable success. He created a system of social welfare in the depths of the dark ages by applying the teachings of Avraham on a national scale: Whereas Avraham opened his tent to tend to those in need, Yosef anticipated and responded to the needs of an empire,[8] all the while remaining true to the faith of Avraham, he had learned from his fathers, never losing sight of the hand of God that made his accomplishments possible.

Is this split—in Yosef's personality, and between Yosef and his brothers—ever healed? The final chapter of Yosef's life story is one of true reconciliation:

---

8. See Rabbi Joseph B. Soloveitchik, *Vision and Leadership: Reflections on Joseph and Moses*, Toras HoRav Foundation, Ktav 2013, page 28ff.

בראשית פרק נ, כד-כו

וַיֹּאמֶר יוֹסֵף אֶל־אֶחָיו אָנֹכִי מֵת וֵאלֹהִים פָּקֹד יִפְקֹד אֶתְכֶם וְהֶעֱלָה אֶתְכֶם מִן־הָאָרֶץ הַזֹּאת אֶל־הָאָרֶץ אֲשֶׁר נִשְׁבַּע לְאַבְרָהָם לְיִצְחָק וּלְיַעֲקֹב: וַיַּשְׁבַּע יוֹסֵף אֶת־בְּנֵי יִשְׂרָאֵל לֵאמֹר פָּקֹד יִפְקֹד אֱלֹהִים אֶתְכֶם וְהַעֲלִתֶם אֶת־עַצְמֹתַי מִזֶּה: וַיָּמָת יוֹסֵף בֶּן־מֵאָה וָעֶשֶׂר שָׁנִים וַיַּחַנְטוּ אֹתוֹ וַיִּישֶׂם בָּאָרוֹן בְּמִצְרָיִם:

> Yosef said to his brothers, "I am about to die. God will surely take notice of you and bring you up from this land to the land that He promised on oath to Avraham, to Yitzchak, and to Yaakov." So Yosef made the sons of Israel swear, saying, "When God has taken notice of you, you shall carry up my bones from here." Yosef died at the age of one hundred and ten years; and he was embalmed and placed in a coffin in Egypt. (*Bereishit* 50:24-26)

On his deathbed, in his final words to his brothers, Yosef begs them to promise that they will take his remains with them when they leave Egypt; he longs to be a part of the family, and not a part of the Egyptian pantheon. At last, there is peace—not only because the man they fear is on death's door, but because a real change has occurred. If we listen carefully, as the brothers most certainly did, we hear a different Yosef. Yosef finally understood what his father Yaakov had known before he came to Egypt; this would not be a five-year visit to wait out the famine. This is not the story of Yosef. This is the start of a long, difficult exile. Yosef's dreams are no longer the point; history has moved on. They are now all characters in the dreams and visions of Avraham, Yitzchak, and Yaakov. The Children of Israel—Yosef included, will be in Egypt for a very long time—but God will redeem them, and when He does, Yosef wants to be a part of it. He wants to leave with his brothers—the brothers who may never have loved him, who certainly never displayed love for him; the brothers for whom he had cared for the past seventy years.

Now, something has changed: Yosef, who had always been so brash, so confident, was suddenly vulnerable. For the first time, he needed them—not as pawns or marionettes in his show, but as brothers. When he acknowledges that, their relationship changes: At last, they are equals. They promise Yosef that they will see that his remains are returned home. And the moment they make this vow, the family finally becomes whole. They are brothers at last, equals, the founders of one nation.

Pharaoh would forget Yosef, but his brothers, who finally felt like brothers, would never forget Yosef. And the brothers who sold him into slavery would bring him back home, as brothers, forever, at last.

The Death of Yaakov

Parashat Vayechi is different from the other *parshiyot* of the Torah. The beginning of every other *parashah* is delineated by a new paragraph, or at least an indentation in the text of the Torah; only *Vayechi* is *satum* ("sealed" or blocked by text). Rashi quotes the Midrash which explains this idiosyncrasy.

> **רש"י בראשית פרק מז:כח**
> ויחי יעקב - לָמָּה פָּרָשָׁה זוֹ סְתוּמָה? לְפִי שֶׁכֵּיָוָן שֶׁנִּפְטַר יַעֲקֹב אָבִינוּ נִסְתְּמוּ עֵינֵיהֶם וְלִבָּם שֶׁל יִשְׂרָאֵל מִצָּרַת הַשִּׁעְבּוּד, שֶׁהִתְחִילוּ לְשַׁעְבְּדָם; דָּבָר אַחֵר: שֶׁבִּקֵּשׁ לְגַלּוֹת אֶת הַקֵּץ לְבָנָיו, וְנִסְתַּם מִמֶּנּוּ. בְּבַ"ר:

> Why is this portion not divided off [*satum*, literally, "sealed"]? The death of Yaakov caused a closing of the eyes and hearts of Israel, due to the troubles of the oppression which began [with Yaakov's death]. An alternative explanationis that [Yaakov] wished to reveal the end of days to his children, but he was blocked from doing so. (Rashi, *Bereishit* 47:28, based on *Bereishit Rabbah* 96:1)

The death of Yaakov marks the end of an era. With his demise, the patriarchal age comes to a close and a new generation begins. *Parashat Vayechi* is the end of *Sefer Bereishit*, literally as well as ideologically. It is the end of the beginning, an end to the epoch of the founders of Judaism, namely the patriarchs and matriarchs. Rashi's comments establish *Vayechi* as not only the close of a book, but as a closed book: At the end of his life, Yaakov wanted to reveal the future to his children, but at the moment this revelation was to take place, Yaakov's clairvoyance was obscured.

בראשית פרק מט, א-ג

וַיִּקְרָא יַעֲקֹב אֶל־בָּנָיו וַיֹּאמֶר הֵאָסְפוּ וְאַגִּידָה לָכֶם אֵת אֲשֶׁר־יִקְרָא אֶתְכֶם בְּאַחֲרִית הַיָּמִים: הִקָּבְצוּ וְשִׁמְעוּ בְּנֵי יַעֲקֹב וְשִׁמְעוּ אֶל־יִשְׂרָאֵל אֲבִיכֶם: רְאוּבֵן בְּכֹרִי אַתָּה ...:

Yaakov called to his sons and said, "Gather, and I will tell you what will happen to you in the end of days. Come together, sons of Yaakov, and listen to your father, Israel. Reuven, you are my firstborn..." (*Bereishit* 49:1, 3)

Yaakov gathers his children around him; his stated intention is to inform them what the future holds for them and their descendants, but instead of this prophetic revelation, he proceeds to speak about the personalities and traits of each of his sons, and of the tribes that will descend from them. What happened?

רש"י, בראשית מט:א

וְאַגִּידָה לָכֶם - בִּקֵּשׁ לְגַלּוֹת אֶת הַקֵּץ וְנִסְתַּלְּקָה מִמֶּנּוּ שְׁכִינָה וְהִתְחִיל אוֹמֵר דְּבָרִים אֲחֵרִים:

Yaakov wished to reveal the end of days but the *Shechinah* [God's Presence] left him, so Yaakov began to say other things. (Rashi, *Bereishit* 49:1, based on *Pesachim* 56a)

Yaakov's response to this loss of vision is fear. The Gemara describes the scene:

תלמוד בבלי מסכת פסחים דף נו עמוד א

כְּדִדְרִישׁ רַבִּי שִׁמְעוֹן בֶּן לָקִישׁ, דְּאָמַר רַבִּי שִׁמְעוֹן בֶּן לָקִישׁ, (בראשית מט) "וַיִּקְרָא יַעֲקֹב אֶל בָּנָיו" וְגוֹ', בִּיקֵּשׁ יַעֲקֹב לְגַלּוֹת לְבָנָיו קֵץ הַיָּמִין, וְנִסְתַּלְּקָה מִמֶּנּוּ שְׁכִינָה, אָמַר, שֶׁמָּא חַס וְשָׁלוֹם יֵשׁ בְּמִטָּתִי פָּסוּל, כְּאַבְרָהָם שֶׁיָּצָא מִמֶּנּוּ יִשְׁמָעֵאל, וְאָבִי כְיִצְחָק שֶׁיָּצָא מִמֶּנּוּ עֵשָׂו? אָמְרוּ לוֹ בָּנָיו, "שְׁמַע יִשְׂרָאֵל, ה' אֱלֹהֵינוּ, ה' אֶחָד", אָמְרוּ, כְּשֵׁם שֶׁאֵין בְּלִבְּךָ אֶלָּא אֶחָד, כָּךְ אֵין בְּלִבֵּנוּ אֶלָּא אֶחָד. בְּאוֹתָהּ שָׁעָה, פָּתַח יַעֲקֹב [אָבִינוּ] וְאָמַר, "בָּרוּךְ שֵׁם כְּבוֹד מַלְכוּתוֹ, לְעוֹלָם וָעֶד."

Yaakov wished to reveal the end of days, but the *Shechinah* left him. He said, "Perhaps there is a defect in my bed [i.e., with my children], Heaven forbid, like there was with Avraham, who fathered Yishmael, and with my father, Yitzchak, who fathered Esav." His sons said to him, "*Shema Yisrael, Hashem Elokeinu, Hashem Echad* — Hear, Yisrael, God is our Lord, God is One.... Just as in your heart there is only One [God], so, too, in our hearts there is only One [God]." At that moment, Yaakov responded, "*Baruch Shem kevod malchuto le-olam va'ed* — Blessed be the glorious Name of His Kingship forever and ever." (*Pesachim* 56a)[1]

When Yaakov's desire to share his knowledge with his children was frustrated, he feared that this was indicative of some lack in his childre— and by extension, in himself, and in *Knesset Yisrael* (the congregation of Israel). As we have seen in earlier sections (particularly *Vayeitzei*), the children of Yaakov are no longer individuals; they represent the nation

---

1. The context of this Talmudic passage is a debate over the propriety of reciting the verse *"Baruch Shem kevod malchuto le-olam va'ed."* This sentence is not found in the text of the Torah; why, then should it be inserted into our recitation of the *Shema*? The midrashic tradition that Yaakov uttered this verse as a response to the *Shema* on his deathbed suffices for a compromise to have been reached: the *Baruch Shem* is not spoken out loud, it is whispered. In fact, one midrashic tradition reports that Yaakov himself said the *Baruch Shem* in a whisper. (*Bereishit Rabbah*, Theodor Albeck edition, *Vayechi* 96).

In a *shiur* I attended, Rabbi Soloveitchik suggested that when Yakakov saw and heard that his sons were outwardly devout, he began to fear that they were merely putting on a show of faith for his benefit. When his sons declared *Shema Yisrael* out loud, in a public declaration of belief, Yaakov taught them, by whispering his response, that they must accept God in their hearts, in their thoughts, in their inner world. Rabbi Soloveitchik mentioned the similarity between the Hebrew words *Baruch Shem kevod malchuto le-olam va'ed* and the Aramaic formulation *"Yehai shmei rabbah mevorach l'oalam ul'olmei olmaya"* – which is the central phrase in the *Kaddish*, the mourner's prayer. Was Yaakov perchance teaching his children to say the *Kaddish*? Was he saying *Kaddish* for himself? See *Targum Yerushalmi* 49:1. For other versions of this teaching see *Sifri Va-etchanan*, *piska* 31, which seems to be Rambam's source. Also see Rambam, *Hilchot Kri'at Shema* 1:4, where he describes the "Baruch Shem" as "praise."

of Israel. If something is lacking in Yaakov's children, the repercussions will be felt by the entire nation. For Yaakov, this possibility is frightening: On his deathbed, it seems to him that he has failed his mission.

As we have seen, the Talmud connects Yaakov's fear to his own family's history: Both his trailblazing grandfather and his saintly father had sired errant offspring; could he expect his own children to be greater than theirs? If Avraham could father a Yishmael and Yitzchak could father an Esav, why should Yaakov expect that all his own children would be righteous?[2] This question is closely related to the Kabbalistic

---

2. See Rav Yeshaya Halevi Horowitz, *Shla Ha-Kadosh, Parashat Toldot*, and his son, Rav Shabtai Sheftel ben Yeshaya Halevi Horowitz, in *Shefa Tal, Hakdamah: Ben Me'ah Shanah*:

ספר השל"ה הקדוש - ספר בראשית - פרשת תולדות תורה אור (ה)

כבר כתבתי בפרשת חיי שרה ענין בכל מכל כל, מאברהם יצא קליפת ישמעאל, ובן בנו הוא עשו, ומיצחק יצא קליפת עשו. וענין יציאת הקליפות מאבות הקדושים, הוא כמו קדימת הקליפה לפרי, שאי אפשר לפרי בלא הקדמת קליפה שהוא הנץ והפרח, ויעקב הוא הפרי. אבל יש סוד בדבר, כי הקליפה יש לה אחיזה בקדושה בשרשה, ובשרשה למעלה נדבקת בקדושה, והטומאה היא בהתפשטותא. ולעתיד תחזור ותטהר על ידי הצדיקים הקדושים המכניעים אותה, בסוד איזהו גבור הכובש את יצרו (אבות ד, א), שבארתי בכמה מקומות שהענין הוא אינו הורג את יצרו הרע רק כובש תחתיו ומטהרו, שלוקח מדת היצר הרע ומשתמש בהם עבודת השם יתברך. כגון קנאה קנאת סופרים, חמדה חומד חמודה גנוזה, וכיוצא באלה הרבה. וזהו ענין שאמרו לאברהם אבינו נשיא אלהים אתה בתוכינו, כלומר בתוכיות שלנו, דהיינו בשרשינו אתה נשיא, ועל ידך נטהר לעתיד. וכל האומות הודו לזה, כמו שאמרו רז"ל (עי' ב"ר מג, ו) עמק השוה, שהשוו כולם והמליכו את אברהם על עצמם. זהו בחינת יציאת הקליפות מאברהם. אבל אברהם בעצמו הוא עצם מעלת ישראל, ויותר מעלתו ממעלת שאר האבות. והענין שמו ישראל הוא יותר בנעלם ובייותר עליה ודקות למעלה, ושם אברהם הוא על שם אב המון נתתיך בגוים, והוא ענין נשיא אלהים אתה בתוכינו, שפירשו כי כן נאחזים בשרשם. והנה אברם נקרא בעודו אברם, רק עתה נתוסף בהולידו את יצחק שיצא ממנו עשו נמצא הותחל בו הסוד של אב המון בעודו אברם, רק עתה נתוסף בהולידו את יצחק שיצא ממנו עשו שהוא כולל כל הקליפות. והנה ראה בעיניך הגלות הזה נקרא על שם אדום, אעפ"י שיש מלכיות גדולות מלכות ישמעאל ועוד הרבה, וכולם נכללים בשם גלות אדום. והרמב"ן האריך בזה בפרשת בלק (כד, כ). הרי מבואר אברם נקרא אברהם:

ספר שפע טל - הקדמה בן מאה שנה

בכל עת יהיו בגדיך לבנים ושמן על ראשך לא יחסר שהם תורה ומצות וכן מנח נולד שם צדיק כמוהו מאברהם יצחק וכן מיצחק יעקב עם כל זה לא היו מלאים בסלת ההוא כי מכל אחד מהם יצא קליפה וסיג ופסולת מאוד מאברהם יצא קין מאדם ישמעאל מיצחק עשו אף הגם שהצדיקים בעצמם היו סלת נקי ולא נמצא בעצמותן שום פסול וחטא עם כל זה לא היו ממולאים בסלת הנקי ההוא כי היה סיג הקליפה ופסולת מעורב במטנן שלא היתה שלימה ומפני זה לא נאמר בהם מלאים אבל אצל כפות זהב מלאה נאמר מפני שהם רומזים על מטתו

discussion of the three *avot* (forefathers), specifically the importance of the number three. Why were there three patriarchs and not two or, for that matter, six? What delineates the era of the patriarchs, which, as we have noted, comes to an end in our *parashah*?

According to Kabbalistic thought, each of the three patriarchs awakened a unique spiritual awareness in the world; each established one of the three pillars necessary to support the establishment of the nation. Avraham brought the Godly attribute of *chesed* (kindness) to the world.[3]

של יעקב אבינו ע"ה כי היה סלת נקי כלה נקי טהור כלה מלאה קטרת להקטיר קטורת לפני ולפנים לעשות רצון אביהם שבשמים וכלן שבטי יה עדות לישראל שעל כלן העיד הקב"ה בעצמו כמה שהחתי' שמו יה' חלק חצי השם מעצמותו השם יד"וד בהם כדפירשנו בעניין חלק י"י עמו והוא אמרו הראובנ"י החנוכ"י הפלא"י וכל זה שיהיה לעדות ולראייה גלוייה ומפורסמת שהם בניו ממש חלק אלוה חלק מעצמותו ב"ה:

3. The association of Avraham with the attribute of *chesed* is based on a verse in *Micha* 7:20. While it is referenced in Midrashic sources, Avraham's identification with *chesed* is stronger in mystical sources and later Chasidic and non-Chasidic literature. See *Zohar Bereishit* 213b, *Sefer ha-Bahir* section 135:

מיכה פרק ז פסוק כ
תִּתֵּן אֱמֶת לְיַעֲקֹב חֶסֶד לְאַבְרָהָם אֲשֶׁר־נִשְׁבַּעְתָּ לַאֲבֹתֵינוּ מִימֵי קֶדֶם:

מסכתות קטנות מסכת כלה רבתי פרק ט
דרש רבא, כל מי שיש בו שלש מדות הללו, בידוע שהוא מזרעו של אברהם, רחמן וביישן וגומל חסדים; בשלמא גומל חסדים, שנאמר תתן אמת ליעקב חסד לאברהם; בישן נמי כדדרש רבא, דדרש רבא הנה נא ידעתי כי אשה יפת מראה את, ולא עד עכשיו; אלא רחמן, הא אברהם לא רחים על בריה, היינו רבותיה דאברהם, להודיעך חיבתו בהקדוש ברוך הוא.

בראשית רבה (וילנא) פרשת חיי שרה פרשה נח:ט
אַחֲרֵי כֵן קָבַר אַבְרָהָם (בראשית כג, יט), הֲדָא הוּא דִכְתִיב (משלי כא, כא): רֹדֵף צְדָקָה וָחֶסֶד יִמְצָא חַיִּים צְדָקָה וְכָבוֹד. רֹדֵף צְדָקָה, זֶה אַבְרָהָם, שֶׁנֶּאֱמַר (בראשית יח, יט): וְשָׁמְרוּ דֶּרֶךְ ה' לַעֲשׂוֹת צְדָקָה. וָחֶסֶד, שֶׁגָּמַל חֶסֶד לְשָׂרָה. יִמְצָא חַיִּים, (בראשית כה, ז): וּשְׁנֵי חַיֵּי אַבְרָהָם מְאַת שָׁנָה וְשִׁבְעִים שָׁנָה וְחָמֵשׁ שָׁנִים. צְדָקָה וְכָבוֹד, אָמַר רַבִּי שְׁמוּאֵל בַּר יִצְחָק, אָמַר לוֹ הַקָּדוֹשׁ בָּרוּךְ הוּא אֲנִי אֻמָּנוּתִי גּוֹמֵל חֲסָדִים, תָּפַשְׂתָּ אֻמָּנוּתִי בּוֹא לְבֹשׁ לְבוּשִׁי (בראשית כד, א): וְאַבְרָהָם זָקֵן בָּא בַּיָּמִים.

בראשית רבה (וילנא) פרשת חיי שרה פרשה ס:ב
וַיֹּאמַר ה' אֱלֹהֵי אֲדֹנִי אַבְרָהָם וגו' (בראשית כד, יב). וַעֲשֵׂה חֶסֶד עִם אֲדֹנִי אַבְרָהָם, הִתְחַלְתָּ גְּמֹר. רַבִּי חַגַּי בְּשֵׁם רַבִּי יִצְחָק אָמַר הַכֹּל צְרִיכִין לְחֶסֶד אֲפִלּוּ אַבְרָהָם שֶׁהַחֶסֶד מִתְגַּלְגֵּל בָּעוֹלָם בִּשְׁבִילוֹ, נִצְרַךְ לְחֶסֶד, שֶׁנֶּאֱמַר: וַעֲשֵׂה חֶסֶד עִם אֲדֹנִי אַבְרָהָם, הִתְחַלְתָּ גְּמֹר.

Yitzchak represents *gevurah* or *din* (justice).[4] The *din* of Yitzchak is, in

מדרש תנחומא (בובר) פרשת חיי שרה

עמד אברהם ודיבק במדת חסד, א"ל הקדוש ברוך הוא שלי היתה המדה הזאת, ואתה אחזתה בה, חייך שאני עושה אותך כיוצא בי, מנין שנאמר חזה הוית עד די כרסוון רמיו ועתיק יומין יתב לבושיה כתלג חיור וגו' (דניאל ז ט), מה כתיב למעלה מן הענין, ואחרי כן קבר אברהם את שרה אשתו (בראשית כג יט), עמד ונטפל בה, א"ל הקדוש ברוך הוא ראוי אתה לעטרה, שנאמר ואברהם זקן.

זוהר כרך ג (דברים) פרשת ואתחנן [דף רסב עמוד ב]

תָּנֵינָן, וְאָהַבְתָּ מַאן דְּרָחִים לֵיהּ לְמַלְכָּא, עָבֵיד יַתִּיר טִיבוּ חֶסֶד עִם כֹּלָּא. וְחֶסֶד יַתִּירָא, הַהוּא דְאִקְרֵי חֶסֶד דֶּאֱמֶת, דְּלָא בָעֵי אֲגַר עֲלֵיהּ, אֶלָּא בְּגִין רְחִימוּתָא דְּמַלְכָּא, דְּרָחִים לֵיהּ יַתִּיר, וּבְרֶחִימוּתָא דְּמַלְכָּא תַּלְיָא חֶסֶד. וְעַל דָּא אִקְרֵי (ישעיה מא) אַבְרָהָם אוֹהֲבִי. וּבְגִין דְּרָחִים לֵיהּ יַתִּיר, אַסְגֵּי חֶסֶד בְּעָלְמָא. וְעַל דָּא, הָכָא, וְאָהַבְתָּ. וּבִרְחִימוּתָא תַּלְיָא חֶסֶד, וְדָא הִיא בֵּיתָא תְּלִיתָאָה.

זוהר חלק א דף ריג/ב

תָּא חֲזֵי, מְנַיִן שֶׁקָּרָא קוּדְשָׁא בְּרִיךְ הוּא לְיַעֲקֹב אֵ"ל, אַתְּ בְּעֵלְאָה, וַאֲנָא אֶהֵא בְּתַתָּאָה, (נ"א את תהא בתתאה, ואנא אהא אלהא בעלאה), מַאי קָא מַיְירֵי. (בראשית יז) וַיַּעַל אֱלֹהִים מֵעַל אַבְרָהָם, אֲבָהָתָן אִינוּן רְתִיכָאן דְּקוּדְשָׁא בְּרִיךְ הוּא. תָּנָא, (מיכה ז) תִּתֵּן אֱמֶת לְיַעֲקֹב חֶסֶד לְאַבְרָהָם, הָא תְּרֵין סְפִירָן, בִּתְרֵין רְתִיכָן, רַבְרְבָן עִלָּאִין: תְּלִיתָאָה יִצְחָק, מַאי (בראשית לא) וַיִּשָּׁבַע יַעֲקֹב בְּפַחַד אָבִיו יִצְחָק. וּבְגִין פַּחַד יִצְחָק דְּהֲוָה סְפִירָה, וְקוּדְשָׁא בְּרִיךְ הוּא דְּהוּא יָקָרָא כָּרְסֵי רְתִיכָא עִלָּאָה, וּסְפִירָה דְיִצְחָק הִיא מֵעֵלָּאָה, מְפָרְשָׁא יַתִּיר מִכָּל סְפִירָן דַּאֲבָהָתָא, הֲדָא הוּא דִכְתִיב וַיִּשָּׁבַע יַעֲקֹב בְּפַחַד אָבִיו יִצְחָק:

ספר הבהיר - המיוחס לרבי נחוניא בן הקנה ז"ל

קלה. אמר ר' יוחנן מאי דכתיב (שמות י"ז יא) והיה כאשר ירים משה ידו וגבר ישראל (שמות י"ג יא) וכאשר יניח ידו וגבר עמלק, מלמד שהעולם מתקיים בשביל נשיאות כפים, מאי טעמא, משום דאותו כח שניתן ליעקב שמו ישראל, לאברהם ליצחק וליעקב ניתנו כוחות, אחד לכל אחד ואחד, ובמדה שהלך כל אחד ואחד דוגמתם ניתן לו, אברהם גמל חסד לעולם שהיה מזמין לכל באי עולם ועוברי דרכים מזון וגומל חסד ויוצא לקראתם דכתיב (בראשית י"ח ב) וירץ לקראתם, ועוד וישתחוו ארצה (שם) זאת היתה גמילות חסד שלימה, והקב"ה מדד לו במדתו ונתן לו מדת החסד דכתיב (מיכה ז' כ) תתן אמת ליעקב חסד לאברהם, אשר נשבעת לאבותינו מימי קדם, מאי מימי קדם, מלמד שאם לא היה אברהם גומל חסד וזוכה למדת חסד לא היה יעקב זוכה למדת אמת, שבזכות שזכה אברהם למדת חסד זכה יצחק למדת פחד דכתיב (בראשית ל"א נג) וישבע יעקב בפחד אביו יצחק, אטו יש איש שישבע כך באמונת פחד אביו, אלא עד כאן לא ניתן ליעקב כח, ונשבע בכח שניתן לאביו שנאמר וישבע יעקב בפחד אבי יצחק, ומאי ניהו, הוא דכתיב (מ"א י"ח לח) ותפול אש ותאכל את העולה ואת העצים ואת האבנים ואת העפר ואת המים אשר בתעלה לחכה, וכתיב (דברים ד כד) כי ה' אלהיך אש אוכלה הוא אל קנא:

4. While the association of Yitzchak with the attribute of *din* is considered a "given" in many later sources, an explicit statement of this association is not easily found in Talmudic or Midrashic sources. In my opinion, though, this association is implied in *Vayikra Rabbah* 29. Also see *Zohar Bereishit* 72a, *Zohar Bereishit* 213b, (cited in note 3, which refers to *Pachad Yitzchak*) and *Tikkunei Zohar* 139a:

Vayechi: The Death of Yaakov

a sense, antithetical to *chesed*, but each is required as a counterbalance for the other. Yaakov represents *tiferet* (splendor, or beauty), the result of the balance of *chesed* and *gevurah*. To borrow the Hegelian model, we may say that the patriarchs represent thesis, antithesis, and synthesis. Once synthesis is achieved, the nation can emerge.

There is, however, another side to this coin, another philosophical thread that is woven through our history but is not a part of this synthesis: Avraham also fathered Yishmael, and Yitzchak fathered Esav.

Who was Yishmael? What was his spiritual "personality"? According to Rabbinic teaching, Yishmael was the counterfeit of Avraham.[5] Rather

---

זוהר כרך א (בראשית) פרשת נח עב

תָּא חֲזֵי, אַבְרָהָם אַתְקִין צְלוֹתָא דְצַפְרָא וְאוֹדַע טִיבוּ דְמָארֵיהּ בְּעָלְמָא. וְאַתְקִין הַהִיא שַׁעְתָּא בְּתִקּוּנָהּ כְּדְקָא יָאוּת דִּכְתִיב, (בראשית כב) וַיַּשְׁכֵּם אַבְרָהָם בַּבֹּקֶר. יִצְחָק אַתְקִין צְלוֹתָא דְמִנְחָה וְאוֹדַע בְּעָלְמָא דְּאִית דִּין וְאִית דַּיָּין דְּיָכוֹל לְשֵׁזָבָא וּלְמֵידָן עָלְמָא.

תיקוני זוהר נספח (מעמ' קלט) דף קלט עמוד א

בְּרֵאשִׁית בָּרָא אלהי"ם, בְּרֵאשִׁית בָּרָ"א תַּ"י/שׁ, דָּא אֵילוֹ דְיִצְחָק. בְּרֵאשִׁית תַּמָּן א"שׁ לְעוֹלָה דְיִצְחָק, וְרָזָא דְמִלָּה (ועל אלין תלת גלגולין אתמר (שיר ז ב) מה יפו פעמיך בנעלים בת נדיב, (רות ד ו) וזאת לפנים בא אימא עלאה עלמא דאתי, ד"א לגביה צריך חליצה, והדא הוא דכ תיב (שמות ג ה) של נעליך וגומר, ואם לאו לית לון רשו לרווחא רמתאה (נ"א לרוחא דמיתא) לסלקא לעלמא דאתי, ובגין דאיהו יום הכפורים אסיר בנעילת הסנדל), (בראשית כב ז) הִנֵּה הָאֵשׁ וְהָעֵצִים וְאַיֵּה הַשֶּׂה לְעֹלָה, נָפַק קָלָא וְאָמַר מְשִׁיחַ בְּרֵאשִׁית יוֹמֵי אִתְבְּרֵי לַעֲקֵדָה דְיִצְחָק. ד בְּגִין דְּלָא אִית קָרְבָּן דְּבָטִיל מוֹתָנָא כַּעֲקֵדָה דְיִצְחָק, דְּאִתְּמַר בֵּיהּ (שם) וַיַּעֲקֹד אֶת יִצְחָק בְּנוֹ, אִתְקַשַּׁר מִדַּת הַדִּין (מלאך המות) וְאִתְעַקַּד לְעֵילָא, וְלָא הֲוָה לֵיהּ רְשׁוּ לְקָרְבָא לְגַבֵּי דִינָא רַבְרְבָא דְאִיהוּ גְבוּרָה, לְתַבְעָא דִינָא, וַעֲקֵדָה דְּנָא מוֹעִילָה לְגָלוּתָא, דַּהֲוָה עָתִיד לְאִתְקַטְלָא מָשִׁיחַ בֶּן יוֹסֵף, וְקָלָא נָפִיק מֵהַהוּא זִמְנָא (שם) אַל תַּעַשׂ לוֹ מְאוּמָה (שם יב), בְּגִין דְּאִתְגַּבְּרוּ רַחֲמֵי עַל דִּינָא, וְרָזָא דְמִלָּה (תהלים צח א) הוֹשִׁיעָה לּוֹ יְמִינוֹ, וּלְבָתַר זְרוֹעַ קָדְשׁוֹ, דְּגָבַר יְמִינָא עַל שְׂמָאלָא.

---

5. See commentary of Rav Moshe Zachut on the *Zohar, Shemot* page 224b; commentary of *HaChayat* on *Maarechet Elohut*, chapter 10; Rav Shneuer Zalman of Lyadi, *Torah Or* on *Megillat Esther*:

פירוש הרמ"ז על זוהר שמות - עמוד 421

ואין קושיה מאברהם שהוליד את ישמעאל, כי הוא היה חלק הקליפה שדבק בו מצד אבותיו ואחר כך נפרד ממנו. ועוד כשהוליד את ישמעאל עדיין היתה הערלה דבוקה בו וכשנימול זכה לאות ה' שה"ס ה' חסדים. דא אתפשט לטב וכו', פי' שאפילו החיצונים צריכים לשפע להתקיים.

פירוש החיי"ט על ספר מערכת האלהות - פרק עשירי

מפני כי גם נגד חסד חוץ למרכבה יש קליפה והוא ישמע

than emulating his father or blazing his own spiritual path, Yishmael imitated his father in a superficial, external manner, and the result was a perversion of the spiritual awareness Avraham brought to the world. Thus, Avraham expressed *chesed* by giving to others, emulating the God of *chesed* who creates and sustains the world. Yet Avraham understood that although the act of giving is Godly, *chesed*, too, must have limitations. Taken to extremes, *chesed* can lead to immorality and sexual licentiousness. In fact, the Torah describes incest as *chesed*—perhaps better described as *chesed* gone amok.

ויקרא פרק כ:יז
וְאִישׁ אֲשֶׁר־יִקַּח אֶת־אֲחֹתוֹ בַּת־אָבִיו אוֹ בַת־אִמּוֹ וְרָאָה אֶת־עֶרְוָתָהּ וְהִיא־תִרְאֶה אֶת־עֶרְוָתוֹ חֶסֶד הוּא וְנִכְרְתוּ לְעֵינֵי בְּנֵי עַמָּם עֶרְוַת אֲחֹתוֹ גִּלָּה עֲוֹנוֹ יִשָּׂא:

If a man takes his sister, daughter of his father or daughter of his mother, and sees her nakedness, and she sees his nakedness, it is "*chesed*." They shall be cut off before their nation. His sister's nakedness he uncovered, and he shall bear his sin. (*Vayikra* 20:17)

Chesed that is not governed by some type of moral system is destructive—and that is precisely the indictment of Yishmael found in rabbinic literature: Yishmael made cynical use of his father's teachings, disconnecting the attribute of *chesed* from its moral moorings.[6]

ספר תורה אור - על מגלת אסתר <דף קיט/ד>:
ואמנם לא כל אדם זוכה למעלת אברהם בתחלה כי לבבו נאמן זה הוא שנשלם אברהם במעלה ונק' אברהם בתוספת ה"א והיינו לאחר שנימול משא"כ קודם שנמול שנק' אברם הרי יצא ממנו ישמעאל שהוא בחי' קליפה דחסד עליון דקדושה לפי שאברהם היה מרכבה לבחי' חסד עליון דקדושה ולכך אמר לו ישמעאל יחי' לפניך שהן בחי' מותרי החסד דהיינו שיהא אור החסד מתפשט גם למטה להיות ישמעאל לפי שבכח החסד העליון לירד ולהתפשט עד תכלית המדרגה היותר תחתונה כי לפ"ע הרוממות והגדולה שנק' חסד אינו תופס מקום לפניו כחשיכה כאורה כו' וכעניין שממית בידים תתפש והיא בהיכלי מלך משום דהשממית לעוצם ערכה היא בהיכלי מלך המרומם ולא מקפיד עליה כו' וד"ל. וזהו הטעם שצריך ת"ח להיות בו גסות הרוח חלק א' מס"ד כו' כי הנה ידוע דע"י אתעדל"ת אתעדל"ע נעשה באותה הדוגמא ממש כי רוח אייתי רוח ואמשיך רוח כו'. והנה באתעדל"ת זה בת"ח נעשה אתעדל"ע להיות למעלה ג"כ בחי' גיאות והתנשאות בקדושה העליונה כי ע"י שנמצא בת"ח גסות בחי' במה שאינו :

---

6. Avraham's ne'er-do-well nephew Lot, who also grew up in Avraham's tent, had a twisted understanding of *chesed*: He invites strangers into his home, but offered up his daughters to the marauding crowd outside his door.

בראשית רבה (וילנא) פרשת וירא פרשה נג סימן יא
וַתֵּרֶא שָׂרָה אֶת בֶּן הָגָר הַמִּצְרִית (בראשית כא, ט), אָמַר רַבִּי שִׁמְעוֹן בֶּן יוֹחָאי רַבִּי עֲקִיבָא הָיָה אוֹמֵר בּוֹ דָּבָר לִגְנַאי, וַאֲנִי אוֹמֵר בּוֹ דָּבָר לְשֶׁבַח, דָּרַשׁ רַבִּי עֲקִיבָא וַתֵּרֶא שָׂרָה וגו', אֵין מְצַחֵק אֶלָּא גִּלּוּי עֲרָיוֹת, הֵיךְ מָה דְאַתְּ אָמַר (בראשית לט, יז): בָּא אֵלַי הָעֶבֶד הָעִבְרִי אֲשֶׁר הֵבֵאתָ לָּנוּ לְצַחֶק בִּי, מְלַמֵּד שֶׁהָיְתָה אִמֵּנוּ שָׂרָה רוֹאָה אוֹתוֹ לְיִשְׁמָעֵאל מְכַבֵּשׁ גִּנּוֹת וְצָד נְשֵׁי אֲנָשִׁים וּמְעַנֶּה אוֹתָן.

"Sarah saw the son of Hagar the Egyptian" (*Bereishit* 21:9) — [he was guilty of] sexual immorality... this teaches us that our matriarch Sarah was aware that Yishmael conquered young maidens and hunted married women and abused[7] them. (*Bereishit Rabbah* 53:11)

Yishmael twisted Avraham's great teachings; it is not difficult to imagine how he misused the concept of *chesed* to satisfy his own desires: "My father teaches that *chesed* is what is important. If you are really dedicated to the idea of *chesed*, of giving to others, then you should certainly give your body to me." Where Avraham taught the idea of love, Yishmael espoused "free love." If Avraham taught people to "love your neighbor as youself," Yishmael taught that people should love their neighbors' spouses. The counterfeit—in the language of the mystics, the *klipah*—of *chesed* is sexual immorality, and this was Yishmael's domain.

Yitzchak endeavored to create a spiritual balance to his father's *chesed*. His greatness was *gevurah*, strength, a second aspect through which God is revealed in this world. The Jewish teaching of *gevurah* is encapsulated in the words of the Sages:

---

7. See above, *Parashat Vayeitzei*, for a discussion of the word *innui*, and the probability that it should be translated as "violation" or "rape." Also see Tosefta *Sotah* 6:6, and the comments of Professor Saul Lieberman in *Tosefta Ki-fshutah*, (Sotah p. 670):who suggests that the phrase used in the Tosefta מכבש את הגגות may indicate anal sex, and possibly homosexual relations.

תוספתא מסכת סוטה (ליברמן) פרק ו הלכה ו
רבי אליעזר בנו של ר' יוסי הגלילי אומר אין שחוק האמור כאן אלא גלוי עריות שנאמר בא אלי העבד העברי וגומר מלמד שהיתה אמנו שרה רואה את ישמעאל מכבש את הגגות ומענה את הנשים:

משנה מסכת אבות פרק ד:א

אֵיזֶהוּ גִבּוֹר, הַכּוֹבֵשׁ אֶת יִצְרוֹ.

Who is strong? He who controls his desires. (*Avot* 4:1)

As God controlled His infiniteness to create a finite world, man must control himself, and a beautiful world will emerge. The *klipah* of *gevurah*, the counterfeit of this attribute, is the individual who tries to control or dominate others. The "worst-case scenario" is when the desire to control others leads to bloodshed. This was Esav's forte, as is suggested by the name by which he and his descendents were known: Edom.[8]

Esav, like his uncle Yishmael, was superficial.[9] He did not deeply understand his father's teachings. He twisted the idea of *gevurah*

---

8. See Rashi, *Bereishit* 25:25:

רש"י בראשית פרק כה פסוק כה
אדמוני - סִימָן הוּא שֶׁיְּהֵא שׁוֹפֵךְ דָּמִים:

"He was red" — this is a sign that he will spill blood.

9. This superficiality is intimated (or foreshadowed) in the name Esav—which indicates "complete," "fully formed," a strange name indeed for a newborn. Like his father, Esav married at the age of forty, but the difference between them is evident in their choice of partners: When it was time for Yitzchak to wed, a complicated process ensued, because Yitzchak was not to marry a local girl. Yet Esav, immediately upon reaching forty years if age, married not one, but two local girls. When he finally understood that his father was displeased with his choices, Esav took a third wife. See *Bereishit* 26:34-35; 27:46; 28:8-9:

בראשית כו: לד-לה
וַיְהִי עֵשָׂו בֶּן־אַרְבָּעִים שָׁנָה וַיִּקַּח אִשָּׁה אֶת־יְהוּדִית בַּת־בְּאֵרִי הַחִתִּי וְאֶת־בָּשְׂמַת בַּת־אֵילֹן הַחִתִּי: וַתִּהְיֶיןָ מֹרַת רוּחַ לְיִצְחָק וּלְרִבְקָה:

בראשית כז: מו
וַתֹּאמֶר רִבְקָה אֶל־יִצְחָק קַצְתִּי בְחַיַּי מִפְּנֵי בְּנוֹת חֵת אִם־לֹקֵחַ יַעֲקֹב אִשָּׁה מִבְּנוֹת־חֵת כָּאֵלֶּה מִבְּנוֹת הָאָרֶץ לָמָּה לִּי חַיִּים:

בראשית כח: ח-ט
וַיַּרְא עֵשָׂו כִּי רָעוֹת בְּנוֹת כְּנָעַן בְּעֵינֵי יִצְחָק אָבִיו: וַיֵּלֶךְ עֵשָׂו אֶל־יִשְׁמָעֵאל וַיִּקַּח אֶת־מָחֲלַת ׀ בַּת־יִשְׁמָעֵאל בֶּן־אַבְרָהָם אֲחוֹת נְבָיוֹת עַל־נָשָׁיו לוֹ לְאִשָּׁה:

from the concept of self-control into a mandate to control others, and ultimately to take life. The fact that Esav married the daughters of Yishmael should come as no surprise: The two had more in common than mere ancestry, and the result of their union was the combination of their negative forces.[10]

Yaakov, on the other hand, internalized the positive aspects of the teachings of Avraham and Yitzchak, and he came to represent the combination of their two traits, *chesed* and *gevurah*, forming the third philosophical pillar, *tiferet* (splendor). The trait of *tiferet* sees beauty in all things, in differences and distinctions, and is able to create a harmonious synthesis. Yaakov, who becomes Yisrael, father of the nation, must have the ability to combine disparate ideas, experiences, and outlooks. This is

---

10. See *Hadar Zekeinim, Bereishit* 28:9 for one particularly nefarious plan which Esav had concocted with this marriage. (However, see *Bechor Shor, Bereishit* 28:9, who points out that Yishmael was already dead at this juncture):

הדר זקנים על התורה בראשית פרשת תולדות פרק כח פסוק ט
וילך עשו אל ישמעאל. בשעה שהודה יצחק על הברכות ליעקב אמר עשו אלך ואתחתן לישמעאל ואתן לו עצה להרוג את יצחק מפני הבכורה כי הוא הבכור ואבי ירש הכל ואהיה גואל הדם ואהרוג את ישמעאל ולא יהיה ליעקב שום קרוב ואהרגהו בסתר שלא יראני שום אדם. ובאותה שעה שחשב עשו אותה מחשבה עבר לפני מדרשו של שם. א"ל שם. רשע מתי חשבת זאת המחשבה הרעה. א"ל עשו מי הגיד לך. א"ל הקדוש ברוך הוא הגיד לי שהיה שם בשעת מחשבתך. והיינו דכתיב ביחזקאל יען אמרך על שני הגוים ועל שני הממלכות לי הם וה'' שם היה. שני הגוים יצחק וישמעאל. ובקשת לך כל הממלכות. אבל ה' שם היה שהגיד הדבר: (אט"ה לפ"ז א"ש הא דקאמר עשו יקרבו ימי אבל אבי שכל זה עלה במחשבתו של עשו שילד ויתחתן עם ישמעאל כדי שיהרוג יצחק אביו ולבסוף יהרוג יעקב ודבר זה הוגד לרבקה ברוה"ק ואמרה לו ליעקב קום ברח לך וכו' והשתא לק"מ ממ"ש בד"ה יקרבו ימי וכו' ונכון):

ר' יוסף בכור שור בראשית פרשת תולדות פרק כח פסוק ט
וילך עשו אל ישמעאל. לפי הפשט לבית ישמעאל, כי כבר הוא נפטר, שהרי זה היה כשהלך יעקב לחרן היה בן עז' שנה, שהרי חי יעקב אחר שהלך ללבן ל"ו שנה, כ' שעמד בבית לבן, ויוסף היה בן שש כשיצא מבית לבן, ונמכר בן י"ז, וי"ד קודם שנולד יוסף הרי ל"א [מ]שבא ללבן, ואחר כ"ב שנה למכירתו הלך יעקב למצרים, וחי י"ז [שנה] במצרים, הרי ע'. ויעקב חי קמ"ז שנים, נמצא בן ע"ז כשבא לחרן, כי ע' וע"ז קמ"ז, וכשמת ישמעאל לא היה יעקב כי אם בן ס"ג, נמצא כשבא לחרן כבר נפטר [ישמעאל] זה י"ד שנה. ורבותינו פירשו אל ישמעאל דוקא, כי אז היה חי, ובאותו פרק מת ואותם י"ד שמש בבית עבר, ובן ע"ז בא לחרן, וסדר שני יעקב: בן ס"ג היה כשמת ישמעאל, ובן ע"ז בא לחרן, ובן פ"ד נשא רחל ולאה. ובן צ"א נולד לו יוסף ובן צ"ז יצא מחרן, ובן ק"ח כשנמכר יוסף, ובן ק"כ כשנפטר יצחק ובן ק"ל כשהלך למצרים, ועשה י"ז במצרים הרי קמ"ז, ויוסף בן נ"ו כשנפטר אביו.

in contradistinction to Avraham and Yitzchak, whose traits represented spiritual building blocks, but not the spiritual building.[11]

Once this synthesis is in place, the nation should emerge. Yaakov's children should be complete; there is no counterfeit among them.[12] The

---

11. See the commentary of the Ben Yehodaya, *Berachot* 64a: *mi-kan le-baal ha-korei...*

ספר בניהו בן יהוידע על ברכות דף סד/א
מכאן לבעל הקורה שיכנס בעוביה של קורה. י"ל למה קרי ליעקב אבינו עליו השלום בעל הקורה טפי מאבותינו אברהם ויצחק, ועוד למה עשו המשל בקורה ולא במשוי אחר, ועוד מה ענין אומרם שיכנס בעוביה והוה ליה למימר שישא הקורה, ונראה לי בס"ד כי יעקב אבינו עליו השלום אחיזתו בתפארת שהוא קו האמצעי הנקרא גופא, אבל אברהם ויצחק אחיזתם בחסד וגבורה הנקראים ידים, כמ"ש בזוהר הקדוש חסד דרועא ימינא גבורה דרועא שמאלא תפארת גופא. נמצא התפארת היא דוגמת הקורה שסומכין עליה עצים מכאן ומכאן ולכן קרו ליעקב אבינו עליו השלום בעל הקורה, ומ"ש שיכנס בעובה של קורה הנה העובי הוא רמז על המילוי, כי מילוי האות הוא עובי האות, והנה אותיות קורה במילואם כזה קו"ף ו"ו רי"ש ה"ה המילוי לבדו עולה מספר זית, וידוע שאמרו רבותינו ז"ל ישראל נמשלו לזית מה זית בסווטא בין בקייטא לא אתאבידו טרפוי, כן ישראל אפילו קטנים שבהם אין להם ביטול לא בעולם הזה ולא בעולם הבא, ולזה אמר על יעקב אבינו עליו השלום הוא יכנס בעוביה של קורה הרומז לישראל, כלומר זכותו יעמוד להם מפני שאם יעמוד זכות אברהם ויצחק בעת צרה יהיה לזה תובעין אחרים שהם עשו וישמעאל ולכך נאמר על עת צרה [תהלים כ' ב'] ישגבך שם אלהי יעקב:

12. The sons of Yaakov, however, saw Yosef as a *klipah* of *yesod*. See *Sefer Likkutim*, *Vayeshev* chapter 37; *Yalkut Reuveni*, *Vayeshev* section 73:

ספר הליקוטים - פרשת וישב - פרק לז
דע, כי חשבו אחי יוסף שהוא שירים לשירים, קליפה מה שנפרדה מאברהם ויצחק בצאת מהם ישמעאל ועשו, ועדיין לא נטהרו. ומה גם בחשבם שיוסף פגם ביסוד, והטהו לצינור שמאלי ח"ו, במה שהביא רעה דבתם עם הפך השלום. והיסוד סוד הלשון, והדיבור פגם בו. ועוד מפרשים הרבה יש שאומרים, אוכלים אבר מן החי ותולין עיניהם בבנות הארץ, כל זה תלוי ביסוד. וכן זלזלו בבני השפחות, הפך שלום, וקראו עבד שהוא בן חורין הפך העבדות. והיסוד נקרא כל, כולל כל המדות, וחשבו שהם ישלימו חסרונם ביניהם, ואז ויתנכלו אותו, חשבו להיות בעלי האחוה שלו. ועוד שהם, עשרה להשלמות אור ישר, ובנימין המשלים אור חוזר. וטעותם היה, כי דעת, אעפ"י שכולל כל המדות, הוא ג' כ' מדה בפני עצמה. ועוד, שזה טעות מפורסם, כי השבטים אינם דוגמת י"ס, אלא י"ב גבולות, מה שיש במלכות סוד שנים עשר בקר, כמ"ש במ"א:

ילקוט ראובני על התורה - פרשת וישב [אות עג]:
ויתנכלו אותו להמיתו, דע כי חשבו אחי יוסף שהוא שירים לשיורי קליפה שנפרדה מאברהם בצאת ממנו ישמעאל ויצחק בצאת ממנו עשו, ושמא לא נטהרה העזרה בשלימות, ומה גם ביוסף שיוסף פגם במדת יסוד והטה אותו אל צינור שמאלי ח"ו במה שהביא דבתם רעה והנה חשבו להשלים חסרונו ביניהם, וזהו ויתנכלו עם הכולל בגי' בשל"ם ר"ם בגי' פי' תקלי"ו כו', ועוד שהם היו עשרה מבלעדיו להשלמת האור הישר, ובנימין הוא המשלים את ערוות לתתאי:

Vayechi: The Death of Yaakov | 341

klipah of the newly emergent Jewish nation is the *eirev rav*, who were responsible for the worship of the golden calf. These people who were not the descendants of Yaakov, but rather Egyptians who had joined the Jewish people in their victorious march out of Egypt.

The *eirev rav*, like Esav and Yishmael, had a superficial grasp of the philosophical underpinnings of Judaism. To them, the trait of *tiferet*, this all-inclusive outlook, encompassed all types of worship. Their perversion of Yisrael's ability to synthesize lead them to embrace idolatry; their error was in assigning such worship any meaning at all. *Tiferet* is the inclusion of many different attributes in the service and worship of the one God; idolatry is the inclusion of other gods, which are, in fact, non-entities.

Time and again throughout our history, this perversion of *tiferet* has resurfaced, and the books of the prophets tell of many "movements" within Judaism that attempted to synthesize foreign forms of worship with authentic Jewish practice. It begins begins at the foot of Mount Sinai, carries on through the period of the prophets, continues through the Hellenistic period, and is alive and well to this very day.

The spiritual dynamics unleashed by Yishmael, Eisav, and the *eirav rav* respectively, are the *klipot* of our patriarchs' teachings: sexual immorality, murder, and idolatry, the three sins that eventually caused the destruction of the First Temple. When the Jews follow the counterfeited teachings of their forefathers instead of internalizing the true messages presented by the pillars of our nationhood, their mandate to lead by example comes to an end. The Temple cannot stand when these pillars fall; the Jewish commonwealth is laid to waste, and the Jewish people scattered.[13]

This was the fear that gripped Yaakov on his deathbed: Had he misread the spiritual dynamics of the nascent Jewish nation? Was there a counterfeit among his children that was causing the *Shechinah* to be

---

13. See *Yoma* 9b:

תלמוד בבלי מסכת יומא דף ט עמוד ב
מִקְדָּשׁ רִאשׁוֹן מִפְּנֵי מָה חָרַב? מִפְּנֵי שְׁלֹשָׁה דְבָרִים שֶׁהָיוּ בוֹ - עֲבוֹדָה זָרָה, גִּלּוּי עֲרָיוֹת, וּשְׁפִיכוּת דָּמִים:

suddenly distant? If so, perhaps the time had not yet come for the nation to be formed. Yaakov's sons, recognizing their father's fear, respond by saying *Shema*; they declared their acceptance of one God.[14] They hoped to allay his fears that their belief was counterfeit.

There is, however, a deeper meaning behind their choice of words. By saying *Shema*, they were actually referring to an earlier episode in their father's life and trying to communicate something very specific to Yaakov.

According to the Midrash, during the entire period that he mourned for Yosef, Yaakov was denied prophecy; the *Shechinah* left him. Yaakov mourned not only the death of his son, but the failure of his own spiritual mission.[15] Believing that Yosef was dead, Yaakov spent years mourning his son, and awaiting his own bitter punishment in the World to Come.

When the message arrives that Yosef lives, the Torah comments:

בראשית פרק מה, כז
...וַתְּחִי רוּחַ יַעֲקֹב אֲבִיהֶם:

...The spirit of Yaakov, their father, lived. (*Bereishit* 45:27)

---

14. See Rav Avraham Zioni, *Zioni al ha-Torah, Parashat Vayechi*:

ספר הציוני על התורה - פרשת ויחי
ונסתלקה שכינה מיעקב מאיש זך ונבר. כי כבוד אלהים הסתר דבר. כשראה זה אמר שמא יש פסול במטתי כמו אברהם שיצא ממנו ישמעאל ויש בה קליפה או יצחק שיצא ממנו עשו איש שדה. ענו כולם ואמרו שמע ישראל ה' אלהינו ה'

15. Midrashic sources inform us that in an earlier prophecy, Yaakov had been told that if none of his sons died in his lifetime he would be spared from Hell. See *Midrash Aggada Bereishit* (Buber) 37:35, Rashi, *Bereishit* 37:35:

מדרש אגדה (בובר) בראשית פרשת וישב פרק לז סימן לה
כי ארד אל בני אבל שאולה. אלא אמר יעקב לפני הקדוש ברוך הוא תן לי אות שלא ארד לשאול, אמר לו הקדוש ברוך הוא סימן זה יהיה בידיך שלא ימות אחד מבניך בימיך, ועל כן אמר כי ארד אל בני אבל שאולה:

רש״י בראשית פרק לז:לה
אבל שאולה - כְּפָשׁוּטוֹ לְשׁוֹן קֶבֶר הוּא – בְּאֶבְלִי אֶקָּבֵר, וְלֹא אֶתְנַחֵם כָּל יָמַי וּמִדְרָשׁוֹ, גֵּיהִנָּם, סימן זה היה מסור בידי מפי הגבורה אם לא ימות אחד מבני בחיי מובטח אני שאיני רואה גיהנם:

Rashi explains that this was more than the normal joyous reaction:

רש"י בראשית פרק מה:כז
ותחי רוח יעקב - שָׁרְתָה עָלָיו שְׁכִינָה, שֶׁפָּרְשָׁה מִמֶּנּוּ:

The *Shechinah* which had left him returned. (Rashi, *Bereishit* 45:27)

When Yaakov and Yosef reunite after twenty-two years, the Torah describes their embrace:

בראשית פרק מו:כט
...וַיֵּרָא אֵלָיו וַיִּפֹּל עַל־צַוָּארָיו וַיֵּבְךְּ עַל־צַוָּארָיו עוֹד:

... [Yosef] saw [Yaakov], and fell on his neck and cried on his neck. (*Bereishit* 46:29)

Rashi provides more details of the scene:

רש"י בראשית פרק מו:כט
ויבך על צואריו עוד - ... ; אֲבָל יַעֲקֹב לֹא נָפַל עַל צַוְּארֵי יוֹסֵף וְלֹא נְשָׁקוֹ, וְאָמְרוּ רַבּוֹתֵינוּ, שֶׁהָיָה קוֹרֵא אֶת שְׁמַע:

...Yaakov did not fall on the neck of Yosef, nor did he kiss Yosef. Our Sages explain that he [Yaakov] was saying Shema. (Rashi, *Bereishit* 46:29)

Yaakov's response to seeing his long-lost son was the recitation of *Shema*. At first glance this seems strange: He has not seen his son in years, and now, at the moment of reunion, Yaakov feels that it is time to say *Shema*! A closer look at the words of *Shema* explain Yaakov's response.

דברים פרק ו:ד
שְׁמַע יִשְׂרָאֵל יְהוָה אֱלֹהֵינוּ יְהוָה | אֶחָד:

Hear, O Israel, God is our master, God is one. (*Devarim* 6:4).

A statement of faith in one God, or even a statement of praise and thanks to the Almighty for reuniting him with his beloved son, should have consisted of the words "*Hashem Elokeinu, Hashem echad,*" but Yaakov added something more: "*Shema Yisrael.*" Years later, when Yaakov's sons allay his fears on his deathbed with the words "*Shema Yisrael,*" it is clear that they are addressing their father, Yisrael. But why does Yaakov say "*Shema Yisrael*" when he is reunited with Yosef? Can he be addressing himself, or are these words superfluous?

In fact, Yaakov addresses Yisrael—not himself, but the entire *Knesset Yisrael*, the totality of the Jewish people, who are reunited at that moment. Upon seeing Yosef alive, Yaakov knows that *Knesset Yisrael* is complete, and the *Shechinah* returns to him. So he recites *Shema* because the Nation of Israel may now emerge.

With this background, we understand why his children say *Shema* when, on his deathbed, he loses the *Shechinah* again. They wish to assure him that they all accept one God, that they are complete, and that he should not fear. They repeat his own prayer, echoing his reference to a united *Knesset Yisrael* while at the same time referring directly to their father.

However, there is another aspect of the recitation of *Shema*. The Midrash teaches:

מכילתא דרבי ישמעאל בשלח - מסכתא דשירה פרשה ג
ישראל אומרים שמע ישראל ה' אלהינו ה' אחד (דברים ו ד) ורוח הקדש צווחת ואומר' מן השמים [ומי כעמך ישראל גוי אחד בארץ (שמואל ב' ז כג)

The Jewish people say, "*Shema Yisrael, Hashem Elokeinu, Hashem echad* — Hear, Yisrael, God is Lord, God is One,*"* and the *Ruach ha-Kodesh* cries out and says from Heaven, "Who is like Your nation Israel, a unique nation on earth" (2 *Shmuel* 7:23, and 1 *Divrei ha-Yamim* 17:21). (*Mechilta, Beshalach* 3)

Vayechi: The Death of Yaakov

When we recite *Shema*, there is a response in Heaven. We accept God's oneness, and God declares our oneness—our uniqueness.

The Gemara entertains the possibility that God wears *tefillin*, as it were. The question is then posed, what is the content of God's *tefillin*? Surely it is not *Shema*, as in man's *tefillin*. The Gemara (*Berachot* 6a) explains that again it is the verse, "Who is like Your nation Israel, a unique nation on earth."

תלמוד בבלי מסכת ברכות דף ו עמוד א

אָמַר רַבִּי אָבִין בַּר רַב אַדָּא אָמַר רַבִּי יִצְחָק, מִנַּיִן שֶׁהַקָּדוֹשׁ בָּרוּךְ הוּא מַנִּיחַ תְּפִלִּין? שֶׁנֶּאֱמַר, (ישעיה סב) "נִשְׁבַּע ה' בִּימִינוֹ וּבִזְרוֹעַ עֻזּוֹ", בִּימִינוֹ זוֹ תוֹרָה, שֶׁנֶּאֱמַר, (דברים לג) "מִימִינוֹ אֵשׁ דָּת לָמוֹ". אֵלּוּ תְּפִלִּין, שֶׁנֶּאֱמַר, (תהלים כט) "ה' עֹז לְעַמּוֹ יִתֵּן". ... אָמַר לֵיהּ רַב נַחְמָן בַּר יִצְחָק לְרַב חִיָּא בַּר אָבִין, הַנֵּי תְּפִלִּין דְּמָארֵי עָלְמָא, מַה כְּתִיב בְּהוּ? אָמַר לֵיהּ, (דה"א יז) "וּמִי כְּעַמְּךָ יִשְׂרָאֵל גּוֹי אֶחָד". וּמִי מִשְׁתַּבַּח קוּדְשָׁא בְּרִיךְ הוּא בְּשִׁבְחַיְיהוּ דְּיִשְׂרָאֵל? אִין, דִּכְתִיב, (דברים כו) "אֶת ה' הֶאֱמַרְתָּ הַיּוֹם, וַה' הֶאֱמִירְךָ הַיּוֹם". אָמַר לָהֶם הַקָּדוֹשׁ בָּרוּךְ הוּא לְיִשְׂרָאֵל, אַתֶּם עֲשִׂיתוּנִי חֲטִיבָה אַחַת בָּעוֹלָם, וַאֲנִי אֶעֱשֶׂה אֶתְכֶם חֲטִיבָה אַחַת בָּעוֹלָם. אַתֶּם עֲשִׂיתוּנִי חֲטִיבָה אַחַת בָּעוֹלָם, דִּכְתִיב, (שם ו) "שְׁמַע יִשְׂרָאֵל ה' אֱלֹהֵינוּ ה' אֶחָד" וַאֲנִי אֶעֱשֶׂה אֶתְכֶם חֲטִיבָה אַחַת בָּעוֹלָם, דִּכְתִיב, "וּמִי כְּעַמְּךָ יִשְׂרָאֵל גּוֹי אֶחָד בָּאָרֶץ".

R. Abin son of R. Ada in the name of R. Yitzchak says [further]: How do you know that the Holy One, blessed be He, puts on *tefillin*? For it is said, "The Lord has sworn by His right hand, and by the arm of His strength. 'By His right hand' — this is the Torah; for it is said, 'At His right hand was a fiery law unto them.' 'And by the arm of his strength' — this is the *tefillin*; as it is said, 'The Lord will give strength unto His people.'" ...R. Nahman b. Yitzchak said to R. Hiyya b. Abin: What is written in the *tefillin* of the Lord of the Universe? He replied to him, "And who is like Your people Israel, a nation one on the earth." Does, then, the Holy One, blessed be He, sing the praises of Israel? Yes, for it is written: "You have avouched the Lord this day . . .

and the Lord has avouched you this day." The Holy One, blessed be He, said to Israel, "You have made me a unique entity in the world, and I shall make you a unique entity in the world." You have made me a unique entity in the world," as it is said, "Hear, O Israel, the Lord our God, the Lord is one." "And I shall make you a unique entity in the world," as it is said, "And who is like Your people Israel, a nation one in the earth."

Just as the Jewish people are dedicated to God, God is dedicated to the Jewish people. Yaakov understood this, and therefore when his sons said *Shema* he responded with the declaration is said in the Temple on Yom Kippur by the people, after they hear the Ineffable Name uttered by the *kohen gadol*, "*Baruch Shem kevod malchuto le-olam va'ed.*"[16] Yaakov realized that his children were complete as the *Shechinah* returned to rest upon him, and he responded just as the entire nation would respond to the *Shechinah* in the future.

According to the Midrash, the slavery in Egypt could not commence until the Jews were a unified, independent nation; otherwise, they would have been unable to withstand the challenge of assimilation.[17]

---

16. See Mishnah *Yoma* 3:8 (also found in 4:1,2, 6:2):

משנה מסכת יומא פרק ג:ח

וְכָךְ הָיָה אוֹמֵר, אָנָּא הַשֵּׁם, עָוִיתִי פָּשַׁעְתִּי חָטָאתִי לְפָנֶיךָ אֲנִי וּבֵיתִי. אָנָּא הַשֵּׁם, כַּפֶּר נָא לָעֲוֹנוֹת וְלַפְּשָׁעִים וְלַחֲטָאִים, שֶׁעָוִיתִי וְשֶׁפָּשַׁעְתִּי וְשֶׁחָטָאתִי לְפָנֶיךָ אֲנִי וּבֵיתִי, כַּכָּתוּב בְּתוֹרַת מֹשֶׁה עַבְדֶּךָ, (ויקרא טז) כִּי בַיּוֹם הַזֶּה יְכַפֵּר עֲלֵיכֶם לְטַהֵר אֶתְכֶם מִכֹּל חַטֹּאתֵיכֶם לִפְנֵי יְיָ תִּטְהָרוּ. וְהֵן עוֹנִין אַחֲרָיו, בָּרוּךְ שֵׁם כְּבוֹד מַלְכוּתוֹ לְעוֹלָם וָעֶד:

17. See *Eliyahu Rabbah* 21:

אליהו רבה (איש שלום) פרשה כא

כשהיו ישראל במצרים תמימי דרך (הן) [היו], כשעמדו אבותינו על הר סיני לקבל עליהן תורה מסיני היו תמימי דרך בדבר, פייסן תחילה ואחר כך ערך לפניהם נזיקין וכל מידות הדין, ואחר כך אמרו, ברוך ה' אלהים אלהי ישראל אלהי צבאות יושב הכרובים, <u>אתה הוא האלהים לבדך על כל ממלכות הארץ, אתה עשית את השמים (ואת) [ושמי] השמים בתבונה, נתקבצו וישבו שהיו כולם אגודה אחת, כרתו ברית שיעשו גמילות חסדים זה עם זה, וישמרו בלבבם ברית אברהם יצחק ויעקב, שלא יניחו לשון בית יעקב אביהם וילמדו לשון מצרים, מפני דרכי עבודה זרה. כאיזה צד עבדו ישראל את אבינו שבשמים במצרים, שלא שינו את לשונם, והיו המצריים אומרים להם, למה אתם עובדים אתו, אם תעבדו אלהי מצרים יקל עבודתו מכם, משיבין ישראל ואומרים להם, שמא עזב אברהם יצחק ויעקב את אלהינו שבשמים שיעזבו</u>

Now *Sefer Bereishit* may come to its end; although the slavery and eventual Exodus will follow, leading up to the giving of the Torah on Mount Sinai, *Shema* will remain the "pledge of allegiance" of this nation for all time. Generations of Yisrael's descendants will say *Shema* in so many different circumstances, and the *Shechinah* will never fail to take notice[18]—as it did in what may be the most famous *Shema* of all:

תלמוד בבלי מסכת ברכות דף סא עמוד ב

בְּשָׁעָה שֶׁהוֹצִיאוּהוּ לְרַבִּי עֲקִיבָא לַהֲרִיגָה, זְמַן קְרִיאַת שְׁמַע הָיָה, וְהָיוּ סוֹרְקִין אֶת בְּשָׂרוֹ בְּמַסְרְקָאוֹת שֶׁל בַּרְזֶל, וְהָיָה מִתְכַּוֵּן לְקַבֵּל עָלָיו עוֹל מַלְכוּת שָׁמַיִם בְּאַהֲבָה. אָמְרוּ לוֹ תַּלְמִידָיו, רַבֵּנוּ, עַד כָּאן? אָמַר לָהֶם, כָּל יָמַי הָיִיתִי מִצְטַעֵר עַל הַפָּסוּק הַזֶּה, "בְּכָל נַפְשְׁךָ" - וַאֲפִלּוּ הוּא נוֹטֵל אֶת נַפְשְׁךָ, אָמַרְתִּי, מָתַי יָבוֹא לְיָדִי וַאֲקַיְּמֶנּוּ, וְעַכְשָׁיו שֶׁבָּא לְיָדִי, לֹא אֲקַיְּמֶנּוּ? הָיָה מַאֲרִיךְ בְּ,אֶחָד' עַד שֶׁיָּצְתָה נִשְׁמָתוֹ בְּ,אֶחָד'.:

When Rabbi Akiva was taken out for execution, it was time to say *Shema*, and while they combed his flesh with iron combs, he was accepting upon himself the kingship of heaven. His students said to him, "Our teacher, even to this point?" He said to them, "All my days I have been troubled by this verse, 'with all your soul' [which I interpret,] 'even if He takes your soul.' I said, 'When shall I have the opportunity of fulfilling this?' Now that I have the opportunity shall I not fulfill it?" (*Berachot* 61b)

When the Romans tortured Rabbi Akiva, the Gemara notes it was "time to say *Shema*"—it was time to uplift the nation from the Roman oppression and rekindle a sense of nationhood. The *Shechinah* had

---

בניהן אחריהן. אמרו להן, לאו, אמרו, כשם שהם לא עזבו אותו כך לא נעזבנו. והיו ישראל מלין את בניהם במצרים, אמרו להם מצריים, מה שמא תקל עבודה קשה מכם, משיבין ישראל ואומרים להם, שמא שכח אברהם יצחק ויעקב את ברית אלהינו שבשמים שישכחו בניהן אחריהן, אמרו להן, לאו, אמרו להן, כשם שלא שכח אברהם יצחק ויעקב ברית אלהינו שבשמים כך לא ישכחו בניהן אחריהן.

18. The expectation that one may see the *Shechinah* when the *Shema* is recited may be the reason we cover our eyes when reciting this prayer.

been exiled with the destruction of the Second Temple, and now the glimmer of hope of rebuilding the Temple had been extinguished. Rabbi Akiva's *Shema* echoes throughout the generations. It was heard by Jews in countless situations, giving them the strength to make the most difficult decisions. It is fascinating that the name *Akiva* is derived from the name *Yaakov*; both were married to women named Rachel, who in turn both excelled in self-sacrifice. The *Shema* of Rabbi Akiva is certainly connected to the *Shema* of Yaakov.[19]

---

19. See *Shaar ha-Gilgulim*, introduction 36 (and 31), *Kehilat Yaakov* entry *Ein Kuf*, See commentary of Rav Moshe Zachut on the *Zohar Bamidbar* (page 811), *Megaleh Amukot Parashat Vayechi*, Rav Yonatan Eibeshitz, *Yaarot Devash* 1:2. Yaakov Avinu and Rabbi Akiva are interrelated on a soul level:

שער הגלגולים - הקדמה לו
גם א"ל מורי ז"ל כי שלשה היו שטעו בענין הקץ, הא' יעקב אבינו ע"ה, כשקרא לבניו ואמר האספו ואגידה לכם את אשר יקרא אתכם באחרית הימים ונעלם ממנו הקץ. הב' הוא שמואל הנביא ע"ה, שטעה בענין אליאב, ואמר אך נגד ה' משיחו, כי חשב שממנו יצא המשיח. הג' ר' עקיבא, שטעה וחשב כי בן כוזיבא היה משיח ה'. ולכן אותיות יעקב הם עקיבא, לרמוז כי טעותם שוה, ולכן שלשתם נתגלגלו כדי לתקן טעות זה

שער הגלגולים - הקדמה לא
ונשמת ר' עקיבא בן יוסף. ונשמת עקביא בן מהללאל. וכמו שיבאר פרטיהם לקמן. ושלשלת יחוס נשמת השרש הזה. ואמנם בחי' טפת הזרע, הנמשכת ממקום העקב הזה עד היסוד, לפעמים נעשת יעקב, ולפעמים נעשת עקביא בן מהללאל, ולפעמים עקיבא, וכיוצא ב

ספר קהילת יעקב ערך עק
עקיבא היה מניצוץ של יעקב אבינו, עקיבא אותיות יעקב (ליקוטי תורה ויחי), ויעקב אבינו פגם קצת ביחוד במה ששלח ליוסף בלא לויה, לפיכך הוצרך לרבי עקיבא לתקן היחוד, וזה שאמרו (ברכות ס"א ע"ב) אשריך רבי עקיבא שיצאת נשמתך באחד לתקן היחוד, ילקוט ראובני פרשת וישב בשם כוונת אר"י זצ"ל (ספר הגלגולים פרק מ"א):

פירוש הרמ"ז על זוהר במדבר - עמוד 118
ונראה לי עוד שכשבאו עשרת הרוגי מלכות להתקן אז נתעבר יעקב אבינו ע"ה ברבי עקיבא כנזכר בח"ב מספר הגלגולים קיא, ויעקב לא התפלל שלא יבוא שם מפני שהיה לתיקון שלהם ולתיקון העולמות כנזכר אצלנו בפסוק קיב, א) (תהלים צד, א) אל נקמות ה', אבל בכאן שלא יצליחו התפלל בסודות אל תבוא נפשי:

ספר מגלה עמוקות על התורה - פרשת ויחי
או שגילה יעקב ליוסף סוד כ"ה אתוון דיחודא שכן כשבא יעקב ליוסף ארז"ל שקרא קריאת שמע לפי שביחודא דקריאת שמע מבטלין כה אחר שהוא שרו של עשר וכמ"ש יעקב למלאכים כ"ה תאמרון לאדוני לעשו ר"ל כשרוצים אתם לבטל כח עשו שהוא אדוני צריכין אתם ליחד פסוק שמע ישראל כמד"א (דברים ט) שמע ישראל אתה עובר היום את הירדן ר"ל כשרוצה

...יָצְתָה בַּת - קוֹל וְאָמְרָה, אַשְׁרֶיךָ רַבִּי עֲקִיבָא שֶׁיָּצְתָה נִשְׁמָתְךָ בְּאֶחָד. ...
יָצְתָה בַּת קוֹל וְאָמְרָה לוֹ, אַשְׁרֶיךָ רַבִּי עֲקִיבָא שֶׁאַתָּה מְזֻמָּן לְחַיֵּי הָעוֹלָם הַבָּא

A *bat kol* went forth and proclaimed: Fortunate are you, Akiva, that your soul has departed with the word *ehad*! ...A *bat kol* went forth and proclaimed, 'Fortunate are you, Rabbi Akiva, that you are destined for the life of the World to Come. (*Berachot* 61b)

אדם לעבור מקום דין שהוא סוד ירדן סוד דין בזה צריך לומר שמע ישראל וכן אמרו לעולם ירגיז אדם יצה"ט על יצה"ר וכו' עד ויקרא קריאת שמע ז"ש ואני נתתי לך שכ"ם של אח"ד שהוא יחוד שמע ישראל אשר לקחתי מיד אמורי שהוא עשו כי בזה נעשו בית עשו לק"ש כשקורין ק"ש. או ע"פ דרכי הראשון שהשבטים יחודם ה' שמע אז אמר הזקן יחוד ברוך שם כבוד שהוא ברזא דעלמא תתאה דרגיה דיוסף שהוא מטטרו"ן עז"א יעקב ואני נתתי לך אותו היחוד אשר אמרתי הנה אחיך רועים בשכ"ם ז"ש נתתי לך שכ"ם שהוא יחוד של שם כבוד מלכותו לך דייקא שהוא בדרגיה והוא על אחיך כי ביחוד של שמע ישראל כ"ו אתוון וביחוד שם כבוד כ"ד אתוון אחד פחות ז"ש אחד על אחיך גם יוסף הורד מצרימה לתקן ר' של אחד ולהאריך באחד ומי שגרע קוצו של ד' עושה מאחד אחר וז"ס שאמר דוד ליהונתן (שמואל א) כפשע בני ובין המות רזא דדוד שכינתא ויהונתן הוא צדיק יסוד וצריך להרחיק א"ח מן ד', ומי שגורע קוצו של ד' הרי המות יפריד ורגליה יורדת מות (משלי ה) ז"ש כי כפשע הוא על ההוא קוצו של ד' בינו לבין המות. ז"ש ואני נתתי לך שכם א' (איוב כג) והוא באח"ד ומי ישיבנו נפשו איותה ויעש. או סוד של ר' עקיבא שיצאת נשמתו באחד לפי שכל ימיו היה מצטער על אותה המחשבה ז"ש והוא באחד שיצאת נשמתו באחד והטעם שנפשו אותה כל ימיו מתי יבא לידו ויקיימנה לכן עתה ויעש כי רצון יראיו יעשה (תהלים קמה) וענין הריגת ר' עקיבא באה ע"ס מי' ניצוצין שיצאו מיוסף מתחת ציפורניו טובה ציפורנם של ראשונים מכריסן של אחרונים שיוצא מכרס שלהם הזרע שיצא הולד מן האשה מבטן. רזא שהרי י' הרוגי מלכות יצאו מציפורני ידיו ואין כל בריה יכולה לעמוד במחיצתן אף בלא הרוגי מלכות ז"ס ותשב באיתן קשתו ויצא הזרע ויפוזו זרועי ידיו זה גרם מיד"י אבי"ר יעק"ב קרי ב' ר' עקיבא לפי שיצאו י' ניצוצין בלא נוקבא משם רועה אבן ישראל גדולי עולם. ז"ש ואני נתתי לך שכם אח"ד על אחיך אשר לקחתי מיד אמורי כי באמת לא שלט אמורי על הרוגי מלכות רק לקחם אלקים ולופטים בא תמורתו מ"שם ר'ועה א'ב'ן י'שראל ר"ת ארמ"י. תרגום מפרש אב"ן אב ובן יש לומר שני פרושים על אשריך ר' עקיבא שיצאת נשמתך באחד הא' שהוא עבור יוסף שגרמה אביר יעקב אותיות ר' עקיבא שהוא גרם בעצמו לאותו חטא או עבור השכינה שנשתתפה עמהם או עבור יעקב בעצמו שחטא בזה ששלחו בלא לויה יוסף יסוד צדיק ועשה עון שהפריד היחוד לכן הוצרך לתקן אח"כ ותקן וקרא ק"ש בשעה שנפל יוסף על צואריו לתקן זווג שהפריד בשליחות יוסף בלא לויה שזה גרם המכירה וע"כ ז' לא הספיק לעשות הזווג לגמרי והוצרך אח"כ להתגלגל בר' עקיבא בהיפך אתוון אבי"ר יעק"ב לכן אמר ר"ע כל ימי הייתי מצטער ע"ז לתקן יחוד וזיווג עד שבמיתתו עשה יחוד ויצאת נשמתו באחד ז"ש משם רועה אב"ן ישראל או עבור אב או עבור בן:

ואני בבואי מפדן מתה עלי רחל בדרך הוצרך יעקב עתה להודיע ליוסף ענין קישור המרכבה של י"ב שבטים למטה לכן מיד כשילדה רחל את יוסף אמר יעקב ללבן שלחני כי ידע יעקב שיוליד י"ב שבטים ותתקשר שכינה בי' למטה בי"ב שבטים ורחל מיתא ונטלה ביתא וכו':

Yaakov said *Shema*, his children said *Shema*, Rabbi Akiva said *Shema*. All of these prayers are connected, and they all address the collective people of Israel—*Knesset Yisrael*. When we say *Shema* we connect to our ancestors and our descendants—the entire community of Israel, transcending time. When our enemies try to break us, or when we take leave of this world; during crusades, pogroms and the Holocaust, Jews said the *Shema*. Israeli soldiers all hear the *Shema* of Yaakov, of his children, and of Rabbi Akiva ringing in their ears. Every day since Yaakov first declared the Jewish faith in the unique, Almighty God, Jews have recited the *Shema* in settings that range from mundane to extraordinary. Jews continue to say *Shema*, and as a result, the children of Yaakov are still here, still alive, still thriving.

Yaakov wished to reveal the future to his children, but his wish was denied. But by saying the *Shema*, the children of Yaakov revealed the future to their father; they showed him that the children of Israel will continue their dialogue with God, and with one another, forever. They revealed to him the secret of Jewish history: Yaakov and his sons addressed their declaration to every Jew, in every generation—to *Knesset Yisrael*—and all of *Knesset Yisrael*, through the millennia, hear, and continue to respond.

In retrospect, Yaakov had nothing to worry about.

יעקב אבינו לא מת – עם ישראל חי!
Yaakov Avinu lo met — Am Yisrael chai!

Our forefather Yaakov never died, for his children live on—
And through them, his faith.

www.ingramcontent.com/pod-product-compliance
Lightning Source LLC
Chambersburg PA
CBHW030134170426
43199CB00008B/60